The American Optic

SUNY series in Psychoanalysis and Culture

Henry Sussman, *editor*

The American Optic

Psychoanalysis, Critical Race Theory, and Richard Wright

MIKKO TUHKANEN

STATE UNIVERSITY OF NEW YORK PRESS

Cover image: David Levinthal, Blackface series (a rear-view of a male minstrelsy figurine in overalls and a top hat). Copyright © The David Levinthal Studio.

Published by
State University of New York Press
Albany

Printed in the United States of America

For information, contact State University of New York Press, Albany, NY
www.sunypress.edu

Production by Eileen Meehan
Marketing by Fran Keneston

Library of Congress Cataloging-in-Publication Data

Tuhkanen, Mikko, 1967–
The American optic : psychoanalysis, critical race theory, and Richard Wright / Mikko Tuhkanen.
p. cm.—(SUNY series in psychaonalysis and culture)
Includes bibliographical references and index.
ISBN 978-1-4384-2763-8 (hardcover : alk. paper)
ISBN 978-1-4384-2764-5 (pbk : alk. paper)
1. Racism—United States—History. 2. Race awareness—United States—History. 3. Psychoanalysis—United States. 4. Wright, Richard, 1908–1960. I. Title.
E185.6.T84 2009
308.800973—dc22

2008050715

10 9 8 7 6 5 4 3 2 1

The whole American optic in terms of reality is based on the necessity of keeping black people out of it. We are nonexistent. Except according to their terms, and their terms are unacceptable.

—James Baldwin in 1987

Thus early I learned that the point from which a thing is viewed is of some importance.

—Frederick Douglass in 1855

Contents

Acknowledgments ix
Introduction: "Richard, Jacques; Jacques, Richard" xi

CHAPTER 1
A [B]igger's Place: The "Racial" Subject in the White Symbolic Order 1

CHAPTER 2
The Grimace of the Real: Of Paranoid Knowledge and Black(face) Magic 29

CHAPTER 3
Unforeseeable Tragedies: Symbolic Change in Wright, Fanon, and Lacan 67

CHAPTER 4
The Optical Trade: Through Southern Spectacles 107

CHAPTER 5
Avian Alienation: Writing and Flying in Wright and Lacan 133

Notes 169
Bibliography 193
Index 223

Acknowledgments

My thanks go, in alphabetical order, to Sandra Adell, Michael Awkward, Carrie Tirado Bramen, Joan Copjec, Tim Dean, Manthia Diawara, Thomas Gardener, Nathan Grant, Sinikka Grant, Elizabeth Grosz, Markku Henriksson, renée hoogland, Shaun Irlam, Tuula Juvonen, Carine Mardorossian, Kobena Mercer, Ralf Norrman, Maarit Piipponen, David Robertson, Matti Savolainen, and Henry Sussman.

Over the past twenty-odd years I have benefited from the support of friends, mentors, colleagues, and students, too numerous to identify, at the following institutions: the Departments of English, the Arts, and Women's Studies at the University of Tampere, Finland; the Departments of North American Studies (Renvall Institute) and Women's Studies (Christina Institute) at the University of Helsinki, Finland; the Finnish Graduate School for North American Studies; the Department of Women's Studies at the Katholieke Universiteit Nijmegen, the Netherlands; Africana Studies at New York University; the Departments of English and Comparative Literature, as well as the Center for the Study of Psychoanalysis and Culture, at the State University of New York at Buffalo; and the Department of English at East Carolina University.

I gratefully acknowledge the financial support of the Finnish Academy, the Finnish Cultural Foundation, Fuseec Finland/Fulbright Commission, Oskar Öflund Stiftelse, the City of Tampere (Tiederahasto), and Weijola Foundation.

Earlier versions of chapters have originally appeared as follows:

- Chapter 1: "'A [B]igger's Place': Lynching and Specularity in Richard Wright's 'Fire and Cloud' and *Native Son*," *African American Review* 33:1 (Spring 1999): 125–33.
- Chapter 2: "Of Blackface and Paranoid Knowledge: Richard Wright, Jacques Lacan, and the Ambivalence of Black Minstrelsy," *diacritics* 31:2 (Summer 2001): 9–34.
- Chapter 3: "Veiling Wright, Veiling Fanon: Visibility and Self-Concealment as Post-Colonial Strategies," in *Mapping African*

America: History, Narrative Formation, and the Production of Knowledge, eds. Maria Diedrich, Carl Pedersen, and Justine Tally (Hamburg: Lit Verlag, 1999), 29–44.

- Chapter 4: "The Optical Trade: From Slave-Breaking in Douglass's Narrative to Self-Breaking in Wright's *Black Boy*," *American Studies* 46:2 (Summer 2005): 91–116.

Introduction

"Richard, Jacques; Jacques, Richard"

We don't know anything about race. Whenever we speak of race, or use the term racial type, we speak, in fact, of a void which cannot be filled.

—Richard Wright, interviewed in 1953

CLARA. They'll never stop looking—the white folks never stop.

—Paul Green and Richard Wright, *Native Son: The Biography of a Young American*

Critical race theorists have long understood that, ever since its emergence in the eighteenth century in Voltaire's and Kant's work, the modern concept of "race" has depended on visual epistemologies.[1] In this, racial definition arguably evinces the ocularcentric legacy of Enlightenment thought, its privileging of sight as the ultimate arbiter of difference. The subhuman place that the African, for example, came to occupy in Western economies and imagination relied on "the epistemologies attending vision and their logics of corporeal inscription" (Wiegman 4). When one considers race's hybrid ascendancy—combining and cross-breeding Enlightenment ideals, aesthetic judgment, economic exigencies, and (pseudo-)scientific discourses—"[t]he importance of the emphasis upon the visual for racial thought cannot be overestimated" (Mosse 24–25). In its contemporary dynamics, race continues to "secure[] itself through visibility": it remains "an aesthetic practice," based on "a regime of looking" (Seshadri-Crooks, *Desiring* 8, 19).

This study argues for the benefit of psychoanalysis in rethinking race as a visible category. Engaging African American literary and theoretical texts with Jacques Lacan's work, it asks what happens when we interrogate "the American optic" (Baldwin, "Last" 210) through what Lacanian theory teaches us about the role of the visible and the scopic drive in the constitution of the human subject. Subsequently, it proposes a shift in race theory, arguing that the visibility of race does not merely assign the subject a social category or discipline one's mobility in society but may have *an ontological status*: in certain symbolic configurations, the subject's emergence, taking place through the visible, may involve "racialization."

The benefit of such a shift is twofold. First, with the psychoanalytic understanding of the visible, one can better delineate not only the ways in which racialization functions, and is contested, in historically specific symbolic orders but also why race remains an indelible category of identification and politics even after critical race theory has demonstrated the groundlessness of most racial categorizations.[2] Second, by engaging psychoanalysis in a dialogue with African American literature and culture, we can open what Houston Baker, Jr., identifies as the "scholarly double bind"—our being constrained by questions and paradigms that, with teleological predictability, guide our work to certain conclusions (*Modernism* 12–13)—and locate "a signifying device sufficiently unusual in its connotations to shatter familiar conceptual determinations" (*Blues* 144). That is, through the dialogue between psychoanalytic and African American texts, we are able to revisit, to cast an awry look on, moments in African American literary history that may have been evacuated of their potential for newness. I suggest that Richard Wright's work is one such site.[3]

What we know of Wright's biography supports a psychoanalytic approach to his work. His association with the psychoanalysts Frederic Wertham and Benjamin Karpman, as well as the texts found in his library—among them books by Karl Abraham, Helene Deutsch, Otto Fenichel, Sandor Ferenczi, Anna Freud, Sigmund Freud, Ernest Jones, Melanie Klein, Theodor Reik, and Géza Roheim—attest to his familiarity with psychoanalysis.[4] According to one biographer, he remained "intensely Freudian"—indeed, "obsessed with psychoanalysis" (M. Walker 286, 245)—throughout his literary and philosophical career.[5]

Yet, proposing a dialogue between Wright and psychoanalysis invokes inevitable methodological problems. Given that psychoanalysis often comes to us as yet another one of the master's tools, is it possible to approach questions of race from a psychoanalytic perspective? More specifically, considering psychoanalysis's historical ties to the discourses of the unprecedented colonial expansion of late-nineteenth-century Europe, as well as the seeming irrelevance of late-twentieth-century Lacanianism to the concerns of African American culture, how are we to open a dialogue between Lacan and Wright, to introduce Jacques to Richard, as I propose to do here?

In terms of psychoanalysis's relation to Wright's work, nothing may be more decisive than the fact that his writings have been seen as a precursor to the militant black movements of the 1960s and was adopted by numerous Black Panthers and Black Muslims as the emblem of black male rage.[6] That psychoanalysis was among the "white" solutions to be rejected in favor of more authentic African American approaches is mediated by Eldridge Cleaver, who recalls his encounters with a prison psychiatrist in *Soul on Ice* (1968):

> I had several sessions with a psychiatrist. His conclusion was that I hated my mother. How he arrived at this conclusion I'll never know, because he knew nothing about my mother; and when he'd ask me questions I would answer him with absurd lies. What revolted me about him was that he had heard me denouncing the whites, yet each time he interviewed me he deliberately guided the conversation back to my family life, to my childhood. That in itself was all right, but he deliberately blocked all my attempts to bring out the racial question, and he made it clear that he was not interested in my attitude toward whites. This was a Pandora's box he did not care to open. (11)

Suggesting the bad faith that informs psychoanalysis's encounter with politics, Cleaver articulates African American writers' and thinkers' distrust of such white disciplines. In the prison psychiatrist, he offers us the stereotypical image of a (psycho)analyst who imposes family romances on everything and hears repressed Oedipal secrets in every word communicated by the analysand, while remaining stubbornly blind to the life-and-death concerns of the latter's everyday existence. As Gilles Deleuze and Félix Guattari write, there remains "a fundamental relation to the outside of which the psychoanalyst washes his hands, too attentive to seeing that his clients play nice games" (*Anti-Oedipus* 356). Consequently, psychoanalysis appears for Cleaver not only irrelevant but directly oppressive: concertedly disregarding cultural and political specificity, it ignores the reality of disenfranchisement.

Cleaver makes a telling comparison in that, immediately before recounting the above dismal scene, he writes of his first encounter with Wright's work: "In Richard Wright's *Native Son*, I found Bigger Thomas and a keen insight into the problem [of black men's desire for white women]" (10). Whereas the psychiatrist will not listen to Cleaver, the problems with which the latter is struggling are brought into relief through an encounter with two "authentic" black men, Bigger Thomas and Richard Wright; the issues that take Cleaver to prison and to the psychiatrist are in fact better illuminated by Wright than by psychoanalysis. Contrasting the psychiatrist's myopic impositions to Wright's "keen insight," he effectively disassociates the two and implies that Wright, as a black man, can speak of African American experience where psychoanalysis remains impotent, blind, and oppressive.

Cleaver's example illustrates the argument that psychoanalysis is either impervious to the urgency of political questions or directly racist in its basic assumptions. For example, a number of writers point out psychoanalysis's colonial loyalties by referring to its analogy between "savagery" and infantilism. While examples abound in Freud, this is perhaps best evidenced by Octave Mannoni's *Prospero and Caliban* (1950), whose theorization of colonialism as a response to the psychic "dependence complex" (40) of the natives has become, fairly or unfairly, an exemplary case of the political misappropriation of psychology and psychoanalysis.[7] Already in 1955, Aimé Césaire notes that the Eurocentric investment in these disciplines is evident in their insistence on depicting "Negroes-as-big-children" (40).[8] In addition to Mannoni's work, psychoanalytic anthropology has produced numerous other case studies that have elicited vehement criticism.[9] In Deleuze and Guattari's famous estimation, "Oedipus is always colonization pursued by other means" (*Anti-Oedipus* 170). At worst, psychoanalysis is seen as "conceal[ing] realities and legitimiz[ing] oppression" (Hartnack 233; qtd. in Seshadri-Crooks, "Primitive" 183), while Freud is identified as "the great colonizer of psyches" (Torgovnick 198).[10] Wright himself offers similar reservations, writing that any discussion of psychology of the colonized is usually rejected by enlightened commentators because it carries "an air of the derogatory" (*White* 41).

Yet, the last two decades have seen the emergence of studies that, without "exonerating" psychoanalysis, complicate these charges. In Freud scholarship, two trends have developed: one exploring questions of racialization in Freud, the other appropriating (aspects of) Freudian psychoanalysis to read "black" texts. For a number of scholars, Freud's anthropological texts, such as "Moses and Monotheism," "Totem and Taboo," and the early "cocaine papers," suggest "the historical importance of racial categories in Freud's work" (Marez 68).[11] Focus is placed on the significance of Freud's own racialized position in fin-de-siècle Europe, where, as Sander Gilman points out, the Jewish "race" was associated with effeminacy, disease, and "criminal perversions" ("Sigmund" 47).[12] Daniel Boyarin similarly argues that Freud's shift from the so-called seduction theory to the theory of oedipalization was precipitated by the racialization of the Jew, the invention of the homosexual, and the acceleration of racism and homophobia at the end of the nineteenth century (*Unheroic* 189–220).[13]

While Gilman and Boyarin tease out the historical complexities in psychoanalysis's emergence, others have accused Freud of purposefully utilizing the representations of the "savage," widely circulated in the rapidly expanding colonial Europe, to escape his own racially stigmatized position. In contradistinction to the "primitive," the argument goes, Freud could claim the privileges of whiteness and civilization, much like Jewish entertainers in early twentieth-century Hollywood could disappear, according to Michael Rogin's thesis, into racial unmarkedness by donning blackface.[14] Thus the significance of Freud's "race" to the formation of psychoanalytic knowledge is generally acknowledged, but its implications remain contested. While Marianna Torgovnick, for example, finds in Freud a more or less self-serving mechanism of displacement (199),[15] for Boyarin the necessity for such negotiations suggests Freud's "postcolonial anguish," making him "both the object and the subject of racism" ("Jewish" 42, 40). Jacqueline Rose similarly remarks that, because of his own racial markedness, Freud could not "unproblematically or unequivocally embody the master narrative of the West" (50), and Barbara

Johnson locates in Freud's position something akin to the Du Boisian "double consciousness" (*Feminist* 10).

Apart from considering Freud's racialized status, or the repression of racial difference in other early psychoanalytic texts,[16] critics have involved psychoanalysis in their readings of African American texts and culture, thereby attempting to redress "the poverty of language offered by psychoanalysis for addressing issues of race and culture" (Luciano 158). A number of biographies of African American literary figures, for example, are allegedly "quite Freudian" (Murray 163).[17] Similarly, given the psychoanalytic emphasis on family relations, it is not surprising that slavery's violent disruption of familial ties has been discussed in psychoanalytic terms. Without explicitly engaging psychoanalysis, Hortense Spillers's influential essay "Mama's Baby, Papa's Maybe" (1987) pointed the way for subsequent theorists to explore the forms of relatedness that African slaves created during their captivity.[18] In *Mastering Slavery*, for example, Jennifer Fleischner considers women's slave narratives as examples of the self-narration that psychoanalysis, according to her, solicits from the analysand with the hope of his or her "liberation" from childhood traumas (5 and passim).[19]

The question that more immediately concerns me in this study, however, is the precise way we can engage Lacanian psychoanalysis with African American literature. While Freud's anthropological texts have provided an obvious starting point for a consideration of his implication in colonialism, Lacan's possible contribution to an investigation into race is harder to tease out: as opposed to issues of sexual difference, there is very little in Lacan's writing that explicitly relates to questions of race or seeks to explain racism. Nevertheless, the recent turn in Lacanian criticism to politics suggests an opening for this investigation. Antonio Viego, for example, reads Lacan's abhorrence of ego psychology's adaptive models, especially their prevalence in the United States, in terms of a critique of "North American coercive assimilatory imperatives working on ethnic-racialized subjects . . . that demand of them a certain mandatory adjustment and adaptation to North American 'reality'" (5) and suggests an "overlap" between Lacan's antiassimilatory critique in the 1950s "and the similar critique of assimilation crafted by early Chicano movement activists" (25). Ernesto Laclau and Slavoj Žižek have similarly suggested some ways in which we can approach politics from a Lacanian perspective.[20] Recent examples of Lacanian scholarship that engage questions of race and colonialism include the collection *The Psychoanalysis of Race* (1998), edited by Christopher Lane, Kalpana Seshadri-Crooks's theory of racialized subjectivity in *Desiring Whiteness: A Lacanian Analysis of Race* (2000), Abdul JanMohamed's study of Wright, *The Death-Bound Subject: Richard Wright and the Archaeology of Death* (2005), and Viego's psychoanalytic reading of Latino/a cultures and literatures, *Dead Subjects: Toward a Politics of Loss in Latino Studies* (2007). Seshadri-Crooks, and some contributors to Lane's volume[21] may be seen as "the New Lacanians" of psychoanalytically inflected critical race theory, given their "emphasi[s on]

Lacan's late notions of drive, *jouissance*, and the real at the expense of his early concepts of desire, the imaginary, and the symbolic" (Mellard 395).[22] Perhaps because of the vagaries of Lacan translations into English, the question of the real, with which Lacan was increasingly concerned in the late 1960s and 1970s, has until recently been neglected in Anglo-American scholarship. If the impact of this shift in Lacanian theory from the imaginary and symbolic aspects of subjectivity to the nonhuman, asubjective realm of the real "has not yet fully registered with [Anglo-American] psychoanalytic theorists of gender" (Dyess and Dean 738), its ramifications for psychoanalytic theories of race has remained similarly unexplored. It is this question that Lacanian race theory needs to concern itself with. The current study is a contribution to this emergent field of scholarship.

Yet, the specter Cleaver evokes—of psychoanalytic arrogance that dismisses the concerns of African American subjects or texts—is not completely exorcised by the proliferation of these psychoanalytic studies of race and racialization. Given the history of psychoanalysis and race, any attempt to read Wright psychoanalytically will conjure up the threat of inflicting on him the reductive readings to which Cleaver was subjected. Predictably enough, this has been the exact outcome of many a psychoanalytic attempt at Wright scholarship. Two examples of this are Margaret Walker's psychobiography *Richard Wright, Daemonic Genius* (1988) and Allison Davis's chapter on Wright in *Leadership, Love, and Aggression* (1983): both demonstrate the necessity of relentless suspicion in the face of psychoanalytic approaches to questions of race. Apart from the many inaccuracies Michel Fabre points out in his "Margaret Walker's Richard Wright," Walker stands as a representative of a reductive tradition in psychoanalytic criticism that misreads not only the literary (or [auto]biographical) texts under consideration but also psychoanalysis.[23] Similarly, Davis's reading of Wright's autobiography exemplifies an elision of the social and political specificity of the "analysand's" situation. Davis writes that while "Wright may have allowed his public to believe that his character and behavior were formed by the impact of racial oppression by Mississippi whites," "[o]ne only needs to read his *Black Boy* . . . to understand that Wright considered his family the primary source of his anger and his hatred." In a reading that is both authoritarian and misogynist, Davis insists that Wright's revolt and anger were not primarily directed against his racist environment, or even that the family structures might have been determined by or mediating such oppressive social structures. Instead, Wright, like his father, was rebelling against his maternal family, "a long, grim line of puritan matriarchs," which "consisted of a clan of obsessively religious and sadistic women" (156–58). At the very least, Davis fails to realize that "[r]acism becomes a part of the subject's unconscious because the parents consciously and unconsciously reflect the racist values of the culture onto the subject from the first moment of life" (Tate, *Psychoanalysis* 133).

We may approach the thorny relation between race and psychoanalysis by noting how it echoes many other interdisciplinary encounters in which the latter has been involved. Discussing its relationship with feminism, Jane Gallop writes: "the worst tendency, the inherent constitutional weakness of psychoanalysis, is to be apolitical (which is to say, to support the institutions in power)" (*Daughter's* 101). "One of psychoanalysis's consistent errors," she continues, aptly describing Cleaver's situation, "is to reduce everything to a family paradigm. Sociopolitical questions are always brought back to the model father-mother-child. Class conflict and revolution are understood as a repetition of parent–child relations. This has always been the pernicious apoliticism of psychoanalysis" (144).[24] Interrogating the link between literature and psychoanalysis, Shoshana Felman suggests that, to avoid such traps of psychoanalytic application—in which, according to her, psychoanalysis stands as the Hegelian master over the bondsman of literature ("To Open" 5)—we must "engage in a real *dialogue* between literature and psychoanalysis." We begin this by reversing the master–slave positions and by "consider[ing] the relationship between psychoanalysis and literature *from the literary point of view*" (6). The objective in establishing this dialogue, Felman continues, is not, however, simply to overturn the positions, but, rather, "to disrupt this monologic, master–slave structure" (6) altogether so that one can "avoid *both* terms of the alternative" and "deconstruct the very structure of *opposition*, mastery/slavery" (7). Yet, skeptical about the possibility of nonreductive psychoanalytic approaches to other disciplines, Françoise Meltzer, in her introduction to *The Trial(s) of Psychoanalysis* (1988), sees psychoanalysis as an inherently colonial project, a form of "empire-building"—what Deleuze and Guattari in *Anti-Oedipus* call "the analytic imperialism of the Oedipus complex" (23)—that seeks to incorporate all other disciplines within its own paradigm and assumptions (Meltzer 7). According to her, Felman's attempted reversal of the master–slave relationship of psychoanalysis and literature betrays the constitutive reductiveness and "totalizing teleology" of the psychoanalytic approach. For what guarantees that such a reversal has any deconstructive effects on the dialectic hierarchy? According to Meltzer, Felman's unstated assumption is that the positions of the master (for psychoanalysis) and that of the slave (for literature) are so "*natural*" that any role reassignment would, by its sheer absurdity, quickly abolish the structure itself (3). At bottom, Felman's argument is a mere variation of psychoanalytic narcissism in which all other disciplines are but mirroring surfaces for psychoanalysis to discover its inalienable and unchangeable truths: "Not content to see itself as one in a number of enterprises, the psychoanalytic project has at its foundation a vision of itself as the meaning which will always lie in wait; the truth which lies covered by 'the rest'" (2). According to Meltzer, psychoanalysis must be reduced from its position of metadiscursive arrogance: "Psychoanalysis is not on trial in order to be attacked," she writes, "but in order to be put back into its place—or, at least, into *a* place" (5). For her, the only way to bring psychoanalysis and other disciplines together is to return the violence of the previous encounters in the exact same form onto psychoanalysis.

Meltzer's response to Felman indicates the difficulty in engaging ethically and productively with any constellation of discourses contaminated by histories of violent hierarchies. (And we may suspect that all such encounters are marked by a certain degree of violence.) She correctly admonishes us that, rather than applying psychoanalytic theory to other disciplines, we must *interrogate* it. This does not mean primarily that we are to criticize it—rather, we must not assume that we are already familiar with its insights, which can then be applied to other fields of knowledge. Yet, what should give us pause is Meltzer's desire to repeat the dialectic of violent reduction of which psychoanalysis stands accused. Here we should ask, what is the ethics of a justice that announces the defendant's incarceration and confinement to "its place" in the opening statement of the trial? Moreover, wanting to "put [psychoanalysis] *back* into its place" (emphasis added), Meltzer assumes that *we already know what this place is.* In this, we are reassured that nothing unexpected will be uncovered during the trial, nothing new unearthed. The testimony will not complicate notions of guilt or responsibility; the whole procedure is committed to a rigid politics of foreseeability.

It is precisely an opening to the unexpected that Gallop points to as ethical engagement in analysis. She suggests that, as a way to negotiate the difficult division between psychoanalysis and politics—which Cleaver's example perfectly illustrates—we must involve the analyst in the scene of interpretation: "Analysis, if it is not to be a process of *adapting the patient* to some reigning order of discourse, must include the risk of unseating the analyst" (*Daughter's* 102; emphasis added).[25] For Frantz Fanon and James Baldwin, for example, the adaptive aims of psychiatry and psychoanalysis reveal the disciplines' colonialist and racist allegiances.[26] Always insisting on what may be called the maladaptive aims of treatment, Lacan, too, refers to the dangers of misdirected analysis when he writes that "the inability to authentically sustain a praxis results, as is common in the history of mankind, in the exercise of power" ("Direction" 216). Yet, while critics such as Deleuze and Guattari condemn psychoanalysis tout court—"It is certain that psychoanalysis pacifies and mollifies, that it teaches us resignation we can live with" ("Deleuze" 229)—Lacan identifies the adaptive methods of ego-psychology as *inauthentic* practice.

Hence, while observing the reductive approaches in the history of psychoanalysis—where psychoanalytic knowledge appears as an uncontested master interpreting its objects—we should note with Lacan that such a rigid postures of self-identity belong to the unethical subject whose relationship to the other is characterized by imaginary misrecognition. The ethical subject, for Lacan, is the mobile subject of desire or, increasingly in his later work, of the drive. That the institution of psychoanalysis is often characterized by rigid, masterly interpretative ambition should not prevent us from seeing what remains unfixable and mobile—that is, inherently ethical—in psychoanalytic discourse. Our inability to rest in one position long enough for it to materialize into a master's throne or the voyeur's keyhole constitutes the *ethics of psychoanalysis.* In this ethical perspective, moreover, lies psychoanalysis's availability for political work. "Psychoanalysis," as Tim Dean writes, "is political precisely to the extent that the position of the analyst diametrically opposes that of the master" (*Beyond* 108). Correspondingly, Meltzer's assumption of already knowing what psychoanalysis can do and her ambition to firmly locate psychoanalysis—to "be actively reductive with psychoanalysis" (7) and to "put [it] back into its place" (5)—appear in this context as decidedly unethical. As Adam Phillips observes, "the fact that psychoanalysis is difficult to place . . . may be one of its distinctive virtues" (3).

One should nevertheless remain doubtful about all claims to "good-natured" exchanges between discursive fields. Edward Said argues that the seemingly neutral setting of "discursive situations" usually masks the fact that "far from being a type of idyllic conversation between equals, [these situations are] more usually of a kind typefied [*sic*] by the relation between colonizer and colonized, the oppressor and the oppressed" ("Text" 181–82; see also Gandhi 28). Like all exchanges established across disciplines, discourses, and knowledges, the dialogue between African American and psychoanalytic literatures is inevitably marked by disparities. Establishing such encounters is an effort where we find our "good intentions" always compromised and endlessly betrayed. However, while violence may indeed be unavoidable in these encounters, we must resist letting this violence solidify into a structure. Furthermore, in all their inherent dangers and pitfalls, such dialogues are precisely what psychoanalysis is all about. Through its engagement with an other, psychoanalysis—and, importantly, other disciplines participating in this dialogue—retains the mobility characteristic of the ethical subject of desire.

I am not the first to see such troubled encounters as potentially productive. The editors of *Female Subjects in Black and White: Race, Psychoanalysis, Feminism* (1997) observe in the intersection of race and psychoanalysis (and, in their project, of feminism) as many "transformative possibilities" as "stubborn incompatibilities" (Abel et al. 1). Encounters that take place or erupt in this treacherous middle-ground, they warn, must not be considered entirely reconcilable. Yet, through such implication we can avoid, however momentarily and without any guarantees of success, reductive psychoanalytic readings that, in their insistence on "reduc[ing] everything to a family paradigm" (Gallop, *Daughter's* 144), bypass sociopolitical questions of power and disenfranchisement. It is, exactly, this *reductive* analytical reading to which Cleaver objects in his account of his sessions in prison—not the fact that analysis implicates the family: "each time [the psychiatrist] interviewed me he deliberately guided the conversation back to my family life, to my childhood. *That in itself was all right*, but he deliberately blocked all my attempts to bring out the racial question" (11; emphasis added). (Psycho)analysis's emphasis on the familial is not necessarily oppressive; Oedipus becomes "the fountainhead where the psychoanalyst washes his hands of the world's inequities" (Deleuze and Guattari, *Anti-Oedipus* 128) only when the analyst refuses everything outside the family, turns a blind eye to the possibility that the family may be imbricated in society and its politics. Thus, if psychoanalysis has participated in the Western projects of colonialism, Fanon's example clearly shows that its historical role in *anti*colonial and *anti*racist struggles is anything but negligible. Similarly, in African American thinking, Du Bois's disillusionment with the ability of objective, scientific knowledge to fight race prejudice coincides with his discovery of racism's unconscious support. In his autobiographical texts, he suggests that this "twilight zone" of "stronger and more threatening forces" that remain in excess of "conscious and rational" motivation behind race prejudice can be explored through Freud's insights (*Dusk* 282, 283, 296). I thus suggest that the question, *What can psychoanalysis do?*, can and must be answered only through the future encounters in which it will be engaged.

One way to think about the transformative potential of these encounters is to give the term its Deleuzian specificity. That is, we can think of the dialogue between psychoanalytic and African American texts as an *encounter between bodies*, as an opening onto an unforeseeable becoming that may transform the encountering bodies beyond recognition—with all the violence that this phrase suggests.[27] Deleuze teaches us that, unlike what Meltzer assumes in her trial scenario, encounters cannot be legislated. For him, bodies are always defined by their relations to other bodies, by their ability to be transformed by the "resonance" that exists between their internal and external relations. Our regarding bodies as autonomous betrays the fact that we have misunderstood their interimplication, have missed their profound resonance. Bodies, consisting of smaller bodies and their relations to one another, are separable yet interconnected: separable in the specificity of their internal relations, yet connected through the bodies they inevitably share with other bodies, in which they enter into a different relation. In their encounter, bodies are never completely compatible, never pieces of a puzzle that snugly complement one another, but are always held together by a certain friction, gravitational pull, or violent harmony. Our success in joining two separate bodies (of work) seamlessly cannot but betray the fact that we have dismissed their true complexity.

I suggest that the Deleuzian understanding of bodies' interimplication, eschewing any notions of harmonious compatibility, characterizes the most productive work emerging from the encounter between psychoanalysis and race. Conversely, the understanding of the necessary transformation that takes place in all encountering bodies reveals some problems in the recent studies on psychoanalytic and African American texts. I take Claudia Tate's *Psychoanalysis and Black Novels* as an example: her work warrants detailed attention because of the centrality it accords to Wright and the largely favorable reviews it has drawn as a timely opening between psychoanalysis and African American writing.[28]

As Tate notes in her introduction, many commentators, "demanding manifest stories about racial politics," have marginalized African American texts that engage questions not directly dealing with society's racial and racist structuring. Texts that "focus on the inner worlds of black characters without making that world entirely dependent on the material and psychological consequences of a racist society" (5) have been rejected for neglecting to interrogate and critique racism and, consequently, considered "not black enough" (4). Tate counters this critical history by reading a number of novels that, from the perspective of the African American canon, have appeared "anomalous" in the output of their authors. She argues that these texts in fact reveal what has been implicit in the more canonical works: according to her, they are central to their authors' oeuvre and the concerns of the black canon in that they "not only inscribe[] but exaggerate[] a primary narrative, an 'urtext,' that is repeated but masked in the canonical texts" (8).

Tate in effect proposes that, rather than continuing what Henry Louis Gates, Jr., calls the "curious valorization of the social and polemical functions of black literature" that has stunted black literary criticism ("Criticism" 5–6),[29] critics of African American texts should pay attention to the workings of unconscious processes, which can neither be explained as effects of a (racist) environment nor contained by the authors' or readers' political designs. In her impressively researched readings, she shows how black texts are amenable to analyses that pay attention to what she calls "textual subjectivity . . . structured by the mediation of desire and prohibition" (25) or the "implicit narrative fragments of desire and pleasure inscribed in the rhetorical organization and language of the text" (27). Her range of references in psychoanalytic theory is similarly ambitious: she draws from Lacan, Freud, and Melanie Klein while gesturing to Karen Horney's and Marie Bonaparte's theories of femininity.

Although demonstrating her familiarity with the field of psychoanalysis, however, Tate does not extend to its theories the kind of detailed investigative effort with which she reads African American texts. This is a conscious choice: she writes in her introduction that, because her audience consists mainly of scholars and readers of African American literature, she is "not interested in consolidating and privileging the theoretical demands of individual schools of psychoanalysis" (12). For her, the numerous psychoanalytic theories "facilitate [her] analysis of unconscious textual desire in the novels as unacknowledged fantasies of lost and recovered plenitude" (13). What she ends up doing, however, is not merely refusing to take sides in intra-disciplinary debates around different psychoanalytic approaches. Rather, her neglect of critical engagement with psychoanalysis leads not only to a reductive theoretical understanding, but also to psychoanalysis's approximating the kind of "narcissistic," "ubiquitous subject, assimilating every object into itself," that Meltzer sees it as. In the mode of psychoanalytic "facilitat[ion]," where what is being read are the black novels, not the psychoanalytic texts, Tate unwittingly perpetuates a familiar hierarchy between literature and psychoanalysis: their potential dialogue is reduced to an application where *our understanding of psychoanalysis is not affected by its encounter with African American writing.*

Similarly, in *Mastering Slavery*, Fleischner, while sympathetic to a psychoanalytic approach to slave narratives, ultimately fails to achieve (what Deleuze would call) an *encounter* between, or (in Felman's terms) the *implication* of, psychoanalytic and literary texts.[30] For Tate and Fleischner, psychoanalysis never emerges as *a body of text to be read*; rather, it surfaces as received theory, "enabl[ing] an approach" to literature (Fleischner 4). Immobilizing psychoanalysis as a body of texts with transparent meaning, texts that need not be read, such an approach reduces the "mutually illuminating and interpenetrative" (Spillers, "'All'" 77) encounter to an application. A failure to engage psychoanalysis allows it to function as a master discourse through which the meaning of other texts can be glossed. Such a dynamic can be discerned in the history of the institutionalization of psychoanalysis: psychoanalysis becomes most oppressive and normative precisely when it congeals into institutions with a received and well-understood canon; at the moment of institutionalization and canonization psychoanalysis loses its capacity for the kind of self-interrogation that I argue marks psychoanalytic approaches proper.

It is to avoid the kind of unintentional reduction that Tate and Fleischner exemplify that I will spend a fair amount of time considering psychoanalytic texts in this study, beginning with the first chapter, which outlines in detail Lacan's theory of the visible. Lacan allows us to understand how the process of racialization, in immobilizing the racial(ized) subject, also enables the "imaginarization" of the white symbolic order—a concept I will explicate as the study progresses—whereby the symbolic is rendered blind and vulnerable to challenges. Understood psychoanalytically, subject formation is not predetermined by societal or historical contingencies but opens a space for the subject's "incalculability" (Copjec, *Read* 208), premised on the unpredictable interventions of the unconscious and the real. Mobilizing such incalculability, Bigger Thomas—the protagonist of Wright's debut novel, *Native Son* (1940)—disappears from the disciplinary radar of the white symbolic order. Even though he is soon arrested in and by his own strategies of subversion, his "flight," in repeating the dynamics of dissemblance and performance familiar from African American history, opens the possibility of understanding contingency and unpredictability as politically salient strategies.

In Chapter 2, "The Grimace of the Real: Of Paranoid Knowledge and Black(face) Magic," I trace one strand of these volatile strategies by focusing on twentieth-century discussions of blackface minstrelsy and particularly African American actors' roles therein. I connect the dynamics of blackface to Bigger's game of paranoid identification. This allows us to further theorize the white symbolic order. As Žižek and others have pointed out, all symbolic constellations are supported by an inassimilable foreign body that simultaneously enables and threatens symbolic structures; this *objet a* marks the site where the real, whose foreclosure is the condition of the emergence of the subject and the symbolic, bleeds into the symbolic. I argue that in the white symbolic, this *objet a* is the mask of blackness, too close proximity to which is signaled by anxiety and the terror of symbolic disintegration.

Chapter 3 strictly speaking exceeds the parameters of "the American optic" in turning to Frantz Fanon's post-colonial work. In "Unforeseeable Tragedies:

Symbolic Change in Fanon, Wright, and Lacan," I continue sketching a Lacanian theory of racialization and symbolic change by bringing together the "tragic" female figures in the work of Fanon (the Algerian women of "Algeria Unveiled"), Wright (Aunt Sue in "Bright and Morning Star"), and Lacan (Antigone in *The Ethics of Psychoanalysis*). I argue that, when engaged with Lacanian psychoanalysis, Fanon's and Wright's work allows us to intervene in two ways in contemporary debates in psychoanalytic theory, particularly its feminist and critical-race-theoretical strands. First, Fanon's and Wright's characterizations of sexuation and racialization suggest, contrary to what a number of the New Lacanians have argued, that in symbolic constellations where race is of paramount importance, not only sex but also race can function as a real difference. We must, in other words, consider Luce Irigaray's argument that "[s]exual difference is one of the major philosophical issues, if not the issue, of our age" (*Ethics* 5) in conjunction with W. E. B. Du Bois's observation, "The problem of the twentieth century is the problem of the color-line" (*Souls* 17). In Fanon and Wright, certain racialized positions can precipitate access to (what Lacan calls) Other jouissance. As such, these positions are potentially analogous to the ethical persistence that Lacan locates in the figure of Antigone. Consequently, Lacan's theory of symbolic subject positions around the real allows us to theorize racialized symbolic structures; furthermore, Fanon's, Wright's, and Lacan's tragic female figures represent psychoanalytic ethics in pointing to the possibility of a radical symbolic overhaul. With the Algerian guerrillas, the lone terrorist Aunt Sue, and the unbending Antigone, the three male writers whose work concern me here attempt to theorize *becoming* beyond existing symbolic possibilities.

Second, an analysis of the descriptions of female resistance by Wright and Fanon suggests that the models of subversion described by the two strands of psychoanalytically inflected feminist theories that have developed since the early 1990s—namely performativity (linked to Judith Butler's work) and the ethics of the real (propounded by the New Lacanians)—are not as incompatible as is often argued. A psychoanalytic reading of Fanon's and Wright's female figures of resistance and subversion shows that performativity, or what Lacanians would call acting, bears an unpredictable relation to the potentially violent rupture of the ethico-real act.

Exploring further the possibilities of symbolic change, the final two chapters turn to Wright's autobiography.[31] "The Optical Trade: Through Southern Spectacles" considers how, in *Black Boy* and the slave narratives that its structure follows, the experiences of reading and writing enable perspectives beyond "Southern spectacles"—a term I adopt from Pauline Hopkins—that is, beyond the enforced perspectives of white supremacy inculcated, in large part, through the threat of the public terror of lynching. I argue that the experience of the literary—an eminently maladaptive art—sustains what Lacan would call the mobility of desire. In the final chapter, "Avian Alienation: Writing and Flying in Wright and Lacan," I propose that in Lacanian terms this mobility can also be described as that of "alienation." In this, my argument diverges from Orlando Patterson's influential theory of the enslaved subject's "natal alienation" in his *Slavery and Social Death* (1982). I suggest that the dangerous and unpredictable, yet potentially productive, experience of the literary is described by slave narrators (and, following them, Du Bois and Wright) as providing an alienated distance from the Other's nonnegotiable demands. Lacan's discussion of alienation's role in subject formation suggests the reasons behind slave narrators' and Wright's ambivalence about the effects of reading and writing (both of which are described in the tropes of "flight" and "flying" in African American culture as well as in Lacanian psychoanalysis). In providing no definitive form for the potentially different symbolic world it points toward, the experience of the literary also functions as something like the drive, dangerously seeking the beyond—which is to say, the internal, implosive impossibility—of symbolic actualizations. As such, it courts, or demands, symbolic death. Consequently, I argue that, in Wright's, Du Bois's, and Booker T. Washington's discussions of the effects of "book learning," we find reconfigured the slave narrators' choice of self-destruction over enslavement. Unlike what Russ Castronovo claims in "Political Necrophilia," the choice of (symbolic) death should not be seen as a renunciation of worldly struggles, an orientation beyond the embodied exigencies of living. If we are to take seriously the psychoanalytic notion of *Todestrieb*, which Castronovo alludes to, we must understand the choice of death in terms of *the becoming of the death drive*. This becoming plays a central role in Lacanian ethics, whose contribution to critical race theory I seek in this study.

While I discuss a number of writers and issues in African American and postcolonial theories, literatures, and cultures in this study, Wright is the central figure to whom I return in every chapter. His centrality is warranted for two reasons. First, of all African American writers, even above Ralph Ellison, Wright is most consistent in dealing with the American optic—the questions of race and visibility—beginning with his early short stories and debut novel. Second, his reception seems to repeat, with uncanny precision, the racist strategies of confinement and (in)visibility that he himself explores in his texts. Ellison describes these strategies when he notes that black invisibility is inextricable from the curious condition of "'high visibility,'" which "actually render[s] one *un*-visible" ("Introduction" xxv). Similarly, I contend that Wright's presence in American letters is like that of "a purloined letter": as perhaps the most influential and visible work by a twentieth-century African American writer, his texts have become invisible on the literary scene, texts whose circulation is independent of their content. It is for this reason that, notwithstanding some exceptions, I will not take up Paul Gilroy's call for a reassessment of Wright's later work, namely, the texts he produced after his exile to France in 1947 (see Gilroy, *Black* ch. 5), where Wright increasingly distanced himself from the strictly African American subject matter and style of writing he had become associated with through *Native Son*, his autobiography, and the short story collection *Uncle Tom's Children* (1938/1940). By concentrating on his earlier writings, I too may be seen to be giving credence to the argument that Wright only ever produced worthwhile material while living in the United States and concentrating on "what he knew best," that is, the situation of the African Americans.[32] Yet, I argue that, given his status as "the purloined letter," there may be good reasons for returning to the most familiar texts of Wright's corpus.

Wright has been vilified for his depiction of women,[33] denounced for "gratuitous" violence,[34] and degraded as the author of programmatic protest literature.[35] While his work does continue to be read, within academia and outside it, he has become more of a political and cultural than a literary figure; it is precisely such overexposure that has made it difficult to approach his texts—especially the most influential ones—without already knowing what one will read, without already being sutured into a fixed perspective as a reader. As Johnson argues, this is exactly what happens with canonized texts: they become the already-read. Consequently, critics such as Paul de Man suggest that the canon need not be dismantled but *(re)read*: "While critics of the university are claiming that campus radicals are subverting the literary canon and that students are no longer reading it," Johnson writes, "de Man is . . . claiming that really *reading* the canon is what is subversive, because students in traditional 'humanist' classrooms are usually taught *not* to read it but to learn ideas about it" ("Double" 30).[36] J. Hillis Miller's observations concerning the fate of canonical works are equally resonant here: "The canonical texts are as strange as any texts uncovered by anthropologists or by students of minority cultures. They are so odd, in fact, that one wonders whether they can ever really have been dominant at all, that is, whether they have ever actually been read. Has what they say ever been, or could it ever be, or ought it ever to be, institutionalized in social practice? Something else may have been put in their place all along" (4). If indeed Wright's early texts—most notably *Native Son* and *Black Boy*—have become part of the canon, we can return to them, assuming that our canonical readings of them may in fact be but inherited preconceptions.[37] Turning Wright's texts from being the already-read to the read-again is one of the tasks of the present study.

CHAPTER 1

A [B]igger's Place

The "Racial" Subject in the White Symbolic Order

> *[Bigger] doubted if Max could make him see things in a way that would enable him to go to his death. He doubted that God Himself could give him a picture for that now. . . . He did not want his feelings tampered with; he feared that he might walk into another trap.*
>
> —Richard Wright, *Native Son*

> *In this matter of the visible, everything is a trap. . . .*
>
> —*Jacques Lacan,* The Four Fundamental Concepts of Psycho-Analysis

According to one version of black literary history, *Native Son* was the first African American novel which dropped "the mask that grins and lies" (Dunbar 402) and allowed the white audience to look behind the minstrel apparel. This is not to claim that all African American writing previous to 1940 should categorically be seen as "humble novels, poems, and plays" (Wright, "Blueprint" 37); it is, however, to recognize the unprecedented impact that Wright's book had on the American imagination. Irving Howe's estimation that "[t]he day *Native Son* appeared, American culture was changed forever" (63) is a view shared by numerous other critics.[1]

If Wright's debut novel has had almost inestimable social and political effects, its literary value remains contested.[2] Numerous readers have objected particularly to what they consider the crippling effects of the narrative's extremely limited point of view. The consequent flaws are said to be evident, for instance, in the unconvincing fictional characters. Howe voices a common criticism in saying that "the characters have little reality, the Negroes being mere stock accessories and the whites either 'agitprop' villains or heroic Communists" (66). They are "stereotypical beyond belief" (Bradley 2018), while Bigger is merely "a symbolical monster," "an incarnation of a myth" (Baldwin, "Many" 72).[3]

Wright attributes a degree of authorial intentionality to the "unrealness" of the fictional characters: "I gave no more reality to the . . . characters than that which Bigger himself saw" ("How" 45). If the characters lack depth, this does not indicate a failure of Wright's skills as a writer—as Howe deduces—but arguably points to something crucial about the black protagonist's lived experience. In "How 'Bigger' Was Born" (1941), recalling his deliberate attempts to have the reader adopt Bigger's *point of view*, Wright emphasizes the importance of "perspectives": "as much as I could, I restricted the novel to what Bigger saw and felt. . . . I had the notion that such a manner of rendering made for a sharper effect, a more pointed sense of the character, his peculiar type of being and consciousness. Throughout there is but one point of view: Bigger's" (44). Wright sensed that, for the narrative to work, the reader had to identify with Bigger's position in the field of vision. Representing the reader as a film viewer—captured by "a movie unfolding upon the screen" (44)—Wright suggests that an acute appreciation of *looking relations* and of the way in which the subject is posited within visibility is critical to understanding the structures of subjection peculiar to African Americans. Consequently, the observation that has been articulated as criticism—that *Native Son*'s structure as a novel is hopelessly damaged and the social "message" of the text compromised by its limited point of view—can be understood as the central insight in the text. Wright deploys perspectival strategies to describe the black man's position in a world as Manichean as anything Frantz Fanon analyzes.

This emphasis on seeing and perspectives is a constant in Wright's work. Calling for black writers to abandon the tradition of "Negro writing of the past" (37) and to adopt new ways of looking at black life, Wright propounds on the importance of angles of vision in his manifesto "Blueprint for Negro Writing" (1937): "Perspective," he writes, " . . . is that fixed point in intellectual space where a writer stands to view the struggles, hopes, and sufferings of his people. There are times when he may stand too close and the result is a blurred vision. Or he may stand too far away and the result is a neglect of important things" (45). Similarly, nearly twenty years after the publication of "Blueprint," he writes in the foreword to George Padmore's *Pan-Africanism or Communism* (1956) of the African American and the colonized subject: "The black man's is a strange situation; it is a perspective, an angle of vision held by oppressed people; it is an outlook of people looking upward from below" (xxii). The problems and possibilities of perspective occur in the earliest moments of literacy and reading in Wright's life. Recounting his childhood experiences of reading in *Black Boy* (1945), he recalls how he was instinctively absorbed in the narratives' perspectives: "The plots and stories in the novels did not interest me so much as the point of view revealed" (238).[4] Like the autobiographical narrator, the protagonist of the posthumously published, unfinished novel *A Father's Law* (2008) seeks a slant that would render what he observers readable and meaningful: "what was hovering tantalizingly beyond his reach were not the facts of the case but a meaningful interpretation of them, an angle of vision from which to see and weigh them" (111). What perspective allows is not the unveiling of that which is hidden but the motivating force of a symbolic logic that would organize the world for the subject.

Wright shares this understanding of the importance of perspective with a number of post-colonial writers, among them the Caribbean novelist and critic George Lamming. Because, as Lamming writes in "A Way of Seeing," "what a person thinks is very much determined by the way that person sees" (*Pleasures* 56),[5] modes of looking become central sites in anticolonial struggle. Sandra Pouchet Paquet writes: "Perspective is expressive of resistance, commitment, and self-celebrating creativity. It emphasizes the substance and method of the writer's calculated decentering of colonial discourse." Referring to Wright's "Blueprint," she argues that in Lamming's work "perspective is demystified as an intellectual process that resituates the colonial writer as an active agent of decolonization" (x).

What Paquet underemphasizes, however, is the ways in which the effects of such anticolonial and emancipatory strategies remain beyond the subject's "calculated" or "intellectual" control. Indeed, the discovery of the subject's coercive embeddedness within perspectives marks Wright's work after "Blueprint." If, in 1937, Wright anticipates Lamming's emphasis on subversive seeing as a form of liberation, he may have been overly optimistic about the redemptive potential of his project. He speaks of the proper perspective as being enabled by a "fixed point in intellectual space," thus implying that there is an unequivocally productive viewpoint for the Negro writer to adopt. It is telling, especially in the light of his subsequent texts, that the word "fixed" can evoke captivity and confinement (or even castration) as much as mastery and control. Indeed, already in his debut novel, Wright interrogates not only questions of seeing but also the ways in which the subject is situated within the "picture." In this move from the subject-as-look to the subject-as-spectacle, Wright's project of finding a proper perspective turns into one of describing one's violent subjection to others' perspectives. Consequently, ten years after "Blueprint," he observes in an interview, "To be American in the United States means to be white, protestant, and very rich. This excludes almost entirely black people and anyone else who can be *easily identified*" ("I Feel" 126; emphasis added). Casting the backward glance of a recent expatriate, Wright suggests that, in the United States, such things as citizenship are determined to a large extent by how the subject—more precisely, his or her body—is positioned within the national perspective; authority and disenfranchisement in American society are premised on the subject's location within the regimes of (in)visibility.[6]

His argument thus anticipates a more recent one in critical race theory. Robyn Wiegman, for example, writes: "Modern citizenship functions as a disproportionate system in which the universalism ascribed to certain bodies (white, male, propertied) is protected and subtended by the infinite particularity assigned to others (black, female, unpropertied). . . . [T]his system is itself contingent on certain visual relations, where only those particularities associated with the Other are, quite literally, *seen*" (6). Similarly, Lauren Berlant suggests that, in the United States, corporeality and citizenship (and the consequent rights) are incompatible with one another: "white male privilege," she writes, "has been veiled by the rhetoric of the bodiless citizen, the generic 'person' whose political identity is a priori precisely because it is, in theory, non-corporeal" (112). Unable to approximate the "ideal model of bodily abstraction," gendered and racialized subjects are, in their corporeal materiality, marked out from what Wiegman calls "the privileged ranks of citizenry" (94): "American women and African-Americans have never had the privilege to suppress the body" (Berlant 113). Like Wiegman and Berlant, Wright describes the racially marked subject as coercively enveloped and immobilized within visibility, within a fixed perspective.

In what follows, I propose that we take seriously Wright's emphasis on the importance of perspectives in understanding formations of race and subjectivity. While often the immediate reference in Wright's discussions of perspective—such as his foreword to Padmore's *Pan-Africanism or Communism*—is to Friedrich Nietzsche, I suggest we approach this question through psychoanalysis,[7] in particular as it has been elaborated by Lacan, who himself, as Jacques-Alain Miller argues, found the Husserlian "science of perspective" of "capital importance" ("Introduction" 9, 11). I suggest in this chapter that Lacan's theory of the visible, which he develops through a reading of the Renaissance accounts of perspective, helps us delineate Wright's understanding of how racialization affects subjectivity and mobility. Taking as my example the intertextual moments of *Native Son* and the early short story "Fire and Cloud" (1938), I begin by showing how Wright's work anticipates critical race theory's historicizing account of the character of the modern concept of "race" as a category of visibility. This emergence of modern "race" can be, and has been, theorized through Michel Foucault's famous delineation of the modern society's disciplinary and panoptic character. While largely in agreement with critical race theory, Wright's work describes and analyzes a societal and libidinal structure where racial difference is an organizing principle. Moving from critical race theory's historicist account to psychoanalysis, I argue that Lacan's theory of perspective allows us to see how this structure—the white symbolic order—is grounded not in any (ethical) symbolic mobility but a rigidity that is characteristically imaginary. This imaginary position is exemplified in Lacan's perspectival theory by Denis Diderot's blind observer and the two colonial masters in Hans Holbein's *The Ambassadors*. For Wright, the white liberals of the Dalton household become the exemplary subjects of imaginary immobility and blindness, which momentarily allow Bigger to disappear from and manipulate the white symbolic order.

THE RACIALIZING GAZE AND CRITICAL RACE THEORY

Considering Wright's insistence that the narrative of *Native Son* proceeds from the black protagonist's perspective, it may seem surprising that Bigger is described in the novel mostly as a visible, tangible entity, lacking in any significant depth of character. That is, although Wright evokes Bigger's "peculiar type of being and consciousness" in "How Bigger Was Born," in the novel itself he seems to depict this "type" in terms of a depthless surface. While Howe extends his complaint of the author's crude brush to all characters, it is true that in particular Bigger seems to be devoid of convincing psychology.

This lack of depth corresponds to the lack of private interiority that Bigger himself experiences in the opening of the narrative. His defenseless, exposed position within visibility becomes obvious during his first visit to the house of his white employers, the Daltons. In this crucial scene, Bigger is led into the hall by the Daltons' maid, Peggy, and uncomfortably sits down on an armchair to wait for the master of the house. Conscious of his awkward corporeal presence and unable to find a comfortable position for his body in the white environment, he feels disturbed by the unreadability of the surrounding inanimate objects, "whose nature he tried to make out, but failed" (39). Then there is a sudden interpellative call that surprises the visitor. Under the eyes of Mr. Dalton, Bigger is immediately turned into a visible entity, a racially marked body:

> "All right. Come this way."
>
> He started at the sound of a man's voice.
>
> "Suh?"
>
> "Come this way."
>
> Misjudging how far back he was sitting in the chair, his first attempt to rise failed and he slipped back, resting on his side. Grabbing the arms of the chair, he pulled himself upright and found a tall, lean, white-haired man holding a piece of paper in his hand. The man was gazing at him with an amused smile that made him conscious of every square inch of skin on his black body. (39)

Like the white gaze that, according to W. E. B. Du Bois, contemplates the Negro with "amused contempt and pity" (*Souls* 11),[8] the look attributed to Mr. Dalton racializes the black man's body such that Bigger becomes conscious not only of his skin but of his entire corporeality, of "every square inch of skin on *his black body*." In other words, the white gaze does not merely assign Bigger a skin color but simultaneously determines something beyond the epidermal surface: it racializes the subject such that his blackness becomes "connected to the organic coherence of the organism as a whole" (Wiegman 31).

That Mr. Dalton's racializing gaze penetrates the depths of Bigger's body becomes evident when we compare the above scene to the description of lynching in Wright's short story "Fire and Cloud." In this comparison, we detect the differences and similarities between two practices of subjugation with varying emphases on violence and visibility. In the story, Reverend Dan Taylor is approached by communist activists to endorse their cause. When he will not promise the town's law enforcement officers to tell his starving parishioners not to take part in a march organized by the communists, a white mob kidnaps him and drives him to the outskirts of the town, where he is savagely beaten. Taylor's hesitant ideas of justice are galvanized by his beating, and he makes a stand: as the starving members of his community gather at the church, he addresses them, saying that they have to show a united front if they are to defeat the white law that keeps them in poverty and hunger. As the crowd marches from the black section of the town, they are joined by the poor white population. Reaching City Hall, they are met by a blockade of policemen and other white people, including the mayor. The threat of further violence is deflected as the mayor, persuaded by the multitude of the crowd, prepares to address the people, apparently ready to compromise. The story ends with Taylor, seeing the mayor hushing the crowd, saying to himself: "'*Freedom belongs t the strong!*'" (154).[9]

"Fire and Cloud" has usually been read as a straightforward depiction of the beginnings of politicized, interracial class consciousness—whose necessity Du Bois, for example, emphasized (*Autobiography* 232)—rendering the story a piece of political propaganda where Wright shows how the disenfranchised, poor black and white people "split by the color line" (Du Bois, *Autobiography* 234) are able to confront their oppressors as a united front under the banner of communism. Michel Fabre, for instance, writes that the story "was expressly designed to show the development of political awareness among Negroes" (*Unfinished* 134), while Stanley Edgar Hyman refers to it as one of Wright's "Stalinist tracts and caricatures" (2010). As I will argue throughout this study, one needs to remain thoroughly suspicious of such propagandistic readings of even Wright's 1930s work. This is not only because Wright explicitly questions the use of literature as propaganda in such early texts as "Blueprint for Negro Writing" (47–48), but also because the reduction of his fiction—whether "Fire and Cloud" or "Bright and Morning Star" (see Chapter 3 below)—to textbook pieces of communist consciousness-raising blinds us to its complexity and craft. To go beyond such simplistic readings, I here contrast Taylor's beating to the scene where Bigger finds himself for the first time face to face with his white employer.

Having been kidnapped and driven by a group of white men to an uninhabited place outside the town, Taylor is dragged out of the car. Mr. Dalton's words to Bigger—"'All right. Come this way'"—are echoed in the abusive address by one of the white men:

> "Aw right, nigger!"
>
> [Taylor] stopped. Slowly he raised his eyes; he saw a tall white man holding a plaited leather whip in his hand, hitting it gently against his trousers' leg. (197)

Told to take off his vest, he has no option but to comply: "He stripped to his waist and stood trembling. A night wind cooled his sweaty body; he was conscious of his back as he had never been before, *conscious of every square inch of black skin there*" (198; emphasis added). Encountering a mob of men who, in the darkened woods, threaten him with a whip, Taylor experiences bodily affects strangely similar to Bigger's, who comes face to face with a wealthy, sympathetic white man in broad daylight in the latter's respectable home: "Grabbing the arms of the chair, [Bigger] pulled himself upright and found a tall, lean, white-haired man holding a piece of paper in his hand. The man was gazing at him with an amused smile that made him *conscious of every square inch of skin on his black body*" (emphasis added).

The mirroring of the two scenes, explicit in the nearly identical phrasing, is too poignant to be coincidental, especially as the texts were written approximately at the same time. With the two scenes, I suggest, Wright exemplifies two overlapping strategies of racialization. In one, a whipping racializes the subject; in the other, visibility takes over the role of overt violence. The function of the beating in "Fire and Cloud" is to show the insurrectionary black man his "place" by making him, quite literally, conscious of his black skin: the member of the mob holding the whip tells Taylor, "'When we get through with you tonight youll know how to stay in a nigger's place!'" (197). As Wiegman argues, the practice of lynching sought to deny African Americans their citizenry and to keep them to their place by reimposing corporeality on (particularly) black men by "deterring the now theoretically possible move toward citizenry and disembodied abstraction" (94; see also 83).[10] In this, it worked to confine African Americans in the same way as enforced visibility: both have as their effect "the imposition of an extreme corporeality," which is precisely what "define[s] . . . the distance [of African Americans] from the privileged ranks of citizenry" (94). Correspondingly, the intertextuality between the scenes from "Fire and Cloud" and *Native Son* reveals the violence inherent in the strategies of racializing visibility described in Bigger's first visit to the Dalton's.

We must nevertheless heed the differences between the strategy of marking the body through lynching (as in the scene from "Fire and Cloud") and that of enforced visibility (exemplified in Bigger's encounter with Mr. Dalton). In the former, "the sign of lowly status takes its form from an exterior branding, imposed at a precise point in time and performed by a disciplinary system readily available to the [subject's] immediate (however disempowered) return gaze" (Wiegman 213n13). Whereas the imposition of corporeal markings—in Taylor's case, the welts from the beating—makes the counter-discourse of a "return gaze" possible, this is prevented when such visible markings are naturalized and encompass more than a particular, definable part of the corporeal surface: "the application of disciplinary power to the entire surface of the body . . . is the product of a different technology, one in which the processes of organization are similarly imposed but wholly veiled. In this dispersion of the locus of power, the body is made the productive agent, a sign wrapped in the visibility it cannot help but wear" (213n13). The comparison between Wright's two texts illustrates exactly, and quite literally, that "[t]o mark the body is not the same as *being* a bodily mark" (25). This is inscribed in the minor inflections that differentiate the two scenes. The impending lynching makes Reverend Taylor "conscious of *every square inch of black skin* [on his back]"; under Mr. Dalton's gaze, Bigger, on the other hand, becomes "conscious of *every square inch of skin on his black body*." Whereas Taylor's painful consciousness of his black skin is physically located and contained in "the square inches" on his back where the lashes will land, Bigger is entirely enveloped by this "skin consciousness." Crucial ramifications follow in the respective position of the two men. Initially, after the beating, Reverend Taylor seems to be entirely engulfed by his branding and his existence to be defined by the pain: "He seemed to have only a head that hurt, a back that blazed, and eyes that ached. In him was a feeling that some power had sucked him deep down into the black earth, had drained all strength from him." However, he immediately recognizes these as momentary sensations that will pass, inevitably giving way to the "life" before and beyond the beating: "He was waiting for that power to go away so he could come back to life, to light" (201). If Taylor escapes the "nigger's place," Bigger, in his place—the [B]igger's place—is more thoroughly fixed and determined; his relation to white people remains lodged deeper. In an early scene in *Native Son*, he rhetorically asks his friend,

> "You know where white folks live?" . . . Bigger doubled his fist and struck his solar plexus.
>
> "Right down here in my stomach," he said. "Every time I think of 'em, I *feel* 'em," Bigger said. (18)

As he visits the Daltons', we are further told that "[t]here was an *organic conviction* in him that this was the way white folks wanted him to be when in their presence" (42; emphasis added). His position under the white gaze has become a corporeal, "organic" part of his existence; in Alice Walker's terms, he has "whitefolks on the brain" (*In Search* 35). Such corporealization of blackness is evident in other African American characters in the novel. Looking at his sister, Bigger thinks, "The very manner in which she sat showed a fear so deep as to be an organic part of her; she carried the food to her mouth in tiny bits, as if . . . fearing that it would give out too quickly" (93).

The comparison between the short story and the debut novel illustrates critical race theory's argument about the shifts that took place as the modern concept of race emerged at the turn of the eighteenth and nineteenth centuries. Visible differences had crucially figured in early discussions of race by European commentators. François-Marie Voltaire, for example, notes in 1765 that "[*n*]*one but the blind* can doubt that the whites, the negroes, the Albinoes, the Hottentots, the Laplanders, the Chinese, the Americans, are races entirely different" (5; emphasis added).[11] However, while in seventeenth and eighteenth centuries visible traits such as skin color and hair texture denoted human variation for Western observers, it wasn't until the late eighteenth and early nineteenth centuries that racial determinants began to signify "inherent and incontrovertible difference[s]" in humans (Wiegman 31). Winthrop Jordan and Wiegman argue that, for the seventeenth-century travel writer François Bernier and the eighteenth-century scientists Carolus Linneaus and Johann Friedrich Blumenbach, racial differences did not order human beings into the hierarchies whose establishment and maintenance became the central occupation of nineteenth-century racial sciences. Jordan writes that, in Linneaus's theories of the organization of nature, human races were distinct yet did not compose a hierarchy (217–28).[12] Similarly, Blumenbach "was not without his preferences, for he argued that the original type of man was Caucasian. Yet at this critical juncture [of writing *On the Natural Variety of Mankind* (1795)] he made no attempt to seize the obvious opportunity for constructing a hierarchy of variations. . . . The white man was the 'primeval' type and stood at the center; but there was no indication that he was on top" (223).[13] Following Jordan, Wiegman suggests that, in the seventeenth and eighteenth centuries, the most prominent and authoritative figures in natural sciences to comment on questions of race considered racial differences impermanent and nonhierarchical, most of them remaining "tied to an understanding of race as mutable and of the human species as part of a larger continuity of order and meaning" (29). With the emergence of comparative anatomy in the late eighteenth and early nineteenth centuries, however, racial differences began to designate something beyond the strictly visible characteristics of the human organism. Rather than signaling merely visible differences induced by climate conditions, racial traits—skin color, hair texture, cranial measurements, and physiognomy in general—became manifestations of deeper, permanent differences between human races.

According to Wiegman and Jordan, the new understanding of differences as lodged "more than skin deep" (Wiegman 30) in the human organism justified the hierarchization of races: "The move from the visible epidermal terrain to the articulation of the interior structure of human bodies . . . extrapolated in both broader and more distinct terms the parameters of white supremacy, giving it a logic lodged fully in the body" (31). With the emergence of the technologies of comparative anatomy, visible traits remained crucial in signaling racial differences, but these differences now betrayed an incontrovertible essence that allowed human beings to be ordered into an evolutionary hierarchy. The racializing gaze of comparative anatomy, in other words, determined the racially marked subject beyond skin color, hair texture, and cranial peculiarities by connecting these traits to one's permanent character. According to the logic of post-eighteenth-century human sciences, once observers determine a person's blackness, they can infer any number of genetic, psychic, or social traits pertaining to that person. As Stuart Hall writes, "Even in racist discourses, where the evidence of racial difference appears to be figured so *obviously* on the surface of the body, so plain for all to see . . . , [physical traits] are capable of carrying their negative connotations *only* because they function, in fact, as the signifiers of a deeper code—the genetic—*which cannot be seen* but which, it is believed, has the power of a science to fix and stabilise racial difference" (21).

Not surprisingly, African American thinkers and philosophers of history have been aware of such shifts. Even if his periodization differs from that of more recent theorists, Du Bois, for example, observes the recent emergence of racial categories: "The discovery of personal whiteness among the world's peoples," he writes in *Darkwater*, "is a very modern thing,—a nineteenth and twentieth century matter, indeed. The ancient world would have laughed at such a distinction" (30). He argues that, while the distinction of us/them may be inherent in human beings, "[i]t has been left . . . to Europe and to modern days to discover the eternal world-wide mark of meanness,—color!" (42). In "Big Black Good Man" (1957), Wright illustrates African Americans' recent imprisonment in visibility by showing how, for the contemporary white imagination, the blackness of African American subjects refers to "depths" well beyond the epidermis. Set in Copenhagen, Denmark, and told from the point of view of Olaf Jenson, an owner of a local hotel, the story describes the phobic reactions of the white proprietor to what in his eyes seems like a monstrous apparition of a huge black man. Encountering the visitor who comes in and asks for a room in the hotel, Olaf finds himself "staring at the biggest, strangest, and blackest man he'd ever seen in all his life" (95). The unexpected appearance of the black man in his daily surroundings incites an unexplained terror in Olaf, who finds himself "filled . . . with fear of this living wall of black flesh" (103). Here, again, blackness is transposed from the skin to the blackness of the whole body, "black flesh." Subsequently, the white protagonist has a violent dream of the black man drowning in which he imagines "the decomposing mass of tarlike flesh" and "picture[s] the giant's bones as being jet black and shining" (106).

Unlike Reverend Taylor, Bigger, hailed by Mr. Dalton and racialized by his gaze, exemplifies this racially marked subject whose characteristics penetrate beyond, yet remain intimately tied to, his visible difference. That Bigger's blackness is not reducible to any notion of epidermal pigmentation is suggested during his subsequent encounter with Mrs. Dalton, whose blindness does not stop her from discerning Bigger's race. If for Voltaire only the blind can escape the categorizing imperative of racial differences, by the mid-nineteenth century, as the truth of race had migrated from bodily surface to interiority, impaired vision did not impede the process of racialization. Mrs. Dalton exemplifies this blind observer who nevertheless is perfectly capable of discerning race. Even though she is blind, Mrs. Dalton, as her husband notes, "'has a very deep interest in colored people'" (41). The seeming easiness with which "color" and "depth" are conjoined suggests precisely the nineteenth-century shift from superficial to deep, immutable differences. In a later scene where Bigger encounters Mrs. Dalton in the kitchen, he has the same visceral response to her presence as he had to her husband's looking: "He went to the sink, watching her as he walked, feeling that she could see him even though he knew that she was blind. His skin tingled" (52). Reminding us of Bigger's "tingl[ing]" skin, Wright describes the effects of the proximity of white people on African Americans in his *12 Million Black Voices*: "The muscles of our bodies tighten. Indefinable sensations crawl over our skins and *our blood tingles*" (100; emphasis added). Intertextually linking "skin" with "blood," the supposed carrier of genetic racial qualities, Wright suggests that the white gaze constructs not only visible racial differences, but, more radically, imposes an involuntary self-consciousness of inherent racial characteristics.

This envelopment within visibility renders Bigger and other racially marked subjects knowable in their "place." It may seem questionable to insist that, for an individual subject at a given occasion, it would be less detrimental to be subjected to extreme physical violence—like Reverend Taylor is—than to be caught in a situation where one is uncomfortably positioned, like Bigger, within a regime of visibility. However, Wright's two texts suggest that this, in all its disturbing implications, is indeed a legitimate conclusion. For whatever reservations one might pose against reading "Fire and Cloud" as a politically encouraging story at the conclusion of which one witnesses the first stages of a powerful interracial labor movement, as the result of his harsh treatment Taylor does stand up to the white law and lead his parishioners to fight against poverty and social inequality. Taylor, that is, comes to possess (political) agency that Bigger lacks. Having been made conscious of his black skin by the branding of his back, he is able to establish a counter-strategy by looking back at the beating—in Wiegman's words, by giving it a "return gaze"—from a vantage point different from the "nigger's place" into which the mob violence has attempted to fix him.

A "[B]igger's place"—the enforced African American place within visibility—seems more restricting and confining than the "nigger's place" that the lynch mob promises to show Taylor. We can see this shift from corporeal brutality to the violence of the visible, evident in the intertextuality of "Fire and Cloud" and *Native Son*, in its historical dimension when we recall Frederick Douglass's argument, in 1894, that instead of punished by lynchings, the crimes that were imputed to blacks should be dealt with "in open court and in open daylight" ("Why" 762). However, as Bigger is captured and brought to trial, he becomes aware of how visibility—the "open daylight" of the law—replaces overt violence as a more effective means in his subjugation. Having been led to the courtroom, he is faced with a crowd of people anxious to see the killer. Recalling his capture by the white vigilante group some days earlier, he thinks: "If they had killed him that night when they were dragging him down the steps, that would have been a deed born of their strength over him. But he felt they had no right to sit and watch him, to use him for whatever they wanted" (237). In the courtroom, he resents the people "watching him as he sat here. . . . Why could they not just shoot him and get it over with?" (312–13). Becoming aware of the differences between the crude power exercised by a lynch mob and the more subtle and legitimate forms wielded in such institutions as courts of law, Bigger feels it more debilitating to be caught within visibility, in front of a crowd of spectators, than it would have been to be subjected to mob violence. With this, Wright shows how the mutations in racist procedures of confinement have responded to the partial success of Douglass's and others' projects of outlawing racial violence.[14]

The [B]igger's place is defined, first of all, in terms of concrete, lived geography. While in the North this geography is not circumscribed by the Southern ethos of Jim Crow, it is nevertheless, as Benjamin Quarles (194) observes, strictly divided into black and white areas.[15] In *Native Son*, the line between blackness and whiteness is drawn in the segregation of black and white populations within the unnamed city where the novel is set. Whereas Mr. Dalton can own property within the Black Belt, "Bigger could not live in a building across the 'line.' Even though Mr. Dalton gave millions of dollars for Negro education, he would rent houses to Negroes only in this prescribed area, this corner of the city tumbling down from rot" (148). African American women have their own particular cages: looking at his girlfriend Bessie, Bigger senses "the narrow orbit of her life: from her room to the kitchen of the white folks was the farthest she ever moved" (118). In *12 Million Black Voices*, Wright similarly describes the female domestic servants as inhabiting an "orbit of life [that] is narrow—from their kitchenette to the white folk's kitchen and back home again" (131). He further links this narrowness of life, concretized in the way that the black population is forced to live in small, overpriced kitchenettes, to white supremacist terror: "The kitchenette is our prison, our death sentence without trial, the new form of mob violence that assaults not only the lone individual, but all of us, in its ceaseless attacks" (106). As Wiegman notes, "The panoptic violence of the slave system, its various practices of surveillance and observation, have in this century reconfigured in the disciplinary mechanisms of urban space" (210n3).

Conscious of the confinement imposed on him and other African Americans, Bigger muses that white people "'make us stay in one little spot'" (300), in the ghetto with its "empty buildings with black windows, like blind eyes" (147). The fact that he and other African Americans are confined to this "cramped environment" blinds him, makes him "str[ike] out blindly" (204). Frustrated by the cost of living, Bigger exclaims, "'They gouge our eyes out!'" (211). The concrete, societal confinement thus has both a blinding effect on racially marked subjects and makes possible their economic exploitation.[16]

In terms of the African American "place," then, more is at stake than the physical confinement of urban geography. If we bear in mind Wright's emphasis on the limited point of view as a textual strategy in *Native Son*—that everything in the narrative is apprehended through Bigger's eyes—we can observe that what is described in the scene of Bigger's first encounter with Mr. Dalton is not necessarily how Mr. Dalton sees Bigger, but how Bigger sees Mr. Dalton seeing him. In other words, the African American place in the field of the visible is as much a psychic location as a geographical or spatial one. We need to understand, then, the ways in which subjection takes place within and through the domain of the visible, a task in whose pursuit I turn to psychoanalysis. The following discussion of Lacan's theory of subjectivity and the visible establishes some parameters to help us not only describe the dynamics of racialization, but also consider the ways in which the (white) symbolic order, through its very operations, is open and vulnerable to counter-strategies, which I will discuss in more detail in the following chapters.

THE RACIAL SUBJECT IN PERSPECTIVE

Insisting on the centrality of perspective to a discussion of nineteenth- and twentieth-century formations of race, I follow Hubert Damisch's observation that "[w]ithout any doubt, our period is much more massively 'informed' by the perspective paradigm . . . than was the fifteenth century" (28).[17] This continuing importance is reflected not only in Wright's discussions of perspectives but also in Lacan's detailed engagement with theories of Renaissance painting, which constitutes one of his numerous dialogues with disciplines outside the psychoanalytic domain. It is important to note that philosophical texts, such as theories of perspective, do not merely provide material for Lacan to illustrate psychoanalytic concepts. Rather, as Charles Shepherdson writes, with these dialogues, he "seems to be transforming his own conceptual apparatus" ("Lacan" 126). In his engagement with Renaissance perspective and geometry, Lacan primarily seeks to conceptualize further the subject's relation to the symbolic and the real. I suggest that, by engaging Lacan's reading of perspective with Wright's understanding of racial difference, we can theorize (what I will call) the white symbolic order in more detail.

To prepare for this dialogue with Wright, I revisit Lacan's triangular schematizations of the field of the visible in *The Four Fundamental Concepts of Psycho-Analysis.* While Kaja Silverman has discussed in detail these diagrams ("Fassbinder"; *Threshold,* chaps. 4–6), I suggest that we must more firmly link them to the question of the Lacanian real. As I argue in Chapter 3 below, the real allows us to understand what the Lacanian ethics of racialization might look like.

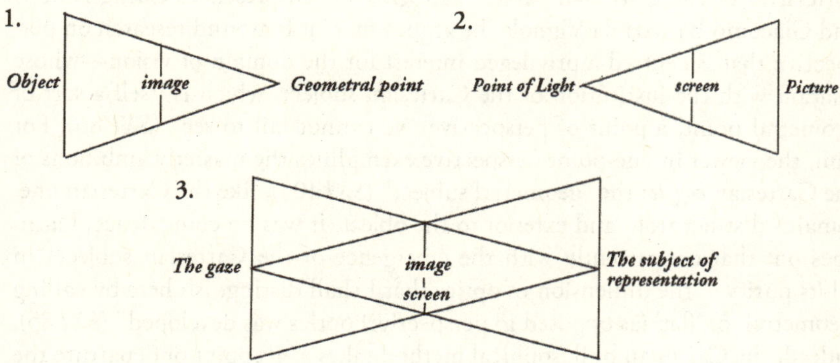

Lacan's schemas recapitulate yet complicate our usual understanding of Renaissance perspective and its cultural impact. As Silverman writes, Lacan's first triangle seems to represent "artificial perspective" ("Fassbinder" 146–47, 408n24), invented by Filippo Brunelleschi in the second decade of the fifteenth century and mathematically formulated some twenty years later in Leon Battista Alberti's *On Painting* (1435).[18] According to received opinion, Alberti's account, which Damisch calls "one of the fundamental texts of western culture" (xxiii), had a revolutionary impact on the West. During the following two centuries, one-point perspective not only became naturalized in Western art (Kemp 53), but also allowed the Western man to position himself, as Alberti asserts in his treatise, as "the measure of all things" (52). In *Perspective as Symbolic Form* (1927), his classic twentieth-century essay on perspective, Erwin Panofsky writes that "the history of perspective may be understood . . . as a triumph of the distancing and objectifying sense of the real, and as a triumph of the distance-denying human struggle for control; it is as much a consolidation and systematization of the external world, as an extension of the domain of the self" (67–68). More recent readers of the Renaissance have echoed Panofsky in emphasizing the cultural influence of Renaissance perspective, where the observer/painter, situated at the apex of the triangle of the Euclidean "cone of vision," "seemingly surveys the world from an invisible, and hence transcendental, position" (Silverman, *Threshold* 132). As John Berger writes, with the invention of perspective "[t]he visible world [was] arranged for the spectator as the universe was once thought to be arranged for God" (16). Subsequently, "[a]ided by the political and economic ascendance of Western Europe, artificial perspective conquered the world of representation under the banner of reason, science, and objectivity" (W. J. T. Mitchell 37). The mapping of space through artificial perspective, it is argued, covers over its own functioning and disguises the incorporative impulses of the subject occupying the geometral point: "Through perspective subjectivity can claim itself to be entirely objective all the while it works in concert with the conquest of space" (Conley 48).

Lacan, too, begins with this reading of Renaissance perspective. He suggests that the exterior position of the subject-as-painter in the first triangle is correlative of the Cartesian subject of *cogito*, of self-presence. Citing Alberti and Giacomo Barozzi da Vignola, he argues that "it is around research on perspective that is centred a privileged interest for the domain of vision—whose relation with the institution of the Cartesian subject, which is itself a sort of geometral point, a point of perspective, we cannot fail to see" (*SXI* 86). For him, the viewer in one-point perspective exemplifies the masterly ambitions of the Cartesian *cogito*: the "geometral subject" (*SXI* 105), like the Cartesian one, remains distinct from and exterior to the object. It was no coincidence, Lacan goes on, that concurrently with the emergence of the Cartesian subject "in all its purity," "the dimension of optics that I shall distinguish here by calling 'geometral' or 'flat' (as opposed to perspective) optics was developed" (*SXI* 85). Indeed, the Cartesian philosophical method takes as its point of departure the outside position of one-point perspective. As Descartes writes in his *Discourse on Method*, the philosopher should "try[] to be a spectator rather than an actor in all the dramas that are played [in the world]" (24).

Yet, Lacan goes on to complicate our understanding of Renaissance perspective and what it suggests about the field of the visible. As Peter de Bolla writes, his purpose is to undermine "the inherent Cartesianism in the model, that which precisely equates seeing with being" (68). Lacan begins by arguing that the optics exemplified in the simple schema for one-point perspective does not necessarily entail sight at all. For example, in the sixteenth century, to allow artists to construct perspective correctly, Vignola and Albrecht Dürer designed contraptions where visual rays were concretely represented with strings stretching from the apex of the cone of vision through a "window" where the three-dimensional image was reproduced on flat surface.[19] Citing also Denis Diderot's "Letter on the Blind for the Use of Those Who Can See," Lacan argues that in these instances geometral perspective is reducible to spatial coordinates and visualizable (or, more appropriately, *graspable*) by the blind: "at issue . . . is simply the mapping of space, not sight" (*SXI* 86; see also 93). Indeed, "[t]he geometral dimension of vision does not exhaust, . . . far from it, what the field of vision as such offers us as the original subjectifying relation" (*SXI* 87). Thus, while critics have traditionally seen in Brunelleschi and Alberti a shift from "tactile-muscular intuition" of Euclidean geometry to the "visual intuition" of the Renaissance (Ivins 8–13), for Lacan, Vignola's and Dürer's instruments reveal that at question here is still tactile space.

To move from tactile space to the visible world proper, Lacan complements the first triangle with an inverted one and, finally, presents a schema where the two triangles are conjoined. While the apex of the first triangle designates the position of the "geometral subject," the second schema "turns *me* into a picture" (*SXI* 105). The third figure, which is an amalgamation of the previous two triangles, gives us the field of the visible proper. In the "scopic register" represented here, the gaze emerges "outside" the subject-as-the-geometral-point. Consequently, the subject's objective, exterior positioning to the field of the visible turns out to be an unsustainable fiction and the subject is forced to realize that "I am looked at, that is to say, I am a picture" (106). While geometral or flat perspective—the first triangle—is based on Euclidean geometry, Joan Copjec has argued that the visible that Lacan alludes to relies on *projective geometry* ("Strut"). According to this argument, Brunelleschi's and Alberti's painterly practices, schematized in the first triangle, were posited on Euclidean geometry. Victor Burgin, too, writes that Brunelleschi and Alberti utilized classic Greek geometry in their mathematization of perspective. In having the picture plane intersect the Euclidean "cone of vision," "Renaissance perspective took its most fundamental concept from Euclid's *Optics*" (106).[20]

Euclidean geometry relies on "a vision in the first person that is coherent, that evinces mastery, and that would imply as its condition the position of a subject that could eventually reclaim it for its own, as its own property, its own representation" (Damisch 32); Euclidean space is "homogeneous, universal, and regular" (Grosz, *Space* 94). Lacan's third triangle, however, is constructed according to the breakthrough in perspectival theories that is associated with Girard Desargues's work in the seventeenth century. As Copjec points out, Desargues's 1636 treatise on painting instructed (as the title itself puts it) how to "*draw[] in perspective without using any third point, a distance point or any other kind, which lies outside the picture field*" ("Strut" 11).[21] There is no space outside the field of vision; perspective emerges according to lines internal to the visible world. The practical advantage of the new model was that, while Alberti's strategy necessitated drawing lines beyond the picture plane, which made things particularly cumbersome in fresco paintings (Field, "Perspective" 239), Desargues's method required no such exterior point to the picture field. For Lacan, the payoff exceeds breakthroughs in painterly practices. When perspective is understood as the field of vision figured in the third triangle, it undoes the mastery of the Cartesian *cogito* by situating the viewer inside the picture. For Lacan, the third triangle encapsulates the field of the visible in which the gaze of the Other operates.

According to Lacan's famous analysis, Hans Holbein's painting *The Ambassadors* (1533) illustrates the dynamics of the scopic drive, figured in the third diagram. This discussion of anamorphosis, I suggest, allows us to theorize the racializing gaze in Wright's work. Lacan's analysis begins when the viewer-subject, having partially turned away from the painting, finally discerns, in an awry glance, the anamorphotic skull in the foreground of Holbein's painting (*SXI* 88). It is at this moment that, our geometral perspective destroyed, we find ourselves drawn into the picture, thrown out of our position of exteriority that flat geometry has allowed (*SXI* 92). For Lacan, the skull, representing the lost object—the gaze as *objet a*—captures us in the destabilizing trajectory of desire:

> at the very heart of the period in which the subject emerged and geometral optics was an object of research, Holbein makes visible for us here something that is simply the subject as annihilated—annihilated in the form that is, strictly speaking, the imaged embodiment of the *minus-phi* [(-ø)] of castration, which for us, centres the whole organization of the desires through the framework of the fundamental drives. (*SXI* 88–89)

The skull as the *objet a* cannot be registered by or in the geometral field of vision. When it comes into view, not only is the geometrically organized picture eclipsed, but we as spectators are captured by the image, called into it. While in the visible world organized according to projective geometry the subject is within the picture (*SXI* 96), in paintings executed according to Alberti's dicta, "the illusion [within the painting] . . . does not reach out to me in order to capture or seduce me" (Marin 32; qtd. in Bersani and Dutoit 45; Bersani and Dutoit's brackets and ellipsis). The visual field organized around Alberti's geometral perspective does not solicit the viewer's participation in the image.

What remains less often noted about Lacan's analysis of Holbein is that, apart from capturing the viewer-subject within the *symbolic* circuits of desire, the painting also illustrates another form of entrapment in the visible, one that is markedly *imaginary*. In speaking of the subject who is "caught, manipulated, captured, in the field of vision" (*SXI* 92), Lacan refers not only to the viewer-subject but also to the two "splendidly dressed" (*SXI* 92) male figures of the painting. In other words, in *The Ambassadors* we discern *two traps*: an imaginary one set by Euclidean vision, and a symbolic one organized around projective geometry. Whereas the viewer-subject is captured through projective geometry and anamorphosis, the ambassadors are effectively entrapped by the "flat," geometral perspective. Surrounded by objects and inventions that symbolize the proper, scientific perspective,[22] the two men are "immobile," "frozen, stiffened in their showy adornments" (*SXI* 92, 88). Representing the colonial authority of proper vision and worldview, the two regal subjects are immobilized in their grand imperialist postures. Geometral perspective, in other words, rigidifies, "imaginarizes," the subject of representation who arrogates himself to the position of the self-possessing, objective observer.

In *Native Son*, we see not only the simultaneous operation of these two traps but also the way in which the subject's getting caught in the symbolic circuit of desire may register, ambivalently, as mobility. In the opening of the narrative, Bigger is fixed within a scheme where the (white) onlookers occupy the position of the Cartesian viewer-subject—represented by the two men in *The Ambassadors*—and in which he is relegated to the place of the object. Given the flat geometry organizing his world, he is perfectly right in assuming that the blind Mrs. Dalton can "see" him, like Diderot's blind man is able to map space from the geometral point. In the Euclidean space of whiteness, Bigger's racially marked position makes it easy for anyone to know him and "his place." He intuits this himself. As he faces Mary for the first time, he "felt that she knew every feeling and thought he had at that moment and he turned his head away in confusion" (56). And, later: "He tightened with hate. Again she was *looking* inside of him and he did not like it" (70; emphasis added). The question here is not only of Bigger's perceptions; as he is driving Mary to school, she says to him:

> "I'm going to meet a friend of mine who's also a friend of yours". . . .
>
> "Friend of mine!" he could not help exclaiming.
>
> "Oh, you don't know him yet," she said, laughing. (56)

Similarly, as Bigger answers Peggy's question as to why he has not touched his meal, saying, "'I wasn't hungry,'" she urges him, "'You're hungrier than you think'" (158–59). Others have ready access to Bigger and assume an immediate and intimate knowledge of him. Moreover, Bigger himself is convinced that they possess an insight into or knowledge of him.

Bigger's extremely confined place does not represent either one of the two forms of capture Lacan illustrates with Holbein. Rather, what Lacan refers to as the entrapment of the viewer-subject through the dissolution of traditional perspective becomes a moment of mobility for Bigger. As he discerns the point of failure in the white symbolic order—that which renders its solid structures fluid, anamorphotic—he learns how to transgress the rigid place it has assigned him. Simultaneously, much like Holbein's ambassadors, the white spectators, whether overtly racists or liberal-minded, become immobilized in their postures of self-knowledge, which Bigger's murderous transgression reveals as imaginary delusions. I will pursue this uncanny moment of double entrapment—which for Bigger is also one of momentary emancipation—in the next chapter. Here, I want to explore in more detail not only the functioning of the white symbolic order but also its slippage into the imaginary, a dynamic that ultimately points to the similarity between Wright's white characters and Holbein's ambassadors.

Mary's knowledge of Bigger depends on her having spectatorial access to him, on her being able *to look*. She points to the causality between looking and knowing when she tells Bigger that she wants to visit the black district of the city: "'You know, Bigger, I've long wanted to go into those houses . . . and just *see* how your people live. . . . We know so *little* about each other. I just want to *see*. I want to *know* these people'" (60).[23] However, here we must carefully delineate what is referred to by the terms "seeing" and "knowledge." Clearly, Mary's assumption that, in order to *know* black people, she *must be able to look* into the hidden recesses of the black district illustrates what Lacan terms "the realist's imbecility" ("Seminar" 40). Visiting the Black Belt, Jan and Mary are like the "pack of idiots" Du Bois writes of having to cart around "the Negro slums" during his instructorship at the University of Pennsylvania (*Dusk* 58). Mary assumes that there is some concealed presence in the Black Belt that she has to seek out and that, having found it, she will unproblematically be able to recognize and "know." She fails to see that the dividing line between her world and the black district functions in a far more complicated manner. There is nothing in the Black Belt which she would not be able to *already have seen* were she to change her *way of looking*, her perspective. The "knowledge" of African Americans is inscribed into her own privileged position which enables her to flirt with the ideas of "subversion" and "revolution" that fill Bigger with anxiety and anger. The knowledge sought by Mary, then, can be described as imaginary knowledge.

Yet, paradoxically, Mary's specular knowledge does function in the realm of the symbolic. Here, we begin to recognize how, because of the violent hierarchies of any historical context, symbolic *savoir* can mask imaginary blindness. Obviously, even though Mary's "seeing-knowing" renders her knowledge imaginary, such looking is effectively symbolic in the racial(ized) field of the visible. That is, while her knowledge may be imaginary (*connaissance*), it also functions as symbolic knowledge (*savoir*) according to *the (Euclidean) coordinates of the white symbolic order*. Furthermore, to define Mary's knowledge as simultaneously symbolic and imaginary is to point to the possibility of troubling, perhaps subverting, the white symbolic order by rendering it blind, by denaturalizing its structures. Whereas her knowledge pertains to the white symbolic order, it can be rendered imaginary when Bigger learns to transgress his place.

What I call the white symbolic order, then, can be sustained only by the rigid organization of subject positions in which racial difference to a large extent determines the form of jouissance available to one.[24] Of course, if the symbolic is the realm of ethical mobility for Lacan, the rigidity of the white symbolic betrays its unethical—hence un-symbolic—character. Bigger's subsequent, momentarily successful manipulation of its structures indeed reveals its imaginary character. My point here is analogous to that of feminist critics who have argued that what in a patriarchy passes off as the symbolic order may be nothing but a masculine imaginary (Tyler 41). While the danger of "pictur[ing] the symbolic order as some sort of extension of the imaginary" is that we profoundly misunderstand their discontinuities and differences (Dean, *Beyond* 86), insisting on the proximity of the imaginary and symbolic formations allows us to show how Jan's and Mary's assumption that structures can be seized and redistributed can only be the result of their own privileged positions within the networks of power and visibility. When they insist that they are "on [his] side" (55), Bigger feels uneasy: "Why was Mary standing there so eagerly, with shining eyes? . . . [T]hey made him feel his black skin by just standing there looking at him, one holding his hand and the other smiling" (58). Bigger knows that subject positions are not as easily negotiable as the young white couple assume. As I will go on to argue in the following chapters, they can be attacked, but this requires something more than white liberals' willingness to be on the same "side" as Bigger. Instead, despite their good intentions, Jan and Mary repeat the gestures of white inattention and condescension exhibited by her (equally well-intending) parents. Like Mr. and Mrs. Dalton (40), they patronizingly discuss Bigger in his presence without addressing him directly ("'They've got so much e*mo*tion! What a people!' . . . 'They've got to be organized. They've got spirit. . . . ' [ellipsis in original] 'And their songs—the spirituals! Aren't they marvelous?'" [66]). Unsurprisingly, their liberal antiracism in fact perpetuates the structures whose symptoms it purports to alleviate, exacerbating their violence, a fact to which Bigger's uneasy reactions attest. As Bigger later tells his lawyer Boris Max, who tries to insist that Mary acted out of kindness: "'Mr. Max, we're all split up. What you say is kind ain't kind at all. I didn't know nothing about that woman. . . . We live apart. And then she comes and acts like that to me'" (297).

As the object of Jan and Mary's racializing gaze, Bigger "fe[els] naked, transparent; he fe[els] that this white man, having helped to put him down, having helped to deform him, held him up now to look at him and be amused" (58). In other words, because they are in a position where they can hold on to their illusion of mastery, Jan and Mary are unable to see that their interventions only reiterate the very conditions of Bigger's subordination.[25] Yet, as their *inability to see* suggests, the two young radicals, because of their positions of privilege, are also rendered blind: they cannot see Bigger's position any more than they can discern the effects of their actions on him. As I will argue in the next chapter, Bigger learns to utilize this *structural blindness*, which he discovers to entail white people's privilege. To anticipate the argument, we can note that his helpless feeling of being held up as a "deformed" object to the looks of the young white couple is depicted as something which turns him into a spectacle yet simultaneously makes him all but disappear. Feeling both "naked" and "transparent," he seems to be in a position that is paradoxically marked both by a specular overexposure or vulnerability *and* by of invisibility. This doubleness of "transparency"—a term which refers to an object that is both obvious or readily knowable and simultaneously looked through and missed—suggests what Lewis Gordon calls "the existential dynamics of black invisibility" ("Existential" 71). That is, while Bigger is identifiable as an embodiment of Ralph Ellison's nameless "invisible man" whose "'high visibility'" renders him invisible ("Introduction" xxv), this transparency of the black subject paradoxically enables a certain defensive concealment. When Bigger mobilizes racial visibility to his advantage, the white people find themselves, like Holbein's ambassadors, immobilized and blinded in postures of self-knowledge.

In the lectures that comprise *The Four Fundamental Concepts of Psycho-Analysis*, Lacan exemplifies this dynamic by implicating himself in such imaginary arrogance. Problematizing the critique of psychoanalysis as stubbornly insensitive to societies' material groundings, he illustrates the way class privilege renders one an unethical subject in his well-known anecdote of "Petit-Jean." In this "true story," he recalls how, as a student in his early twenties, "desperately [wanting] to . . . see something different," he briefly visited a small fishing village. The young intellectual enjoyed taking part in the villagers' fishing trips to the sea on the "frail craft[s]" that the fishermen had to use "at [their] own risk." Taking the often unfavorable conditions as a chance for an adventure, our hero, who "loved to share" "this risk, this danger" with the fishermen, recalls almost lamenting that "it wasn't all danger and excitement—there were also fine days"—days which, supposedly, the fishermen would welcome much more than the "adventure" of having to go out in heavy storms and risk death at sea (*SXI* 95).

Among the villagers, there was a young man whom "we"—Lacan and the fishermen—called Petit-Jean, who, Lacan says almost parenthetically, "like all his family, . . . died very young from tuberculosis, which at that time was a constant threat to the whole of that social class." As a member of a better-off section of society, Lacan recalls how, during one fishing trip, Petit-Jean points out a sardine can floating on the waves, "a witness to the canning industry, which *we*, in fact, were supposed to supply" (emphasis added). "*You see that can?*" Jean asks the young guest. "*Do you see it? Well, it doesn't see you!*" While Petit-Jean finds "this incident [*Ce petit épisode*] highly amusing," the guest refuses to smile. And why? "To begin with, if what Petit-Jean said to me, namely, that the can did not see me [*ne me voit pas*], had any meaning, it was because in a sense, it was looking at me [*elle me regarde*], all the same. It was looking at me at the level of the point of light, the point at which everything that looks at me is situated" (*SXI* 95/89).

"The point of this little story"—and note how the story itself remains diminutive for Lacan, as much as "little Jean" does—

> . . . derives from the fact that, if I am told a story like that one, it is because I, at that moment—as I appeared to those fellows who were earning their livings with great difficulty, in the struggle with what for them was pitiless nature—looked like nothing on earth. In short, I was rather out of place in the picture. And it was because I felt this that I was not terribly amused at hearing myself addressed [*m'entendre interpeller*] in this humorous, ironical way. (*SXI* 95–96/89)

Lacan initially includes himself in the communal *we* that feeds the canning industry whose unseen presence the lone object suggests. The appearance of the can—a metonymic reference to an entire structure of economy under whose dictates the fisherman toil—denaturalizes for the narrator the idyllic scene of the fishing community. The can's *looking* reminds Lacan of the drive, of the libidinal economy that not only makes up the fishing community but also suggests its dependence on a conceivably exploitative industry. At the same time, its *not seeing* shows the young intellectual that he does not belong to, or make sense in, that economy; he remains outside the picture. With Petit-Jean's observation, the young Parisian loses his pretensions to the collective "we" in whom he had included himself earlier—the "we" who had christened Jean with the diminutive, the "we" whose livelihood was dependent on the canning industry. It exposes his unethical position as the outside observer, untouched by the engagement and ambivalence of desire. The comparison of the villagers' and, in particular, little Jean's harsh existence with Lacan's leisurely activities suggests that the latter's discomfort was elicited by the realization of his own "power of annihilation" (*SXI* 81) as a privileged subject.

We may note the similarity of the young Lacan's assumptions about the fishermen and their community to Jan's and Mary's assumptions about the collectivity or "side" they constitute with Bigger. Like the young intellectual who visits the village craving to "see something different" (*SXI* 95), the youthful radicals of *Native Son* wish to go slumming in the Black Belt, seeking the exotic, authentic other. Such projects, however, are possible only if one begins from the assumptions of geometral vision—that one is an outside observer unaffected by and, importantly, *innocent of* the (exploitative) symbolic economy. What such tourism misses is the fact that "I am not simply that punctiform being located at the geometral point from which the perspective is grasped. No doubt, in the depths of my eye, the picture is painted. The picture, certainly, is in my eye. But I am in the picture" (*SXI* 96; translation modified). What the young Lacan realizes with Petit-Jean's remark is that, in the attempt to get a glimpse of the exotic other, he has reduced himself to a geometral point that remains external to the scopic field. This position is characteristic of the unethical, annihilating subject who remains outside the trajectory of the drive.

THE BIGGER PICTURE

Apart from Jan and Mary, also Boris Max, Bigger's communist lawyer, exemplifies the detached, undesiring, unethical viewer-subject in *Native Son*. Critics have unhesitatingly interpreted Max's courtroom speech as solving Bigger's "riddle," which the text recurrently evokes and whose meaning constantly eludes Bigger. For most commentators, Max's lengthy speech for the defense is the most embarrassing failure in Wright's novel, a heavy-handed gesture by the author to articulate his social "message" and ideological stance.[26] I agree with Laura A. Tanner, however, that "[t]hose who cite Max's speech as an example of Wright's overwhelming political didacticism surely do injustice to Wright's technical skill" (144; see also James Miller 501), as well as with Barbara Johnson's observation that Max, far from voicing any definitive insights into Bigger's situation, misreads his client ("Re(a)d"; see also Scruggs 90–95). Rather, through Max's (mis)understanding of Bigger, Wright further elaborates on the latter's problematic situation.

In his closing argument for the defense, Max admonishes the judge to show leniency by sentencing Bigger not to death but to a life in prison. According to him, this would be the perfect corrective for his client since prison life would constitute an ordered form of sociality which he has so far been deprived of. "'To send him to prison," Max says, "would be more than an act of mercy. You would be for the first time conferring *life* upon him. . . . He would have an identity, even though it be but a number. He would have for the first time an openly designated relationship with the world. . . . The other inmates would be the first men with whom he could associate on a basis of equality'" (338). Max considers prison a place of relief for Bigger because of its orderly organization. However, if he seeks to embed the black subject in a clearly delineated network of relations, his answer provides us what Lacan identifies as a *utilitarian* solution to the problem. In the early essay on the mirror stage, Lacan, discerns a "utilitarian function" underpinning the "society's historical enterprise" as it was embodied in the recently defeated Nazi regime. Advocating "the concentration-camp form of the social link," utilitarianism, according to Lacan, proposes "a freedom that is never so authentically affirmed as when it is within the walls of a prison" (8). If he implies that the existentialist response to the political ideologies in 1930s and 1940s Europe were inadequate, Wright similarly suggests Max's inability to read the racially specific history of penal institutions in the United States. According to Angela Davis, "slavery's underlying philosophy of punishment insinuated itself into the history of imprisonment" (102). Not surprisingly, Bigger explicitly compares his position as an African American man within the society to incarceration: "'We live here and they live there.

We black and they white. They got things and we ain't. They do things and we can't. *It's just like living in jail*'" (17; emphasis added). Hence, the imprisonment that Max would like to see conferred on Bigger as "*life*" would be nothing other than a repetition of his "life" within the society. As Foucault writes, "by locking up, retraining and rendering docile, [the prison] merely reproduces, with a little more emphasis, all the mechanisms that are to be found in the social body" (*Discipline* 233).[27] The prison provides a particularly concrete example of the strategies that confine the racial(ized) subject into a [B]igger's place—the enforced African American place within visibility.

Max continues to misread his client throughout the trial. He begins his closing argument with bravado: "'I shall put no witnesses upon the stand. *I* shall witness for Bigger Thomas. I shall present [the] argument'" (318). The entire courtroom drama unfolds as his dilemma: "'Night after night, I have lain without sleep. . . . How can I, I asked myself, make *the picture* of what has happened to this boy show plain and powerful upon *a screen of sober reason*. . . . Dare I, deeply mindful of this boy's background and race, put his fate in the hands of a jury'" (325; emphases added). Max's repetitive, italicized *I* compares drastically with Bigger's own stunted efforts at witnessing for himself. Apart from being completely incapable of uttering a word in the courtroom, he finds it hard to voice his "I" even in Max's presence. Having received the death sentence, he makes one last effort to express his thoughts and feelings: "'I—I . . . ,'" he stammers, uttering what sounds more like an exclamation of pain than an assertion of the first person singular (352; ellipsis in original).

In his speech, Max makes telling slips that link him to the other white characters in the novel. He constantly refers to his client as "son" or "boy," thus infantilizing him in the customary manner of the white people. Like Mary before him, he conflates specular access and "knowledge," telling the court, "'our decision as to whether this black boy is to live or die can be made in accordance with what actually exists. It will at least indicate that we *see* and *know*'" (338; original emphases). (After making this linkage between "seeing" and "knowing," Max makes the assumption of panoptic surveillance as conferring "*life*" upon Bigger.) Furthermore, when Max finishes his eloquent address, Bigger realizes that "[h]e had not understood the speech, but he had felt the meaning of some of it from the tone of Max's voice" (339; see also 350). His speech recalling Bigger's experience of having the Daltons discuss his "case" in his presence without addressing him (40), Max, like other white characters, thus views the world through the white symbolic order.

Talking with Max before the court's final ruling, Bigger requests that his mother not be there to see him receive the sentence. Max says that her presence would, nonetheless, strengthen his case. The stakes, furthermore, are higher: "'Well, this thing is bigger than you, son,'" he says. "'In a certain sense, every Negro in America's on trial out there today'" (312). Du Bois's observations about the Scottsboro case characterize Max's defense: the lawyer's efforts to situate the crime in a political and sociological context that would make it comprehensible inevitably exclude Bigger.[28] Even when the "thing" that Max refers to coincides with the very name of the accused ("This thing is [B]igger") it somehow, though correctly naming him, already exceeds him: "This thing is [B]igger than you." Max, in using Bigger as the example of the plight of African Americans, the underprivileged, and the poor in white capitalist society, effectively forces his client into a predetermined "place" in the "bigger" scheme of things.

Recalling Lacan's discussion of painting, we may note that what allows Max to re-present (in both senses of the word) yet, by that very method, miss Bigger is his reliance on a realistic method in which he dispassionately, albeit with some agonizing, unfolds the "picture" "upon a screen of sober reason." From a distance, he paints the image of Bigger's situation for the jury, an image that, like those of geometral optics, are to be "contemplated and appraised dispassionately" (Bersani and Dutoit 45). The viewers' and critics' position—their geometral perspective—allows them to remain external to representation: "Not being in the painting, we can judge its adequacy to the reality or the idea it 'imitates.' . . . If realism requires that we, as viewers, educate ourselves in order to earn our position of superiority, the work itself demands nothing of us except that we be its dispassionate judges. It doesn't look out at us, it doesn't call to us; *it awaits our verdict*" (45; emphasis added). Geometral perspective demands that we "educate" ourselves about the rules of art and the reality that it purports to represent. This may prove a formidable project in itself, but such art does not interrogate *us*, does not destabilize *our self-knowledge*, does not return the look with which we probe and measure its verisimilitude. Safely disconnected from the trajectories of desire, it allows us to remain dispassionate and objective; like the jurors, we are only asked to give our "verdict."

Such spectatorial position describes the white liberal approach to the Negro problem. While Mary, Jan, and Max realize their necessity of "learning" about black people, they can remain "sober" observers. (Unbeknownst to themselves, Mary and Jan make a paradigmatic transgression of catastrophic results when they lose their sobriety in their excursion to the ghetto.) If Mary and Jan wish to experience, to get a realistic representation of, their black chauffeur's world, it turns out that this wish for gritty realism only repeats, for Bigger, the violence of the structure that had enabled the Black Belt in the first place. According to Lacan's reading of the ethics of the scopic drive, this is the unethical external position of the disengaged tourist whose role Lacan takes on in his anecdote of the fishing village.

My reading is here diametrically opposed to Yoshinobu Hakutani's interpretation of Max's courtroom speech. In Hakutani's opinion, the lawyer's efforts "contrast sharply with the talk of Mr. and Mrs. Dalton, which is larded with sociological jargon" (81); Max is "an entirely trusted, altruistic, and extremely compassionate defender of Bigger" (179). Our opposing readings result from different ideas of how to access the meaning of Bigger's life. For Hakutani, an understanding of Bigger's position requires "distance" and "impersonality."

According to him, Max succeeds in speaking for Bigger because he "establish[es] a distance from life and create[s] an impersonal vision" (71).[29] Max's point of view is indeed an impersonal one in that it resists any implication which would make his autonomous spectatorial position untenable. As Slavoj Žižek argues, if one adopts a "disinterested" perspective of mastery, one remains blind to the "object" of the interpretation. According to Žižek, "true" looking is possible only from the biased viewpoint of *desire*: "if we look at a thing straight on, i.e., matter-of-factly, disinterestedly, objectively, we see nothing but a formless spot; the object assumes clear and distinctive features only if we look at it 'at an angle,' i.e., with an 'interested' view, supported, permeated, and 'distorted' by *desire*" (*Looking* 11–12). An objective point of view, as opposed to one that allows our subjective bias—our desire—eclipses the object. In psychoanalytic terms, disinterested, objective looking does not allow one to discern the truth of one's desire; it can only lead to an accumulation of knowledge. Considering Hakutani's linkage between "objectivity" and "distance from life," it is telling that the District Attorney Buckley, too, relies on a demand for objectivity to condemn Bigger to death: "'the law is strong and gracious enough to allow all of us to sit here in this court room today and try this case with dispassionate interest'" (341). Here we find one example of Frantz Fanon's insight that "objectivity is always directed against [the colonized]" (*Wretched* 77). Positioning himself to his client like a masterly interpreter to a riddle, Max remains tied to the traditional concept of visibility and knowledge. He sees himself in a position of an objective observer—the position, that is, of "geometral point" in Lacan. By the same reason, we can suggest that he becomes an "annihilating subject," the unethical subject who has immobilized desire and positioned himself outside its trajectory.

Assumptions about Bigger's being and "place" have been made not only by the fictional characters in the novel. Donald B. Gibson notes that readers of *Native Son* have consistently posited the novel in a social perspective in which the protagonist's individuality has been drowned out by the features of "whatever category a reader might have placed him in" (102): "Few have seen [Bigger] as a discrete entity, a particular person who struggles with the burden of his humanity" (97). He admonishes readers not to follow the fictional characters in (over)interpreting his "blackness": "readers need to avoid [this] error . . . by distinguishing between Bigger's qualities as a representative figure and his qualities as a particular person" (97). When such a distinction disappears and Bigger is seen merely as a part of a structure, one sutures him into an inflexible place that he himself cannot negotiate.

Considering our present discussion of Bigger's sequestered place within visibility, Gibson's attempt at displacing Bigger's rigorous position of representativeness seems laudable. However, the difficulties in such a strategy are immediately demonstrated by Gibson's own efforts. Notably, his argument starts to sound suspiciously familiar when he goes on to advise the readers "to lift Wright's novel out of the context of the racial problem in America and to place it in larger perspective" (97). With this gesture, Gibson uncannily reenacts the problem itself. Does he not propose to do for Wright's novel what he has condemned Max for doing for Bigger? What is this "larger perspective" if not a repetition of Max's argument that the issues in the court case are beyond his client, bigger than Bigger?

Gibson is certainly right in claiming that *Native Son* has been misread because of its reception as "a 'Negro' novel or a protest novel" (97). However, in trying to avoid Max's elision of Bigger as merely exemplary, he paradoxically ends up doing the same. What matters to him is not Bigger's position as the object of racism nor his class status but his "humanity." Suggesting that the proximity of death undermines Max's attempts at making his client see himself as a "test symbol" (*Native* 324), Gibson writes that "about to die in the electric chair, Bigger ceases to be representative of the Negro and becomes every man whose death is imminent—that is, every man" (103). However, Gibson here again repeats, with staggering precision, Max's mistaken reading of Bigger. After the verdict of death, when he is exchanging his last words with Bigger, Max demonstrates that the perspective which scotomizes his client is that of "humanity." Just as Bigger is "on the verge of believing that Max knew, understood," the white man's words show him otherwise: "'You're human, Bigger . . . ,' he says. "[I]n the work I'm doing I look at the world in a way that shows no whites and no blacks, no civilized and no savages . . . When men are trying to change human life on earth, *those little things don't matter. You don't notice 'em. They're just not there. You forget them*'" (354; emphasis added; second ellipsis in original). Max becomes a blind, unethical subject, who doesn't "notice" things like race. Curiously, Gibson does not discern Bigger's telling reaction to Max's words (Bigger realizes that "Max didn't even *know*!"; rather, "the white man was still trying to comfort him in the face of death" [354]).[30] Instead, like the white lawyer, he remains blind to Bigger when he looks at the situation from the perspective of "humanity." Max, Hakutani, and Gibson "drown [Bigger] in the universal" (Fanon, *Black* 186).

CONCLUSION

Many critics have pointed out that Max's understanding of Bigger's situation—which they more often than not see as identical to Wright's own position—is didactic and, at times, patronizing; his exegesis is an "embarrassment" because it is so "obvious." Yet, reading a text that consistently questions our specular access to truth, that is, the too-readily assumed causality between what we "see" and what we "understand," should we as readers not remain thoroughly suspicious when we are presented with answers that seem obvious to the point of triteness? I would argue that, by conflating Max's answers with what the text "itself" is saying, readers repeat the very structures of reading/being read, observer/observed, and objectivity/partiality that are illustrated in Bigger's relation with other characters in the novel. By assuming that Bigger's voice can be heard through his lawyer—that the "riddle" of his life is solved on the courtroom stage—we as readers are situated in the privileged yet blind position of a Boris Max, a Mr. Dalton, a Jan Erlone.

Such elisions are perhaps not surprising. Jane Gallop points out that analytic scenes (or scenes of reading) which are structured according to the dialectic of objective analyst/partial analysand, or reading/being read—that is, the Euclidean space of identity—are easier to tackle than ones which would require another kind of involvement: "The technique of mastery—one unconscious (the patient's) and one neutral, scientific interpreter/reporter (the analyst)—is 'easier.' Such case-histories remain within the classical discourse of science, with its separation between subject and object" (*Daughter's* 102). In his deployment of topology and projective geometry, Lacan seeks to complicate the Euclidean coordinates of intersubjectivity. He attempts to short-circuit the almost automatic processes based on such geometries of subjectivity by, for example, recommending to analysts in training that they defer hearing a meaning in the patient's discourse. He speaks of "this inconsistent mirage called the relation of understanding—as if there were anything that could ever be grasped in this order!" (*SIII* 7). The critics' knowledgeable readings of Bigger's riddle, and of *Native Son*, are perhaps descriptive of the kind of rush to understanding that Lacan warns his audience against:

> Begin by thinking you don't understand. Start from the idea of fundamental misunderstanding. . . . You will observe in the training we give to our students that this [the point of "understanding"] is always a good place to stop them. It's always at the point where they have understood, where they have rushed in to fill the case in with understanding, that they have missed the interpretation that it's appropriate to make or not to make. This is generally naively expressed in the expression—*This is what the subject meant*. How do you know? What is certain is that he didn't say it. (*SIII* 20, 22)

"I have always told you," Lacan reminds his audience years later, "that it is important not to understand for the sake of understanding" (*SVII* 278). One must not, he warns the trainees, proceed to understand too quickly; the "I see" of the observer may belie that s/he has been captured within the imaginary structures of visibility/knowledge where the other's discourse is rendered mute, where s/he is trapped in the postures of self-knowledge that characterize the colonizing subjects of *The Ambassadors*. Gallop cautions against the reductive readings that such unequivocal "solutions" produce: "A 'solved' riddle is the reduction of heterogeneous material to logic, to the homogeneity of logical thought, which produces a blind spot, the inability to see the otherness that gets lost in the reduction" (*Daughter's* 61). Max's reduction of Bigger's riddle in the courtroom, as well as the critics' acceptance of his speech as an unmediated interpretation of authorial intentions, thus functions to reduce Bigger's otherness.[31] In this way, Max's speech and the critics' reading of the courtroom scene reproduce the reductive strategies of confinement illustrated in Bigger's relation to other fictional characters and even, as Laura Tanner (132) points out, the narrative voice in the text.

But if such authoritative self-knowledge relies, as I have been suggesting, on perspectival strategies of exteriority and control, the masterful positions assumed are also to a certain extent vulnerable. They are strategies of the blind, for, as Lacan observes, the geometral optics illustrated by Alberti and Diderot "allow that which concerns vision to escape" (*SXI* 92): the Euclidean organization of early Renaissance perspective is merely "a partial dimension in the field of the gaze, a dimension that has nothing to with vision as such" (*SXI* 88). Lacan suggests that the construction of geometral perspective, exemplified in the first triangle, is always compromised by, because implicated in, the field of vision represented in the more complicated diagrams. Anamorphosis, for example, is already present, "immanent in the geometral dimension" (*SXI* 88). Thus, before embarking on an elaboration of the three diagrams, Lacan, taking his cue from Maurice Merleau-Ponty, cautions that everything designated as distinct in such representation of the visible remains always "*entrelacs*," a term that is translated into English as "interlacing," or "intertwining," or "*chiasm*[*ic*]" (*SXI* 93, 95): "As we begin to distinguish [the] various fields [of the visible]," he observes, "we always perceive more and more the extent to which they intersect" (*SXI* 93). Similarly—as the following chapter details—in *Native Son* Bigger discovers that the hierarchical organization of the white world betrays its imaginary, and consequently manipulable, character.

CHAPTER 2

The Grimace of the Real

Of Paranoid Knowledge and Black(face) Magic

Only the subject—the human subject, the subject of the desire that is the essence of man—is not, unlike the animal, entirely caught up in this imaginary capture. He maps himself in it. How? In so far as he isolates the function of the mask and plays with it. Man, in effect, knows how to play with the mask as that beyond which there is the gaze.

—Jacques Lacan, *The Four Fundamental Concepts of Psycho-Analysis*

There is a danger of corrosion of the self in this pretense, and surely a rending of integrity. How, and when does one call upon the real self to dispel the make-believe and claim humanity and dignity?... It was just possible that the trick had been too perfect; legerdemain *had undone itself in a disappearance act where the self had vanished, but also the incantation to call it back again.*

—Nathan Irvin Huggins, *Harlem Renaissance*

In late November 1998, a teacher in New York City's Public School 75 introduced an acclaimed children's book called *Nappy Hair* to her third-grade students as extracurricular reading material. The book, written by Carolivia Herron, is a transcript of a piece of oral history passed on in the author's family. It tells the story of a black girl with "the kinkiest, the nappiest, the fuzziest, the most screwed up, squeezed up, knotted up, tangled up, twisted up . . . hair you've ever seen in your life" (Herron n.p.). According to the author, the book aims to celebrate diversity and encourage pride in black children. Some parents of the (mostly black) pupils saw it differently, however. In the days following the introduction of the book, photocopies of parts of the book were circulated among the parents, some of whom were enraged when they saw what they considered demeaning, stereotypical, and "racially insensitive" depictions of black people. A meeting was called with parents and school officials. Threats were made by the parents, and the 27-year-old teacher, a white woman, was put on desk duty while an investigation was launched. Even though the school ended up backing the teacher, she refused to return to the classroom, citing fears for her own safety (L. Holloway, "School"; "Teacher"; "Threatened"; "Unswayed").

The incident received a fair amount of commentary, including a *New York Times* op-ed article by Jill Nelson. In the article, Nelson argues that what the *Nappy Hair* controversy illustrates is not the racial insensitivity of the white teacher or the school system—as the black parents argued—but that the "barriers to . . . self-esteem are perpetuated not by the white community but by the black one." For Nelson, the black community remains overly sensitive about certain representations of blackness. She suggests that such attitudes may have their origin in slavery and in the valorization of white physical features, which the enslaved Africans adopted from their masters. In this, she follows critics such as Kobena Mercer, who writes in "Black Hair/Style Politics" that "black people's hair has been historically *devalued* as the most visible stigmata of blackness, second only to skin" (101). Inevitably, representations such as those at stake in the classroom controversy find their historical background in minstrelsy: "In the minstrel stereotype of Sambo . . . the 'frizzy' hair of the character is an essential part of the iconography of inferiority. In children's books and vaudeville minstrelsy, the 'woolly' hair is ridiculed, just as aspects of black people's speech were lampooned in both popular music hall and in the nineteenth-century novel as evidence of the 'quaint folkways' and 'cultural backwardness' of the slaves" (102). Nelson concludes: "Too many African Americans have internalized and passed down these beliefs, as if proximity to whiteness inherently enhances our worth."

Nelson's reading of the controversy is neither incorrect nor adequate. Certainly, the parents' outrage with the book—more precisely, with the selected pages which were circulated among them as poor-quality photocopies—seems like an embarrassing case of ill-conceived censorship. The fury seems particularly misdirected in that the book seeks to negotiate a history of negative stereotyping by celebrating bodily features which have been demonized. But Nelson's mistake lies in her assumption of a clean break between minstrel images of the past and the impact of more current representations. Contrary to her understanding, the recent controversy shows that recognizing representations as socially and ideologically constructed and manipulated stereotypes may do very little to diminish their efficacy. As James Baldwin puts it, often "one does not . . . cease playing a role simply because one has begun to understand it" ("Black" 291). The pain and anger which the images of the little black girl elicited attest to the current valence of these representations. That the minstrelsy-related images recurred in the context of education may have contributed to the parents' outrage. As Patricia A. Turner notes, minstrelsy images of black children have had their impact on public policies. "It seems safe to assume," she writes in *Ceramic Uncles and Celluloid Mammies* (1994), "that in making decisions and forming policies about educational entitlement and support for underprivileged families, some elected and appointed public servants [who grew up with and absorbed the images of African Americans in the popular culture of the 1930s, 1940s, and 1950s] still envision the undeserving raucous, ill-kept black children prominently displayed in advertising copy and picture postcards" (17–18). It is against this background that we must evaluate responses that call the accusations of racism against the teacher "knee-jerk and baseless" (Haberman).[1] If the response is a kind of a cultural reflex, as is suggested here, recognizing racist images and recoiling from them are precisely not without base but, rather, constitute a response according to a deeply—even *organically*—lodged cultural memory. Of course, one may even argue that, as a reflex, such a "knee-jerk" reaction is also potentially life-saving.

Yet, addressing this history does not require that one remain hostage to, or, in Manthia Diawara's terms, a "custodian" of ("Blackface" 17), its dynamics. While the children's book deals with the often painful legacy of minstrelsy, its purpose—encouraging positive self-images in African-American children—also tells us that the abusiveness of minstrel images can under certain circumstances be turned around and mobilized for self-affirmative purposes by African Americans. Such strategies are familiar from colonial encounters, as David Theo Goldberg notes: "parameters and paths of resistance and emancipation are initiated by forms oppression assumes. Yet, once initiated, they are not limited by or to oppressive direction or determination. Even when the oppressed assume categories of degradation in the name of resistance, stand inside them as a place of combat, the categories assumed are invested with novel, resistant, redirected and redirecting significance" ("In/Visibility" 187). In his famous analysis of the anticolonial movement in Algeria, Frantz Fanon observes that "it is the action, the plans of the occupier that determine the centers around which a people's will to survive becomes organized" (*Dying* 47). In her study on the strategies of African American resistance during slavery, Saidiya V. Hartman similarly argues that "too often the interventions and challenges of the dominated have been obscured when measured against traditional notions of the political and its central features: the unencumbered self, the citizen, the self-possessed individual, and the volitional and autonomous subject" (61). However, as the "nappy hair" controversy suggests, the outcome of these strategic reappropriations is never guaranteed. The black parents' reactions to the book also tells us that the dangers of misreading—or, perhaps more precisely, those of *reading*—are inherent in such negotiations.

Indeed, if the master's tools can begin the work of dismantling the master's house, then any agency thereby constructed must remain tenuous and difficult to own. Consequently, while I will here trace the ways in which minstrel representations have been mobilized by African Americans for potentially emancipatory ends—very much like *Nappy Hair* was meant to engender self-respect in black children—I will also point out the dangers in such strategies of resistance, dangers embodied in the parents' reaction to the book. To do this, I will discuss what I consider representative examples of the proliferating historical and theoretical studies on minstrelsy. What interests me in the work of these theorists of minstrelsy is the ways in which, in their texts, the effects of blackface and the minstrel mask on African Americans become *ambivalent* in the sense in which Homi Bhabha uses the psychoanalytic term to describe colonial mimicry. I propose that, to understand the political leverage of this ambivalence, we begin to engage Lacan's theory of mimicry and paranoid knowledge in our reading of minstrelsy. This helps us further theorize the white symbolic order.

By discussing *Native Son* and *Nappy Hair*, I also want to suggest that, while the precise forms of its appearance have shifted, the dynamics of blackface should not be considered a thing of the past. Contrary to Alain Locke's optimism in 1925, "Uncle Tom and Sambo [may not] have passed on" (5). Rather than being confined to a period in the history of U.S. race relations, the minstrel mask perhaps continues to organize racial visibility in the United States. Tracing this genealogy, W. T. Lhamon writes, "the minstrel show has seeped well beyond its masked variants into vaudeville, thence into sitcoms; into jazz and rhythm 'n' blues quartets, thence into rock 'n' roll and hip hop dance; into the musical and the novel, thence into radio and film; into the Grand Old Opry, thence into every roadhouse and the cab of every longhaul truck beyond the Appalachians" (56).[2] *Native Son*'s alleged status as the first African American novel which had the courage to halt the minstrel show in front of its white audience and to *tell it like it is* (see Gates, "Preface" xii–xiii) suggests the centrality of Wright's debut novel in this history.

THE MASTER'S FOOLS

Research into blackface minstrelsy and its cultural, historical, and political significance has since the beginning of the twentieth century bred controversial, passionate, and insightful studies, whose political urgency is evident in their polemical nature. The sometimes sharp disagreements between scholars stem not only from the scarcity of primary material on the shows and their audiences (playbills, testimonies, and other documents); what makes minstrelsy such a controversial topic is its implication in questions of race, ethnicity, and the role of culture in the constitution or abrogation of citizenship and civil rights.

The most notable break in minstrelsy studies occurred with Ralph Ellison's 1958 essay "Change the Joke and Slip the Yoke." However, the contested nature of the field becomes evident in the disagreements between the most recent studies. While Lhamon, in *Raising Cain* (1998), shares important aspects with Eric Lott's *Love and Theft* (1995)—most notably the insistence on the (con)fused, unpredictable character of the blackface tradition, whatever its constitutive thrust and intention—he nevertheless argues that his reading of nineteenth-century minstrelsy differs crucially from those of his contemporaries (6).[3] William J. Mahar, in *Behind the Burnt Cork Mask* (1999), echoes Lhamon in stressing the "significant[]" differences between his studies and "the standard works in minstrelsy studies" (namely, Nathan's, Toll's, and Lott's) (6).[4] Such repetitive dismissals of earlier studies as biased, insubstantial, or politically motivated recur in the history of minstrel studies. I suggest that what these accumulating references to earlier works bespeak is the fact that, like blackface performance itself, minstrel theory has evolved with the twists and turns of its own "lore cycle," to borrow Lhamon's term. Like the hybrid phenomena it studies, it assimilates contemporary concerns to its reading of historical evidence and reenacts in modernized forms the very issues that were expressed on the minstrel stage. Minstrel theory's lore cycle, I propose, tells us as much about racial formations and negotiations as do the original, first-hand documents themselves. In what follows, then, rather than attempt to adjudicate between the historical veracity of the different interpretations, I delineate blackface minstrelsy's lore cycle as a potential articulation of *strategies of resistance* that are never clearly distinguished from *forms of collaboration*.

In some ways, my reading of minstrel theory echoes Lott's and (in particular) Lhamon's understanding of the fluctuating character of blackface performance. Lhamon writes that deciding whether blackface articulates a cross-racial or -ethnic identification or whether it congeals into racist, antiblack discourse and practices is important but "also diversionary" (141). That is, the politically necessary work of pointing out the racism in blackface performance may prevent us from understanding the unpredictable ways in which "cultural work [can] produce liberatory change even through racism, and in spite of it" (141). The seemingly most toxic areas of cultural production such as blackface performance *necessarily* provide us an opening for strategic intervention whose outcome may not be calculable from or contained within the existing horizon of possibilities. Such areas of toxicity may contain a more radical potential for symbolic reconfigurations than do more "level-headed" projects such as multiculturalism and identity politics, which, as David A. Hollinger (107) and Kalpana Seshadri-Crooks (*Desiring* 12, 49, 158–59) point out, rely on the sustenance of race as a stable category of identification.

We should, then, pay close attention to hybrid forms of culture such as blackface. According to Dale Cockrell, the blackface tradition emerged among the lower classes whose ranks were not racially segregated in the early days of minstrelsy (84–86). Similarly, such forms of cultural expression as music and dance were "creolized at the level of common urban people" (86). We can indeed understand minstrelsy as a creolized cultural form, in the sense in which Édouard Glissant uses the term. Put simply, creolization refers to the kind of ongoing cultural mixing, "unceasing process of transformation" (*Caribbean* 142), that is distinctive to the Caribbean, whose "history [is] characterized by ruptures and . . . began with a brutal dislocation, the slave trade" (61). However, Glissant's theory is not unique to the Caribbean: while the latter "may be held up as one of the places in the world where Relation [another term for creolization][5] presents itself most visibly" (*Poetics* 33), "no people has been spared the cross-cultural process" (*Caribbean* 140). Minstrelsy is a similarly unstable cultural form bred by an encounter of unimaginable violence. It expresses the trauma of this encounter and its incalculable consequences while also enabling a variety of (subaltern) responses, for, as Glissant writes, one cannot participate passively in creolization (*Poetics* 137). Like creolized cultures, the forms of resistance and negotiation that blackface gave rise to are also necessarily unstable, cross-bred, and contaminated. Cockrell's description of blackface's urban ascendancy is instructive: "The cities were a machine for acculturation, and the popular theater both invested in the enterprise and benefited from it. New rituals issued from the wedding of old ones, as cultural manners came to know and like each other: Pure blood lines mixed with the stuff of the Other, procreating the new" (58).[6]

But one must also note the dangers in such strategies and politics based on hybridity and creolization. The unease that theories of post-colonial hybridity have elicited is telling in this respect. Critics such as Abdul JanMohamed and Benita Parry have responded to these dangers in their opposition to Bhabha's work (JanMohamed, "Allegory"; Parry, "Problems," "Resistance").[7] They reject Bhabha's understanding of the hybridity of the colonial encounter, fearing that it disables all oppositional politics of resistance. For Bhabha, clear party lines and lines of combat no longer hold; forms of resistance are no longer readily distinguishable from potentially destructive mimicry. In lieu of oppositional tactics, we are left with the uncontainable forces of what can be called the strategies of *pharmakon* or those of *viral resistance*.[8] These unstable practices, whose implications for post-colonial studies disturb JanMohamed and Parry, guide my reading of blackface minstrelsy as a creolized form of culture that has produced a cross-bred species of resistance and negotiation.

Let me now turn to the evolving (hi)story of minstrel studies. I necessarily take up the cycle in mid-shift. The first studies of minstrelsy written after the disappearance of the minstrel show as it was known in the nineteenth century are Dailey Paskman and Sigmund Spaeth's *"Gentlemen, Be Seated!"* (1928), Carl Wittke's *Tambo and Bones* (1930), and Constance Rourke's chapter "That Long-Tail'd Blue" in her *American Humour* (1931). As many subsequent commentators have noted, these early accounts are largely blind to the ways in which sociopolitical tensions necessitated and were expressed in nineteenth-century minstrelsy representations. Rourke does briefly suggest the connection between the popularization of minstrelsy and the struggle for black emancipation in the 1840s and 1850s, but does not explore the question further (98). Paskman and Spaeth's cursory references suggest that for them blackface's origin in African (and African American) culture is self-evident. (When they do refer to the tradition's black origins, their comments, tongue in cheek or not, speak volumes. Speculating on the origin of Mr. Bones's instrument, they write: "The cannibals of Africa probably originated the idea when they wanted a little music after having feasted thoroughly upon their enemies" [28].)[9] Wittke locates the origins of minstrel routines onboard the slave ships, whose "captains sometimes forced their black cargoes to dance and sing on shipboard on the way across the Atlantic from Africa, and plantation owners in America kept their Negroes happy and productive in the same way" (6). Few minstrel theorists would disagree with Wittke: Boskin, for example, notes that "slavers utilized entertainment as a means of exerting strict control, ensuring stamina, and warding off depressed spirits" (44). Yet, while Wittke seems to discerns the disciplinary coerciveness behind these performances, he goes on to suggest that they were *at the same time* expressions of the character of the African slaves: continuing in the same paragraph, he writes that "the Negroes danced and sang because of their own innate and irrepressible fondness for rhythmic and musical expression. . . . These Negro performances were spontaneous and almost instinctive" (6–7). For Wittke, the practices of the Middle Passage smoothly meld into the "innate and irrepressible" expressions of the slaves. In this, he repeats the ways in which slave traders and masters insisted on seeing their cargoes and property as happy and contented (see Boskin 44–45). In this slippage from coerced to "spontaneous" self-expression, Wittke illustrates how, through interiorization, the disciplinary practices of subjection may become the subject's genuine, "instinctive" expressions (see also Hartman 32–48).

While Ellison's seminal essay "Change the Joke and Slip the Yoke" pointed to a new turn in the evolution of minstrelsy theory's cycle, it was only in the 1960s and 1970s that the uncritical views of minstrelsy, exemplified by Paskman/Spaeth, Wittke, and Rourke, were challenged in more formal, scholarly studies. A crucial shift took place with the reassessments by Hans Nathan, Nathan Irvin Huggins, Robert C. Toll, and Alexander Saxton. While making no reference to "Change the Joke," Nathan follows Ellison in noting the origins of white minstrelsy in politically motivated, "malicious parod[ies]" of slave culture and African Americans' celebrations of the Emancipation (49). He suggests that white minstrels borrowed or adapted their material from black culture (e.g., 70–71, 81, 129, and chs. 7 and 8), but also insightfully points to what we could call the hybrid origins of blackface routines (95, 166, 186–88, 207). In this, he is closer to Lott and Lhamon than to Huggins, Toll, and Saxton, who followed in his footsteps in the early 1970s.

In the last chapter of *Harlem Renaissance* (1971), Huggins, explaining the lack of African American "ethnic theater" in the first two decades of the twentieth century, emphasizes the psychological effects of minstrelsy representations on blacks and, in particular, black artists. On the evidence of playbills and contemporary accounts, Toll's *Blacking Up* (1974) not only delineates the social, political, and psychological framework in which minstrelsy emerged in the nineteenth century, but also provides a theoretically insightful account of African American blackface performance. Saxton, in "Blackface Minstrelsy and Jacksonian Ideology" (1975), argues for the political significance of minstrelsy in the early and mid-nineteenth century: "Minstrelsy's political stance," as he puts it, "was a defense of slavery" (18).[10] According to him, antiabolitionists and proponents of Jacksonian ideology found in the emergent mass media and the minstrelsy tradition two ways of disseminating and propagating their ideology (21); he claims that "blackface minstrelsy acted out the most appalling aspects of Jacksonian ideology" (28).[11]

We can thus divide twentieth-century minstrel theory into three separate but inevitably overlapping stages in the cycle of its evolution. Paskman/Spaeth, Wittke, and Rourke articulate the first one, in whose most uncritical moments blackface representations were assumed to be the transparent results of simple cultural borrowing. The second stage is initiated by Ellison and confirmed by Nathan, Huggins, Toll, and Saxton. These writers argue that, rather than mirroring African American culture, blackface functions as a reflecting surface in which the image of the white audiences is projected according to social, political, and psychological exigencies—and at a considerable expense to African Americans.[12] Recent readings—mostly in the 1990s—have begun to question the status of nineteenth-century blackface performance as an unequivocally racist, antiblack practice, both in intentions and effects. While careful not to underestimate the presence of racism in blackface that their predecessors stressed, the representatives of this third shift break away from the "intentionalistic" concept of minstrelsy and, instead, emphasize its hybrid, creolized nature. Best exemplified by Gubar, Lott, Lhamon, and Cockrell, this third generation is characterized by its hesitance to attribute blackface dynamics to one social group or another, or to argue that minstrelsy constituted a controlled, strategic program. While Gubar stresses "the blatant racism of minstrelsy" (xvii) and notes that one should not "romanticize racial masquerades that indubitably discount African American subjectivity" (xviii), she goes on to argue that the motivation behind and the effects of "racechanges" cannot be articulated in the form of a self-conscious project, whether antiblack or antiracist: "throughout the twentieth century white impersonations of blackness functioned paradoxically both as a deeply conservative (even racist) as well as a shockingly radical (sometimes anarchic) mode of cultural production" (12; see also 43, 44). Indeed, "the long history of racechange demonstrates that no single effect, no simple ideology can be said to emanate from a trope that embodies the slipperiness of metamorphosis in its adoptions and adaptations as well as in its historical evolution" (41).

Gubar and others of her "generation" locate the promise and danger of blackface in its hybrid constitution. Cockrell writes that it is precisely the open, unpredictably changing character of blackface minstrelsy that yielded an expressive medium in the negotiations of race: "When the institution of American slavery required a national dialogue, blackface minstrelsy might have been one of the most effective of all the forms it took, for it was . . . implicitly paradoxical and dynamic" (54). Lott similarly emphasizes the ambiguities of "love and theft," as he calls the interracial dynamic of antebellum blackface performances. Lhamon, too, eloquently argues for the early, pre-1850s minstrel stage as a site for what he calls "cross-racial charisma." Like Roediger, he sees minstrelsy as a working-class phenomenon, but, more than *The Wages of Whiteness*, his study emphasizes the cross-racial identification that blackface promoted (44–45). Suggesting that "the tradition of minstrel criticism has reduced a vastly popular and multiply meaningful form to one-dimensional simplicity" (134), he emphasizes the importance of readings "that admit ambiguity and outright conflict" in blackface representations and images (163–64). Noting, controversially, "the relative lack of racism in early blackface delineations" (191), he suggests that, rather than necessarily marking their distance from black culture, early blackface performers and audiences at times embraced it enthusiastically (203). Consequently, despite its notorious embodiment as the figure of segregation, Jim Crow emerges for Lhamon as "an imp of crossing, not of separating." It is only in later manifestations that "the imp of links has become . . . the monster of segregation" (204).

But more than the debate over the thrust behind white minstrels' performances, the place of the black blackface artist delineates the ambivalence I wish to interrogate here. While African Americans began to take to the stage themselves already in the mid-nineteenth century, black minstrel performers, according to most accounts, gained wider success later in the century.[13] By the time African American performers became common on the minstrel stage, blackface had already been thoroughly hybridized into an expressive, vernacular form of its own that had no *necessary* connection with the black Atlantic culture. Nevertheless, minstrel theorists suggest that black performers took the tradition to a new direction, creolized it for ends that were not foreseeable from the vantage point of blackface history. We can thus suggest that, although blackface has more often been considered as a dehumanizing, distorting mask imposed on African American and colonized subjects, this mask, when actively deployed, can also denote the racially marked subject's becoming inaccessible to the culture otherwise bent on determining him or her.

According to Mel Watkins, black minstrels could initially not but reaffirm the "distorted black spectre already dominat[ing] the stage" and offer white audiences a kind of "comfort and reassurance" in their beliefs on blacks' "natural" inferiority (123–24): "Black minstrelsy was regarded not as performance but as a kind of peep show that offered an unobstructed view of Negroes in their natural and preferred environment—servitude and the Southern plantation" (121; see also Huggins, 246). Ellison even suggests that the damage done to African Americans through the demeaning representations to which minstrel images greatly contributed exceeded the effects of slavery: "The physical hardships and indignities of slavery were benign compared with this continuing debasement of our image" ("Change" 48).[14] Why, then, did black Americans, not far removed from slavery and painfully aware of everyday racism, partake as performers and audience in the construction of these demeaning stereotypes? To begin with, the minstrel stage was perhaps the only venue in which black performers could earn a living at a time when African Americans were otherwise severely disenfranchised.[15] Blackface presented similar opportunities to the spectators, too. Watkins submits that, for black audiences, African American performers "were living reminders that it was possible to escape at least partially the poverty and degradation that was so common among blacks" (126). As Toll writes, "a number of Negroes must have gotten 'a glimpse of another world' and realized that minstrelsy was one of the few ways they could reach it. . . . Minstrelsy was one of the few opportunities for mobility—geographic, social, and economic—open to nineteenth-century Negroes" (222–23). The mastery of minstrelsy, an engagement with its representations, may also have been the only way by which African Americans were able to partake in public discourse (Baker, *Modernism* 15–41).

Following Ellison's insight, a number of writers further argue that, by embodying the blackface persona, black performers were able to parodically reconfigure racist representations and challenge the oppressive logic on which they were based. Huggins notes that black performers "tried to use the stereotype as an instrumental satire" by distancing themselves from damaging representations through exaggeration (259). Toll and Gubar, too, suggest that, within the narrow limits of minstrelsy representations, black performers were able to modify and challenge the stereotypes: from behind the mask, some black performers acted out "white people's conceptions of the stage Negro with a defensive irony that called attention to the artifice of the role" (Gubar 96–97).[16]

In other words, even as one must concede the (at least partially) racist motivation of minstrel representations as well as their damaging results for black Americans, seeing in white blackface the simple expression of white supremacy is far too simplistic. Such an instrumentalist view neglects the necessarily contradictory investments that any cultural form as successful as minstrelsy relies on and produces. While Lott and Lhamon focus on antebellum minstrelsy by white performers, their perspicacious remarks on the undecidability of its effects deserve to be repeated in the present context: if the "dominative intentions [of white blackface] were continually compromised by the return of unwanted meanings, gestures, and relationships" (E. Lott 101), then despite whatever (conscious or unconscious) ambitions black performers brought to the minstrel stage, the results of these performances were finally unpredictable.

Not surprisingly, such unpredictability does not easily enable political strategies. As JanMohamed's and Parry's reactions to strands in contemporary postcolonial theory suggest, it may indeed be inassimilable to the ways we have become accustomed to thinking of political activity. There are several ways, however, in which we can approach the politics of unforeseeability. For example, Michel Foucault's rejection, particularly in his final interviews, of any programs that assume a continuity between the present and the future gestures towards an understanding of politics as "a state of becoming," informed by what he calls "pessimistic activity" ("History and Homosexuality" 370; "On the Genealogy" 343). Similarly, Elizabeth Grosz suggests that the dimension of time, and its problematic articulations in Western metaphysics, can be rethought politically through such various thinkers as Charles Darwin, Friedrich Nietzsche, Henri Bergson, and Gilles Deleuze (*Nick*; *Time*). In what follows, however, I suggest we turn to Lacan's understanding of mimicry and paranoid knowledge to conceptualize the possibilities in blackface representations and performance. In this, my reading departs from most contemporary understandings of paranoia, which remain largely in agreement with the spirit of Gilles Deleuze and Félix Guattari's assessment, according to which "paranoiac investment" arrests the flow of desire and immobilizes molecular becomings into the stability of molar groupings (*Anti-Oedipus* 364, passim).[17] As opposed to "revolutionary schizophrenia," "capitalist paranoia" (Deleuze, *Negotiations* 24) reduces the world to an imaginary counterpart to the ego, which, as Rosi Braidotti tells us, "is a temple to narcissism and paranoia" (136). It also pre-empts becoming, according to Eve Kosofsky Sedgwick: as a consequence of the dominance of "paranoid" readings, queer criticism, for example, has been confined to repeating the discourses of power it has sought to contest. In contrast to the paranoid approach, Sedgwick advocates what she calls "reparative" reading practices, which, rather than articulating the constraints and violence that the queer subject is faced with in his or her environment, seek to locate resources that are as yet unactualized in the present material existence. In reparative readings, Sedgwick argues, we find a productive relation to futurity which the "paranoid imperative" ("Paranoid" 6) disenables.

I suggest, however, that, in Lacan's discussion of anamorphosis in painting, "paranoid ambiguities," exemplified for example in Salvador Dali's "paranoia criticism" (*SXI* 87),[18] enable the mobility of desire, as opposed to the imaginary capture of geometral optics exemplified in Brunelleschi's and Alberti's perspectives. Paranoia in the face of what is seen—the suspicion that the image can at any point reorder itself, turn the profile of a young woman into the sunken features of an old lady—undermines the certainties of geometral vision. Consequently, the Lacanian notion of paranoia enables us to negotiate the ambivalence—the openings as well as the dangers—of blackface strategies. While paranoia is usually understood as a pathology, Lacan splits the concept into two by suggesting that, apart from (and in conjunction to) pathological paranoia, we must consider paranoid identification as a constitutive feature of intersubjectivity. As Jerry Aline Flieger, too, observes, in Lacan the paranoid structure does not always entail psychosis "but is also a mode of discovery" ("Listening" 103): "paranoid knowledge may be read from two angles: it may be considered as either the province of the 'errant' psychotic in error—hopelessly adrift from human symbolic interaction; or as the grounding of intersubjectivity, the daily double dealings of all-too-human dupes with their fellows" ("Postmodern" 103). This malleable line between the two paranoid constructions delineates also the ambivalent and unpredictable dynamics of blackface minstrelsy. We should note that Lacan's distinction between the two forms of paranoia hinges on notions that echo concepts familiar from the history of African American philosophy and cultural theory. That is, what demarcates the two forms of paranoia is a certain distance that the subject has from itself—distance that one can translate in the African American idiom as "double consciousness." This distance, as François Roustang notes in "How Do You Make a Paranoiac Laugh?," is often marked by laughter. For W. E. B. Du Bois, it is precisely this "divine gift" that has enabled African American survival (*Darkwater* 21).

MIMICRY, THE MIRROR STAGE, PARANOIA: PLAYING (LIKE) AN IDIOT

I propose that we begin by conceptualizing the historical functioning of blackface through the concept of the mirror stage. There is a sense in which I hesitate to suggest this, for, as Stephen Melville writes, "Lacan has been over-read as the theorist of 'the mirror stage" (111). Apart from simplifications of his theory, this overemphasis has resulted in the critics' concentration on the early, structuralist phase in Lacan's work and the relative neglect, until quite recently, of his 1960s and 1970s texts. As I argue throughout this study, it is important to consider the possible contribution of Lacan's later work—with its focus on the questions of the real, the drive, and the *objet petit a*—for a psychoanalytically informed critical race theory. Nevertheless, I here risk a return to the theory of the mirror stage in order to highlight the concepts of mimicry and paranoid knowledge, which have not received as much attention as those of, say, *méconnaissance* and body-in-pieces. Furthermore, the reappearance and reinvention of these early concepts in his subsequent texts demonstrate "the multifaceted and nonlinear evolution of Lacan's thought" (Chiesa 107).

The concept of mimicry in Lacan refers to the kind of multiple mimesis that we find in white and black blackface minstrelsy. In "The Mirror Stage as Formative of the *I* Function as Revealed in Psychoanalytic Experience," mimicry designates the moment when the human infant (mis)recognizes itself in the mirror and comes to experience its body through the specular image as a totality, more coordinated than bodily experience would suggest. Lacan describes this (mis)recognition as "the illuminative mimicry of the *Aha-Erlebnis*" (3). Here, mimicry names a fundamental alienation that, nevertheless, is crucial for the functioning of the human subject. As the infant catches its image on the reflecting surface, the human subject is simultaneously *captured* by this very image: Lacan speaks of "the spatial capture manifested by the mirror-stage" (6). Dylan Evans writes that this capture—which some of Lacan's translators render as "captation"[19]—designates the fascinating, arresting effect of the specular image (20). Because of this double valence—identification/alienation, or identification-as-alienation—mimicry never refers to anything like the subject's assimilation or adaptation to its surroundings. The human subject remains in an irreducible discord with his/her environment. As Evans points out, the human subject is, in Lacan's view, "essentially maladaptive" (4).

For Lacan, there exists a continuity not only between animal and human mimicry but also between animal and human psychology in general,[20] the similarities and differences between which can be conceptualized in the dimensions of the imaginary and the symbolic. While the dimension that both animals and humans share is that of the imaginary, in human psychology (and, consequently, mimicry), this is further complicated by the symbolic dimension. According to Lacan, animal mimicry is essentially imaginary mimicry: "the imaginary is surely the guide to life for the whole animal domain" (*SIII* 9). Such mimicry is characterized by (illusory) one-to-one relations to the (imaginary/specular) other and a belief in similarity, unity, and correspondences. In the imaginary, the subject is captated by its image or counterpart. As Evans writes, "The imaginary exerts a captivating power over the subject, founded in the almost hypnotic effect of the specular image." In imaginary mimicry, the subject is entirely captated, "imprison[ed] . . . in a series of static fixations" (83).

Human mimicry has a much more complicated relation to such acts of mimesis than does animal mimicry. Even while positing imaginary mimicry as part of human psychology, Lacan emphasizes that, for the human subject, the imaginary order is always already structured through the symbolic: "in man, the imaginary relation has deviated [from that which it is in nature]," he says in the third seminar (210). "While the image equally plays a capital role in our own domain, this role is completely taken up and caught up within, remodeled and reanimated by, the symbolic order" (9). The human subject, in other words, is capable of escaping the "static fixations" characteristic of imaginary and animal mimicry through its capacity for "play." As Lacan continues in the eleventh seminar, humans are "not, unlike the animal, entirely caught up in this imaginary capture. . . . [The human subject] isolates the function of the screen and plays with it. Man, in effect, knows how to play with the mask as that beyond which there is the gaze" (107).

Crucial for the functioning of human mimicry is the irreducible human characteristic of paranoia. Paranoia is not only an exclusively human form of behavior but, more precisely, the human subject, for Lacan, is inescapably paranoid.[21] Whereas, for Freud, paranoia is always linked to repressed homosexuality, Lacan sees paranoia as structurally necessary for the human subject. As he asserts, the mirror stage "reveals . . . an ontological structure of the human world that fits in with my reflections on paranoiac knowledge" ("Mirror" 4). The paranoid subject emerges when, in the mirror stage, the ego is constituted as a specular other and as an object of paranoid identification. The mimicry of the mirror stage constitutes the "specular I" which is turned with the intrusion of the symbolic into the "social I." Entry into the symbolic inevitable entails what Lacan calls the "paranoiac alienation" of the subject. As John P. Muller and William J. Richardson write, "captivation by the image of the other in transitivism leads to paranoiac identification" (*Lacan* 40).

Anticipating his famous discussion of Edgar Allan Poe's detective story, which he gave later the same year (and which I will return to in the final chapter),

Lacan, in his second seminar, speaks of a game of "even and odd" as a parable for the structure of all human knowledge as paranoid. The human subject is like a player who manages to win his/her opponent by identifying with the logic of the other's strategy. In the game, there are three stages. In the first one, the player assumes that there is one-to-one correspondence between him/her and the opponent, and that s/he can effortlessly guess the other's moves: "I suppose the other subject to be in exactly the same position as me, thinking what I am thinking at the very moment that I am thinking it." This period is characterized by an unmediated identification and undifferentiation between the two subjects—characterized, that is, by the imaginary. In the second period, a certain alienation occurs, in that the subject can now "mak[e] himself other," thus realizing that "the other, being himself an other, thinks like him." Thus, there has to be a third position for him/her to occupy if s/he wants to guess the other's planned move. "As third party, I realise that if that other doesn't play the game, he fools his opponent. And from then on I'm ahead of him, by opting for the position opposite to the one which seemed to me, in the first period [*temps*], to be the most natural" (brackets in original English translation). From the introduction of a third element follows a third period, which is characterized by a kind of a return, a folding-back into the first period: "someone of superior intelligence can in fact understand that the trick is . . . to play like an idiot, that is to return to the first formula" (*SII* 180–81).

We can read the development of the infant during the mirror stage as analogous to the dialectic of the game of even and odd. As much as the game strategies constitute a certain "*identification of the reasoner's intellect with that of his opponent*" (*SII* 180),[22] the mirror stage is also defined by Lacan "*as an identification*" ("Mirror" 4). In the symbolic domain, paranoia becomes a necessary structure for the social dialectic. The third period in the game of even and odd would thus correspond to the final stage of paranoid alienation in the mirror stage.[23]

Mikkel Borch-Jacobsen asks, "what guarantees that the so-called normal personality is not fundamentally paranoid?" (32). Lacan's answer is that a form of paranoia is a sign of a healthy subject and the aim of analysis: speaking of the "paranoiac structure of the ego," Lacan suggests in "Aggressiveness in Psychoanalysis" (1948) that the aim of analysis is to "induc[e] in the subject a guided paranoia"; the healthy subject is characterized by a paranoia which is "highly systematized, in some sense filtered, and properly checked" (21, 17). According to Slavoj Žižek, there is only a nominal difference between the functional, healthy human subject who manages the social dialectic through paranoia and a subject who has lost his/her ability to negotiate the symbolic order. "When faced with such a paranoid construction," he writes, "we must not . . . mistake it for the 'illness' itself: the paranoid construction is, on the contrary, an attempt to heal ourselves" (*Looking* 19). As Lacan points out, clinical descriptions of paranoia, including those by Freud, can easily be indistinguishable from "the most wonderful descriptions of the behaviour of everyone" (*SIII* 19).

Here, we can begin to conceptualize the strategies and counterstrategies of blackface by linking them to Lacan's game theory. I suggest that, in the latter, the return to the first period, which characterizes the third strategy of the player—that is, "to play like an idiot"—presents precisely the dangers and indeterminacies that theorists of minstrelsy tackle with. Initially, Lacan proposes that this third period is the masterly strategy of "a superior intelligence." However, if this stage entails a return to the first period, the player's position in the game comes perilously close to that which inevitably leads to him being open to the other's perception. Thus, such a reversal can also signify a loss of control in the game. This, then, is the trap in what Lacan calls double deception: when the truth is hidden on the surface, the other needs only to realize that his/her opponent is deceiving him/her by telling the truth, to take his/her strategy at face value—s/he really *is* playing like an idiot—in order to win the game. The third period is where the game turns the tables on the players who are suddenly in danger of being possessed by their strategies and who become something like structural positions in the game. I suggest that this slippage is characteristic of blackface strategies: the black performers who have put on the masks created for and by the white gaze can fool their audience by "playing (like) an idiot." Avital Ronell points out the political necessity of such moves: "sometimes ducking into stupidity offers the most expedient strategy for survival" (7). Yet, as the theorists of minstrelsy without fail emphasize, in such strategies the minstrel mask threatens to possess the subject. What I call *black(face) magic* is impelled by—to quote Jacques Derrida's discussion of the *pharmakon*—"the magic virtues of a force whose effects are hard to master, a dynamics that constantly surprises the one who tries to manipulate it as master and as subject" (*Dissemination* 97). As soon as the player, whether of even and odd or of the minstrel stage, begins to believe in his/her own deception, the game spins out of control. Similarly, in his "Seminar on 'The Purloined Letter,'" Lacan emphasizes that when the human subject plays symbolic games to avoid being caught in an imaginary posture in front of the gaze, the deception may be only temporary (44). As Muller and Richardson observe, a certain "sliding effect" is almost inevitable whereby the subject's insight into the symbolic structure turns into another imaginary entrapment ("Lacan's" 63).

BEING POSSESSED

Having delineated them in the second seminar, "The Mirror Stage," and the "Seminar on 'The Purloined Letter,'" Lacan returns to the questions of paranoia, mimicry, and identification in the mid-1960s seminar *The Four Fundamental Concepts of Psycho-Analysis*. If, in his earlier work, he emphasizes mimicry's imaginary pull—the ways in which the subject is caught by "the lure of spatial identification" ("Mirror" 6)—in the 1960s he follows how mimicry engages the *real* aspect of human experience. In the early work, in other words, Lacan theorizes mimicry largely as an intersubjective phenomenon; later, it increasingly becomes a function that entails—that constitutes an engagement with—the Other, the symbolic constellation which itself is discovered to be fundamentally riddled with the real.

In both the early and later texts, Lacan turns to Roger Caillois's work to illuminate what is at stake: the subject's maladaptive character. Referring to Caillois in "The Mirror Stage," Lacan emphasizes that "attempts to reduce [mimicry] to the supposedly supreme law of adaptation" must unequivocally be regarded as "ridiculous" (5); in *The Four Fundamental Concepts*, he similarly denies that "the phenomenon of mimicry can be explained in terms of adaptation" (73). Lacan seeks to redefine the function of adaptation such that it ceases to be a phenomenon of the intersubjective world. He suggests that the subject reacts to the gaze with "adaptation": "From the moment that this gaze appears, the subject tries to adapt himself to it, he becomes that punctiform object, that point of vanishing being with which the subject confuses his own failure" (*SXI* 83). Adaptation does not refer to the organism's imitation of its environment, the kind of defensive self-concealment that one supposedly finds in the animal world. Rather, it is an adaptation *to the gaze itself*: "Whenever we are dealing with imitation, we should be very careful not to think too quickly of the other who is being imitated. To imitate is no doubt to reproduce an image. But at bottom, it is, for the subject, to be inserted in a function whose exercise grasps it" (*SXI* 100). To understand the way in which mimicry immobilizes, or "grasps," the subject, we should turn, with Lacan, to Caillois, whose remarks in "Mimicry and Legendary Psychastenia" (1938) on the mimetic behavior of animals help us to elaborate the connections between Lacan's theory of mimicry and the function of blackface. More precisely, Caillois's understanding of animal mimicry and its correlation with forms of human behavior outlines for us the ambivalence that blackface performance as a counterstrategy poses for the racialized subject.

Like Lacan after him, Caillois dismisses arguments according to which animals mimic their environment for either predatory or defensive reasons ("Mimicry" 23–25). Mimicry does not serve the survival of the species but is "a *luxury* and even a dangerous luxury": some insects resembling pieces of shrubbery are unintentionally mutilated by gardeners; others end up practicing cannibalism when they mistake each other for leaves (25). We must look for reasons for such behavior elsewhere. Caillois suggests that, in imitating their environment, insects respond to "*temptation by space*" (28). Rather than an effort to resemble a particular organism (an inedible insect; a beast of prey), mimicry is an attempt to disappear into the environment (27). As a result of this disappearance, the distinction between the organism and its surroundings is blurred if not lost. The organism loses the "privilege" of occupying a clearly circumscribed perspective vis-à-vis its environment: "the living creature, the organism, is no longer the origin of the coordinates, but one point among others; it is dispossessed of its privilege and literally *no longer knows where to place itself*" (28).

Caillois suggests a connection between the realms of the animal world and human psychology—a connection on which Lacan elaborates. Noting that "there seems to exist in man psychological potentialities strangely corresponding to these facts [of mimicry in animals]" (25), he presents two human analogies for the mimetic behavior of insects: the phenomena of psychosis and magic. Both mimicry and psychosis entail the disappearance of the self into the environment, the blurring of bodily boundaries, and the loss of a perspectival point. "To these dispossessed souls," Caillois writes of psychotics, "space seems to be a devouring force. Space pursues them, encircles them, digests them. . . . It ends by replacing them. Then the body separates itself from thought, the individual breaks the boundary of his skin and occupies the other side of his senses. He tries to look at *himself from* any point whatever in space. He feels himself becoming space, *dark space where things cannot be put*" (30). Like the mimetic insect that aims not to resemble any particular organism but to disappear into its environment, the psychotic becomes "similar, not similar to something, but just *similar*" (30). At stake is the loss of perspective. Elizabeth Grosz suggests that we understand animal mimicry as "a kind of 'natural psychosis'": "Both the psychotic and the insect renounce their rights to occupy a perspectival point, abandoning themselves to being spatially located by/as others. The primacy of one's own perspective is replaced by the gaze of another, for whom the subject is merely a point in space and not the focal point organizing space" (*Volatile* 47; see also "Lived" 193). The nonpsychotic subject is characterized by a location from which it organizes its field of vision. The psychotic subject, on the other hand, has relinquished its place in, its perspective onto, the symbolic order and has become a nonprivileged point in the field of the other's gaze, without distinct boundaries and coherence. With the crumbling of imaginary anatomy, the subject's "lived spatiality" evaporates:

> The subject can take up a position only by being able to situate its body in a position in space, a position from which it relates to other objects. This anchoring of subjectivity in its body is the condition of a coherent identity and, moreover, the condition under which the subject has a perspective on the world, becoming a source of perception, a point from which vision emanates. In psychasthenia, this meshing of subject and body fails to occur. Psychotics are unable to locate themselves where they should be: such subjects may look at themselves from the outside, as others would; they may hear the voices of others inside their own heads. (Grosz, "Lived" 191–92)

This potentially psychotic loss of positionality describes Bigger's strategy. In other words, the way in which the racialized subject can transgress its "place" in the white symbolic order approximates the loss of self in mimicry and psychosis. We can understand this confluence between transgressive practice and psychotic loss of subjectivity by noting how Caillois sees mimicry and psychosis as forms of magic gone awry. He suggests that mimicry may have begun "at a time when [the insects'] organisms were more plastic" ("Mimicry" 27) and that, subsequently, the organisms were immobilized in their mimetic poses. "Mimicry," he writes, "would thus be accurately described as *an incantation fixed at its culminating point* and having caught the sorcerer in his own trap. . . . What else but *prestigious magic* and *fascination* can the phenomena be called that have been unanimously classified under the name of mimicry . . . ?" (27).

If mimicry, for Caillois, resembles magic of which the sorcerer has lost control and that consequently engenders effects that turn against the magician, minstrel theorists too propose that we understand black blackface performance as a form of *dangerous magic*. Huggins suggests that acts of minstrelsy threaten to defeat the intentions of the black(face) magician: "It was just possible that the trick had been too perfect; *legerdemain* had undone itself in a disappearance act where the self had vanished, but also the incantation to call it back again" (263). Similarly, while Bigger, after Mary's killing, manages to deceive the white gaze—which had previously "possessed" him (72)—he soon begins to lose control. Meeting Bigger outside the Daltons', Jan wants to hear the truth of Mary's disappearance but drastically misreads the situation. He tells Bigger, "'Don't be scared. . . . Listen, now. Let's go somewhere and get a cup of coffee and talk this thing over'" (146). Jan repeats his and Mary's previous mistake of thinking that they can be on "Bigger's side," share a [B]igger's place with him. His (geometral) perspective does not allow him to see how inadequate his "solutions" (wanting to be on Bigger's "side," having a good talk over a cup of coffee) are.[24] Bigger is impelled to draw a gun on him, "fe[eling that] he had to act as he was acting" (146). Even at this early stage, then, the idiot's game threatens to take control of Bigger in ways that may not be very different from how his possibilities, (im)mobility, and place had earlier been dictated for him. When Jan leaves, Bigger feels that "[h]e was coming back into *possession of himself*; for the past three minutes it seemed he had been under *a strange spell*, *possessed by a force* which he hated, but which he had to obey" (147; emphases added). The confrontation with Jan, in other words, puts him in a position where his black(face) magic—his "playing (like) an idiot"—unexpectedly "possesses" him like he was earlier possessed by the racializing gaze.

After he has been exposed as the killer, Bigger goes to Bessie and, fearing that, if questioned, she will divulge information which will lead to his capture, forces her to accompany him to a deserted, condemned house. When he proceeds to plan her murder, he again feels that he has no other option, that he is being caught in a situation out of his control: "He thought of it calmly, as if the decision were being handed down to him by some logic not his own, over which he had no control, but which he had to obey" (194). Later, explaining his crimes to Max, he says, "'I knew what I was doing, all right. But I couldn't help it. . . . It was like another man stepped inside of my skin and started acting for me . . .'" (298; last ellipsis in original). No sooner has Bigger transgressed his place than he finds himself in a place "over which he ha[s] no control."

These repeated moments of possession in *Native Son* illustrate the similarity between Bigger's black(face) magic and the subject's psychotic/mimetic disappearance into its environment. Like Bigger, who feels that after Mary's murder he becomes indiscernible to others, the mimetic subject blends in with its surroundings. Bigger's mimicry illustrates the fact that, while the "psychotic" dimension is inevitable in animal mimicry, mimicry in humans is crucially modified by the introduction of the dimension of the symbolic. In animal mimicry, the subject can no longer place itself in the environment; it does not experience the distinction between itself and its surroundings; it becomes a point in the field of another's gaze, a point that has lost its perspectival privilege of ordering the field of vision. But the human subject's mimetic "play" may avoid the psychotic trap. As Lacan notes, human mimicry does not *necessarily* lead to the psychotic capture by space that Caillois sees in the insect world (*SXI* 107)—but this danger remains. Amidst his successful deception, Bigger, to his surprise and terror, finds himself re-possessed.[25]

The black(face) magic of minstrelsy can be thought of as an active response to the ghosts that haunt the racialized subject in the white symbolic order. Minstrelsy, then, would amount to an act of exorcism, and blackface comes to function as the mask of a conjurer. Wright and minstrel theorists illustrate the precariousness of such conjurations, however, as they immediately go on to point out the danger of such rituals: the spirits called out to exorcise those of the white symbolic order are not readily distinguishable from the demands imposed by the white world. That Bigger "fe[els] strange, possessed" (72) not only as his black(face) sorcery spins out of control but also before Mary's murder further suggests that this position is already the place of the racialized subject in the white symbolic order. For Lacan, psychosis is, precisely, a form of possession: "If the neurotic inhabits language, the psychotic is inhabited, possessed, by language" (*SIII* 250). Language speaks the psychotic subject, much in the same way that, encountering Mr. Dalton for the first time, Bigger finds himself "whisper[ing]; not speaking really; but hearing his words issue involuntarily from his lips, as of a force of their own" (39). In transgressing his place, Bigger turns his psychotic possession by the symbolic into an emancipatory disappearance from its radar. But then he learns that the danger in this mimetic absenting of self is that the "the trick had been too perfect"—that in his disappearing act he loses his perspective that defines him as a subject.

COMPOUNDED DUPLICITIES

To further illustrate the link between mimicry, the mirror stage, and Bigger's black(face) magic, let us return to the scene of the crime.

As Mrs. Dalton approaches Bigger and her semi-unconscious daughter in the latter's darkened bedroom, he pushes a pillow onto Mary's face to keep her from stirring. Although her mother initially appears to him as a "white blur," immediately after Mary's death—even before Bigger consciously realizes that he has suffocated her—the woman comes clearly into view: "Then suddenly her fingernails did not bite into his wrists. Mary's fingers loosened. He did not feel her surging and heaving against him. Her body was still. . . . He could see Mrs. Dalton plainly now" (74). As Mrs. Dalton approaches the bed, Bigger doubles her movements: "With each of her movements toward the bed his body made a movement to match hers, away from her, his feet not lifting themselves from the floor" (74). By mimicking Mrs. Dalton's actions, Bigger conceals his presence. The next morning, Bigger realizes that it is indeed this kind of *doubling of others* that he needs in order to be able to hide himself, to make himself secret: "The thing to do was to act just like others acted, live like they lived, and while they were not looking, do what you wanted" (91).

Here we perhaps witness the "fertile moment" of paranoia,[26] marking the entry into the ("healthy") social dialectic and the emergence of the paranoid subject. Mimicry—his doubling of others—allows Bigger to escape full, disempowering visibility and creates a space of mobility and agency for him: he "feel[s] free, that his life was his, that he held his future in his hand" (161–62). A mirror stage of sorts follows: after the accidental murder, there occurs another scene of looking, which, although reminiscent of those in which Bigger is racialized by Mr. Dalton's gaze, nevertheless differs from them significantly. The day after the murder, Bigger rides to his employers' house in a street car. Amidst the white people Bigger "looked anxiously at the dim reflection of his black face in the sweaty window pane. Would any of the white faces all about him think that he had killed a rich white girl? No! . . . He smiled a little, feeling *a tingling sensation* enveloping all his body. He saw it all very sharply and simply" (96; emphasis added). We can briefly compare this scene to a passage in *The Souls of Black Folk* (1903) in which Du Bois visualizes the African American subject's incipient awareness of being caught in the specular "double consciousness": "In those sombre forests of his striving his own soul rose before him, and he saw himself,—darkly as through a veil, and yet he saw in himself some faint revelation of his power, of his mission. He began to have a dim feeling that, to attain his place in the world, he must be himself, and not another" (14). Both scenes are moments of self-recognition that stir vague feelings of empowerment. Even though Du Bois goes on by renewing his call for an integrity of being—"he must be himself, and not another"—notably, the feeling of empowerment does not come from, nor does it necessarily result in, any newly attained unity of the subject. On the contrary, the subject's empowerment is possible only through the "second sight" that the black American subject is "gifted" with (10):[27] after all, "his power, his mission" is revealed only at the moment of the subject's *seeing himself*, of being faced with the ghostly apparition of "one's soul."

Bigger's sense of empowerment is similarly initiated at a moment of mirroring—a moment when Bigger sees himself as others might see him, sees himself as other. He becomes to a certain degree invisible, unreadable: he realizes that none of the other passengers is able to intuit that "he had killed a rich white girl." Unlike in earlier scenes with the Daltons, the bodily sensation of his "skin tingl[ing]" (52) is initiated through his recognition of his own reflection: the "tingling sensation" now comes from his own looking rather than from that of any white person. A reorganization has thus taken place in the (looking) relations between Bigger and others. His new perspective provides him with what the text calls "a queer sense of power" (203). Whereas he has previously been easily accessible to others, he now feels he has become, at least partially, invisible to them. The white people whose eyes he had felt turning on him on the previous day are all described as unseeing: "Jan was blind. Mary had been blind. Mr. Dalton was blind. And Mrs. Dalton was blind; yes, blind in more ways than one" (91). His new perspective provides Bigger a self-determining agency: "Now that the ice was broken, could he not do other things? What was there to stop him?" (91). Like the African American in Du Bois who gets a glimpse of "his power, his mission" as he learns to see himself, Bigger "felt that he had his destiny in his grasp. He was more alive than he could ever remember having been; his mind and attention were pointed, focused toward a goal" (127).

A feeling of secrecy, then, is at the core of Bigger's empowerment: he acquires a sense of freedom and agency when he feels he is beyond others' looks, which have previously assigned him to a rigorous, inflexible place. In his inaccessibility to those around him, Bigger is able to see without being seen: "if he could see while others were blind then he could get what he wanted and never be caught at it" (91). Indeed, not only does "the whole blind world" (115) lose its easy access to Bigger; through his crime, Bigger begins to see things "very sharply and simply" (96). During breakfast with his family on the morning after the killing, "[h]e looked around the room, seeing it for the first time" (89). As he enters the Daltons' basement later that morning, he encounters the maid Peggy "peering hard into the furnace" in which he has incinerated Mary's body (99). He immediately thinks that he has been caught by the white woman's inquisitive looking. However, he soon realizes that, whereas he had previously felt "shame and fear" when immobilized by white eyes, Peggy is now to a certain extent in his position: rather than turning her eyes on him, she feels "ashamed of having been seen in the basement in her kimono" (100). In other words, she is very much like the Sartrean subject who, peering through a keyhole, is suddenly caught in her act of voyeurism: as much as the voyeur is ashamed of having been surprised by the (Sartrean) Other (*Being* 259–61), Peggy, caught looking, feels "ashamed."[28]

Bigger realizes that others are in effect "blind to what did not fit" (91)—that they operate according to perspectival optics which render them blind to anomalies and inconsistencies. He begins to use white people's assumptions to hide himself in the picture that they expect to see. Assuming that they are in control of their and others' position in the visual field—that is, arrogating to themselves the position of an autonomous voyeur, the Cartesian cogito—the white people always miss and misinterpret the stain in the picture before them (see *SXI* 74). In "objectifying" what is within their visual field, the white spectators inevitably misrecognize what they see *and* their own position in the field of vision: "objectification in psychological matters is subject, at its very core, to a law of misrecognition that governs the subject not only as observed, but also as observer" (Lacan, "Freudian" 123).

This new sense of vision that Bigger acquires after the killing corresponds to the Du Boisian "second-sight." Indeed, reminding us of Du Bois's trope of the "veil," Wright concretizes Bigger's protective concealment and second sight in the terms of the "wall" or the "curtain." After the murder, Bigger looks at his family, thinking, "He had a natural wall from behind which he could look at them" (90). Yet, the fact that the wall/curtain figures in his life also previous to Mary's killing suggests that, like double consciousness, it is paradoxically debilitating *and* empowering. We find that the wall/curtain has always been there as a way for Bigger to distance himself from the otherwise unbearable realities of his existence:

> He hated his family because he knew that they were suffering and that he was powerless to help them. He knew that moment he allowed himself to feel to its fullness how they lived, the shame and misery of their lives, he would be swept out of himself with fear and despair. So he held toward them an attitude of iron reserve; he lived with them, but behind a wall, a curtain. (9)

In this early scene, the wall/curtain figures as a defense against the psychic effects of poverty and oppression. After the killing, something happens to his relation to the wall/curtain: as he is having breakfast with his family, he thinks, "No, he did not have to hide behind a wall or a curtain now; he had a safer way of being safe, an easier way" (91). Yet, in the same scene, Bigger's empowering sense of concealment is again given in the same trope: "He had a natural wall from behind which he could look at them" (90).

These ostensibly paradoxical descriptions of Bigger's deployment of the curtain suggest that it has a double function. As the above passage from *Native Son* implies, the curtain initially muffles the effects of poverty that would otherwise make Bigger's life unbearable, that would "swe[ep him] out of himself with fear and despair." Yet, Bigger's ability to reorganize the field of vision through the curtain suggests the possibility of unexpected effects. Previously, he has experienced being "on stage" as disempowering and exhausting, while simultaneously using the curtain as an inadequate way to distance himself from the misery of his life. After the murder, he recognizes that he can consciously remobilize the curtain. As such, the above passage does not suggest Bigger's abandonment of the curtain, but, rather, his realization that it can be deployed in more sophisticated and productive ways than for a mere obstruction of others' looks. Thinking of his new-found method of concealment, Bigger says this quite explicitly: "In a certain sense he had been doing just that in a loud and rough manner all his life, but it was only last night when he had smothered Mary in her room while her blind mother had stood with outstretched arms that he had seen how clearly it could be done" (96). Having transgressed his place, Bigger can do the most violent things under the blind white gaze. Rather than merely hiding something from others' eyes, the curtain starts *showing* things in ways that Bigger is in control of. What has been an obstacle to the white gaze now becomes a lure inviting it—and, by that very invitation, tricking it.

Bigger deploys the curtain in a masterful game of paranoid knowledge. When Jan is told that Bigger has implicated him in Mary's disappearance, he immediately assumes that this is a plot by the Establishment to get him. "'Is this a game?'" he asks, to which Mr. Dalton replies in the negative (144–45). What both of them fail to see is, of course, that it *is* a game—a game controlled by Bigger. "'Say, what *is* this!'" Jan exclaims, hearing the accusations leveled against him. "'What're you making this boy lie for?'" (142). He misses Bigger's involvement in the lies because he, in a typically patronizing attitude, aims for some "deeper" motivation that is hidden *behind* his actions—Bigger, that is, functions for him like a screen through which he tries to make out what is really going on (the Old Regime plotting against the Communists). What he does not realize is that the truth is closer to the surface, that the truth is *on* the surface: it is Bigger who is framing him. Similarly, the white investigators are fooled by Bigger in assuming that behind him there lies a hidden meaning to Mary's disappearance: a communist plot. This bypassing of Bigger by white people recurs several times. The newspaper men ask Britten whether Bigger is telling the truth, supposing that it is another white man, rather than Bigger himself, who can vouch for Bigger's words (170). Bigger's position as the "fool" gives him access to others' thoughts as they assume that they don't have to hide anything from him: "'Aw, he's a dumb cluck. He doesn't know anything,' one of the [reporters] whispered in a voice loud enough for Bigger to hear" (181). "'You going to pull the dumb act on us?'" (168), one reporter asks Britten, blind to the fact that it is in fact Bigger who is fooling them by playing (like) an idiot. Britten similarly misses Bigger's involvement because he looks for some other, hidden significance (Bigger's involvement with "Communists" or "jews") (163).[29] Suddenly, Bigger realizes that "his hands held weapons that were invisible" (111)—invisible, that is, from the (white) geometral perspective.

During the interview, Bigger employs paranoid identification to anticipate white people's moves. He wonders how much they know, what they are trying to get at, what their strategy is, and how he should best respond to their moves. He plays the "dumb black boy" for the investigators: playing (like) an idiot, he repeats the moves of the Lacanian gambler of "superior intelligence" or the black minstrel performer. However, there are moments when his strategies of paranoia and identification do not let him correctly anticipate what the white people are after. Britten surprises Bigger by accusing him of being a communist. It is at that moment that Bigger gets his first lesson in the instabilities of (paranoid) identification: "He had not thought that this thing could cut two ways" (137). His playing (like) an idiot allows him to escape his persecutors but may simultaneously put him in a position he could not have foreseen. When, in a similar moment of insight, Cross Damon, the protagonist of *The Outsider* (1953), realizes the dangers in his games of deception, he articulates the unforeseeable repercussions in these strategies in ways which are applicable to Bigger's game:

> His past life had prepared him for participating in . . . compounded duplicities. His temperament made him love to understand those who thought that they were misleading him and it was fun to use his position of being misled to, in his turn, mislead them into a position where they thought he was misunderstanding them. He knew, of course, that such complicated games carried a risk of *his* misunderstanding those whom he was supposed to understand, but he was willing to shoulder such handicaps. (572–73)

Indeed, *Native Son* reminds us that, even if the subject can remobilize the curtain, this says nothing about the ultimate outcome of such negotiations. The subject is likely to be recaptured by the very means by which he attempts to deceive; black(face) magic will hex the conjurer. We can see the limitedness of Bigger's agency in orchestrating others' interpretations of the situation in the fact that his perspective is not one of unobstructed, concealed looking. Even though he feels that "a natural wall" conceals him and his look from others, he is surprised time and again in the act of looking. As he looks at his slow-moving, tired mother, she, although described in many ways as having an extremely limited vision, "saw him looking at her" (92) and asks if there is something wrong with him (85, 87). Catching him "star[ing] vacantly in her direction," his sister Vera accuses him of stealing looks at her while she is getting dressed (88, 93). "'How come you looking at me that way, Bigger?'" asks his little brother, Buddy, a little later (92). Buddy, to whom the text attributes the same "shining eyes" (94) that had made Bigger so uncomfortable in the presence of Mary and Jan (58), runs after Bigger and queries if he "'was in trouble . . . '" (94; ellipsis in original). Similar, unanticipated and unsettling reactions come also from his girlfriend Bessie (117, 123).

Having briefly managed to use the curtain protectively, Bigger eventually falls back on its previous function as something that he uses simply to hide behind. This redeployment of the curtain occurs in the concluding scenes to the second part of the novel, where, having been exposed as the murderer, he is being hunted by the white vigilante groups. In the passages, the terms "his curtain, his wall" circulate insistently. That Bigger eventually regresses back to the old strategy of the curtain becomes obvious as he is finally cornered by the search party, having been hiding on rooftops in freezing weather: "He was surprised that he was not afraid. Under it all some part of his mind was beginning to stand aside; he was going behind his curtain, his wall, looking out with sullen stares of contempt" (226). His pursuers use a powerful water cannon to force his surrender. As the icy stream of water hits him, "[h]e was behind his curtain now, looking down at himself freezing under the impact of water in sub-zero winds" (227). Finally, he succumbs, nearly losing consciousness: "He opened his eyes and saw a circle of white faces; but he was outside of them, behind his curtain, his wall, looking on" (228).

ANAMORPHOSIS AND TROMPE L'OEIL

The double function of Bigger's curtain—as an inadequate strategy of survival, and as a form of mimicry that enables (however limited and short-term) guerrilla tactics—exemplifies one of the forms of ostentatious obsequiousness that black Americans have had to adopt to survive, particularly in the segregated South. I will discuss such forms of acting and subversion, and their implications for Lacanian theory, in the next chapter. For now, I wish to locate in more detail Bigger's black(face) magic in Lacan's theory by moving from Lacan's early texts—"The Mirror Stage" and the second seminar—to his later work. The similarities and differences between the discussion of mimicry in these texts allow us to see Lacan as "paradoxically *systematic* thinker" (Chiesa 4). On the one hand, his earlier and later delineations of the subject and the symbolic order are recognizable as part of the same oeuvre: for example, his discussion of the subject of the mirror stage—where one finds psychoanalytic theory "at odds with any philosophy directly stemming from the *cogito*" ("Mirror" 3)—clearly anticipates his deployment, in the eleventh seminar, of theories of Renaissance perspective to delineate the subject that is not a Cartesian consciousness outside the picture. On the other, in the later work he theorizes the subject in terms of the *objet a*, a shift in emphasis with crucial ramifications.

One of the best-known recent attempts at a theory of visibility and resistance is Kaja Silverman's reading of Lacan's eleventh seminar, *The Four Fundamental Concepts of Psycho-Analysis.* If I have argued that, for Bigger, the curtain has a double function, Silverman too suggests that the Lacanian screen, which stands between "point of light" and "picture," determines the subject while at the same time potentially allowing some protection for him/her. Describing the function of the screen as that of "the thrown-off skin, thrown off in order to cover the frame of a shield" (*SXI* 107), Lacan, in Silverman's reading, suggests that it "can . . . not only be abjected, but also put between me and the world of others as a protective device" (*Threshold* 202). There may be no escape from the gaze but "some limited power is available to the subject who recognizes [his or] her necessary subordination to the gaze, but finds potentially transgressive ways of 'performing' before it" ("Fassbinder" 128). According to Silverman, although the screen as the site of the subject in the field of vision is always determined by the gaze over which the subject has no control, it can be reappropriated by the human subject who is not entirely captated by the gaze. Similarly, I suggested that, faced with the white detectives investigating Mary's disappearance, Bigger starts consciously to act the part that he has been obliged to embody all his life. Previously, being fixed by others' looks had elicited uncontrollable bodily reactions from him. Now, however, as the eyes of the white interrogators turn on him, his response is one of excitement at the recognition of his agency in the situation: "They wanted him to *draw the picture* and he would draw it like he wanted it. He was trembling with excitement. In the past had they not always drawn the picture for him?" (135; emphasis added). This time, that is, Bigger feels that he is in control of his situatedness in the "picture."

While her deployment of Lacan in visual studies—film and photography—offers immediate ways to understand Bigger's negotiation of his place in "the picture," I want to insist on a more detailed dialogue than the one Silverman produces between Lacanian theory and other bodies (of work).[30] That is, to theorize Bigger's disruption of the white symbolic order, we must understand the role of the *objet petit a*, whose function Silverman neglects but which is central to any consideration of the later, "post-structuralist" Lacan.

Discussing trompe l'oeil painting, Lacan asks,

> What is it that attracts and satisfies us in *trompe-l'oeil*? When is it that it captures our attention and delights us [*nous captive et nous met en jubilation*]? At the moment when, by a mere shift of our gaze, we are able to realize that the representation does not move with the gaze and that it is merely a *trompe-l'oeil*. For it appears at that moment as something other than it seemed, or rather it now seems to be that something else. (*SXI* 112/102)

Lacan points out the satisfaction in the subject's realization, achieved at the moment when s/he shifts his/her look and sees that the perspective does not move accordingly, that the representation is in fact a trompe l'oeil. There is an intense "pleasure" (*SVII* 135) in the denaturalization of representations. Why? Because, simultaneously, the subject's own place and perspective are denaturalized, and s/he gains an insight into the functioning of the field of vision. As Anne Trubek points out, trompe l'oeil paintings, first mimicking and then denaturalizing realist representations, draw their viewers into the painting—much like, according to Lacan, Renaissance paintings do. As Trubek writes, "the lack of perspective in *trompe l'oeil* leads to an uncanny sense of immanence, a *merging* of subject and object" (43). The effect of such absorption is a sense of mobility: even though trompe l'oeil "'invade[s]'" the subjects' space, it simultaneously, in releasing the viewers from the illusion of the necessity of one proper perspective, gives them "'freedom of movement'" (50).[31] Thus trompe l'oeil's "calling out" to the viewer is "a gesture toward communication and dialogue": the painting, in destroying the illusion of one perspective, "seeks out that viewer to supply the meaning it does not provide" (51).

Lacan suggests that, with this transgressive movement of our look, the trompe l'oeil "seems to be something else." "This other thing," he specifies, "is the *petit a*, around which there revolves a combat of which *trompe-l'oeil* is the soul" (*SXI* 112). In other words, when the look changes its position, the trompe l'oeil intimates the presence of the *objet petit a*, the remainder (and reminder) of *das Ding*, the symbolic order's constitutive outside. According to Lacan, the art of perspective—which both anamorphosis and trompe l'oeil play havoc on—conceals the nothingness on which the subject, like a piece of "primitive architecture," is grounded (*SVII* 135). This emptiness is the void of the real, or *das Ding*, whose leftover piece in the symbolic, the *objet a*, impels the subject on its trajectory of desire.[32] In painting, perspective's "illusion of space" domesticates the "emptiness that designates the place of the Thing": "painting progressively learns to master this emptiness, to take such a tight hold of it that painting becomes dedicated to fixing it in the form of the illusion of space" (*SVII* 140). In denaturalizing perspective, anamorphosis and trompe l'oeil undermine such strategies of domestication, showing the abyss on which rests whatever image perspectival illusion has enabled. As Lacan says, "the interest of anamorphosis is described as a turning point when the artist completely reverses the use of that illusion of space, when he forces it to enter into the original goal, that is to transform it into the support of the hidden reality—it being understood that, to a certain extent, a work of art always involves encircling the Thing" (*SVII* 141). Anamorphosis and trompe l'oeil, in other words, loosen the "tight hold" that perspectival illusion of space—as a symbolizing mechanism—has laid on *das Ding*.

Given that they conjure up the *objet a* in representation, trompe l'oeil paintings elicit what Lacan would call an ethical engagement with the symbolic, where the subject-viewer is not able to retain his/her distance from representations but is instead, through a dizzying multiplication of perspectives, drawn into the picture. While such a shift in positions is disorienting, it simultaneously opens new interpretative possibilities for the subject. In Lacan's terms, it places the subject in the mobile field of desire. Such mobility is possible by showing the lack, the nothingness of *das Ding*, at the heart of representations.

In killing Mary in front of her mother, Bigger experiences a shift in perspective that corresponds to that of the viewer of trompe l'oeil paintings, who "must experience two temporally sequential moments: the moment of *being* fooled and the subsequent realization that he or she *has been* fooled" (Trubek 37). The latter moment constitutes the pleasure of the paranoid subject, a pleasure that Bigger feels immediately after the murder.[33] He realizes that what others are looking at, that the "reality" of what they see, is merely the trompe l'oeil of representations, and discovers a perspective that, in distorting what he had earlier taken as reality, opens another space for him, a space in which to reconstitute symbolic reality. His is a "paranoid vision which refutes the accepted authoritative or consensual version of reality" (Flieger, "Postmodern" 89).

While Lacan says that this denaturalization of perspective is pleasurable, we need to add that, like the gaze itself, this distortion has double effects for the subject: its pleasure easily turns into anxiety as an intuition of the real's proximity. Furthermore, I submit that the subject's reaction to such paranoid realization may be partially contingent upon his or her positioning in the culturally inscribed circuits of the field of vision. Because structures of visibility at a given historical moment are organized so as to yield power to certain subject positions while rendering others subordinate, dominant subjects experience anxiety over losing their masterly position while others can gain satisfaction in realizing that their position is subject to change when the field of the visible is denaturalized.

THE MASK AS *OBJET PETIT A*

Lacan suggests that, discerning the object-cause of desire, the subject functions like an eye under a harsh light, an eye whose squint resembles a "grimace" (*SXI* 94). Elsewhere, he refers to something he terms "the grimace of the real" (*Television* 6).[34] I propose that we understand this "grimace" in terms of the double function of the gaze for the subject. That is, pertaining to the real, the "grimacing" gaze as *objet petit a*—the grimace of the skull that comes into view in a sideways glance—destabilizes the subject, producing anxiety. The subject consequently reacts like an eye under a glaring light, shielding itself with the "grimace" of the eyelids. This doubleness (the grimace of the real or the gaze as *objet petit a*, and that of the eye/I), is, I submit, exemplified by the minstrel mask in the context of the white symbolic order.

Bigger learns to squint, to grimace, as he actively deploys the blackface mask in his momentarily successful bid for mobility in the white symbolic order. While seemingly supporting symbolic logic, his blackface persona simultaneously marks the point of the symbolic's internal failure, an opening where violent alterity floods its circuits. From the white geometral perspective, that is, Bigger functions like Lacan's "grimace of the real," like the anamorphotic skull in Holbein's painting. If the racialized subject can deploy blackface paranoiacally (in the "healthy" social dialectic) or be entirely determined by it (leading to psychosis), for the white audience, too, the mask functions doubly. First, it is necessary to sustain the symbolic order. According to Žižek's well-known formulation, "the symbolic mechanism [must] be hooked onto a 'thing,' some piece of the real . . . because the symbolic field is in itself always already barred, crippled, porous, structured around some extimate kernel, some impossibility. The function of the 'little piece of the real' is precisely to fill out the place of this void that gapes in the very heart of the symbolic" (*Looking* 33). Second, as the *objet petit a*, this unsymbolizable leftover of the traumatic real is the point of the symbolic order's internal inconsistency: "The role of the Lacanian real is . . . radically ambiguous: true, it erupts in the form of a traumatic return, derailing the balance of our daily lives, but it serves at the same time as a support of this very balance" (29). It is precisely subjects in a [B]igger's place who function as this "necessary/impossible" (Stavrakakis 49) stain of the real that simultaneously sustains the symbolic *and* radically undermines it. The return gaze of the stain exposes the traumatic contingency of the symbolic.

The symbolic order's structuration around the radical otherness of the real has usually been mapped through sexual difference. Here, too, we find the figures of the mask and the veil. The concept of the mask of femininity originates in Joan Riviere's essay "Womanliness as Masquerade," where it refers to the fact that the two sexes meet only through the masquerade of "womanliness." Lacan partially borrows from Riviere in conceptualizing the "*travesty*" of the (non)encounter of the sexes, which takes place "through the mediation of masks" (*SXI* 107). His theory is later echoed in Luce Irigaray's notion of masquerade [*la mascarade*] as "[a]n alienated or false version of femininity arising from the woman's awareness of the man's desire for her to be his other [which] . . . permits woman to experience desire not in her own right but as the man's desire situates her" (*This* 220). For Irigaray, masquerade is potentially superseded by the more subversive mimicry [*mimétisme*], through which the woman "tr[ies] to recover the place of her exploitation by discourse, without allowing herself to be simply reduced to it" (76; see also 220).[35] In feminist psychoanalysis, then, the mask approximates the veil with which the phallus, in order to function symbolically, is necessarily covered (Lacan, "Signification" 277). ~~Woman~~ is the repository of the veiled phallus and thus the site that guarantees the masculine jouissance. As an example of such jouissance, Lacan discusses courtly love, which is characterized by the unattainability and exchangeability of the Lady whose virtues the troubadours extol (see *SVII* 139–54; *SXX* 69). The position of the Lady is that of the veiled phallus whose lack sustains yet troubles masculine libidinal economy. Embodying the *objet a* and consequently partaking in the nothingness of the real, ~~Woman~~ can be said not to exist. Yet, we should remember that this "does not mean that the place of woman does not exist, but rather that this place remains essentially empty. The fact that this place remains empty does not mean that we cannot find something there. But in it, we find only masks, masks of nothingness" (J.-A. Miller, "On Semblances" 14).

Given Lacanian scholarship's focus on the phallic economy of the symbolic order, a number of Lacanians conclude that sexual difference, unlike other, including racial, differences, is of the order of the real. Yet, as I will argue in the next chapter, Wright and Frantz Fanon suggest that race may be understood as a real difference: it allows the functioning of the symbolic order while simultaneously threatening its logic with the intrusion of the real. James Baldwin indicates precisely this when he writes that "the black man has functioned in the white man's world as a fixed star, as an immovable pillar: and as he moves out of his place, heaven and earth are shaken to their foundation" (*Fire* 336). We can anticipate this argument by noting how, in *Native Son*, the minstrel mask that Bigger learns to deploy figures as the *objet a*. Mr. Dalton tells Britten that he hired Bigger to give the "boy" another chance: "'He's here to try to get a new slant on things,'" he says (139). While Bigger does, of course, get his new angle or perspective on things, this "slant" obviously is not what Mr. Dalton would have anticipated. Having realized his "new slant"—having perverted his perspective and produced a new grimace—Bigger also realizes the vertiginous and devastating potential of his new position for white people. He wishes he could tell them how he had killed a "rich white girl":

> He wanted the keen thrill of startling them, but felt that the cost was too great. He wished that he had the power to say what he had done without fear of being arrested; he wished . . . that *his black face* and the image of his smothering Mary and cutting off her head and burning her could hover before their eyes like a terrible picture of reality which they could see and feel and yet not destroy. (110; emphasis added)

Bigger wishes that white people would receive his message as the indestructible "answer of the real." The "terrible picture of reality," then, is the mask (precisely, "his black face")[36] that has sustained the white symbolic order but which Bigger longs to turn into the frightening grimace of the real that would hover, like the skull in the foreground of Holbein's painting revealing its deadly contours in a sideways glance, in front of the representation that what white people thought they saw.[37] As Stephen Greenblatt writes, the skull in *The Ambassadors* distorts and cancels out all the culturally valued objects sustaining the proper, geometral perspective (17–18). For the white symbolic order, recognizing Bigger's grimacing mask would similarly render the proper perspective impossible. Comparing *The Ambassadors* to *Native Son*, we can further suggest that, in recognizing the answer of the real, the white symbolic order would also have to realize that it has always been implicated in such a terrifying alterity—as much as, on a closer inspection, the spectator of Holbein's painting can discern a figure of the skull also in the brooch worn by one of the men in his hat (Greenblatt 18).

Like Bigger, other racially marked subjects are to a greater or lesser degree aware of the dynamics of the visible and the *objet a* in the white symbolic. Fleeing the white vigilante groups, Bigger eavesdrops on two black men—"Jim" and "Jack"—discussing his case. While one of them would turn the perpetrator in to normalize the situation, the other advocates a suicidal counterstrategy by means of a violent appropriation of white fantasies of blackness: "'Ah'd die firs'!'" he says, to which his partner responds: "'Man, yuh crazy!'" Embracing the *insanity* of his position, the first man avers: "'We's all black 'n' we jus' as waal *ack* black, don' yuh see?'" His interlocutor, however, argues that it is necessary for blacks to defuse the acute crisis in the city by retaining a proper perspective: "'Aw, Jim, it's awright t' git mad, but yuh gotta *look at things straight*'" (213; last emphasis added).

In advocating "acting black," Jim suggests that, because, in the eyes of the white world, the Black Belt is inhabited by sub-human savages, criminals, and rapists—"the sprawling forms of dread," as Boris Max puts it in his courtroom speech (324)—the racialized subject should answer back by adopting and embodying that very violence, by turning its blinding force back on the white world. "Acting black" constitutes an insane rearticulation of the terms of the [B]igger's place in the white symbolic order; as Jack suggests, it requires that one go "crazy." As the irrationality of a probable suicide, it would comprise what Žižek has called "the answer of the real." Žižek suggests that we encounter such an answer when the world begins to play our game, mimic the fantasies we have projected on it and of it. When our symbolic pretenses and fantasies receive an unexpected echo from the world, our daily lives are suddenly paralyzed by sheer terror (*Enjoy* 32). This is precisely how Jim proposes to attack the white world: to reflect back on it its fantasies of "blackness." In these fantasies, as he says, "'[w]e's *all* murderers'" (213).

That Bigger's crime turns out to fit so well into the white symbolic order turn his contingent actions into an answer of the real. Jan and the investigators fail to see Bigger's involvement in Mary's disappearance because they search for some deeper, hidden significance. Like any figuration of the real, Bigger's crime "is . . . not an inaccessible kernel hidden beneath layers of symbolizations, it is *on the surface*—it is . . . a kind of excessive disfiguration of reality, like the fixed grimace of a smile" (Žižek, *Looking* 172–73n2). From the moment our mimicry receives an echo from the real, the game takes on a compulsive, psychotic character: "The answer of the real . . . function[s] . . . as a shock that dissolves the mask of trickery. Once we are seized by panic, the only way out appears to be to 'take seriously' our own pretense and to cling to it" (34). For Jim, "acting black"—violently embodying the grimacing role of the black man—would similarly destabilize the white symbolic order, giving it precisely what it has fantasized about. While Jim advocates a radical reordering of the visible by "acting black," for Jack it is necessary to retain one's place in the (geometral) scheme of things, "look[ing] at things straight."

In *Native Son*, the steady perspective of "looking at things straight" commands most black and white spectators alike. This allows Bigger to "imaginarize" the white symbolic order with his "queer sense of power" (203). Yet, despite their geometral perspective, others are soon onto him. One of the earliest indications of his "fate"—the title of the novel's third part—comes when, after his interrogation, "Bigger [sees] Mr. Dalton *gazing at him queerly*. He [does] not like that look. . . . 'You're telling us the truth about all this, aren't you, Bigger?'" the white man asks (145; emphasis added). Albeit briefly, Mr. Dalton casts an "(in)queering" look at Bigger, intuiting that the latter is not being entirely straight with the investigators. Countering Bigger's tactical moves, his lateral shift disrupts the black man's empowerment, threatening to blow his cover. He steps out of his customary viewpoint and, in an awry glance, glimpses some of the possibilities that are scotomized by his masterful perspective of whiteness. As the master of the house learns, it is only by queering one's perspective that one can exercise "a straight eye," the "ability to see whether an object is placed straight" (*OED*). Jim, too, discerns the benefit for black subjects to renounce their customary perspectives on the world determined by racial economies. Calling Jack to shift his perspective, to look differently—"'don' yuh see?'"—Jim suggests an analogous move to Mr. Dalton's. As an irreconcilable counterpoint to the rational, "straight" perspective that Jack admonishes, "acting black" amounts to a *queer*—a twisted, unexpected, odd, violent—response, coming from left field, to the intolerable realities of one's existence.[38]

Very soon, indeed, Bigger is exhausted by his game. As he is being questioned by the investigators and newspaper reporters alike, he thinks:

> Things were happening so fast that he felt he was not doing full justice to them. He was tired. Oh, if only he could go to sleep! If only this whole thing could be postponed for a few hours, until he had rested some! He felt that he would have been able to handle it then. Events were like the details of a tortured dream, happening without a cause. At times it seemed that he could not quite remember what had gone before and what it was he was expecting to come. (169)

Here we can see a certain breakdown in Bigger's paranoid game. His feeling of things "happening without a cause" implies the breakdown of his symbolic calculations by that which escapes causality and chance. As Lacan says in the second seminar, the real is precisely that which cannot be calculated, into which nothing like chance can be integrated (*SII* 182). The rigor of his game is such that very soon Bigger feels unable to sustain his masterly position in it and loses his sense of "what it was he was expecting to come." He fatally miscalculates his own agency and position in the white symbolic order in that, while he may have gained insight into the structure of the symbolic, the weight of his historically predetermined position is such that it tends to destroy his newly gained position of freedom.

As I suggested above, the streetcar scene following Mary's murder can be read as Bigger's belated mirror stage, his realization of the potential for secrecy inherent in his own image. After he has been found out and begins his flight, there is another scene in a streetcar. This time, however, Bigger becomes aware of his exposure to others' looks: he "watch[es] to see if the conductor was noticing him; then he [goes] through the car, watching to see if any face [is] turned to him" (189). Notably, this scene takes place immediately after his exposure and before his crime is reported in the newspapers; thus, he cannot fear being recognized as the killer on the grounds of newspaper photographs. Rather, he feels his crime is suddenly visible on his body, as much as his black skin must be visible to others' looks. Logically, then, it is suggested a little later that Bigger's mimicry has been strictly *corporeal.* When, after his exposure, he gives up his acting, he feels "tense inside; it was as though he had been compelled to hold himself in a certain awkward posture for a long time and then when he had the chance to relax he could not" (197). His posture may have been adopted because of symbolic exigencies, but, like the corporeal mimicry Caillois discusses, it eventually turns into a lethal, imaginary trap. Rather than allowing the subject's supple negotiation of the symbolic order, it prevents him from successfully responding to changes in his *Umwelt.*

THE GIFT OF LAUGHTER

As Bigger's capture suggests, the danger in paranoid identification is its proximity to pathology. How can one tell the difference between clinical paranoia and the "paranoiac structure of the ego" (Lacan, "Aggressiveness" 21)? Remarking on Lacan's idea of human psychology as inherently paranoid, François Roustang proposes in clinical context that when the analyst can make the paranoiac laugh, the pathology has subsided. While Roustang does not distinguish between the two registers of paranoia, I would like to insist on this difference. When one is faced with the pathology of paranoia, "to think a paranoiac could laugh is absurd; and it is even more absurd to undertake to make a paranoiac laugh, since he could only interpret the attempt as a supplementary persecution" (709). On the other hand, in the paranoid identification that I have been exploring in this chapter, laughter marks the fluidity and suppleness of the subject of desire. Let us compare Roustang's observation to the following scene, in which Bigger, having delivered the kidnap note to his employers, finds himself hesitant to eat the leftover food that he finds in the Daltons' kitchen, even though it is obviously meant for him:

> He rested his black fingers on the edge of the white table and a silent laugh burst from his parted lips as he saw himself for a split second in a lurid objective light: he had killed a rich white girl and had burned her body after cutting her head off and had lied to throw the blame on someone else and had written a kidnap note demanding ten thousand dollars and yet he stood here afraid to touch food on the table, food which undoubtedly was his own. (158)

Seeing himself "for a split second"—that is, for an other, as an other—Bigger, in this flash of insight, "rapidly . . . becom[ing] two persons at one and the same time" (Baudelaire 118), finds himself observing his situation through the eyes of others. Speaking of clinical paranoia, Roustang notes that "the possibility of laughing at oneself is the minimum distance from oneself required at the beginning of the cure" (713). Bigger achieves this "minimum distance" from his "place" with the revelation that elicits laughter from him. For a split second, as a split other, his new position offers him the mobility to identify with himself as an other that characterizes the functional paranoid subject.

Yet Bigger's laughter is ambivalent: while it signals the mobility of paranoid identification, it issues not of his own will, not as something he is in control of, but as a surprise, an unwilled and unwilling reaction. With its ambivalence, the black protagonist's laughter echoes that of African American audiences of minstrelsy, which has troubled many commentators. Lawrence

W. Levine notes that African American humor—which "ha[s] enabled blacks to come into prolonged and intimate contact with white civilization without being annihilated and to emerge from slavery in a comparatively strong state" (299)—has for many blacks dangerously evoked stereotypical blackface representations (300). Watkins suggests further that the distaste of the mainly bourgeois black audiences for minstrelsy signals a more rigid, and hence borderline pathological, attitude than the ability to revel in blackface representations: "one might reasonably argue that educated blacks' *inability* to laugh at minstrel exaggeration reflected some[, in our terms, pathological,] paranoia and self-doubt among themselves. Normally, the ability to laugh even when the joke is at one's own expense is a sign of assurance and confidence" (128). We can understand the different reactions to minstrelsy not only as premised on class distinctions (the middle-class subjects' refusal to laugh being determined by their aspiration to "uplift" themselves to the respectable ranks of the bourgeoisie), but also as expressing the irreducible double conditions of minstrelsy and laughter themselves.

Numerous commentators—among them Du Bois, Jessie Fauset, James Weldon Johnson, and Langston Hughes—have noted the significance of laughter in African American history and culture.[39] Levine observes: "The need to laugh at our enemies, our situation, ourselves, is a common one, but it often exists the most urgently in those who exert the least power over their immediate environment; in those who have the most objective reasons for feelings of hopelessness" (300). When we cannot control our surroundings, when there remain no pretenses to the self-identity and -determination of the Cartesian cogito, we are most compelled to laugh at our condition, our selves. I suggest that this subject of laughter approximates (and hyperbolizes) what Lacan, in his third seminar, refers to as the "normal subject": "What characterizes a normal subject is precisely that he never takes seriously certain realities that he recognizes exists. You are surrounded by all sorts of realities about which you are in no doubt, some of which are particularly threatening, but you don't take them fully seriously" (*SIII* 74). The normal, nonpathological subject allows itself a distance from the "realities" whose existence it nevertheless does not doubt, while "the insane embody what we would be led to if we began to take things seriously (123–24). As Roustang writes, "the paranoiac [in the pathological sense] is overwhelmingly convinced that his certitudes are true. Wanting to introduce laughter—that is, discontinuity—into that self-adhesion is tantamount to insanity. . . . [I]t is certitude about oneself which creates seriousness that prohibits laughter" (709–10). We can suggest that if the sign of the healthy subject is its refusal to take "certain realities" seriously, then the more threatening the subject's environment, the less seriously does it tend to take these realities of annihilation. While we are accustomed to thinking that, when threatened, we most likely take realities seriously in order to negotiate them successfully, I argue that in states of constant, structural potential for annihilation, laughter provides psychic mobility and paranoid flux, without which one would indeed be annihilated as a subject.

We find this ambivalence of laughter in two recent African American texts about intergenerational encounters. In his routine, the black stand-up comedian Warren Hutcherson tells of his childhood in the late 1960s with his Black Muslim father. The father's "job" was "to find all the plots against the black race, no matter how cleverly hidden." Thus even a trip to the supermarket provides an educational outing for the father. "'Look at dis, boy,'" Hutcherson recalls the father saying,

> "every time you go to the grocery store, the white man is playin' with yo mind. It's all subconscious, all subliminal. Ask yourself: why must I be *cuckoo* for Coco Puffs? You see? They're trying to tell you the black shit will make you crazy. See what goin' on here: the frosted flakes—they're white, they're *great*. . . .
>
> "Look at here, this is regular rice but it's brown, so they call it *wild rice*. What's so *wild* about it? Is Uncle Ben chasin' Aunt Jemima 'round the shelf? . . .
>
> "Look at these olives, why these black olives in a can? You see these green olives, they not in a can. The green olives *in a jar*. Why they have to *lock* these black olives *up*?
>
> "They tryin' to tell you you're *cuckoo*, you're *wild*, you need to be *locked up*!"

While the son's laughter suggests that the insight of the previous generation has rigidified into the paranoid litany of antiblack conspiracy, it would be too glib to dismiss the father's reading of racism's embeddedness in American consumerism as mere obsolete ranting. Indeed, the laughter evoked by Hutcherson does not so much repudiate the reading as address in it a kind of rigid literalness that embodies what Norman Podhoretz arrogantly refers to as African Americans' "paranoid touchiness" (qtd. in Staples).[40] As Levine shows, laughter has accompanied the most insightful and pertinent black critiques of racism in American culture. Similarly, I argue, Hutcherson's laughter does not negate the father's interpretation but prevents the insight from being immobilized into a pathologically paranoid posture, a kind of "imaginary trap" that Lacan refers to in the eleventh seminar.

I suggested in my discussion of the *Nappy Hair* controversy that, while correctly identifying the history of racist abuse and ridicule behind the reaction to Herron's book, Jill Nelson does not adequately recognize the complexity of the situation. Comparing her reading to Hutcherson's, we can see what is missing from her gloss. While both see in the parents' reactions a paranoid conspiracy theory, what is crucially different in their respective approaches is Nelson's refusal to engage with these representations, her insistence on distancing herself from them and her demand that others do the same. With the laughter he invites, Hutcherson, too, seemingly repeats the accusations that African

Americans are too serious about the racism they see around them. However, contrary to Nelson's distance from the object of her critique, in Hutcherson's reading, the subject and the object of laughter are arguably joined. According to Roustang, laughter indeed requires intimacy with its object: "laughter must be directed toward ourselves, or at least imply a 'we' in which we are included"; "it must retain the greatest proximity with the very thing from which it breaks. . . . Laughter is the smallest conceivable unit of detachment, of difference, of removal; it is the quantum unit of distance" (712, 710–11). In its "minimal distanciation" (711), laughter allows the subject to split itself from the other but nevertheless joins the two: in this, it repeats the mirror stage's dynamics of identification-as-alienation.

In "The Blackface Stereotype," Manthia Diawara tells of a similar intergenerational encounter; this time the account is narrated from the father's point of view. In preparing the introductory essay for a collection of David Levinthal's photographs of blackface paraphranelia, Diawara shows some of the images to his thirteen-year-old son and explains the oppressive history of blackface representations:

> I told him that whites used to malign black people as watermelon and chicken thieves. They would say that during the night, when it was pitch dark, black people would go to the master's field to steal watermelons, or, like foxes, to the chicken coop to steal chickens. But supposedly, these black people were always betrayed by their white teeth and white eyes which shone in the dark like lightning. They could not hide, even in the darkest of nights, even though they were so black. That was why their smiles were cut like slices of watermelon and they were considered, like chickens, to be cowards. My son laughed and remained pensive for a moment before resuming his mundane activities.
>
> Left alone with Levinthal's pictures, I began to consider the history lesson I had just given my son, his reaction of laughter, and his subsequent boredom with my explanation of the meaning white people had put behind the Blackface stereotypes. (8–9)

Some days later, the son shows the father an image with uncanny similarities to the blackface representations in whose signification the latter wanted to school the thirteen-year-old:

> he brought to my attention two white kids on the cover of the Summer 1998 issue of *Health Diary*, a United Healthcare magazine. Each kid has a slice of watermelon in his hands and is laughing with satisfaction. The hat on the head of one of the kids, their bare feet, and their self-abandonment in the presence of watermelons, all stereotype the stereotype of black people. By bringing the image to my attention, my son made that much of an association. But his act is also challenging me to stop being the custodian of these

> stereotypes, to distance myself from them, and to begin to enjoy the humor in them. Only then will I, like him, become an individual and modern. (17)

Both intergenerational encounters, narrated by Hutcherson and Diawara, are marked by a moment in which the older participant's reading of blackface representations is refigured by the younger one's laughter. Diawara takes up the challenge to reread the oppressive, racist images in ways that negotiate their injurious history without forgetting this past, that is, in ways that appropriate blackface representations for subversive ends. While, following critics like Toll, Saxton, Boskin, and Turner, he observes that "the stereotypes help[ed] to maintain the myth of the gothic Old South and deny the changes in our contemporary society" (9), he nevertheless goes on to discuss Kara Walker's controversial silhouettes and Chris Rock's appearance in blackface on the cover of *Vanity Fair* to argue that blackface representations can be turned against their original intent.[41] What the self-representations by the "so-called neo-Coons" accomplish is similar to what early African American blackface performers gained in donning the mask: "the emphasis," Diawara writes in almost a Lacanian idiom, "is no longer on resistance politics, but on wearing masks that facilitate *one's mobility in the world*": "If the old stereotype is the projection of white supremacist thinking onto black people, the new stereotype compounds matters by *desiring that image*, and deforming its content for a different appropriation" (15; emphases added). Yet, given what I have suggested in this essay, this emancipation—what Diawara calls the move from resistance to mobilization—is never purified from ambivalence but straddles the dangerous edge of paranoid identification and imaginary capture, of playing (like) and idiot and being possessed by one's strategies—a dynamic that ultimately recaptures Bigger.[42]

The sons, then, show the fathers the creolization of American culture in blackface representations. In insisting on a hierarchical or "Manichean" understanding of oppression, one risks losing an insight into the possibilities within the present situation. The ambivalence expressed in the sons' laughter at the fathers' readings—the latter being, like Nelson's take on *Nappy Hair*, pertinent yet insufficient—reveals the contamination, indeed the creolization, that the dynamics of blackface, albeit to varied extents in different historical contexts, have always expressed. If one does not do this, one immobilizes oneself—like, arguably, the parents at PS 75—into the role of a "custodian" of past injuries.

Indeed, Herron's *Nappy Hair* itself constitutes the kind of playful negotiation with the mask that, according to Lacan, prevents one from becoming such a custodian, from being trapped in the imaginary. Joyfully, laughingly engaging with representations of kinky hair and wooly heads, Herron distances herself from this history while nevertheless identifying with it. Similarly, Hutcherson's performance, in repeating minstrel representations of Negroes who take themselves too seriously, refuses the comfort of objectivity and distance and, instead, actively acknowledges and "owns" the history of derogatory laughter. Hutcherson and Diawara suggest the productivity of responding to the stereotype with the acknowledgment of laughter: rather than dismissing them as irrelevant and anachronistic, like Nelson, or censoring them, like the parents of the *Nappy Hair* controversy, one can produce further elaborations of blackface stereotypes, prolong their life with creolizing, paranoid laughter.

CHAPTER 3

Unforeseeable Tragedies

Symbolic Change in Wright, Fanon, and Lacan

> ***. . . tragedy is at the root of our experience [as analysts]. . . .***
>
> —Jacques Lacan, *The Ethics of Psychoanalysis*

> ***. . . in our time, as in every time, the impossible is the least that one can demand.***
>
> —James Baldwin, *The Fire Next Time*

Like the Ibo villager in Chinua Achebe's *Things Fall Apart* who predicts "green men . . . com[ing] to our clan and shoot[ing] us" (142), Wright invites us to consider colonialism by envisioning an alien invasion: "let's imagine a mammoth flying saucer from Mars landing, say, in a Swiss peasant village and debouching swarms of fierce looking men whose skins are blue and whose red eyes flash lightning bolts that deal instant deaths" ("White Faces" 224).[1] Describing what one postcolonial critic calls "the gun-sight of the European observer's viewpoint" (Walder 167), Wright voices the by-now commonplace argument in postcolonial theory that, for the colonized, being caught in the settlers' "devouring, mobile eyes, synecdoches for the cannibalizing world of colonialism" (Bongie 37), is tantamount to being annihilated. Indeed, from the very beginning of his work, Wright anticipates some of postcolonial theory's central themes, perhaps most importantly those of visibility and perspectives. In this, he gestures toward the important similarities in African American and postcolonial situations, identifying not only the ways in which, as he says in an interview, "the [American] Negro is intrinsically a colonial subject" ("Why" 125), but also how the dynamics of visibility that he describes in *Native Son* operate in the colonial world. For example, in a 1956 review of Octave Mannoni's

Prospero and Caliban—which boasts the above sci-fi scenario—he deploys a metaphor of vision to announce the impact of the "new genre" of postcolonial writing: the new theory, according to him, proceeds from or allows "a wider angle of vision" ("White Faces" 223; see also *White* 5). As we remember, it is a similarly new perspective that he called for African American writers to adopt some twenty years earlier, in "Blueprint for Negro Writing." One can argue that, in later endorsing the work of such postcolonial writers as George Lamming, he not only identified with Lamming's description of the shift from agrarian to industrial society, as Michel Fabre suggests (*Unfinished* 400), but also found valuable the Caribbean novelist's consideration of the power of the colonizing gaze.[2]

Given his emphasis on visibility and the gaze, Wright's work obviously shares concerns with Frantz Fanon's. As Stuart Hall writes, *Black Skin, White Masks* (1952), for example, has proven influential for current theories of postcoloniality particularly because of "the association it establishes between racism and what has come to be called the scopic drive" (16). In this chapter, I suggest we reread Fanon's understanding of visibility in the colonial regime by engaging him with Wright and Lacan. While I am certainly not the first to suggest Wright and Lacan as Fanon's interlocutors, the encounter as I stage it seeks to intervene in and clarify debates in both Fanon and psychoanalytic scholarship. Lacan's later work—which has been absent from readings of Fanon—allows us to revisit feminist criticism of Fanon's work. Simultaneously, Lacan's theory of the subject's relation to the real—usually articulated in terms of sexual difference—helps us further sketch the way that "race" functions in the symbolic order. My argument about "the white symbolic order" necessitates a deprivileging of sexual difference as the only "real" difference, in the Lacanian sense of the term. As some recent work in psychoanalytic queer theory has suggested, this can be done by following Lacan's increasing emphasis on the role of the *objet a*, instead of that of phallus, in his later work (Dean, *Beyond*). The emphasis on the real, with its corollary of the *objet a*, also allows us to approach questions that are crucial for theories of oppression: that is, how to effect radical change in the symbolic order. As much as psychoanalysis helps us reconsider Wright and Fanon, the dialogue is of mutual implication: their understanding of anticolonial resistance suggests in turn some ways to reconsider the alleged intractability of the symbolic order in Lacanian theory.

Biographical details confirm the connection between Fanon, on the one hand, and Wright and Lacan, on the other. The dialogue between Wright and Fanon was well established during their lifetimes. They had relocated to France a year apart from each other: Wright—who had been granted a passport only after pressure from the French embassy and such notable exiles as Gertrude Stein—arrived in Paris in May, 1946 (Fabre, *World* 179; *Unfinished* 299–302), while Fanon journeyed to the colonial metropolis from Martinique to study dentistry the following year (Gendzier 16). After his expatriation, Wright had become more influential on the French cultural scene than in the United

States, where his exile to Europe was considered at times with suspicion and, on occasion, regarded as an act of outright traitorousness.[3] His influence in France was established by the translation of *Native Son* in 1947, immediately followed by the French edition of *Uncle Tom's Children* and, in January of the following year, of *Black Boy* (Fabre, *Unfinished* 331).[4] When Wright writes in 1950 that William Faulkner and Edgar Allan Poe were writers whose "greatness had to be established by way of France into the American consciousness" ("A Man of the South" 355), we may suspect that he is also alluding to his own literary fate as an expatriate in Paris.

As a student, Fanon was aware of Wright's presence in France, initiating a correspondence with the American author (Fabre, *Unfinished* 382, 383).[5] In a letter dated January 6, 1953, he expresses an ambition to write a full-length study on Wright. His consequent books, I suggest, can be read as a commentary on Wright's works, produced in lieu of the proposed study. Wright's influence on Fanon, in other words, is not confined to the most obvious and best-known examples, such as the explicit references to *Native Son* in *Black Skin*.[6] While Manthia Diawara has pointed out the echoes of *Black Power* in *The Wretched of the Earth* (*In Search* 67),[7] I will trace the ways in which Fanon's theory of epidermalization (in *Black Skin*) and veiling (in "Algeria Unveiled") elaborate on Wright's theory of racialization. The trope of the "curtain" in *Native Son*, for instance, is comparable not only to Fanon's theory of epidermalized differences in *Black Skin* but also to the veil whose function during the Algerian war Fanon analyzes in "Algeria Unveiled," the first chapter of *A Dying Colonialism*. Similarly, I will argue that Aunt Sue, the female protagonist of Wright's early short story "Bright and Morning Star" (1938), anticipates the Algerian women's strategies of resistance, which are marked by their tragic dimension.

In Fanon scholarship, Lacan is a similarly familiar interlocutor to Fanon. Especially in the 1990s, the appeal of Fanon's work, and particularly of *Black Skin*, was in its seeming amenability to psychoanalytic readings (Mercer, "Decolonisation" 121). However, reacting to the vogue in Fanonism that Homi Bhabha's work has inspired, such critics as Ato Sekyi-Otu, T. Denean Sharpley-Whiting, and Nigel Gibson have deemed psychoanalysis an inappropriate approach to Fanon's understanding of colonialism. Such criticism seems to aim at psychoanalysis's alleged inability to address colonialism's historical and material realities. Writing that "[t]he problems Fanon addresses do not take place in a vacuum, but arise from distinct historical and social situations and the way people think about them," Gibson reproaches Bhabha for focusing on "the apparent ambiguities of identity" in *Black Skin, White Masks* instead of what he calls "lived experience of blackness" (*Fanon* 2).[8] Sekyi-Otu similarly argues that "ideological practices, dominant view of the world, [and] relations of power" (7) should always be prioritized in our discussions of the psychic disorders bred by colonialism. Instead, the psychoanalytic emphasis on the psyche over the social has led to "a reductively psychologizing reading of Fanon" (Sekyi-Otu 6). Others cite Fanon's "own ambivalence" (Sharpley-Whiting 28n21) about psychoanalysis in rejecting Lacanian approaches to his work. The least one should say about psychoanalytic readings, according to the critics, is that they "have in the main produced a very one-sided Fanon" (N. Gibson, "Fanon" 102). Writing in 1995, Kobena Mercer, cannily anticipating the subsequent critique, worries about the violence that too close a proximity to Lacan would do to Fanon, denouncing "certain tendencies of postcolonial criticism that seem to construct Fanon as a black Lacan" ("Decolonisation" 124).

But if we are to argue for the inevitably reductive or unproductive character of the dialogue between psychoanalysis and postcolonial theory, we should make sure that we have understood the specificity of the encountering bodies (of work). It is not clear that Fanon's readers who seek to avoid this dialogue refer to the psychoanalytic theory I am concerned with in this study. For example, Gibson cites Fanon's critique of Mannoni's theory of the native "dependence complex" (Mannoni 40) as an example of Fanon's rejection of psychoanalysis (*Fanon* 53ff.). Crucial distinctions are further blurred with Sekyi-Otu's neglect of the elementary difference between psychology and psychoanalysis, which is fundamental to understanding psychoanalysis and particularly Lacan. A correlate misunderstanding is the critics' (and Fanon's [*Black* 11]) references to the "individual" as the focus of psychoanalysis. Because of Lacan's emphasis on the Other as the primary interlocutor for the subject, the "individual" can only refer to the ego's imaginary defenses and pretensions. To posit the individual as the focus of psychoanalytic inquiry is to miss the Lacanian argument about the characteristically human emergence in language: "The subject of Lacanian theory is an asubstantial category because it preexists being: the subject appears in the discourse of the Other anterior to birth. . . . It is because there is no subject without the Other that the subject remains irreducible to the category of the individual" (Dean, "Wanting" 263).[9]

I suggest the confusion between psychology and psychoanalysis, as well as between the individual and the subject, may have taken place because, when addressing Lacan, Fanon's readers (and, needless to say, Fanon himself) have consistently referred to his early texts, most notably the 1940s work around the subject's misrecognition of his/her gestalt in the mirror image. In other words, whether endorsing or disputing psychoanalysis's suitability to reading Fanon, critics, taking their cue from the long footnote on the mirror stage in "The Negro and Psychopathology" (*Black* 161–64n), have discussed the imaginary/symbolic registers of the mirror stage. I propose that we shift our attention to Lacan's work of the late 1950s and early 1960s, where, addressing the "ethics of psychoanalysis," Lacan moves from considering the symbolic and the imaginary registers to theorizing the real.[10] Here, all psychological references to "individuals" become impossible, given that "the psychoanalytic subject [of the '60s Lacan'] is so far from approximating any notion of the discrete individual person as to be virtually unrecognizable" (Dean, *Beyond* 52). Lacan illustrates this unrecognizability by deploying such counterintuitive topological figures as the Möbius strip, the Borromean knot, and the cross-cap to represent the subject's relation to the Other.[11] These figures clearly place the subject in a field of extimate forces that may include, while being irreducible to, the social and historical formations of colonialism, whose oppressive imperatives, according to Gibson, are neglected by psychoanalysis. There is no simple way to connect Lacan's formulation of the symbolic Other, the structure of language whose incompletion mobilizes the subject's interminable desire, to the material conditions of human existence. Yet, what psychoanalysis, in its Lacanian variant, does argue against is conceptualizing the subject's embeddedness in the world in terms of its self-interests vis-à-vis exterior conditions. Such logic of exteriority and interiority can be supported only by the coordinates of Euclidean geometry, from which Lacan decisively distances himself. Given that the subject's and the symbolic order's inextricability simultaneously signals their profound, and often violent, discord, Lacanian theory can provide a methodology for understanding precisely the complexities of the subject's investment in and ambivalence about dominance and resistance that Fanon deals with.

It is, moreover, worth noting that Lacan's emergent concern with the ethical dimension of psychoanalysis may have been precipitated by the increasingly violent crisis that demanded the attention of the French intellectuals and the French Left in the late 1950s. The *Ethics* seminar, after all, took place during 1959–1960, a time marked by the turmoil of the Algerian resistance to the French occupation and its consequent, brutal repression—a crisis that Fanon famously addresses in *A Dying Colonialism*.[12] It is mindful of this context that we should read Lacan's emphasis, in the introduction to the seminar, on the importance of psychoanalysis for "a certain moment in the history of man, namely, the one we are living in" (*SVII* 1). "Have we crossed the line?" he asks later in the year, referring to "what is happening out there in the world in which we live. It isn't because what is occurring there makes such a vulgar noise that we should refuse to hear about it" (231). With these cautionary, nearly apocalyptic remarks, Lacan prepares the audience for his subsequent discussion of Sophocles's play *Antigone*, a choice of material that becomes particularly significant here. He would not have been the first to find in the play's eponymous heroine a figure of resistance to seemingly insuperable oppression. The most famous twentieth-century examples are the stage adaptations by Jean Anouilh (1944) and Bertolt Brecht (1948) (see Steiner). For their audiences, Antigone's refusal to heed Creon's edict that the remains of her traitorous brother be denied burial rites embodied a call for resistance to the Nazi occupation and the Vichy government. Considering this, the precise timing of Lacan's discussion of *Antigone* is noteworthy: he opened the lectures two weeks after Laurence Bataille, the daughter of his partner Sylvia Bataille, had been arrested for her participation in a group with ties to the Algerian *Front de libération nationale* (FLN). (Bataille was arrested on May 10, 1960 [Roudinesco 187]; Lacan began the first of his three sessions on *Antigone* on May 25.) According to Elisabeth Roudinesco, Lacan saw in Bataille's political radicalism aspects of what he identified as Antigone's ethical stance; visiting her in prison, he brought in the notes for his *Antigone* lectures (187–88). In this context, his suggestion that *Antigone* anticipates "the cruelties of our time" (*SVII* 240), offering "images of our modern wars" (266), can clearly be read as references to the Algerian battle (see also Rooney 53).

However, despite such historical continuities between Fanon and Lacan, we should note that my approach may be incompatible with the historicist methodology of many of the critics mentioned above. Given that Gibson dismisses psychoanalytic readings of *Black Skin* because Fanon would not have had access to Lacan's texts cited by many contemporary critics (*Fanon* 214n2), he certainly would scoff at my suggestion that we introduce the Lacan of the late 1950s and the 1960s into our discussion. Similarly, David Macey's warning against seeing Fanon as "an apprentice Lacanian" (142) silently assumes that the exegesis of Fanon's texts needs to rest on biographical data affirming the author's alleged discipleship. Clearly, then, the most recent turn in Fanon scholarship, represented by Gibson and others, shares a historicist understanding of textuality and culture, which "promotes the thesis that knowledge is totally immanent to a specific sociocultural field or a moment" (Sedinger 120). This in itself points to a profound difference between these critics' methodologies and mine. Psychoanalytic critique argues that, even when they produce works as rich as Gibson's reconsideration of Fanon's influences, "historicist models may be shackled by their insistence on immanence, since it condemns them to chronicity while mystifying the complexity of textual negotiations over time" (Marshall 1208). Furthermore, Tracey Sedinger and Tim Dean maintain that the psychoanalytic argument about the absent core of the symbolic order—an absence that is inconceivable to a historicist understanding of culture—does not denote only a limit but also the possibility of production: the *objet a*, as a placeholder for that which is constitutively missing from any symbolic order, or the lack in the Other suggests a future beyond existing discursive regimes. For Sedinger, historicism's understanding of politics is seriously limited because it eschews any notion of an outside that would not be culturally determined (126–27). On the other hand, psychoanalysis, as Dean writes, sees the Other as amenable to change, precisely in its inconsistency and lack: "Th[e] psychoanalytic argument about positive effects proceeding from an absent cause provides for a nondeterministic concept of causation, a concept Lacan identifies with his category of the real as that which is strictly unsymbolizable." At the same time, however, the properly psychoanalytic understanding of causation does not return us to the concept of the individual: "Lacan's theory of the real is neither determinist nor voluntarist because the way in which the real is symbolized—and therefore the way in which the subject, as subject of the signifier, is produced—is malleable, although not by the individual" (Dean, "Wanting" 269).

If one insists on Lacanian psychoanalysis as a methodology, the appropriate response to Gibson's admonition that we must avoid the psychoanalytic tendency to conceptualize subjectivity and pathology in a "vacuum" (*Fanon*

2) is to point out that the only such zone of nonexistence in psychoanalysis is that which Lacan calls the real. It is this nothingness that, for psychoanalytic ethics, drives the subject off symbolic circuits and onto another trajectory, one whose precise form is yet to come. In this mode of becoming, psychoanalytic ethics is characterized by the very temporality that names the field of *post*colonial theory. Consequently, I suggest that, in complicating our understanding of the subject's cultural immanence, psychoanalysis can respond to Fanon's call, at the end of *Black Skin* and *The Wretched of the Earth*, for the future's radical openness. It is through the examples of tragedy found in Fanon, Wright, and Lacan that I approach the question of symbolic change in this chapter. The fact that the tragic figures in the work of all three male writers are women engages Lacan's theory of the organization of differences around the undifferentiation of the real. Arguably responding to feminist criticism of his earlier work (Luepnitz 227–28), in *Seminar XX* Lacan sees sexual difference as bespeaking the impasses of the real. In the work of recent psychoanalytic critics—"the New Lacanians," as James Mellard dubs them—this question of the real is articulated as an ethical question about the subject's relation to the limits of symbolic intelligibility and, consequently, about the symbolic order's openness to change. Furthermore, posing the question of futurity and change in postcolonial and critical race theory through the question of the real addresses the disagreement between recent Lacanian theorists on sexual difference's possible priority as a real difference vis-à-vis the symbolic nature of other, including racial, differences. While Joan Copjec and Kalpana Seshadri-Crooks insist on sexual difference as the only properly real difference, others, most notably Dean and Charles Shepherdson, have suggested that other forms of difference can be understood as of the order of the real. A dialogue between Lacan's work and the postcolonial theories of Fanon and Wright helps us intervene in these debates.

Suggesting similarities between Fanon's and Wright's understanding of visibility and resistance, I open my discussion by considering the gendered dynamics of (anti)colonial negotiation in *Black Skin*, *A Dying Colonialism*, and *The Wretched of the Earth.* I find it necessary to revisit this perhaps familiar problematic in order to highlight tragedy's role in anticolonial action not only in "Algeria Unveiled" but also in Wright's early short story "Bright and Morning Star." The question of tragedy is prominently featured also in Lacan's discussion of ethics and difference in *Seminar VII: The Ethics of Psychoanalysis* and *Seminar XX: On Feminine Sexuality.* Through tragedy, we can connect Lacan's understanding of sexuation to the theory of racialization and visibility that I have been pursuing in this study. I argue that, as much as the subject's relation to the real is given form through sex, in symbolic orders where race is of profound consequence, racial difference too may determine the subject's relation to that which is beyond symbolization, that is, the form of his or her jouissance. For Lacanian theory, this argument necessitates decoupling the real and sexual difference. To do this, I take my cue from Dean's contribution to psychoanalytic queer theory that argue we shift our focus from the Lacanian phallus to the *objet a*.

I further argue that, in their discussion of the unstable dynamics of "acting," "veiling," and "epidermalization," Fanon and Wright point to the ways in which sex and race affect the "not-whole" subject's negotiation with, and possible disruption of, the symbolic order. These dynamics—Fanon's theory of epidermalization and veiling as well as Wright's description of the morphing of (emasculating, subordinate) acting into a violent, and characteristically tragic, act against the symbolic order—illustrate the Lacanian shift from symbolic to Other jouissance. Finally, connecting Fanon's and Wright's depiction of racialization to the dynamics of Lacanian sexuation allows us to intervene in a central debate in contemporary feminist-psychoanalytic theory, around the possibility of symbolic change.

FROM EPIDERMALIZATION TO VEILING: THE HISTORIC DYNAMISM OF *LIVRÉE*

In *Black Skin, White Masks*, Fanon's theoretical vehicle for understanding racial visibility is the concept of epidermalization. With this coinage, Fanon refers to the dialectic whereby feelings of inferiority, cultivated in the colonized by the colonizing culture, are anchored in appearances, in epidermal differences. The epidermalized subject, "overdetermined" and "*fixed*" (116) by the colonial gaze, finds that his body has become indelibly marked in relation to the white man.[13] This "burden of corporeal malediction" (111) makes it impossible for the colonized to effectively challenge colonial discourse: according to Fanon, counterdiscourses such as negritude are merely stages in the colonial dialectic, themselves caught in the throes of its "Manichean delirium" (*Black* 183).[14]

With allusions to Jean-Paul Sartre's study of anti-Semitism,[15] epidermalization describes what W. E. B. Du Bois and, after him, Wright evoke as the African American experience of being measured with "amused contempt and pity" (Du Bois, *Souls* 11; Wright, *12 Million* 103). The "two frames of reference" that the colonial intrusion forces upon the colonized (*Black* 110) also echo Du Bois's description of double consciousness. Similarly, there are obvious parallels between Wright's and Fanon's descriptions of racialization and epidermalization. As much as "an invisible burden" (*Native* 101) weighs on Bigger Thomas, an encounter with "the white man's eyes" posits "[a]n unfamiliar weight" on Fanon's narrator (110): "I become aware of my uniform [*ma livrée*]. I had not seen it. It is indeed ugly" (114/112).

But what precisely is the uniform that epidermalization weaves? The term *livrée* translates as "livery" or, in zoology, as "coat" (Carney 159). "Livery," according to *The Oxford English Dictionary*, refers in a general sense to "the distinctive uniform style of dress worn by a person's servants," nowadays exclusively male servants. More precisely, the term stands for servants' apparel, "formerly sometimes a badge or cognizance (e.g. a collar or hood)," that allows their identification as the master's property. In zoology, "coat" denotes an "animal's covering of hair, fur, wool, feathers, etc.; rarely the skin or hide." By having to adorn his *livrée*, the narrator of *Black Skin* is thus dehumanized, his skin becoming like an outer layer of the body of an animal, a coat of hair or feathers. His livery brands him the property of his master, the white man. Serving as "a token by which [the servants] may be recognized" (*OED*), *livrée* represents the same kind of visual overdetermination that Wright describes in *Native Son*: it marks its carrier as both nonhuman and possessed. The term thus encapsulates the threefold function of epidermalization in Fanon's work: *livrée* becomes a *livery*, a *coat*, and a *uniform*. In the first function, epidermalization weaves an unremovable, encompassing sign of servitude on the colonized subject. In the second function, it imposes a mark of subhumanity on the colonized, allowing the colonizer to refer to them in "zoological terms" (*Wretched* 42). Finally, *livrée* marks the epidermalized subjects as indistinguishable from one another and absolutely different from the colonizers.

Livrée furthermore points to the confluence of surface and depth in the process of racialization, which I discussed in Chapter 1. According to the *OED*, livery has progressively become a more *encompassing* sign of proprietorship. Whereas it originally referred to "a badge or cognizance," it later came to denote an entire piece of garment, a servant's uniform. In *Peau noire, masques blancs*, Fanon extends *livrée*'s reference not only to the subject's skin but entire corporeality, which cannot be doffed at will but indelibly determines the subject. Thus repeating the logic of racialization that metamorphizes the "black skin" of a Reverend Taylor (Wright, "Fire" 138) into Bigger's "black body" (*Native* 40), the colonized subject's epidermis begins to control him. Moreover, as much as the shift from surface to depth illustrates the disciplinary dynamic of nineteenth-century scientific racism, Fanon's narrator points to the instrumental position of Western science in constructing racial, epidermalized differences: "I am being dissected under white eyes, the only real eyes. I am *fixed*. Having adjusted their microtomes, they objectively cut away slices of my reality. I am laid bare. I feel, I see in those white faces that it is not a new man who has come in, but a new kind of man, a new genus. Why, it's a Negro!" (116). As a result of such operations of racial sciences, the racialized/epidermalized subject is firmly located in his place: like Bigger, whose place seems to allow others intimate knowledge of him, Fanon's racialized subject feels "responsible at the same time for [his] body, for [his] race, for [his] ancestors" (112). As much as Bigger is immobilized, the narrator in *Black Skin* is "unmercifully imprisoned" (112), "told to stay within [his] bounds" (115).[16]

The most notable difference between Bigger and Fanon's narrator is that the latter does not learn to use self-concealment protectively. In *Native Son*, Bigger loses, if only momentarily, the weight of racialization: after killing Mary, he experiences "a lessening of tension in his muscles," feeling that "he had shed an invisible burden he had long carried" (97). Becoming partially invisible to the world that had so effectively imprisoned him, he escapes "the overwhelming corporeality of blackness" (Barrett, "African-American" 415). Moreover, Bigger's transgression is enabled by the unintentional effects of racialization itself: as Stanley Edgar Hyman writes, it is "the terror-inspired muscle tension that unwittingly smothers Mary Dalton" (2011), a crime that in turn allows Bigger's radical shift of perspective. In his consequent guerrilla warfare, Bigger learns how to activate livery's more archaic usage, where it signifies "the uniform of a soldier" (*OED*). On the other hand, for Fanon's narrator, even his possible disappearance from visibility would not allow for the kind of agency that Bigger experiences; his desire for inconspicuousness marks an acceptance of his place: "I slip into corners, I remain silent, I strive for anonymity, for invisibility. Look, I will accept the lot, as long as no one notices me!" (116).

If the narrator of *Black Skin* thus remains inert and fixed, in Fanon's study of the Algerian resistance movement, however, a visible sign similar to that of the black epidermis is mobilized by the colonized. Like blackness for the epidermalized subject, the *haïk*[17] marks a transgressive-yet-contained femininity, showing that the woman, by occupying public *space*, is transgressing her *place*. This encroachment on male space is tolerated only as long as it is made obvious, as long as the veil announces that "women should ideally be inconspicuous" (Odeh 33): "The veil is an expression of the invisibility of women on the street, a male space par excellence. . . . [It] means that the woman is present in the men's world, but invisible; she has no right to be in the street" (Mernissi 51, 84).[18] As Ralph Ellison writes, it is such "high visibility" that secures black *in*visibility ("Introduction" xxv); similarly, while the veil renders the woman conspicuously out-of-place in the public sphere, "[t]he Algerian man has an attitude toward the Algerian women which is on the whole clear. He does not see her. There is even a permanent intention not to perceive the feminine profile, not to pay attention to women" (Fanon, *Dying* 44). The veil in "Algeria Unveiled," like epidermalized blackness in *Native Son* and *Black Skin*, functions as a corporeal inscription that announces the subject's rigid place in the symbolic order.

This emphasis on visibility points to one of Fanon's most original and enduring insights, which bears repeating here: colonial power's demand that nothing frustrate its desire for an all-encompassing surveillance. Others have since corroborated and elaborated on his observations about Western observers' vacillating feelings of "romantic exoticism," "aggressiveness," and "[f]rustration" (*Dying* 43–44) when confronted with the veil. Edward Said, for example, points out the recurrent "metaphors of secrecy, depth, and sexuality" (*Orientalism* 222) in Orientalist descriptions. Judy Mabro similarly writes that, because the veil and the harem have "prevented the observer from seeing and communicating with women," they have "produced feelings of frustration and aggressive behaviour" in Western observers while tantalizing them with "the promise of exotic and erotic with the 'beauty behind the veil'" (2).[19] Mabro echoes also Fanon's argument of the veil's thwarting the colonial occupation by not only hiding but in fact giving women an unreciprocated visual access to the Western visitors (4–5).[20]

In Fanon's famous analysis, the dialectics of (un)veiling and resistance are initiated by the attempt of the French to conquer the Algerian nation by encouraging its women to abandon their traditions. In this, the colonizers recognized the position of women as "the symbolic repository of group identity," "the privileged bearers of corporate identities and boundary markers of their communities" (Kandiyoti 382, 388). Because women were thus the "key symbols of the colony's cultural identity" for both the colonizers and the colonized, "[i]n the colonialist fantasy, to possess Algeria's women is to possess Algeria" (Woodhull 19, 16).[21] The strategy thus employed what Sharpley-Whiting calls "*colonial feminism*," the alleged Western concern for the well-being and rights of Muslim women (5, 67).[22] Calls were made by school teachers and charity organizations, by government officials and social workers, for Algerian women to renounce their male oppressors by doffing their veils:

> The dominant administration solemnly undertook to defend this woman, pictured as humiliated, sequestered, cloistered . . . It described the immense possibilities of woman, unfortunately transformed by the Algerian man into an inert, demonetized, indeed dehumanized object. The behavior of the Algerian was very firmly denounced and described as medieval and barbaric. (Fanon, *Dying* 38; ellipsis in original)

The colonizers sought to disrupt the native cultural economy by refiguring the circulation of its women. According to the French propaganda, the Algerian woman, hidden behind her veil and cloistered in her home, had been withdrawn from circulation, turned into an object devoid of exchange value. By *monetizing* female bodies, the occupiers sought to reconfigure and ultimately collapse the economy of Algerian life, which bred and nourished anticolonial resistance. Algerian women did take up the colonizers' call, abandoning the veil and joining the traffic of the colonial city: "These test-women, with bare faces and free bodies, henceforth circulated like sound currency in the European society of Algeria" (42). Yet, the French failed to see that the Algerians, "radically transformed into [European women], poised and unconstrained" (57), had entered the circulation as counterfeits, passing in the occupiers' economy like *queer money*. Such passing conferred on them what Bigger realizes as his "queer sense of power" (203): in an ingenious strategy of perverting the opponents' perspective, they were able to move in and out of enemy territory, perfectly visible yet unreadable for the colonizers' gaze.

When the French found out about the terrorist tactics of the "Europeanized" women—"since certain militant women had spoken under torture" (61)—the veil was reassumed, again for revolutionary ends: "a new technique had to be learned: how to carry a rather heavy object dangerous to handle under the veil and still give the impression of having one's hands free, that there was nothing under the *haïk*, except a poor woman or an insignificant young girl" (61). In "the intense emotive politics of dress" (McClintock 365), the *haïk* begins to function as a decoy that can be mobilized either way, through its absence or its presence. Wearing the veil, the Algerian woman signals a passivity that would exclude participation in a violent, subversive activity; abandoning the garment, she seems to have adopted Western ideals and the French objectives. The exchange between the French and the Algerians unfolds as a game of paranoid knowledge where the player of "superior intelligence" (Lacan, *SII* 180) remains one step ahead of the opponent's strategies. Like Bigger, who, playing (like) an idiot, learns to mobilize his "curtain," Algerians turn into tricksters in their response to colonial strategies: "In the presence of the occupier, the occupied learns to dissemble, to resort to trickery. To the scandal of military occupation, [s]he opposes a scandal of contact. Every contact between the occupied and the occupier is a falsehood" (65).[23] Lethally queer, the Algerian women hide behind the veil *or* its absence "revolvers, grenades, hundreds of false identity cards or bombs" (58), becoming terrorists in the true sense of the word: they use guerrilla tactics of concealment to deliver their deadly messages to its unsuspecting destination.

In the dynamics of (un)veiling, the *haïk* thus situates the colonized in the picture such that they become invisible to the aggressors' eyes. The latter, arrogating themselves to the position of external observers, are blinded because the picture has ceased to be readable according to the rules of geometral perspective. Algerian women activate in their strategy of (un)veiling what Lacan calls the *dompte-regard*, the taming-of-the-gaze function of painting, whereby "he who looks is always led by the painting to lay down his gaze" (*SXI* 109). Lacan illustrates this function with the tale of Zeuxis and Parrhasios, where the former produces a painting of a cluster of grapes so lifelike that it deceives a flock of birds. Parrhasios, however, "triumphs over him for having painted on the wall a veil, a veil so lifelike that Zeuxis, turning toward him said, *Well, and now show us what you have painted behind it*" (103). Lacan identifies this gaze-taming function of painting with mimicry in animals: "mimicry is no doubt the equivalent of the function which, in man, is exercised in painting" (109). We can continue the analogy by suggesting that, as much as animal mimicry functions like camouflage in warfare (99), *dompte-regard* allows subversive guerrilla tactics in human conflicts. By taming the gaze embodied in the colonizers, the *haïk* seduces the latter to lay down their weapons: as Fanon writes, "Showing empty and apparently mobile and free hands [from under the veil] is the sign that *disarms the enemy soldier*" (*Dying* 62; emphasis added). While Zeuxis's mastery allows imaginary deception—his painting addresses *need*, embodied in the birds—Parrhasios's seduction mobilizes symbolic *desire*. His veil prompts Zeuxis to look for what remains invisible in representation. The painting of the veil functions as a screen behind which the desiring spectator seeks answers that are in fact hidden on the surface. It is such symbolic screening that allows Bigger to frame Jan and that, according to Lacan's reading of Edgar Allan Poe's short story, the Queen and the Minister deploy in their efforts to hide the purloined letter

(Lacan, "Seminar"). Such deceptions depend on an "imaginarization" of the other's perspective.

Hence the veil as the unvarying feminine "uniform," characteristic of Algerian womanhood (*Dying* 36), allows the Algerians' guerrilla tactics of decolonization. While the original French term in *Sociologie d'une révolution* is *uniforme* (17), *Peau noire*'s *livrée*—which Charles Lam Markmann at times translates as "uniform"[24]—suggests that, whatever countertactics are possible for the epidermalized subject, they are more difficult to deploy and more ambivalent in their results than those available for the Algerian women. One can argue, however, that the threefold function of *livrée*—as livery, coat, and uniform—enables the subversive strategies Bhabha has made so much of. If the hide-cum-livery that Fanon's narrator discovers on himself is indeed hideous—"*effectivement laide*," Fanon writes (112)—it may yet hide the epidermalized subject from the colonizing gaze. In all its consequent ambivalence, this *hide-ing* function of epidermalization[25] points to the dynamics whereby the racialized subjects' overdetermined visibility may enable self-concealment. For example, Winthrop Jordan suggests in another context that racial markedness, which, in the eyes of white slave traders, made African captives particularly "suitable" for slavery, had the unintended effect of rendering them nearly invisible. While the Africans "represented something of an answer to the problems of identification," "the very distinctiveness of [their] features tended to overwhelm the white man's ability to discriminate among individuals: some descriptions of the faces of plantation Negroes in runaway advertisements sound as if they might well have fitted every fifth Negro in the region" (108). The function of *livrée* as a uniform, Jordan proposes, led to something like *intraracial passing*, producing the very means by which the subject could fool, in however restricted a sense, the disciplinary regime. *Livrée* may furthermore take on the more archaic connotation of "the uniform of a soldier" (*OED*), thus resonating with the Algerians' mobilization of the veil: "Removed and reassumed again and again, the veil has been manipulated, transformed into a technique of camouflage, into a means of struggle" (*Dying* 61).[26]

Livrée-as-uniform thus suggests that colonial strategies of subjugation incite countermeasures that turn violence against the perpetrators: an imposed livery becomes "the uniform of a soldier," camouflaging the anticolonial guerillas. This function of epidermalization, implicit in *Black Skin*, is foregrounded in *The Wretched of the Earth.* A physical effect of colonization, the "always tensed" condition of the "native's muscles," turns into a precondition of violent action: "He is in fact ready at a moment's notice to exchange the role of the quarry for that of the hunter. The native is an oppressed person whose permanent dream is to become the persecutor" (*Wretched* 53).[27] Jock McCulloch sees in Fanon's insistence on the inevitability of violence in the colonial situation an appropriation of the discourse of ethnopsychiatry which had proposed an inherent, biological tendency for violence in Algerians (106–07, 116). This turning-around of ethnopsychiatry's assumptions against colonialism constitutes the kind of an answer of the real that Bigger delivers to the white symbolic and that Frederick Douglass, writing in 1892, warns will be the black response to lynching: "In arguing upon what will be the action of the Negro in case he continues to be the victim of lynch law I accept the statement often made in his disparagement, that he is an imitative being; that he will do what he sees other men do" ("Lynch" 749).

This shift in the meaning of *livrée*-as-uniform is anticipated by Wright already in the early 1940s. Considering African Americans' existence as "daily warfare," he observes in *12 Million Black Voices* that "the color of our skins constitutes our uniforms" (123). As one of the combatants, Bigger adopts this black uniform to respond to the aggression of the white symbolic order, which had woven and imposed on him the uniform in the first place. Indeed, Boris Max correctly identifies his murderous actions as the exigencies of war (333).

FANON AND FEMINISM

Yet, despite such openings to anticolonial guerrilla tactics by epidermalized subjects, it is clear that, for Fanon, the veil is much more readily available for mimicry and camouflage than any imposed cutaneous liveries. Several explanations for this asymmetry offer themselves immediately. First, the veil obviously constitutes a more mutable layer of the human subject than the skin. While clothing, like epidermalization, categorizes and identifies subjects through visibility—"great areas of civilization, immense cultural regions, can be grouped together on the basis of original, specific techniques of men's and women's dress" (*Dying* 35)—it remains more manipulable than the epidermalized subject's *livrée.*

Yet, I suggest that a more central reason for the different effects of veiling and epidermalization can be found in the ways that the veil and the livery inform the *sexed subject's* corporeal experience or "bodily schema." In *Black Skin*, Fanon describes this schema as "a slow composition of my *self* as a body in the middle of a spatial and temporal world": "It does not impose itself on me; it is, rather, a definitive structuring of the self and of the world—definitive because it creates a real dialectic between my body and the world" (111). Epidermalization disrupts this "real dialectic" for the colonized man, who consequently "encounters difficulties in the development of his bodily schema [*schéma corporel*]" (110/109). As the disciplinary mechanisms of colonialism complicate the subject's bodily experience, his "distorted, recolored" body (113) is reflected back by the colonizing gaze. Finally, the existing "corporeal schema crumble[s], its place taken by a racial epidermal schema" (112).

The veil has a crucially different function for the woman. For Fanon, the *haïk* is an essential part of the Algerian woman's corporeal experience: "The body of the young Algerian woman, in traditional society, is revealed to her by its coming to maturity and by the veil. The veil covers the body and disciplines it, tempers it, at the very time when it experiences its phase of greatest effervescence. The veil protects, reassures, isolates" (58–59). Uncovered, Fanon continues, the woman has hallucinatory experiences of her body being distorted and dismembered:

> Without the veil she has an impression of her body being cut up into bits, put adrift; the limbs seem to lengthen indefinitely. When the Algerian woman has to cross a street, for a long time she commits errors of judgment as to the exact distance to be negotiated. The unveiled body seems to escape, to dissolve. . . . She experiences a sense of incompleteness with great intensity. . . . The absence of the veil distorts the Algerian woman's corporal pattern [*le schéma corporel*]. (59/42)

Whereas the livery disrupts the male subject's corporeal being in the world, the veil mediates the "real dialectic" of the female subject's bodily relation to her *Umwelt*. Consequently, it is *without* the veil that she is threatened with the "crumbling of the bodily schema" which the *livrée* initiates in him.[28] However, while the Algerian woman's corporeality is distorted when the protective shield of the veil is drawn aside, she, unlike the male colonized subject, who experiences a psychotic fragmentation of his body, can nevertheless reorient herself in the reorganized world of the visible.

Fanon's characterization of Algerian women's adaptability must be understood in the context of his earlier views of black women's relation to the colonizers. Rey Chow points to a similar gender disparity in Fanon's description of subaltern responses to colonialism in *Black Skin*. While black men's reactions are characterized by a profound "emotional ambivalence" (42) to colonialism's psychic and cultural assault, women of color can rationally adjust to the white bias by seeking to marry white and thereby "lactif[y]" (Fanon, *Black* 47) themselves and their progeny. Consequently, "the black man is viewed as a helpless victim of his cultural environment, whereas the woman of color is viewed as a knowledgeable, calculating perpetrator of interracial sexual intercourses" (Chow 42). However, if women like Mayotte Capécia effortlessly betray the native community in their embrace of the colonizers' values,[29] such ready adaptability, lacking in men, turns into an asset for anticolonial resistance in "Algeria Unveiled." In the Algerian freedom struggle, women confound the enemy strategies by taking on and dropping white masks, luring the colonizers with the image of triumphant Europeanization that they long to see.

During the anticolonial struggle, then, there emerges "a new dialectic of the body of the revolutionary Algerian woman and the world" (*Dying* 59)—a dialectic that the epidermalized man is unable to initiate. This novel relatedness amounts to the kind of radical shift of perspective that Bigger experiences after killing Mary. The unveiled woman, released from her ordered perspective, has to get accustomed not only to new ways of *being seen* but also of *seeing*: "When the [unveiled] Algerian woman has to cross a street, for a long time she commits errors of judgment as to the exact distance to be negotiated" (59). The unveiled woman's problems in depth perception point to possibilities on which Fanon does not explicitly elaborate in "Algeria Unveiled." Her proprioceptive disorientation arguably suggests that she has been released from a confining perspective, materially embodied in the veil, into a new world that she ultimately learns to negotiate. Here we find the core of feminist criticism of Fanon. A number of writers argue that Fanon is reluctant or unable to recognize that, for the Algerian woman, the veil may signify beyond the meanings posited by the anticolonial movement. Anne McClintock, for example, writes that in "Algeria Unveiled" female agency emerges only as necessitated by the exigencies of the revolution. Having come into existence at the behest of anticolonial resistance, women's agency, she argues, is seamlessly absorbed back into the family after the revolution (367). Jeffrey Louis Decker (184) and Rita A. Faulkner (849) similarly claim that Fanon's account of the women's role in Algerian decolonization is skewed because of his refusal to see the veil as oppressive. Other readers have castigated Fanon for being "clearly masculinist" (J. Butler, "Endangered" 18), one deeming him a "hater of women" (Brownmiller 250; qtd. in Sharpley-Whiting 15).[30] According to these critics, Fanon, blind to the "the patriarchal inflections of Algerian nationalism" (Sharpley-Whiting 21),[31] does not recognize the ways in which women's concerns complicate those of the nationalist struggle. In this, he uncritically participates in the anticolonial discourse of the FLN that made it impossible for Algerian women to question patriarchal practices, including veiling, without sounding treasonous and giving ammunition to the occupiers (Helie-Lucas 108).

The complexities of the colonial encounter are such that if, as Fanon writes elsewhere, colonialism "manages to impose on the native new ways of seeing" (*Toward* 38), the (unpredictable, unintended) effects of such emergent perspectives may not be unequivocally oppressive for women. Failing to consider that the perspective of the veiled woman is molded by a patriarchy that confines her to the domestic space, Fanon, the critics continue, does not see that, necessitating "new ways of seeing," the removal of the *haïk* opens for her possibilities unavailable from behind the veil. In effect, such feminist readings argue that Fanon does not, *will not*, entertain the thought that the unveiled women, having seen unexpected sights beyond the veil and found themselves able to negotiate the world's new coordinates, may not willingly return to the perspective into which the veil had sutured them. When it comes to women, the argument goes, Fanon is reluctant to consider the irrevocable, unpredictable outcome of the colonial encounter, whose implications he so brilliantly theorizes in *The Wretched of the Earth*. Ignoring the irreversible changes that take place through colonialism and the resistance it elicits, he neglects the dimension of temporality, of *becoming*, in his discussion of the women's role in the Algerian resistance movement and society at large. Given his criticism of negritude's denial of these effects in its nostalgic return to the precolonial past, such an omission would be striking indeed.

A crucial moment in "Algeria Unveiled" for many is Fanon's description of the unveiled women's "authentic birth" as street-smart revolutionaries. The female revolutionary, Fanon strangely insists, "is not a secret agent" (50). Without benefiting from formal military training in the art of espionage, or simulating cultural representations she may have found in novels or films, she

> learns both her role as "a woman alone in the street" and her revolutionary mission instinctively. . . . It is without apprenticeship, without briefing, without fuss [*sans récits, sans histoire*], that she goes out into the street with three grenades in her handbag or the activity report of an area in her bodice. She does not have the sensation of playing a role she has read about ever so many times in novels, or seen in motion picture. There is not that coefficient of play, of imitation, almost always present in this form of action when we are dealing with a Western woman.
>
> What we have here is not the bringing to light of a character known and frequented a thousand times in imagination or in stories [*récits*]. It is an authentic birth in pure state, without preliminary instruction. There is no character to imitate. On the contrary, there is an intense dramatization, a continuity between the woman and the revolutionary. The Algerian woman rises directly to the level of tragedy. (50/33)

Diana Fuss suggests that this passage reveals Fanon's anxieties over the unwieldy trajectories of cross-cultural identification, however strategically initiated. If female agency is indeed characterized by a fluid adaptability, what prevents the Algerian woman from becoming too involved in her passing, too engaged in mimicry? How can one prevent the strategic imitation of whiteness from turning into an unconscious identification with the colonizing culture? According to Fuss, Fanon aims to preempt these dangers with his insistence on there being "no character to imitate" for the revolutionary women of Algiers. If there is no substantial model for the native woman's passing, she cannot be seduced by her performance: her imitation cannot tip over into identification with the values or characteristics that she transiently embodies (Fuss 151–53).[32] There is no danger of her disappearing into the Western circulation like a counterfeit bill might be absorbed by the monetary system into which it is passed.

In this, Fanon seems to partake in the masculinist project of nation-building by subsuming women's specific concerns under those of the anticolonial struggle; their wishes and ambitions are not allowed to complicate the process of decolonization. Thus the future of the emergent nation is contained within a clearly defined program: women cannot introduce into the dialectics of decolonization any variables that might precipitate an unexpected turn in FLN's agenda.

However, to better understand the role of sexual difference in Fanon's conceptualization of anticolonial resistance, I propose we explore the Algerian women's emergence as tragic heroines, their ascendancy "directly to the level of tragedy" (Fanon, *Dying* 50). It is notable that, as much as Fanon conceptualizes resistance by moving from the epidermalized male subject of *Black Skin* to the female guerrillas of "Algeria Unveiled," both Wright and Lacan discuss the symbolic order's openness to challenges through tragic female figures: while in Lacan we famously have Antigone, Wright, in his early short story "Bright and Morning Star," gives us Aunt Sue.

TRAGIC ACTS: "ALGERIA UNVEILED" AND "BRIGHT AND MORNING STAR"

Wright's influence on Fanon may be gauged in the fact that Aunt (in Wright's vernacular rendition, "An") Sue, the female protagonist of "Bright and Morning Star," anticipates the women of "Algeria Unveiled": she is not only a tragic heroine but also a figure of subversive veiling.[33] The story, taking place in a rural Southern community, depicts a destructive encounter between Sue and the white law. Her two sons, Johnny-Boy and Sug, have become part of the local communist movement. She too comes to subscribe to the communist perspective, which eventually replaces her Christian view of the world. Sug is in prison as the narrative begins; soon, Johnny-Boy, too, ends up in jail, having been betrayed by a white informer (named, perhaps significantly, Booker) who has infiltrated the communists' ranks. To prevent further information from reaching the sheriff and to avenge her son's torture, Sue goes to the jail, smuggling in a gun under a death shroud, which she brings ostensibly to carry away Johnny-Boy's body with. Having shot the informant, she herself is promptly killed by the law enforcement officers.

"Bright and Morning Star" explores themes that Wright had already dealt with in "Blueprint for Negro Writing" and that he would elaborate on in *Native Son*. Christianity and communism figure in the story as competing *perspectives*, thus repeating the emphasis on (angles of) vision in the contemporaneous writer's manifesto. In the opening of the story, Christian belief functions protectively for Sue. "[F]ocus[ing] her feelings upon an imagery which had swept her life into a wondrous vision" (224), her faith allows her to bear white racism and daily hardships "with a soft smile of *secret knowing*" (225; emphasis added), that is, with something like the concealment that Bigger's curtain offers after Mary's murder. As her two sons become politically active in the communist party, Sue initially tries to make them see things her way: "She . . . sought to fill their eyes with her vision, but they would have none of it." Instead, "they began to boast of the strength shed by a new and terrible vision" (225). Her Christian perspective is subsequently replaced by a politicized worldview. Predictably, this shift in the protagonist's loyalties has been read as Wright's didacticism: the majority of critics regards "Bright and Morning Star," like "Fire and Cloud," as made-to-order propaganda for the American communist movement, examples of the young Wright's naïve belief in the Red cant. Fabre connects the two stories, writing that "Bright and Morning Star" "clarifies the theme of Christianity evolving into political commitment first treated in 'Fire and Cloud,' with the influence of the heroine's sons, who are both Communists, pushing her further in this direction than the Reverend Taylor" (*Unfinished* 163). I argue, however, that those who read the story as propaganda have allowed its tragic dimension to be eclipsed by a dialectical reading. Wright gives us no simple progression from ineffectual Christianity to politically potent communism. Instead, in this early story he clearly implies what a character in his final, posthumously published novel, *A Father's Law* (2008), observes: "'The Communists are rivals of the Church'" (141). By themselves, both perspectives, functioning as faiths, harden into imaginary traps for the subject. Wright demonstrates that radical challenges to the symbolic order require the relinquishing of such perspectives. In Lacanian terms, having traversed all faiths, Sue is driven to *act*.

The misreading of "Bright and Morning Star" as communist propaganda becomes obvious when we consider the fate of the subjects who make sense of the world through the Red angle. When it becomes evident that an informer has infiltrated the communist ranks, Sue insists that it must be one of the recently recruited white people. Her unshakable conviction is premised on racial loyalty that complicates and contradicts the communist perspective: "'Ah knows ever black man n woman in this parta the country. . . . Ah watched em grow up; Ah even heped birth n nurse some of em; Ah knows em *all* from way back. There ain none of em that *coulda* tol!'" Johnny-Boy dismisses her views, instead prioritizing "politics" over "race": "'Ah cant see white an Ah cant see black. . . . Ah sees rich men n Ah sees po men.'" When he asks his mother, "'Why is it gotta be *white* folks?'" she replies, simply, "'Son, look at whuts befo yuh'" (234). Sue realizes that the depth of her son's communist "faith" impairs his vision: "he believes so hard hes blind" (233). Responding to the communist creed, Johnny-Boy, to quote Wright's assessment in "Blueprint," "stands too far away and . . . neglect[s] . . . important things" (45). He is not unlike Max in *Native Son*, from whose myopic perspective one "'look[s] at the world in a way that shows no whites and no blacks. . . . [T]hose little things don't matter. You don't notice 'em'" (354). The informer indeed turns out to be a white comrade. Johnny-Boy's rigorous adherence to a communist perspective—seeing "rich men" and "po men" instead of "white" and "black"—allows a traitor to hide in the picture. He consequently finds himself in a particularly destructive trap: having been incarcerated, he is viciously tortured in the county jail, his kneecaps crushed and eardrums exploded.

The Red perspective fails Sue, as well. Having replaced the protective and sense-making angle of Christianity with that of communism, she makes what she later considers a fatal mistake in standing up to a white mob who, trying to find Johnny-Boy, has broken into her house. As the perpetrators are about to leave, she cannot help shouting after the men, "'Yuh didnt git what yuh wanted! N yuh ain gonna nevah git it!'" The men, irritated by her lack of humility, beat her up. Weakened by the attack, she divulges the names of the secret Party members to Booker, a recent white recruit whom she does not trust and who turns out to be the informer. The strength of her conviction, which makes her stand up to the white men, betrays her: as she begins mocking the men who are about to leave her house, "[h]er faith surge[s] so strongly in her she [is] all but blinded" (240). Later this is described as "a moment of weakness that came from too much strength" (251). She realizes that, in the moment of her defiance of the white mob "[a] part of her life she thought she had done away with forever had had hold of her" (252). While the Red angle had promised an understanding of and agency in the symbolic order that Christianity's otherworldliness could not offer, its gradual strengthening into a rigorous, self-enclosed belief system suddenly ensnares her: "she had *trapped* herself with her own hunger; to water the long dry thirst of her faith her pride had made *a bargain which her flesh could not keep*" (252; emphases added). She realizes that the communist perspective, as a self-assured posture, is after all not much different from the imaginary comfort of Christianity. As she tells Booker the comrades' names, she becomes the casualty of *her body's failing* in programmatic communism's imaginary vise.

Rather than, as critics would have it, showing the dialectical progression from Christianity to communism, Wright illustrates how both angles, when occupied as "faiths," reveal only a partial picture, which is subsequently, and fatally, mistaken for the whole truth. According to Wright, in other words, both Christianity and communism function *imaginarily*: they disable the subject's mobility, offering imaginary solutions to symbolic ills. Rather than being content with illustrating the stages of dialectical materialism, as Fabre assumes, Wright, already in this early stage of his career, identifies programmatic communism, like religion, as an imaginary delusion, rendering one unable to see how race (Sue's "black" and "white") complicates the symbolic order's class dynamics (Johnny-Boy's "rich" and "po"). Such perspectives figure as "faiths" that, by compelling the subject's belief, allow her to make sense of and bear one's impoverished, oppressed existence. As the story progresses, the respective faiths constitute dialectical responses to the conditions of Sue's life: they are "stars" according to which the subject can orient herself in the hostile environment. Yet, as angles of vision, they unfailingly immobilize and blind her without productively reconfiguring her world; they are stages in a dialectical process of actions and counteractions that can merely perpetuate the logic of the (white symbolic) law.

A more productive, and far more dangerous, response to the social dialectic of competing faiths is figured in terms of "the background of rain" (247), whose ceaseless "droning" (221) punctuates the narrative. The white noise of the rain slides in and out of one's attention, like the ticking of a clock, which, as a reminder of duration, is heard only through its anomalies and disruptions. In the opening of the narrative, Sue ponders on the ambiguity of the phenomenon: "'Rains good n bad,'" she thinks. "'It kin make seeds bus up thu the groun, er it kin bog things down lika watah-soaked coffin'" (221). Christianity and communism have allowed her not to be "bogged down" by the hardships of her life.[34] Indeed, the text suggests that all extant perspectives are ways of avoiding drowning—sutured into them, one is "buoyed with a faith beyond this world" (224). Yet, as an escape from "the wet darkness" (226) that Sue contemplates beyond her window, such faiths may also cut one off from the *fecundity* of "the driving rain" (245).

Sue finds herself immersed in its deadly but productive ambit after her beating by the white mob. Blinded, she teeters on the brink of unconsciousness, "[h]er ears . . . filled with the drone of rain" (241). It is in her struggle to surface from this realm of nonidentity, unconsciousness, and undifferentiation that she commits herself, once again, to a faith. Half-conscious, she sees "a vast white blur . . . suspended directly above her. . . . Gradually the blur resolve[s] itself into a huge white face that slowly fill[s] her vision" (241–42). The face is that of the white recruit, Booker, whom she already suspects of being an informant. Yet, she succumbs to the seduction of his voice, whose interpellative address pulls her back from the "droning" to sentient life: "feeling somehow that she existed only by the mercy of that white face, . . . she heard her name being called. . . . It was as if an invisible knife had split her in two, leaving one half of her lying there helpless, while the other half shrank in dread from a forgotten but familiar enemy. *Sue its me Sue its me* . . ." (242; final ellipsis in original). As Booker, extending her a lifeline, proceeds to extract from her the names of the other comrades—ostensibly, to warn the party members of the sheriff's moves—Sue hesitates: "Lawd, Ah don blieve in this man!" (245). Nevertheless, the need for belief is strong enough for her to divulge her information. When, detecting inconsistencies in his story, she becomes suspicious, he asks: "'Sue, don yuh blieve in me?'" (246). Her desire to believe guides her perception: "She stared at him until her lips hung open; she was searching deep within herself for certainty" (246). To prop up her faith, she consequently offers Booker an alibi by asking leading questions: "'You meet Reva? . . . She tell yuh?' . . . She asked the questions more of herself than of him; she longed to believe" (246–47).

Like Christianity and communism before, her faith in Booker is a deadly trap; her longing to believe turns into a yet another specular capture. She later hears from Reva, a white friend, that he has been found out as the informant. At this moment, Sue, relinquishing all faiths, is moved with the realization that she cannot find her support in any given system, whether it be religion, communism, or intersubjectivity. She risks her survival for a future that is beyond the dialectical rationale, unsupported by the network of faiths. Indeed, to avoid the misreadings of "Bright and Morning Star" as propaganda, we should consider Sue not as an embodiment of history's dialectical progression but as a tragic heroine whose necessary action she herself cannot survive. More precisely, to follow the unpredictable convolutions of resistance and change, I suggest we engage Lacan's theory of tragedy. Sue's "weakness that c[omes] from too much strength" (251) names her *hamartia*, her tragic flaw. Realizing the trap that the Red angle has led her to, she stands "[m]ired . . . between two abandoned worlds, living, but dying without the strength of the grace that either gave" (252). She becomes, in Lacan's terms, a tragic heroine "who find[s herself] right away in a limit zone, find[s herself] between life and death" (*SVII* 272). Situated in this impossible in-between location, the tragic heroine acts by striking against herself and thereby the symbolic order: Sue decides to go alone to the county jail and kill Booker, knowing that she herself will not be able to survive the act. Her strategy prefigures the actions of the Algerian women who, like Sue, deceive their opponents by presenting a lure in the form of an image that the latter wish to see. Like the seemingly meek native women who carry explosives under their veils, Sue, concealing a shotgun under her shroud, enters the jail as an unsuspected "mammy," the "nigger woman" that the white mob had interpellated her as. As she comes up with the plan, "[h]er whole being leaped with will; the long years of her life bent toward a moment of focus, a point. Ah kin go wid mah sheet! Ahll be doin whut he said! Lawd Gawd in heaven, Ahma go lika nigger woman wid ma windin sheet t git mah dead son! . . . [S]he had in her heart the whole meaning of her life; her entire personality was poised on *the brink of a total act*" (253; emphasis added). In this moment of clarity and focus, she becomes the tragic heroine: "It is the nature of the tragic hero[ine], at once [her] greatness and [her] doom, that [s]he knows no shrinking or half-heartedness, but identifies [her]self wholly with the power that moves [her], and will admit the justification of no other power. However varied and rich [her] inner life and character may be, in the conflict it is all concentrated in one point" (A. C. Bradley 369–70).[35] In Wright, this "one point," the "total act" Sue courts, is self-annihilation: as Abdul JanMohamed writes, "the willing acceptance of death functions as the most viable form of liberation in [Wright's] fiction" ("Rehistoricizing" 202).[36]

In her decision not to confide her plans to her comrades, Sue is a lone terrorist whose story may never find symbolic recognition. Driving themselves beyond the logic of the structure, tragic figures, unlike the heroes of a "just war," do not seek symbolic inscription for their actions; theirs is not a design to be monumentalized, a story to be passed on. Not acting on behalf of a recognized law nor leaving behind suicide notes, they risk being misread, forgotten, deleted from symbolic memory. Similarly, while Sue's actions can be rationalized—she aims to prevent the names of her comrades from falling into the sheriff's hands—they are not supported by her communist faith. She does not act for the sake of the Party's good; rather, while her suicidal act may benefit the communist movement, we get the feeling she is moved by something else, by a desire to strike blindly at the law. Furthermore, rather than being supported by communism, her act becomes possible only when she sees the imaginary delusion of the Red faith: she acts alone because she realizes that she does not have a readily available framework in which to situate or find her solution. In Žižek's terms, she "take[s] a risk, a step into the open, with no big Other to return [her] true message" ("Afterword" 243).[37]

For JanMohamed, "Bright and Morning Star" is an early example of Wright's life-long illustration of and negotiation with "the dialectics of death."

In *The Death-Bound-Subject: Richard Wright and the Archaeology of Death* (2005), he designates with this term the formation of the subject within the symbolic order organized according to the exigencies of slavery and subsequently mutated into the practices of Jim Crow. JanMohamed argues that Lacan provides us a crucial rereading of Hegel—especially the exchanges between the lord and the bondsman—which pushes the dialectics beyond the arguably conformist logic of the *Sittlichkeit* of Hegelian ethics. Lacan allows one to theorize the slave's futurity other than through the obedient "work" that may lead to subjective recognition. Work in the Hegelian sense becomes that which seals and sustains the death contract between the master and the slave. In order to avoid his "actual-death," the laboring slave, as the death-bound-subject, is preserved but immobilized by "social-death," the condition that for Orlando Patterson results from the slave's "natal alienation." The working slave lives on within the circumscribed temporality of his imminent but repetitively commuted death sentence. He is forced to earn such commutation by acceding to the futureless temporality of labor. Slavery's dialectics of death offers no hope of a future different from the present state of things.

When the subject emerges and is caught in the dialectics of death, "effective freedom derives from negating, indeed destroying, the self formed by hegemony and permitting a new self to emerge in its place" (68–69). What is required, in JanMohamed's Lacanian terms, is "symbolic-death." While he considers "symbolic-death" as the necessary, self-destructive choice for the racialized subject of slavery and Jim Crow, JanMohamed nevertheless does not attend to Lacan's *Ethics* seminar in his discussion of Wright. I insist on this link, for the seventh seminar not only theorizes the choice of death in Antigone's figure, but also marks the turning point in Lacan's work from the ethics of desire to the ethics of the drive. Lacan emphasizes the contrast between the "irrational" doggedness of Sophocles's heroine, Antigone, to give her singular point of existence—the remains of her orphaned brother (*SVII* 278–79; Sophocles, lines 1001–4)—funeral rites and Creon's persistence that no one be above, or beyond, the law. While Creon is thus identified with the Kantian universal good (*SVII* 259), Antigone's demand to bury her brother has to do with the insistence on something that Lacan alludes to as "unwritten laws," "a certain legality which is a consequence of the laws of the gods": "Involved here is an invocation of something that is, in effect, of the order of law, but which is not developed in any signifying chain or in anything else" (*SVII* 278; see Sophocles, lines 503–5). For Lacan, Antigone's ethical call responds to the beyond of symbolization, that is, the realm of the real or the death drive. Consequently, he argues, her refusal to follow Creon's edicts excludes her from the community, plunges her to the limbo of the living dead: "Although she is not yet dead, she is eliminated from the world of the living" (*SVII* 280). By way of her ethical act, she undergoes a symbolic death, withdraws from the symbolic order. In its unyielding insistence on that which is intolerable to symbolic laws, such suicide represents for Lacan the "only successful act": "only such a 'self-destructive' act [can] clear the terrain for a new beginning" (Žižek, "Class" 123).

As a living dead, Sue hardly experiences her physical, "actual" death. Like Antigone, who "gave [her]self to death" (Sophocles, line 630), Sue, "giving up her life before they [take] it from her" (261), withdraws from her position in the structure where the law can locate her. As the sheriff's man shoots her, "[s]he yearn[s] suddenly to talk. 'Yuh didnt git whut yuh wanted! N yuh ain gonna nevah git it! Yuh didnt kill me; Ah come here by mahsef . . .' She fe[els] rain falling into her wide-open, dimming eyes and hear[s] faint voices. Her lips move[] soundlessly. *Yuh didnt git yuh didnt yuh didn't* . . ." (262–63; ellipses in original). Her insistence in this scene on the failure of the law to reach her contrasts with her similar claim earlier in the story. In the previous scene, where, propped up by her communist faith, she defies the white mob ransacking her house—"'Yuh didnt git what yuh wanted! N yuh ain gonna nevah git it!'" (240)—she succumbs to the failure of her imaginary position, her body betraying her. Having undergone a symbolic death, however, she can iterate the same words from a position beyond the law. In this, she becomes a tragic figure, marked by symbolic self-annihilation. The heroine's ethical stance is thus of a completely different order than Creon's embodiment of the law. Precisely because of his level-headedness, the latter cannot be a tragic figure: "tragic heroes are always isolated, they are always beyond established limits, always in an exposed position and, as a result, separated in one way or another from the structure" (*SVII* 271).

Having relinquished all faiths that have allowed her orientation toward a meaningful future, Sue similarly is swept off "beyond the limits of the human" (*SVII* 263). JanMohamed argues that "for Sue, the plan itself is a new morning star, *another resurrection of her faith* and capacity for resistance, and, if successful, it would mean a resurrection of the Party as well" (*Death-Bound-Subject* 72–73; emphasis added). Yet, while her plan does provide her a new "star that gr[ows] bright in the morning of new hope" (251), it is not clear that it functions as a "faith." Indeed, her actions, in their self-destructiveness, are the annihilation of every belief, whose previous configurations have failed the tragic heroine. Having realized the betrayal of all faith, Sue comes "undone" (250). If her desperate belief in Booker pulls her up from the realm of unconsciousness and disorientation that is characterized by the droning of the rain, in her decision to go to the jail she herself becomes *a drone*, an actor that has shed everything marking her human singularity. The text describes Johnny-Boy's crippling with sickening detail to emphasize Sue's inhuman persistence in witnessing the scene of her son's torture; she remains unsupported by all of the forms of faith—Christianity, communism, human relationality itself—on which she has attempted to anchor her symbolic order. In the short story's final passage, she is identified with "the dead," a realm that is both immortal and singular: "She felt rain falling into her wide-open, dimming eyes and heard faint voices. . . . Focused and pointed she was, buried in the depths of her star, swallowed in its peace and strength; and not feeling her flesh growing cold, cold as the rain that fell from the invisible sky upon the doomed living and the dead that never dies" (263). The story thus opens and closes with the immortal, singular droning of "the driving rain" (245): "the dead that never dies" rather than "the dead that never die." JanMohamed's proposition that Sue "does literally die but continues to 'live' in the lives of others who are the political beneficiaries of his death" (68) seems to repeat the structure of belief in futurity that has consistently failed the tragic heroine. Rather, what remains the locus of becoming at the end of the narrative is not identifiable within any extant form of life—the "living" are "doomed"—but in the nonhuman ontology of the "dead," its singular "droning."

WRIGHT'S TWO MASKS

Lacan's discussion of Antigone's as an ethical position points to a shift in his theory from the ethics of desire to an ethics of the drive, concomitant with the move, in his work, from an emphasis on the symbolic to one on the real. James Mellard writes that, in the *Ethics* seminar, "Lacan insists that the true ethical position is not that which abides by the desire of the law of one's culture but that which accords with *jouissance*" (406). Alenka Zupančič, too, notes a shift in Lacan whereby desire is reconfigured as a defense against the real, a "compromise formation": according to his later work, "we escape to the realm of infinite symbolic metonymy in order to avoid the encounter with the Real of enjoyment" (*Ethics* 235). Yet, observing such changes in Lacan's focus from the symbolic to the real, we should not assume too simple a split between desire and the drive. While the two forms of ethics are radically different, indeed opposed, the ethics of the real emerges as the always-already present underside of symbolic ethics. Driven after the missing part, the piece lost in the "primal separation" (*SXI* 83), desire itself always aims at symbolic limits. Consequently, the ethics of desire—"the law of one's culture"—is already complicated by the ethics of jouissance. According to Lacan, tragedy is concerned precisely with this paradox: in the wake of the symbolic law, something else surfaces, something that is intimately tied to the logic of the law yet nevertheless radically opposed to it: "The good cannot reign over all without an excess emerging whose fatal consequences are revealed to us in tragedy" (*SVII* 259). This excess is the remainder of the real that is properly speaking not outside the law or the symbolic order but internal to it: it designates the point of its failing that is identical to its very possibility.[38] While Creon is on the side of the symbolic, the stubborn Antigone quickens this underside of the law, its internal limit. As I suggested in the previous chapter, this internal failing is signaled by the specter of the *objet a*, which designates the grounding and the point of failure of the symbolic. This internal outside—or "intimate exteriority" (*SVII* 139)—at once allows the law's functioning yet insists in its circuits as an inassimilable ghost that continuously prevents its smooth functioning. One can similarly suggest that, like the law and its constitutive failing, the two Lacanian ethics—those of desire and the drive—are intimately conjoined, situated with respect to one another like the surfaces of a Möbius strip.

In this context, it is important to observe that if Sue, as a tragic heroine, embodies something like the ethics of the real, her ethical act is enabled by her performance as a "nigger woman" for the white law, much like the Algerian women's terrorism proceeds through their donning the mask of submissive natives or Europeanized allies. A tactical minstrelization of interracial contact—the mask of the mammy—allows her violent counterattack. We should further note, however, that in Wright's work not all forms of minstrelization open to revolutionary violence; rather, there are two forms of masquerade, as much as the radicalism of subversive (female) veiling is contrasted in Fanon with the immobility of the epidermalized (male) subject. Apart from Sue's, another form of racial masking proves considerably less productive, indeed debilitating. I argue that these two forms of masquerade, like Fanon's epidermalization and veiling, can be understood only through the theory of sexuation. Such understanding of the interlinking of race and sex helps us reconsider the feminist criticism of Fanon I recounted earlier.

In "The Psychological Reactions of Oppressed People," Wright briefly explores what he calls "a whole variety of ironic attitudes" in colonized people, subsuming these under the heading of "acting." There is, he explains, "an almost unconscious tendency [in the colonized] to hide their deepest reactions from those who they fear would penalize them" (*White* 17). Echoing Fanon's observation of the "falsehood" that characterizes all contact between the colonized and the colonizers (*Dying* 65), many have pointed out such exigencies of dissimulation in African American history. Joseph Boskin writes that the "contact between whites and blacks during the long period of slavery almost always involved intricate forms of performing" (45). Others show that such performing has survived to Jim Crow and beyond, becoming "a perfected system" (Wright, *White* 18). Consequently, during segregation, white people "typically felt that they knew 'their' blacks well, since they saw and interacted with them often" (James Davis 64–65). A white character in Du Bois's novel *Dark Princess* exemplifies such assumption: "'I know niggers,'" he announces, "'and I don't mean perhaps. Ain't I white'" (9). This phrase suggests several readings. Not only do white people "know their niggers"; they know them *because* they are white. As Bigger, having entered the Dalton household, intuits, in the racist system of interracial contact whiteness structurally denotes intimate knowledge of blacks. Furthermore, for Du Bois, the white person's assumed knowledge of the racial other guarantees (the degree of) his whiteness ("Ain't I white!").

Wright is extremely ambivalent about such strategies of "enforced duplicity" ("Interview" [with Schmid] 108). According to him, "the sooner all of these so-called secrets are out in the open, the sooner both sides, white and colored, realize the shadows that hem them in, the quicker sane and rational plans can be made" (*White* 19). He continues in an interview: "a society is not very strong when it rests upon a large basis of secret, hidden things, like quicksand. In my opinion, things must be in the open" ("Negro" 237). He repeats his condemnation about black tricksterism also in his fiction. Fishbelly, the protagonist of *The Long Dream* (1958), is initiated into the rigorous etiquette of interracial contact when he sees his father's performance in front of a white officer of the law:

> Fishbelly understood now; his father was paying humble deference to the white man and his "acting" was so flawless, so seemingly effortless that Fishbelly was stupefied. This was a father whom he had never known, a father whom he loathed and did not want to know. Tyree entered the room and looked at him with eyes of a stranger, then turned to watch the retreating white man. When the white man had turned a corner in the corridor, Fishbelly saw a change engulf his father's face and body: Tyree's knees lost their bent posture, his back straightened, his arms fell normally to his sides, and that distracted, foolish, noncommittal expression vanished and he reached out and crushed Fishbelly to him.
>
> "My son," Tyree mumbled in a choked voice. (115)[39]

In *Discourse on Colonialism*, Aimé Césaire repeats Wright's negative views on acting, lamenting the necessity for deceptive subaltern performance. Both theorists wish to end the choreography of postcolonial contact, to put out of business "the obscurers, all the inventors of subterfuges, the charlatans and tricksters, the dealers in gobbledygook" (Césaire 34; see also 9).

Other African American and (post)colonial writers and scholars, however, have been less quick to denounce these acts of dissemblance, which, as C. L. R. James observes in *The Black Jacobins*, may be "the refuge of the slave" (334). In *Incidents in the Life of a Slave Girl* (1861), Harriet Jacobs asks: "Who can blame slaves for being cunning? They are constantly compelled to resort to it. It is the only weapon of the weak and oppressed against the strength of their tyrants" (609). Speaking of what John Brown, in his slave narrative, calls "the systematic deception we practised, in self-defense, on our master" (351), Henry Bibb, too, writes that "the only weapon of self defence that I could use successfully, was that of deception" (15; see also 38). In *To Tell a Free Story*, William Andrews discusses numerous similar slave narratives that show the necessity for, and even celebrate, trickery and dissemblance, "the survival art of self-invention" (93). A character in Wesley Brown's *Darktown Strutters* describes this art form by confessing, "'I know I gotta stretch the truth in order to live'" (134). Henry Louis Gates's theory of signifyin(g) is the best known contemporary reevaluation of these strategies. His theory echoes the dynamics of black(face) magic I discussed in the previous chapter. The "repetition, with a signal difference" (*Signifying* 51 and passim),[40] characteristic of black vernacular cultures, can be compared to subversive possibilities in African American appropriations of blackface.

Why does Wright reject such "weapons of the weak"? He cannot be accused of being unaware of their historical importance. In *12 Million Black Voices*, he observes that plantation slaves "developed a secret life and language of [their] own" that "enabled [them] to speak of revolt in the actual presence of the [plantation owners] without their being aware!" (40).[41] Despite recognizing its subversive potential, Wright immediately links the double-voiced black vernacular to the demeaning and self-defeating acting that he condemns in "Psychological Reactions" (*12 Million* 41). A reason behind the rejection of such strategies is suggested by Wright in the latter essay. He goes on to state that, when "acting," the black man adopts certain ways to signal his submission to the white man: "The Negro's voice is almost always pitched high when addressed to a white man; all hint of aggressiveness is purged from it" (18). Wright suggests, that is, that emasculation—a high-pitched voice—is an essential part of the act from behind which the black man meets the white man. Again, in *The Long Dream*, Wright illustrates what he observes in *White Man, Listen!* As Tyree, Fishbelly's father, is visited by a white man, the son again witnesses his father's transformation: the father addresses the man with a "high-pitched, unnatural" voice (67). This is repeated as Tyree later boasts of his power over the white people in his town, "'Ye see, Fish, these goddamned crazy white folks *respect* me,' Tyree cut him off again in a high-pitched voice, throwing an arm over his son's shoulder. 'I know how to handle these white folks.' Tyree's cracked tenor rose in feigned lyricism. 'Fish, I know these goddamn white folks better'n they know themselves'" (128).[42] Notably, Tyree's voice retains its "high pitch" even when there are no white people present; he addresses his son as he did the law enforcement officer. This suggests the danger that minstrel theorists point out: the game's taking control of the players, the dissemblance act's becoming indistinguishable from the "real" person behind the mask.

If Wright connects such acting to femininity, Lacan similarly writes that "[i]n playing the part of the one who hides," the subject "is obliged to don . . . the attributes of femininity and shadow, so propitious to the act of concealing" ("Seminar" 44). In terms familiar from African American history and culture, we can connect such efforts at concealment to narratives of passing, which are always implicated in questions of sexual difference. As M. Giulia Fabi observes, there is a "close connection between passing and traditional notions of true femininity" (13). Passing, Phillip Brian Harper continues, "is actually constitutive of . . . normative femininity . . . insofar as the very duplicity and inconstancy comprised in . . . passing are part and parcel of an essentially feminine 'nature' that . . . is refigured as the inoffensive frivolity of proper bourgeois womanhood" (118). The masculine ideal of subjectivity, on the other hand, cannot tolerate such duplicity and concealment: it is "impossible . . . for the narrative of the passing man to culminate in his accession to a socially acceptable masculine position" (119), as evidenced, for example, by the masculine failure of James Weldon Johnson's ex-colored man. In many passing narratives, such feminine deception is opposed to open heroic confrontation, which is gendered masculine (Fabi 10, 17). In contrast to a political activity in the public sphere, passing is figured "as a privatized (and thus symbolically feminized) endeavor" (Wald 110). The male passer, then, seemingly repeats the African American blackface performer's "strange, almost macabre, act of black collusion in his own emasculation" (Huggins 245).[43]

Obviously, however, Aunt Sue and the Algerian terrorists problematize the supposed connection between passing and "feminine ideals of passivity and gentility" (Fabi 13). I suggest we approach the instable dynamics of passing through the Lacanian theory of the symbolic order's structuration around (sexual) difference. That is, the two outcomes of passing—represented by Sue's revolutionary act and the emasculating minstrel performance of Tyree, Fishbelly's father—can be mapped onto the symbolic structures that emerge out of the impossibility that sexual difference names for Lacan. For Lacan, sexuated subjects are located in specific positions vis-à-vis symbolic order's "excluded interior" (*SVII* 101), the real. According to him, our assumption of masculine and feminine positions is an effort to come to terms with the primordial trauma as the effects of which subjects emerge in the world. As subjective structures, "man" and "woman" aim (and inevitably fail) "to symbolize the lost core of our being" (Verhaege 147). Given the different stakes that men and women have in the symbolic order, it can be argued that, to a large extent, Antigone's defiance suggests her feminine relation to jouissance and the law. The tragic heroine's symbolic death and disruptive act, possibly precipitating a symbolic crisis, are enabled, at least to an extent, by her feminine structure: as Joan Copjec writes, only through a theory of sexuation can one distinguish "the act of Antigone from the action of Creon" ("Tomb" 237; see also Žižek, *Enjoy* 46).

I proceed by briefly summarizing Lacan's theory of sexuation, drawing out aspects that help us delineate how sexual and racial difference function in Wright's and Fanon's understanding of resistance and symbolic change. Particularly crucial for us are the two forms of feminine jouissance Lacan isolates: they help us understand Wright's analysis, in "Psychological Reactions," of the double role of acting in resisting the white symbolic, as well as Fanon's characterization of postcolonial becoming in *Black Skin*, "Algeria Unveiled," and *The Wretched of the Earth*. Given Wright's and Fanon's description of resistance and symbolic change, I argue that the subjective positions Lacan draws out in *Seminar XX: On Feminine Sexuality*—positions that name different ways of dealing with the traumatic real—may illustrate symbolic responses not only to sexual difference but to other differences too that are of fundamental importance to a particular symbolic constellation. As Renata Salecl writes, "it is the very core of society that we are dealing which when we try to understand the real, the unsymbolizable kernel around which society structures itself. The problem is thus that another culture structures itself differently around some central impossibility" (*(Per)versions* 134). In symbolic orders where other differences, such as race, are constitutive, that is, subjective positionings may be determined by racial difference.

SEXUAL DIFFERENCE, RACIAL DIFFERENCE

In the sexuation graphs of *Seminar XX* (78), the subject positions of men and women are characterized by their differing relations to the symbolic function[44] and jouissance: masculine and feminine subjects are "split differently" (Fink, *Lacanian* 118).[45] Lacan offers two propositions concerning each subject position. For men, he writes:

1. There is one who is not subject to the symbolic function; and
2. All are subject to symbolic function; or, Man as whole is subject to the symbolic function.

For women, he writes:

1. There is not one who is not subject to the symbolic function; or, There are no exceptions to being subject to the symbolic function; and
2. Not all woman is subject to the symbolic function; or, Woman as not-whole (or not-all) is subject to the symbolic function.

The crucial point to note is the different ways that the rule and its exception function on the masculine and feminine sides. While there is one exception—the primordial father—to man's symbolic function, nothing like it exists on woman's side. According to Lacan, who follows set theory here, this one exception produces man as *a closed set*, while woman, in relation to the symbolic function, is produced as *an open set*. Consequently, men are as whole under the symbolic signifier: "[t]he whole here is thus based on the exception" of the primal father, the one not under the sway of the phallic signifier (*SXX* 79–80). When it comes to women, on the other hand, something escapes, or may exceed, the symbolic function, given the openness of the set "woman": "woman is not-whole"; "there is always something in her that escapes discourse" (*SXX* 33).

We consequently find that man and woman have different ways of negotiating the real. While man deals with jouissance through the fantasy supported by the *objet a*, woman has potentially two ways of approaching the real. One of these is characterized as symbolic—or, as it is more widely known in Anglo-American feminism, phallic—jouissance (~~Woman~~'s relation to the symbolic function), the other as nonsymbolic, Other jouissance (~~Woman~~'s relation to the lacking Other, S[Ⱥ]). These two forms of feminine jouissance can be exemplified by feminine masquerade and Antigone's act, respectively. While woman's masquerade (cor)responds to the masculine fantasy, thus producing what Lacan calls the "comedy" of sexual (non)relations ("Signification" 279), Antigone's answer—arguably representing the "tragic" way the sexual relationship fails—is to refuse the validity of symbolic positions. More precisely, her defiance is not even addressed to Creon: rather, she "buries her brother simply because she wants to, simply because she must, and not because she seeks to prove a point to anyone else, or because she aims at some useful or calculated end" (Shepherdson, "Of Love" 70). Antigone neither supplies an answer to nor requests a response from the Other; instead, she "relate[s] to the real or the 'God' face of the Other" (Barnard 8). Acting according to the "unwritten laws," the laws of gods, Antigone accesses Other jouissance, yet one that is internal to the symbolic: "this is not the freedom of a transgressive or a libertine desire. This is a freedom that lies both within and beyond the law. . . . Woman not being all under castration represent the freedom granted by the law rather than a freedom from the law" (Moncayo 231). Nevertheless, according to the symbolic rules of the game, this way of dealing with the real is irrational, possibly psychotic. Ceasing to signify, to make sense, in the symbolic register, she consequently experiences a symbolic death.

I propose that, to understand Wright's and Fanon's ambivalent characterizations of resistance, we not limit ourselves to sexuation in considering the subjective structures impelled by the real that Lacan sketches in *Seminar XX*. In Wright's work, the two forms of passing/acting, represented by Tyree's and An Sue's performances, can be understood as exemplifying two ways of relating to the *point de capiton* of the symbolic order, that is, as symbolic and Other jouissance, respectively. We can argue this, of course, only if we assume that the sexuated subject positions of *Seminar XX* designate the subject's symbolic relation not necessarily, or not exclusively, to the phallus or the real of sexual difference, but to the symbolic function and the *objet a*. To show the productivity of Lacanian psychoanalysis for queer theory, Tim Dean makes a parallel point, arguing that we should "move beyond sexual difference as the principal explanatory framework for theorizing desire" (*Beyond* 88). He accomplishes this by demonstrating that the figure of the phallus, whose insistent specter continues to be problematic for many feminist and queer readers—the phallus that, as Jane Gallop puts it, feminists find "particularly hard to swallow" (*Thinking* 125)[46]—is for Lacan "provisional rather than foundational" (Dean, *Beyond* 45). According to Dean, in Lacan's work since the early 1960s, the phallus becomes "largely obsolete" (45), increasingly replaced by the *objet a*, a point on which Ernesto Laclau agrees ("Identity" 72). Hence, "it is purely . . . arbitrary that the phallus should hold any indisputable priority in relation to the symbolic order's exigencies. . . . [T]he phallus as Lacan's model for the causal principle of desire may be bracketed once the full significance of the object *a* comes into view" (Dean, *Beyond* 50). As Žižek writes, the emphasis on the *objet a* in Lacan's later work signals his attempt "to break *out* of th[e] framework [of the inescapable paternal law], to expose the *fraud* of paternal authority" ("*Da*" 255).

We can see why such a de-emphasis of the phallus, in favor of the *objet a*, is crucial also for the dialogue between Lacan and critical race theory. As I argued in the previous chapter, in the white symbolic order, the figure of the (minstrel) mask or the (Du Boisian) veil comes to occupy the place of the *a*, the (phobogenic) object-cause of desire. For this argument to make sense, we must be ready to assume that what Žižek calls "the traumatic kernel" of the symbolic may congeal not only around sex but also race. It is instructive to note that the tropes of the "mask" and the "veil," repeated in the African American tradition, figure centrally also in Lacan's discussion of symbolic responses to sexual difference (see "Signification" 279–80). While the phallus functions as veiled, the real itself, as Lacan writes in *The Four Fundamental Concepts of Psycho-Analysis*, "reappears, in effect, frequently unveiled" (*SXI* 55). Such confluences between, on the one hand, Lacan's discussion of sexuation and, on the other, Wright's and Fanon's theorization of racialization suggest that structures of desire and alterity, as well as our symbolic negotiations with jouissance and the real, should not be understood exclusively in terms of the phallus and sexual difference. Instead, certain symbolic structures may revolve as much around other forms of difference as sexuation. While the real and the *objet a* are transhistorical, unhistoricizable categories, the precise forms of symbolic structures that mediate our ambivalent relation to the *a*, and consequently the real, are of historical contingency (Dean, *Beyond* 53). The real, precipitating the desiring subject's emergence, is the unnamable ground that is symbolized in the subjective positions that Lacan maps in *Seminar XX*. Where race is of central, constitutive importance, subjective relations to jouissance revolve as much around racial as sexual difference. Jacques-Alain Miller suggests as much when he argues that racism should be understood as a response to the racial other's unfamiliar way of relating to jouissance ("Extimité" 125). The graphs in *Seminar XX* thus have significance beyond questions of sexual difference: they also suggest how raced subjects are positioned in the symbolic. As Dean writes, "the two sides of the graph cannot legitimately be gendered, but instead should be understood as diagramming differential modalities that inform every subject" ("Homosexuality" 141n19).

I thus part company with Lacanians for whom sex names the only real difference. Copjec, for example, writes that, "defined not so much by discourse as by its default, sexual difference is unlike racial, class, or ethnic differences. Whereas these differences are inscribed in the symbolic, sexual difference is not: only the failure of its inscription is marked in the symbolic. Sexual difference, in other words, is a real and not a symbolic difference" (*Read* 207). Put simply, the "real-ness" of sexual difference means that all subjects are sexed but not necessarily raced: while "the organization of the ego and the acquisition of the body image" always entail sexuation, "the visibility of the body does not necessarily have to be a racial visibility" (Seshadri-Crooks, *Desiring* 30). Like Copjec, for whom "[i]t is always a sexed subject who assumes each racial, class, or ethnic identity" (*Read* 208), Seshadri-Crooks writes that "[t]here is no doubt that one can be constituted with a 'unified' bodily ego without necessarily identifying with a racial signifier, or seeing oneself as racially marked. . . . [R]ace is not like sex. Not all are subject to the racial signifier" (35).

Others propose understanding racial difference as a real difference because race, like sex, exceeds symbolic signification: "we cannot adequately conceptualize race or sexual difference," Shepherdson writes, "if we treat them precisely as laws, theories of selfhood, or economic policies. Like sexual difference, race is not a human invention" ("Human" 45). Race, Shepherdson continues, is not "an ideological construction" (61) but must be understood as "something real," precisely "because it exceeds our symbolic grasp" (46). Cynthia Dyess and Dean similarly argue that, "once sexual difference is understood as real in the sense that it is experienced originally as traumatic, then we can start to appreciate how racial difference also operates as a real, not merely symbolic, difference" (752n).[47]

Seshadri-Crooks would presumably respond to Shepherdson, Dyess, and Dean by arguing that the extrasymbolic aspects of race do not signal a real difference. Instead, even though race "produces extra-discursive effects," it "is of purely cultural and historical origin. . . . From a certain perspective, it seems marked on the body, something inherited like sex; from a Lacanian perspective, one might even suggest (erroneously) that it seems to exceed language" (*Desiring* 4). In her theory, race does not entirely belong to the real, like sex, nor is it completely in the symbolic, like class or ethnicity: "Race [unlike sex] is historical and material . . . , but unlike class it is not at all malleable" (4). Consequently, race should be seen as "neither wholly nature nor nurture, essence nor construct" (161n6). Instead, as the "master signifier" of "Whiteness," race figures as that which promises to fill in the gap that is at the heart of subjectivity, "attempt[ing] to compensate for sex's failure in language," "to signify the sexed subject, which is the 'more than symbolic' aspect of the subject" (7, 21). The racial signifier, according to Seshadri-Crooks, undertakes to overcome the split at the heart of sexed subjectivity, "promis[ing] access to being itself. It offers the prestige of being better and superior; it is the promise of being more human, more full, less lacking" (7).

While Seshadri-Crooks names "Whiteness" as the master signifier, Sheldon George, in "Trauma and the Conservation of African-American Racial Identity," takes a different but complementary view in psychoanalytically theorizing black racial identity. According to him, blackness as identity functions to cover over the primordial split in the subject. "Race," he writes, "is an anxious attempt at using fantasy to reestablish the *I* and maintain the subjectivity that is challenged by racism. Fantasy allows African-Americans to replace their lost *being* with a racial identity" (66). Tracing this loss to the trauma of slavery, George suggests that African American identity is a way to negotiate this originating rupture: "Where the traumatic, missed past eludes representation, race arises as the signifier that is its representative. Race is latched onto by African-Americans because it seems to express and explain what defies symbolization: the trauma that is formative for African-Americans" (71). The insistence on the essence of racial identity "hinders the ability of African-Americans to escape the trauma of slavery," which, as "formative trauma," has come to function as "their *real*" (71).

For Seshadri-Crooks and George, whiteness and blackness, respectively, articulate the lost, alienated core of being for the subject. George ends his essay with a note that resonates with Dominick LaCapra's suggestion, in *Representing the Holocaust*, about the possibility of defusing trauma by a process of "working through" (LaCapra 199). According to George, the way forward in terms of race is for African Americans "to become the agency that makes the traumatic *real* of slavery speak, to excise the trauma from its place within the *real* through an articulation of this trauma's interaction with and relation to African-Americans" (72). The constitutive encounter with the real—the trauma of slavery—should be symbolized, articulated in the realm of signifiers and meaning.

Yet, considering the radical foreignness of the real, we need to remember that its articulation must have profound consequences for symbolic structures. Otherwise, we are speaking of *symbolization as a process of adaptation to an existing network of signifiers.* The symbolic becomes an absorbent entity that, in its malleability, is resistant to radical challenges and restructuring. Indeed, seeing the trauma of slavery behind the racial identities of African Americans, George unwittingly naturalizes what I have called the *white* symbolic order. Without a consideration of what happens to the existing symbolic realm when "the Thing itself speak[s]" (*SVII* 132), we are engaged in a project of *adjustment* in which we seek to "speak away" the real of racial constitution, articulating it in symbolic terms and thereby defusing its traumatic aspect. James Baldwin dismisses such projects of adaptation: "I was not even remotely tempted by the possibilities of psychiatry and psychoanalysis," he writes. " . . . [A]nyone who thought seriously that I had any desire to be 'adjusted' to this society had to be ill" ("Here" 688). From his earliest work, Lacan too unfailingly criticizes clinical work that aims at symbolic adjustment and adaptation. What Lacanian psychoanalysis, in its ethical dimension, is interested in is, instead, the becoming of a symbolic order through that which subsists as inassimilable within its framework. In symbolic terms, this goal registers as insanity, as the impossible. Yet, Baldwin and Lacan make this the whole point of their ethics: as Baldwin notes, "in our time, as in every time, the impossible is the least that one can demand" (*Fire* 379); for Lacan, similarly, "[o]ne must not be satisfied . . . with anything less than the impossible" (Penney 35).

Wright, too, suggests in his work that race—the mask-as-the-*objet-petit-a*—is that which sticks in the throat, impedes the smooth functioning of the (white) symbolic order. For him, the ethical answer is not to adjust; in *Native Son*, he ridicules the inadequacy of Mr. Dalton's and Jan Erlone's attempts at problem-solving with their liberal invitations to Bigger to "'talk it over'" (44, 146). Rather, he insists on the radical, violent inassimilability of the real of race into existing symbolic circuits. Seeing race as real allows us to understand the emphasis on the temporal dynamics in Wright's, Fanon's, and Lacan's mobilizations of tragedy. For them, the real may actualize the future anterior of a symbolic constellation, the "will have been" of a future whose contingencies can be narrated only in retrospect.

With the material I engage here, I thus argue for the de-privileging of sexual difference as the sole real difference. If the real does not have content as such—if it is the realm of a primordial splitting around which desire and drive circulate—then a symbolic order's specific organization around this lack need not take the exclusive form of sexuation. I suggest that our experience of lack is determined by the contingencies of the network that comprises the symbolic order. In the examples with which I am concerned here, race functions as the object-cause of the symbolic order; consequently, I have called this the white symbolic order. That race is of primary, real significance in the symbolic constellation I deal with here is suggested by the feminist scholars Barbara Smith and Beverly Smith, who, discussing the lynching of black women, note: "The horrors that we have experienced have absolutely everything to do with them *not even viewing us as women*" (122). In some of the most violent forms of the white symbolic order, racial difference trumps sexual difference. Indeed, Smith and Smith conclude that the symbolic reality they are concerned with revolves as much around racial as sexual difference: "There's hardly a thing in this world in our experience that is not referred to being either Black or white, from animals on—people talking about white dogs" (125). Similarly, as the Daltons' door is opened for Bigger for the first time, the temporal sequence of his perception confirms the priority of race in his symbolic universe: "He saw a white face. It was a woman" (38).

FROM ACTING TO THE ACT

If we thus de-emphasize the connection between the real and sexual difference, we can understand Wright's and Fanon's characterization of resistance in terms of the different subject positions vis-à-vis jouissance. In Wright, the racialized subject's symbolic jouissance emerges as the self-defeating, demeaning masquerade of "acting" that responds to the white fantasy about the (colonized, racialized) other. Such acting stages the "comedy" of a failed relationship in condemning the subject to an endless performance that responds to the white symbolic fantasy. While in Lacanian theory this acting is a symbolic response to the impossibility of (sexual) relation, it also names an imaginary response in that it is doomed to repeat the existing structures of symbolization. Its correlates in Wright and Fanon are Tyree's humble deference to the white law and Mayotte Capécia's compulsive affirmation of her "denegrification."[48] Yet, these examples must be considered in conjunction with another form of response to the racialized symbolic that Wright and Fanon describe—a response embodied in the figures of Aunt Sue and the Algerian women. These tragic heroines morph the *acting* that imaginarily complements symbolic fantasies into the violent *act* of Other jouissance.

The New Lacanians have regarded symbolic acting and the real act as irreconcilable. For Žižek, "[t]he very masculine *activity* is already an escape from the abysmal dimension of the feminine *act*. The 'break with nature' is on the side of woman, and man's compulsive activity is ultimately nothing but a desperate attempt to repair the traumatic incision of this rupture" (*Enjoy* 46).

However, Wright and Fanon see an unpredictable relation between imaginary performances and real violence. For both, men's acting more often functions in the register of symbolic jouissance, supporting racist fantasies. Women, on the other hand, can court Other jouissance, the beyond of symbolization: like Sue, they are less likely to be immobilized in imaginary acting, presumably because their sexuation allows real identifications. As opposed to the jouissance that props up fantasies of difference, such feminine jouissance may precipitate a symbolic rupture.

Thus, if symbolic jouissance figures as a mechanism of *ego identifications*, an act is premised on *an identification with the real*. I suggest that it is to the difficulty of obtaining radical symbolic change through ego identifications that Wright responds in his dismissal of the subaltern performativity that characterizes Tyree of *The Long Dream*. It is here, too, that we can situate the significance of Algerian women's mimicry as "an authentic birth in a pure state, without preliminary instruction" (*Dying* 50). What Fanon describes in the struggle of decolonization is an identification with the real, a strategy that bears a troubled, unpredictable relation to temporality. Anticolonial resistance should not be limited to a reversal of aggression that forces the colonialist regime to encounter its own violence, but should induce what Samira Kawash, after Walter Benjamin, refers to as "divine violence," or what we can call *real violence*. In Fanon, Kawash identifies two forms of violence, one "mythical," the other "divine." The former, which "found[s] a new arrangement of rule within the flow of history," can be located in the imaginary register of performance and resistance. Divine violence, on the other hand, must be understood as "a non-instrumental violence, a sovereign violence that operates outside the means-ends relation": it "would herald the blasting open of history to an order not after but on the other side of colonialism" (241). Lacanian theory—to which Kawash alludes—becomes helpful here, for, as Dean writes, Lacan offers us precisely such "a nonmimetic account of identification based on the concept of the real" (*Beyond* 72). In this, Lacan allows us to flesh out Susan Schwartz's undertheorized suggestion that, in "Algeria Unveiled" and other texts by Fanon, "birth is a figure of rupture . . . which opens a space for imagining social reorganisation" (198). What the tragic heroine's act may elicit is a symbolic reorganization through the real—a domain that we must thus understand as "generative, [and] not simply constraining" (Dean, *Beyond* 51).

Criticizing Judith Butler's notion of performativity, Dean goes on to argue that "the concept of mimicry situates identification at the level of imaginary representations, excluding the real from consideration" and consequently "restrict[ing] vital political questions to the arena of ego identifications" (71). Yet, Wright and Fanon suggest that imaginary and real identifications bear a more ambivalent relation to one another. While we can understand Sue's violent response qua Other jouissance, we should note that her act is enabled by the role of a "nigger woman," her wearing the mask-as-*objet-a* that finds its support in (and sustains) the white symbolic fantasy of racial difference.

Yet, this performance, which is not readily distinguishable from the demeaning, emasculating clowning that arouses Wright's ire, enables the emergence of what we could call, pace Fanon, revolutionary violence. It allows Sue to deliver an "answer of the real" to the white law as she twists the comedy of the failed (racial) relationship into a tragedy that evokes the inassimilable underside of the (racial) symbolic order.

It is crucial to note in this conjunction that, even though Wright denounces acting, he does concede that dissemblance, rather than merely capturing the subject as the master's fool, has facilitated anticolonial revolution. "I must say in all fairness," he writes in "Psychological Reactions," "that this duality of attitude has really aided the Asian and African in his dealing with white Westerners. In almost every instance of colonial revolt, the white Westerner has had absolutely no inkling of the revolt until it burst over his head, so carefully hidden had the rebels kept their feelings and attitudes. In short, oppression helps to forge in the oppressed the very qualities that eventually bring about the downfall of the oppressor" (*White* 21). And as he continues elsewhere, because of the efficacy of subaltern performances, "imperialists of the twentieth century are men who are always being constantly and unpleasantly surprised" (*Black Power* 132). Indeed, "rarely do things work out . . . the way the white man had hoped and thought they would, in the countries he colonized" ("Conversation" 161). A primary example of this unexpectedness is the way in which *acting*, like Sue's performance, may enable *the act* of real, revolutionary violence.

Let us, then, spell out the ramifications that Wright's and Fanon's models of revolutionary becoming have for our understanding of psychoanalytic theory. While recent Lacanian scholarship has assumed the incompatibility of the two forms of feminine jouissance, "Bright and Morning Star" and "Algeria Unveiled" suggest the Möbius-like interimplication of these two modes. Consequently—and perhaps surprisingly—our dialogue between psychoanalysis and critical race theory helps us reassess the fraught relation between two strands of feminist scholarship that, since their emergence in the early 1990s, have been associated with Butler's work and that of the New Lacanians. While Butler argues that the necessary iterability of the law allows inaccurate repetitions that can become "rallying points for a certain resistance to classification and identity as such" ("Imitation" 16), Copjec, Dean, and Žižek insist that Butlerian performativity preempts radical symbolic change. For them, Butler fails to appreciate "the distinction between imaginary resistance (false transgression that reasserts the symbolic status quo and even serves as a positive condition of its functioning) and actual symbolic rearticulation via the intervention of the Real of an *act*," which Antigone embodies (Žižek, *Ticklish* 262; see also "*Da*" 220). That resisting performances are caught in the economy they ostensibly threaten is suggested by Baldwin's comments on "acting": "even a 'bad nigger,'" he writes, "is, inevitably, giving something of a performance, even if the entire purpose of his performance is to terrify or blackmail white people" ("Alas"

281). The performance of the thug repeats the mechanism that produced the minstrel coon caricatures.

Wright's and Fanon's descriptions of acting and revolutionary violence imply, however, that the two models, those of acting and the act, are not irreconcilable. Performativity, that is, may not be irrevocably imaginary, cut off from the ethics of the real. It may, on the contrary, open the temporality of the real, of becoming. Consequently, given the inextricability of the three Lacanian registers, acting, or what Butler calls performativity, may not be essentially inimical to the dynamics that the New Lacanians have identified as the subject's only freedom: the act that can undo, or traverse, symbolic fantasy in an incalculable, unforeseeable way. In Wright and Fanon, acting, in its proximity to the real as the symbolic order's internal point of failure, can induce the kind of symbolic change that Lacan's theory of tragedy is concerned with. The examples of the Algerian women and Sue suggest a link between performativity and the tragic act: performance qua imaginary identification (Algerians as Europeanized or submissive Muslim women; Sue's mask of the mammy) can accelerate into the real act, the becoming-tragic of the Algerian guerrillas and Aunt Sue, that is not, to paraphrase Fanon, supported by ego identifications. Such terrorism, as Kawash shows, figures in Fanon as the opening to a violent, unpredictable becoming. While the New Lacanians have insisted on the absolute distinction between acting qua performativity and the act qua the answer of the real—and while Butler never considers the latter option—my reading of racial and sexed performances in Wright and Fanon suggests their unpredictable inextricability.[49]

Despite the linkage between Butler and the Lacanians, their projects differ in their approaches to the risk of becoming as an unforeseeable emergence.[50] From her earliest work, Butler has consistently posited the Lacanian real as an extrasymbolic realm of radical alterity that prevents any reconfiguring of the symbolic order, that bears no relation to becoming.[51] Instead of understanding it as an unformed zone of radical emptiness and unactualization, she inhabits the real with the abjected and the unrecognized (see also Dean, "Art" 26). In her earlier work, the gender-non-conforming bodies of the effeminate gay man and the butch lesbian are relegated, through social non-recognition, into the real (*Bodies* 96); later, this outside comes to be inhabited also by the transgendered (*Undoing* chap. 3), those living in nonheterosexual kinship arrangements (chap. 5), and lives that are not "grievable" because not "recognizably human" (*Precarious* xiv, 89, and passim). Whereas the New Lacanians seek to politicize the act that may actualize the real, Butler doubts the political viability of symbolic suicide. As she writes in *Antigone's Claim*, in Lacan, "[t]he law that mandates [Antigone's] unlivability is not one that might profitably be broken" (40). In this she is, of course, absolutely correct: a real act can never be undertaken for *profit*; symbolic change through the real must remain incalculable, as much as Antigone cannot have a "calculated end" in mind (Shepherdson, "Of Love" 70). While it seems that Butler's theory of performativity-as-becoming[52] at times courts the ethics of incalculable change,[53] she seems unwilling to relinquish performativity's potential for strategic, "profitabl[e]" symbolic intervention. Arguably, Butler thus evinces the unwillingness of political theorists and activists to consider change that cannot be integrated into their revolutionary calculations, which Elizabeth Grosz speaks of: "politics seems to revel in the idea of progress, development, movement, but the very political discourses that seem to advocate it most vehemently . . . seem terrified by the idea of a transformation somehow beyond the control of the very revolutionaries who seek it, of a kind of 'anarchization' of the future" ("Thinking" 17). Lacanian theory of becoming, on the other hand, insists on the unforeseeability of symbolic change: there are no guarantees that beyond the Oedipal father we find anything better than our current conditions of symbolic existence.

Sue's "actual" death at the end of "Bright and Morning Star" emphasizes the dangerous character of the tragic act and the ethics of the real. Like Antigone, who is walled alive in a tomb for defying Creon's orders, Sue, shot by the sheriff's men, is "buried in the depths of her star" (263), a location which names at once the law's outraged retaliation and its inability to reach her. There are no easy politics of resistance to be drawn from this scene, for Sue's demise does not guarantee what symbolic change, if any, her terrorism has had on the white law. Hers is a real act, which never promises anything beyond its immediate execution. Yet, the raindrops that fall on her as she lays dying, like soil on a coffin, return us to the opening of the story, where Sue, in a moment of foreshadowing, links her watery death to fertility and production (221). Correspondingly, the final lines of the short story fleetingly suggest that her act as the living dead—"the dead that never dies"—may have "doomed" those whose existence is bound up in the existing symbolic configurations.

Similarly, what Fanon's feminist critics have argued is his failure to allow women's concerns to inflect the anticolonial struggle points instead, from the Lacanian perspective, to his troubled efforts to open the realm of becoming, to seek the way in which subaltern performances under the colonizing gaze can precipitate to revolutionary violence. The tragic aspect of the Algerian women as well as Aunt Sue's suicidal act points to strictly unforeseeable shifts in the symbolic order.

CHAPTER 4

The Optical Trade

Through Southern Spectacles

It is hard to have a southern overseer; it is worse to have a northern one; but worst of all when you are the slave-driver yourself.

—Henry David Thoreau, *Walden; or, Life in the Woods*

Living in the South doomed me to look always through eyes which the South had given me, and bewilderment and fear made me mute and afraid. But after I had left the South, luck gave me other eyes, new eyes with which to look at the meaning of what I'd lived through. . . . Books were the windows through which I looked at the world. . . . To me reading was a kind of remembering. . . . [A]t once I was able, in looking back through alien eyes, to see my own life.

—Richard Wright, "*Black Boy* and Reading"

As a number of critics have noted, Wright's autobiography follows African American slave narratives in tracing the flight of its protagonist from the white supremacist South to the relative freedom of the North.[1] The experiences of reading and writing—the experiences of the literary, as I will call them—constitute a central component in such narratives of ascent: as *Black Boy* proceeds, "literate mobility" slowly takes over "illiterate immobility" (Stepto 132). In this, Wright's narrator echoes slave narrators, who "literally wrote [their] way out of slavery" (Gates, *Figures* 13). In the most concrete and immediate sense, having verifiably produced written texts, some slaves—Phillis Wheatley being the best known example—were released, the royalties of their literary products used to trade for their freedom or their masters manumitting them as a reward for such uniquely human pursuits. Moreover, the slaves' written documents played a significant role in reconfiguring the Africans' and their descendants' place in the West. Cultures considered to lack written documents were, as Hegel deemed, immobilized in a limbo outside History (*Philosophy of History* 199). Literacy's importance in contesting views that considered Africans "a race of children" (Hegel, "Anthropology" 40) is underlined by Noah Webster's 1790 admonition for the necessity of education in the new nation: "You have been children long enough, subject to the control and subservient to the interest of a haughty parent" (82; qtd. in Salvino 140). The Africans' ability to write refuted the Enlightenment continuum of logic according to which—as Frantz Fanon puts it—"Negroes are savages, brutes, illiterates" (*Black* 117), allowing the descendants of African slaves "to demonstrate [their] own membership in the human community" (Gates, *Signifying* 128).

Yet, reading and writing proved ambivalent technologies of liberation. Like slave narrators before him, Wright does not find in the literary an experience of an unambiguous freedom, transcendence, or flight. He follows the likes of Frederick Douglass in that he recognizes the true dimensions of his bondage through the literary: reading "open[s one's] eyes to the horrible pit, but to no ladder upon which to get out" (Douglass, *Narrative* 42). The experience of the literary easily becomes "a curse rather than a blessing" (42), an experience of one's immobility and confinement as much as that of an escape. In Jacques Derrida's words, "The god of writing is the god of the *pharmakon*" (*Dissemination* 94). Yet, it is such experiences of ambivalence and promise that characterize the mobility of desire from which the black subject has been excluded in the white symbolic order. It is also here that Wright's continual emphasis on the discovery of new perspectives through reading gains its significance. The experience of the literary allows Wright's autobiographical narrator to shift the perspective into which racial subjection has confined him.

In this chapter, I trace Wright's rewriting of the slave narratives' scenes of racial subjection and experiences of the literary. I begin with Douglass's autobiographical narrator, whose experiences are often recalled when, in discussions of slavery, an optimistic emphasis is placed on the possibility of the subject's resistance to violent regimes of subjugation. In these discussions, the famous scene of the narrator's fight with the slave-breaker Edward Covey is taken as an example of how, by risking his life, the slave is capable of wresting his freedom and "manhood" from the seemingly overwhelming violence and oppression of slavery. However, in his autobiography, Wright, writing exactly hundred years after Douglass, illustrates how such manifestations of resistance have in turn elicited further, unexpected forms of subjection. In recasting Douglass's description of slave-breaking and possible resistance thereto into the early-twentieth-century American South, Wright points to the shifts of racial violence in the American society. He shows how such forms of corporeal violence as slave-breaking and lynching had by the 1920s been taken over by (or all but disappeared into) self-breaking, achieved through the injunctions of what I call, after Wright, *the optical trade*. Naming both an economy of the visible and a historical shift toward disembodied surveillance, the optical trade, as Wright demonstrates, organizes and sustains the racial logic of twentieth-century America.

While in this study my theoretical focus remains on Lacanian psychoanalysis, I propose we begin conceptualizing the differences between these two forms of subjection through Hegelian and Foucauldian frameworks. It is easy to understand why Hegel, with his "all-embracing idea of reason" (Marcuse 24), would invite an optimistic reading of the futurity of slavery. As Judith Butler observes, in its emphasis on the negative the Hegelian system lends itself to a political reading where histories of the oppressed, replete with experiences of loss, open onto a different future: "Hegel provided a way to discern reason in the negative, that is, to derive the transformative potential from every experience of defeat" (*Subjects* 62). Tracing Hegel's influence in subsequent theories of liberation, Herbert Marcuse similarly notes that "Hegel's optimism is based upon a destructive conception of the given" (26). According to Marcuse, Hegel opposed the English empiricists because of their insistence on "the ultimate authority of the fact," of that which exists, which leads to "the conservative and affirmative attitude of their philosophy: it induces thought to be satisfied with the facts, to renounce any transgression beyond them and to bow to the given state of affairs" (27). In the movement of the negative, Hegel found a mode of becoming, whose unfolding in history has had a great appeal for theorists of slavery. Even if history tells us otherwise, the Hegelian system insists that, "[b]y virtue of its own power, reason would triumph over social irrationality and overthrow the oppressors of mankind" (Marcuse 7).

Hegel has become influential for theorists of slavery especially through Alexandre Kojève's reconsideration of the dialectics of negativity and overcoming. As Kojève writes, only the slave, through his experiences of mortal terror and work, is capable of true revolutionary action: "this revolutionary transformation of the World presupposes the 'negation,' the non-accepting of the given World *in its totality*. And the origin of this absolute negation can only be the absolute dread inspired by the given World, or more precisely, by that which, or by him who, dominates this World, by the Master of this World." The Master, on the other hand, can be at best "a 'skillful' reformer, or better, a conformer" (29). For critics of the Hegelian bent, the working slave's overcoming of the idle master is embodied in Douglass's challenge to Covey. The autobiographical narrator's uprising prefaces a "dialectical overcoming" of slavery and hence points towards "authentic freedom." Douglass thus proves to be a true "revolutionary." Having overcome Covey the master, Douglass the slave is on his way to authentic self-consciousness, which is possible only for the subject who has experienced slavery.

The Foucauldian/Wrightian reading of slavery's afterlife in post-Reconstruction America, however, offers no such comforting trust on "historical evolution" (Kojève 51). Instead, Wright points to the panoptic regime's superior efficacy over the spectacle of punishment in ensuring subjection. In this economy, the kind of overcoming that Douglass embodies may indeed lead to another trap where slaves are enslaved even more efficiently, not through their ruthless masters but through their own disciplinary gaze, instituting a kind of an "unhappy consciousness." Wright's recontextualization of slave-breaking thus arguably illustrates the by-now familiar Foucauldian thesis about the enfolding of external injunctions into an internalized code in the modern power/knowledge regimes.[2] While the spectacles of overtly violent racism were partially disappearing by the time of Wright's narrative, forms of subjugation had simultaneously mutated into a more economically disseminated disciplinary regime, whose power rested on the violence of the visible.

In the subsequent sections of this chapter, I illustrate the slave narrators' and (particularly) Wright's negotiation of racial visibility through the experience of the literary. This experience, in all its ambivalence, entails what for Lacan is the mobility of desire. Yet, this mobility is not a stage in the kind of "historical evolution" that Hegelian dialectics posits. Indeed, part of the ambivalence of this experience comes from the fact that it does not constitute a definitive trajectory for the subject to orient him- or herself on. It does not provide a destination for one's flight but retains a dangerously open relation to futurity. It is here that, arguably, the experiences of slave narrators and Wright are incompatible with the constitutive thrust of the Hegelian system, especially as it was articulated in the 1807 manuscript of the *Phenomenology*, where the Spirit's telos in the Absolute becomes more emphasized than in Hegel's earlier work (Marcuse 92). In her consideration of Hegel's influence in subsequent theories of desire, Butler insists: "The negative is also human freedom, human desire, the possibility to create anew. . . . The negative showed itself in Hegelian terms not merely as death, but as a sustained possibility of *becoming*" (*Subjects* 62). At stake, however, is the precise form of this becoming. If we take seriously the paradigmatic tendencies in Hegel, we must concede Spirit's telos in the Absolute. Spirit is "the process of its own becoming, the circle which presupposes its end as its purpose, and has its end for its beginning; it becomes concrete and actual only by being carried out, and by the end it involves" (Hegel, *Phenomenology* 81). As Derrida notes, "Absolute knowledge is *present* at the zero point of the philosophical exposition" (*Dissemination* 20). Consequently, "[t]he *Aufhebung* is included *within* the circle of absolute knowledge, never exceeds its closure, never suspends the totality of discourse, work, meaning, law, etc." (*Writing* 275). The appeal of the Hegelian approach to readings of slavery is in the teleological certainty with which it works toward the synthesis of Spirit. As opposed to Butler, whose work in its entirety can be seen as an effort to recuperate Hegel for a politically inflected philosophy that opens "a futural form of politics that cannot be fully anticipated" (*Undoing* 180),[3] I suggest in this and the following chapter that, formulating an understanding of an open becoming, we turn to Lacan's later work. It is this openness of futurity—which, as I suggest at the end of this chapter, can be seen, despite Lacan's explicit dismissal of Darwinism, in terms of *an evolutionary becoming*—that in the experience of the literary elicits the slave narrators' anxiety and ambivalence.

Before turning to Lacan, I theorize *the historical shift* that I locate in the intertextuality of Douglass's and Wright's autobiographies with Foucault's genealogical work on the disciplinary systems of the West. In a cautionary note about methodology, Richard Brodhead warns against re-cognizing in our readings of nineteenth- and twentieth-century North American culture the epistemic shifts Foucault speaks of (17).[4] He insists that, while engaging in dialogues between theory and history, we should carefully heed "the interplay of forces specific to actual social sites" (17). The primary way in which I hope to disenable the possible Procrustean violence of theoretical frameworks is by attending closely to Douglass's and Wright's literary works. However, while my focus here is on what these two African American texts, a century apart, suggest about the shift in nineteenth- and twentieth-century racial relations, a number of historical accounts of post-Reconstruction America corroborate "the optical trade" that Foucault and Wright suggest to have taken place. Historians make it clear that the violence *Black Boy*'s adolescent narrator would have faced in the early 1920s was obviously different, but not necessarily lessened, from the brutality of slavery that Douglass had struggled with. After the "grand but brief interlude of multiracial democratic experimentation" (West, "Ignoble" 53) of Reconstruction, by the turn of the century a "stiff conformity and fanatical rigidity" had taken over Southern race relations (Woodward, *Strange* 44).[5] C. Vann Woodward mentions Wright's home state Mississippi as the "pioneer of the movement" for black disfranchisement (83) and goes on to point out that segregation showed no signs of easing in the 1920s, the decade that Wright describes in the passages on which I concentrate in the next section. "In fact," he writes, "the Jim Crow laws were elaborated and further expanded in those years" (116).[6] The growth of Jim Crow was made possible by the shifts in the way the color line was policed. Tracing the NAACP's antilynching campaigns, Robert L. Zangrando notes that "[a]s opposition [to lynching] mounted in the 1920s and 1930s, the number of reported lynchings declined, but more subtle forms of brutality evolved" (4). By this, Zangrando points to how lynchings ceased to be widely advertised entertainment for large crowds and instead were carried out by smaller groups of assailants; how news about lynchings was more often suppressed than distributed to the media, as had been done in earlier decades; and how executions were sometimes sanctioned in mock trials preceding the violence. I argue that Wright's autobiography, in describing the optical trade, suggests further ways in which racial violence became less tangible yet more effective in the early decades of the twentieth century.

If my analysis of Douglass and Wright yields a rather pessimistic reading of slavery's afterlife—where "slavery is dead but inescapable" (Rogin, "Francis" 76)—I am not alone in noting such tendencies. Indeed, the problematic I point to has been catalogued in more depth and range by Saidiya V. Hartman in *Scenes of Subjection: Terror, Slavery, and Self-Making in Nineteenth-Century America* (1991). Yet, following a number of his predecessors in the

African American tradition, Wright finds in the experience of the literary a potentially effective tool with which to undercut what Ann Laura Stoler calls racism's "polyvalent mobility" (376). This tool, which will concern us also in the next chapter, mobilizes the racialized subject in a way that, notwithstanding the great danger it poses for the subject itself, may allow a more sustained challenge to the white symbolic order than the one Bigger Thomas mounts.

FROM SLAVE-BREAKING TO SELF-BREAKING

In *Discipline and Punish* (1975), Foucault famously traces the transitions that he claims to have shaped the penal system and the whole of Western societies during the seventeenth and eighteenth centuries. He contends that "the gloomy festival of punishment" of the seventeenth century—characterized by an excess of violence, by the protracted torture of criminal(ized) bodies, and by the public display of the execution proceedings—was slowly superseded by a disciplinary practice where the "body as the major target of penal repression disappeared" (8). Foucault argues that, in the latter form of punishment, disciplinary power "imposes on those whom it subjects a principle of compulsory visibility. In discipline, it is the subjects who have to be seen" (187). He also stresses that the panoptic surveillance that finds its extreme form in the carceral situation is by no means limited to prisons or other disciplinary institutions such as the army, the schoolroom, the orphanage, or the monastery.[7] In these, one can observe in an explicit form the strategies of surveillance and discipline discernible in the society at large: "[the prison] was only the concentrated, exemplary, symbolic forms of all these institutions of sequestration created in the nineteenth century. . . . The prison is the reverse image of society, an image turned into a threat" (Foucault, "Truth" 85).

That slavery included practices that Foucault would name those of the spectacle is clear from Douglass's 1845 narrative. In a crucial, early scene in the *Narrative*, the young narrator describes the sight of a female relative being mercilessly beaten:

> No words, no tears, no prayers, from his gory victim, seemed to move [the master's] iron heart from its bloody purpose. The louder she screamed, the harder he whipped; and where the blood ran fastest, there he whipped longest. He would whip her to make her scream, and whip her to make her hush; and not until overcome by fatigue, would he cease to swing the blood-clotted cowskin. I remember the first time I ever witnessed this horrible exhibition. I was quite a child, but I well remember it. I never shall forget it whilst I remember any thing. It was the first of a long series of such outrages, of which I was doomed to be a witness and a participant. It struck me with awful force. It was the blood-stained gate, the entrance to the hell of slavery, through which I was about to pass. It was the most terrible spectacle. I wish I could commit to paper the feelings with which I beheld it. (18)

Even though the lashes do not land on his back, this "most terrible spectacle" "str[ikes]" the young spectator "with awful force"; even though he is not directly subjected to the beating, the scene he is forced to witness nevertheless ushers him through "the entrance to the hell of slavery." In other words, the violent, public scene of the punishment sutures the narrator into his "place" within the violent economy of slavery.

Clearly, however, the spectacle of the punishment is supported by other strategies of subjugation—strategies which seem to correspond to the Foucauldian concept of disciplinary power. The most famous passages of "slave breaking" are those where Douglass describes his servitude under the "negro-breaker" Covey.[8] Using deception to catch his slaves "neglecting" their duties of constant toil (and thus to justify consequent punishment), Covey surreptitiously watches over his servants: "His comings were like a thief in the night. He appeared to us as being ever at hand. He was under every tree, behind every stump, in every bush, and at every window, on the plantation" (57). Notably, he successfully induces in the slaves a kind of paranoia similar to the disciplinary subject's sense of being under the ubiquitous gaze in Jeremy Bentham's Panopticon: "He had the faculty of making us feel that he was always present" (*Life* 570). Douglass's account suggests, then, that in the African American history, there is an overlap in the two deployments of power: Covey's strategy partakes in both spectacle and panopticism.

We must note, however, that, despite the fact that the slaves seem to be uncertain whether or not they are being watched over, the master's gaze nevertheless fails to become properly panoptic. The slaves, for example, manage to exchange mutinous words among themselves. As Douglass recalls, he and other slaves "never called [Covey] by any other name than '*the snake*.' We fancied that in his eyes and gait we could see a snakish resemblance." For the servants, Covey's "trickery" is a decidedly "unmanly" practice (*My Bondage* 265, 266). Clearly, Douglass is here able to cast a gaze of contempt upon the master's strategies and distance himself from the scene of surveillance.

According to Foucault, the staging of state-sanctioned violence in the seventeenth century invited repercussions by which those wielding the power were themselves threatened. Public execution, he writes, "was . . . dangerous, in that it provided a support for a confrontation between the violence of the king and the violence of the people. It was as if the sovereign power did not see, in this emulation of atrocity, a challenge that it itself threw down and which might one day be taken up" (73). This challenge, of course, is what Douglass's narrator responds to in his counterviolence and resistance to Covey. After several vicious beatings, he decides rather to fight his master to death than to succumb to another flogging. It is here that the power balance between the two men changes: "This battle with Mr. Covey was the turning-point in my career as a slave. It rekindled the few expiring embers of freedom, and revived within me a sense of my own manhood" (*Narrative* 65). The young Douglass's resistance was part of the costly consequences of slave system's sovereign violence that

W. E. B. Du Bois sardonically identifies as one of the driving forces behind abolition: "It was seen, first in England and later in other countries, that slavery as an industrial system could not be made to work satisfactorily in modern times. Its cost was too great, and one of the causes of this cost was the slave insurrections from the very beginning, when the slaves rose of the plantation of Diego Columbus down to the Civil War in America" (*Negro* 159–60; see also Du Bois, *Africa* 47).

In *Black Boy*, Wright illustrates the way in which such problems were resolved in the twentieth century. Indeed, scenes of uprising or rebellion are missing from his autobiography. Instead, he suggests over and again that, for a racially marked subject, a crucial survival skill in the South is the ability to *read* race and to show that s/he is literate in matters of race: to show by demeanor that one knows one's place. The fact that the narrator proves to be less than agile in learning the significance of color leads him to several confrontations with his environment. Among these, there are scenes which vary from the violence exhibited by white people (see, for example, 172–75) to other, seemingly less injurious moments of guidance by his fellow blacks. Here, I want to concentrate on an example of the latter that takes place as one of the narrator's well-meaning friends, a young man called Griggs, instructs him in the importance in learning to *see* color in one's environment and, further, in controlling what one lets white people see. Griggs, whom the narrator meets washing his employer's windows, scolds the narrator for his inappropriate behavior: "'See?' he said triumphantly, pointing his finger at me. 'There it is, *now*! It's in your face. . . .' He paused and looked about; the streets were filled with white people. He spoke to me in a low, full tone. 'Dick, look, you're black, black, *black*, see? Can't you understand that?' (176). Drawing attention to Dick's failure to "look" properly—to see and to show that he is "black, black, *black*"—the friend exhorts him to pay attention to the color of the people around them, to learn to see the racial markedness of his environment: "'You act around white people as if you didn't know that they were white. And they *see* it.'" Griggs has to spell out for Dick the disastrous consequences that being color blind can have: "'White people make it their business to watch niggers,'" he explains. "'And they pass the word around. . . . You're marked already'" (176).

To Griggs's advice that he should be careful not to "'act around white people as if he didn't know they were white,'" the narrator remarks, "'Oh, Christ, I can't be a slave'" (177). For the narrator, acting according to the code proposed by Griggs is tantamount to being enslaved. Yet, acceding to such slavery may be required for survival:

> "But you've got to eat," [Griggs] said.
>
> "Yes, I've got to eat."
>
> "Then start acting like it," he hammered at me, pounding his fist in his palm. "When you're in front of white people, *think* before you act, *think* before you speak. . . ." (176)

The narrator is faced with a choice—whether or not to become literate in the racial code of the South—that is, precisely, an overdetermined and, hence, an impossible choice because at stake is his existence: "I fought with myself, telling myself that I had to master this thing, that my life depended upon it" (186). If he will not conform to the code, he will not make a living and will possibly be killed. Here, the narrator encounters the power and lure of subjection. Butler argues that one of the ways in which power induces subjection is by promising continued existence as its corollary (*Psychic* 20–21). However, as Abdul JanMohamed compellingly argues in *The Death-Bound-Subject*, while Wright's narrator is promised continued existence if he conforms to the Southern, racialized code of conduct (he will be employed and is not immediately threatened with violence), subjection will condemn the racialized subject to a kind of immobility, a living death. As I will argue in the next chapter, while this condition is related to what Orlando Patterson has called the slaves' "social death," the immobility it induces differs from slavery's "profound natal alienation" (38) in naming a kind of a terroristic suture into and by the optical trade, from whose circuits *alienation* offers a way out.

For the narrator, however, it seems impossible to embody this role perfectly: "What Griggs was saying was true, but it was simply utterly impossible for me to calculate, to scheme, to act, to plot all the time. I would remember to dissemble for short periods, then I would forget and act straight and human again, not with the desire to harm anybody, but merely forgetting the artificial status of race and class" (177). Acting properly requires an ability "to calculate, to scheme"—to adhere to the rules of a certain economy. These rules baffle the narrator. However, Griggs knows of a job opening in the vicinity and, having instructed the narrator, informs him: "'There's an optical company upstairs and the boss is a Yankee from Illinois. . . . He wants to *break* a colored boy *into* the optical trade'" (177–78; emphases added). The narrator is given, in other words, another chance to learn "the optical trade," the economy of the visible. Here, the exigencies of capitalist economy form the background of, or at least are ever-present in, the maintenance of social hierarchies based on race as the commonsensical criterion of visibility. Learning to see the right way is potentially a "trade" for the narrator, just as "watch[ing] niggers" is made, as Griggs puts it, by "white people" into "their business."[9]

We must read the verb "to break (in)" in its double meaning in the phrase "to break a colored boy into the optical trade." It signifies not only an act of introduction but also one of a violent, forceful subjugation. "Colored boys" like the narrator have to be broken by breaking them into the optical trade, that is, by teaching them the appropriate way of seeing and being seen, of performing and gazing.[10] The phrase gains its full significance when placed in the context of slavery and Douglass's *Narrative*. As the narrator's anguished words, "I can't be a slave," suggest, "breaking (in)" connotes also the process of "breaking (in) slaves," teaching them their roles and duties by crushing their will with floggings and beatings, a practice in which Covey and such fictional counterparts as Simon Legree excel. Having listened to Griggs's instructions on how to act among white people, the narrator of *Black Boy* says, "'I guess you're right. . . . I've got to watch myself, break myself . . . '" (177; second ellipsis in original). As the shift from Griggs's "breaking into" to the narrator's "breaking oneself" demonstrates, the professionalization of colored boys in and by the optical trade entails violence, which may be most efficacious when self-inflicted. Wright's autobiographical narrator would have us believe that his failure in breaking himself resulted more from a hapless, unwitting nonconformity than from conscious rebellion: "Perhaps I had waited too long to start working for white people; perhaps I should have begun earlier, when I was younger—as most of the other black boys had done—and perhaps by now the tension would have become an habitual condition, contained and controlled by reflex. But that was not to be my lot; I was always to be conscious of it, brood over it, carry it in my heart, live with it, sleep with it, fight with it" (143). Consequently, as Griggs observes, his is a particularly "'tough break'" (183), in all the senses of the phrase.

In the transition from Douglass to Wright, then, the *surveillance* and *slave-breaking* by the master is turned into *self-surveillance* and *self-breaking.* As his later writings clearly show, Douglass was aware of such mutations in the racist procedures of post-Reconstruction America. While writing in 1894 he points to peonage, disfranchisement, and the "mobocratic crimes" of lynching as bespeaking "the determination of slavery to perpetuate itself, if not under one form, then under another" ("Why" 753, 770), I suggest that Wright, in *Black Boy*, observes how slavery had further metamorphosed into practices of self-breaking. In early-twentieth century America, in other words, the racial logic that sustained slavery was not only inscribed into the penal code (as Angela Davis notes) and morphed into the practices of disfranchisement and lynching (as Douglass argues), but also internalized as the injunctions of the optical trade, where the demand for surveillance is posited upon the subject him/herself, hence not allowing any emancipatory syntheses of the master–slave dialectic.

LYNCHING AND THE OPTICAL TRADE

Considering the brutality of lynching practices, which survived well into the twentieth century and the era that Wright describes in *Black Boy*, it would be obscene to argue for a clear break between the modes of spectacle and discipline in the U.S. racial economy.[11] If disciplinary and panoptic strategies are embedded in slavery (Wiegman 39–40), the threat of violence is an integral component of the optical trade. Observing the changes in racial relations in 1920s, Zangrando writes: "With blacks largely disfranchised, segregated, and economically victimized, supremacists could dispense with lynching as an everyday means of manipulation and control. Blacks, however, could never be certain that violence might not recur" (12). In *Black Boy*, Wright suggests the regularity of physical violence in the optical trade by prefacing the scene of Griggs's instruction with examples of white brutality against blacks (two white men assault a black woman, who is consequently arrested for disorderly conduct; the narrator is assailed by a gang of white youths [172–75]).

But above all, in order to learn the optical trade and to act according to its dictates, black boys have to "watch themselves." "'[W]atch yourself and don't get into trouble,'" a white man tells the narrator (181). In Du Boisian terms, he has to learn to utilize "double consciousness," seeing himself through the eyes of others, if he wants to escape becoming a target for violence. While double consciousness entails a visionary potential, in it resides also the violence of the visible that sutures the racialized subject into his/her place much more securely than the spectacle of the punishment, however gruesome and traumatic, that Douglass's young narrator witnesses. Adopting the terminology of trauma studies (see L. Brown), we can say that, in the hundred years that separate the two African American writers, the visible trauma of subjugation in slavery is taken over by the insidious trauma of everyday racism.

However, even though, time and again, the narrator finds himself "resolving to watch [his] every move" (186), he cannot accommodate himself to such self-surveillance but always forgets his place in the optical trade. In working for the optical company, he learns that to occupy his position in the trade is, in a certain sense, to attempt the impossible. The owner of the company tells his two other employees, white men called Pease and Reynolds, "to *break* [the narrator] *in* gradually to the workings of the shop" (179; emphasis added). While Pease and Reynolds seem to agree, the narrator finds himself sweeping the floors and doing other menial tasks, rather than learning to operate the machines with which lenses are ground and polished. When he asks one of the men to guide him in the work so that he could "learn the trade," he gets a hostile response:

> "Nigger, you think you're white, don't you?"
> "No, sir."
> "You're acting mighty like it," he said.
> . . .
> Pease shook his fist in my face.
> "This is a *white* man's work around here," he said. (180)

Finally, the narrator realizes, "I was black; I lived in the South. I would never learn to operate those machines as long as those two men in there stood by them" (184).

As a result of the incident, Pease and Reynolds apparently decide to teach the narrator a lesson. He is confronted by the white men, with Reynolds saying that he heard him refer to his colleague as Pease. This puts the narrator into an unnegotiable double bind. Had he, a black boy, called a white man anything but *mister* or *sir*, he would be beaten. Were he to deny the charge, he would accuse another white man of lying, and would consequently be beaten. In the optical trade, the narrator is positioned in an impossible site where he can make no right move, where violence is inevitable; in Jay Mechlin's folkloric terms, he finds himself faced with a situation of "paradoxical communications" that he cannot negotiate (282).[12] Disoriented, he feels "that the people were unreal, . . . that I had been slapped out of the human race" (182), and resolves to resign from the company. The next day, as he returns to get his final paycheck, the Yankee boss tries to find out what has happened. "An impulse to speak rose in me and died with the realization that I was facing a wall that I would never breech [*sic*]. I tried to speak several times and could make no sounds" (183). Finally, the narrator leaves the optical company, without saying a word to the boss, "[going] into the sunshine and walk[ing] home like a blind man" (185).

The confrontation with Pease and Reynolds reminds the narrator of a lynching of an acquaintance he has heard of. To understand the exact position of black boys in the optical trade, let us consider this scene:

> What I had heard [of the lynching] altered the look of the world, induced in me a temporary paralysis of will and impulse. The penalty of death awaited me if I made a false move and I wondered if it was worth-while to make any move at all. The things that influenced my conduct as a Negro did not have to happen to me directly; I needed but to hear of them to feel their full effects in the deepest layers of my consciousness. Indeed, the white brutality that I had not seen was a more effective control of my behavior than that which I knew. The actual experience would have let me see the realistic outlines of what was really happening, but as long as it remained something terrible and yet remote, something whose horror and blood might descend upon me at any moment, I was compelled to give my entire imagination over to it, an act which blocked the springs of thought and feeling in me, creating a sense of distance between me and the world in which I lived. (164–65)

Hearing of the lynching does something to "the look of the world"—to the narrator's vision of the world and/or the way he feels he is being looked at—and an immobility, "a temporary paralysis," ensues. The narrator wonders whether he should move at all, or just stay where he is, in his place. This paralysis is repeated as he tries to form a response to Pease and Reynolds: "my tongue would not move. . . . I tried to speak several times and could make no sounds" (182, 183). For such paralysis to be induced, it is not necessary for the racial subject to experience a lynching or even witness one—indeed, it seems that the threat of violence works better when it is not experienced first-hand but remains at a remove. Were the narrator to experience the act of violence himself, he might be able to deduce some logic in the way in which it is meted out, to predict its course and recurrence. Now that it remains to a degree invisible, its logic is similarly cloaked, veiled, and becomes more threatening because unpredictable: the narrator, like the colonized subject whom Fanon describes in *The Wretched of the Earth*, "is never sure whether or not he has crossed the frontier" (53).[13] As Richard later muses, "perhaps even a kick was better than uncertainty" (253).

The look of the world here is rendered *in* and *through* Southern spectacles, a term I owe to Pauline Hopkins, who uses it to describe the efforts of Southern proslavery spokespeople at the turn of the century to convince Northerners of history's "misconception" of the slave plantations as places of violence and subjugation.[14] As Hopkins writes, these apologists invite Northerners to view not only the antebellum past but also contemporary racial relations "through Southern spectacles" (*Primer* 21), that is, from a perspective that seeks to unify the nation at the cost of black memory and black lives. Hopkins is undoubtedly aware of her pun: connecting public displays of injury to the production of what is visible and observable in history, the term evokes the antiblack violence, including the practice of lynching, whose resurgence at the end of the nineteenth century Hopkins, in a number of her *Colored American Magazine* articles, connects to the ongoing counterfeiting and obfuscation of black history.[15] Wright describes the imposition of Southern perspectives when he writes: "Living in the South doomed me to look always through eyes which the South had given me" ("*Black*" 81).

Yet, crucially, the phrase "the look of the world" is repeated later in *Black Boy* to describe the effects of reading. The narrator tells how, in his effort to leave the South, he "hungered for books, *new ways of looking and seeing*. It was not a matter of believing or disbelieving what [he] read, but of feeling something new, of being affected by something that made *the look of the world* different" (238; emphases added).[16] Reading, like the news of the lynching, does something to the narrator's perception: "the mood of the book" he read would "linger[], coloring everything [he] saw, heard, did" (238). The narrator's first experience of reading—when his grandmother's lodger reads *Bluebeard and His Seven Wives* to Richard—affects him similarly: "the look of things altered" (38). Both lynching and the literary determine the subject's position *vis-à-vis* others and the gaze: like the literary, which "created a vast sense of distance between me and the world in which I lived" (242), the news of the lynching "creat[ed] a sense of distance between me and the world in which I lived" (165).

Through the literary, the narrator is able to negotiate visibility other than through Southern spectacles. As he writes, books became "the windows through which [he] looked at the world" ("*Black*" 81). "Wright reminds us," Stepto observes, "that reading . . . depends on seeing and knowing and gaining perspective" (146–47; see also Baker, *Blues* 146). The paralyzing, immobilizing "the look of the world," induced by the news of the lynching, is addressed through the experience of the literary, which resituates the narrator and others in the field of vision. Through reading, the narrator "beg[ins] to regard [the people around him] differently" (238), but such mobility of perspectives never entails for the black reading subject the imaginary comfort of seeing without being seen.

BUOYING UP, CASTING DOWN

Reading and race are intimately conjoined even in the earliest experiences of *Black Boy*'s narrator. It is by encountering "the baffling black print" (23) on the pages of a book that Richard comes across the meaning of race for the first time:

> When I had learned to recognize certain words, I told my mother that I wanted to learn to read and she encouraged me. . . . There grew in me a consuming curiosity about what was happening around me and, when my mother came home from a hard day's work, I would question her so relentlessly about what I had heard in the streets that she refused to talk to me.
>
> . . . I soon made myself a nuisance by asking far too many questions of everybody. Every happening in the neighborhood, no matter how trivial, became my business. It was in this manner that I first stumbled upon the relations between whites and blacks, and what I learned frightened me. (23, 24)

This new, frightening knowledge consists of old, familiar concepts, such as "white" people, being given new readings. Before his learning to read, "'white' people" is an empty, even absurd, signifier for the narrator: white people "had never looked particularly 'white.'" He cannot readily accept the new meaning of "whiteness": "It might have been," he muses, "that my tardiness in learning to sense white people as 'white' people came from the fact that many of my relatives were 'white'-looking people. My grandmother, who was white as any 'white' person, had never looked 'white' to me" (24). As in *Native Son*, where Bigger's "blackness" is visible even to eyes that cannot see, it becomes clear that recognizing "color" has very little to do with actual seeing. Poignantly, the narrator speaks of his difficulties in "*learning* to *sense* white people as *'white'* people." The phrase suggests, first, that one has to "sense," rather than to "see," color, just as the blind Mrs. Dalton can intuit Bigger's "blackness"; second, that one has to be able to make whiteness into a cultural metaphor, to use it citationally by putting quotation marks around the word ("white people as 'white' people"); and, third, that the meaning of race has to be "learned": reading race is something that one can begin to understand through schooling—something one has to be broken into.

As I noted, one of the recurrent themes of Wright's autobiography is the narrator's stunted growth as a reader of race. In the primal scene of literacy, the "consuming curiosity" elicited by reading leads the narrator to "ask[] far too many questions." Because of this inquisitiveness, he gets into dangerous situations whose code he cannot master. That he becomes a reader but not a reader of race is signaled by the recurring term *baffling.* Although he learns to read the "baffling black print" on the pages of a book, he remains "baffled" about color, constantly misreading race: "The words and actions of white people were *baffling signs* to me. . . . *Misreading* the reactions of whites around me made me say and do the wrong things" (187; emphases added). While he is unable to master the code of interracial contact, which leaves him "baffled" (180), his reading and writing make him unreadable, baffling to others, black and white alike: having discovered his published work, his classmates approach him with "baffled eyes" (159). As a potential challenge to white supremacy, communism too forces on the black subject a code of proper acting that "baffle[s]" the narrator (335). Correspondingly, the ability of "self-achieved literacy" to allow the subject's mobile perspectives on the world "baffle[s]" the communists Wright knows (352).

As Wright emphasizes in *Black Boy*, reading opens and sustains new "point[s] of view" (238), mobilizing the productivity of double consciousness by giving the black subject "alien eyes" with which to re-member the world ("*Black*" 81). Comprised of reading and writing, *the experience of the literary* enabled the slaves' flight and aided in the reconfiguration of their place, for, as Douglass puts it, "education and slavery were incompatible with one another" (*Narrative* 40). As Lawrence Levine argues, reading and writing helped create new possibilities of subsistence in the traumatic post-Passage existence by precipitating "changes in perception and world view" in the black subject (156–57). The experience of the literary offered a distance from one's immediate bondage, fissuring the seemingly unconquerable edifice of present reality. In *Native Son* and *Black Boy*, the experience of the literary similarly constitutes an experience of flight, an alienating disappearance from the geometral field of vision around which the white symbolic order is organized. If within this visibility Bigger is necessarily a "flat," "depthless" character—as a number of critics have lamented—his paranoid mobility, consequent to his imaginarization of the white field of vision, opens for him a secret interiority. He comes to approximate what D. A. Miller in *The Novel and the Police* (1988) calls the "liberal subject," a subject seemingly free of the surveillance which s/he nevertheless discerns functioning all around him or her.

In his study on the disciplinary technologies of subjection in the Victorian novel, Miller argues for the function of the novel in the constitution of this form of subjectivity. "[T]he experience of the novel," he writes, "provides . . . subjectivity with a secret refuge: a free, liberalizing space in which [the subject] comes into [his or her] own, a critical space in which [one] takes [his or her] distance from the world's carceral oppressions" (215). As a private space for the novel-reading subject, this experience provides the subject a sense of secrecy: "Perhaps the most fundamental value that the Novel, as a cultural institution, may be said to uphold is privacy, the determination of an integral, autonomous, 'secret' self. Novel reading takes for granted the existence of a space in which the reading subject remains safe from the surveillance, suspicion, reading, and rape of others" (162). In *Orality and Literacy* (1982), Walter J. Ong similarly argues that literacy constitutes a "consciousness-raising activity" (151) partially because of the privacy it demands and entails: "in composing a text, in 'writing' something, the one producing the written utterance is . . . alone. Writing is a solipsistic operation" (101).

Miller's and Ong's claims can help us clarify the logic that drove the debates surrounding the dangers of slave instruction (and, subsequently, black education in the post-Reconstruction era) for the white nation. As I noted in Chapter 1, Robyn Wiegman argues that the racially marked subject's access to citizenry is limited by his or her "extreme corporeality" (94), his or her embeddedness in the field of the visible. By carving out a space of privacy that (in however illusionary a manner) renders one free of "the world's carceral oppressions" (D. A. Miller 215), the experience of the literary threatens to constitute the African American subject as a "disembodied abstraction" and consequently to indicate the possibility of his or her inclusion in "the privileged ranks of citizenry" (Wiegman 94). African American reading may be prohibited—constantly interrupted and interrogated, as in *Black Boy*—precisely because the experience of the literary presupposes a private, secluded locale for the reading subject. In this, *Black Boy* echoes Western dystopian narratives, in whose totalitarian worlds all spaces of privacy and secrecy have been destroyed (see Gottlieb 11–12). Like in *Black Boy*, this voidance of privacy is often figured in prohibited reading: for example, in the Republic of Gilead, in Margaret Atwood's *The Handmaid's Tale* (1986), the solitude of reading has become unthinkable for women (219).

The experience of the literary, in other words, would remove the African American subject from his or her fixed position in visibility, from his or her subjection to the "surveillance, suspicion, reading, and rape of others" (D. A. Miller 162). Of course, taking his cue from Foucault, Miller sees such freedom as illusory: he suggests that, seemingly free from surveillance, the "liberal" subject becomes in fact all the more entangled in the networks of power. The experience of the novel constitutes a form of disciplinary subjection that avoids the crudity of blatant, even spectacular, punishment and subjugation. The subject is embedded in the network of discipline that it sees itself avoiding while enjoying the sight of its functioning around him or her. Indeed, while in the cultural imagination of the United States, literacy and education have figured as the passwords for social mobility, they have also functioned as disciplinary methods guaranteeing the continuing existence of a stratified society. Dana Nelson Salvino argues that, despite its promise, the dissemination of literacy among whites and blacks in antebellum America was institutionalized in "an educational system that would not radically alter the existing social balance" (144). The consequences of this tendency for slaves and freedmen were felt in the United States from antebellum to post-Reconstruction time. Salvino argues that "[l]iteracy could lead blacks out of physical, but not cultural and economic, bondage" (153).

For Miller, the novel-reading subject's experience of uninterrupted privacy, his sense of seeing without being seen, is, then, illusory. "It is built into the structure of the Novel," he writes, "that every reader must realize the definitive fantasy of the liberal subject, who imagines himself free from the surveillance that he nonetheless sees operating everywhere around him" (162). Such a confirmation of freedom is, Miller continues, essential for the subject: the liberal subject "seems to recognize himself most fully only when he forgets or disavows his functional implication in a system of carceral restraints or disciplinary injunctions" (x). The distance that the novel-reading subject is able to take from surveillance is, in Miller's phrase, "thoroughly imaginary" (x).

The freedom and voyeurism of the novel-reading subject is *imaginary* also in the Lacanian sense. The subject, imagining himself seeing not seen, is all the more immobilized in the specular capture where he is caught seen without seeing, as Lacan notes in his reading of Edgar Allan Poe's "The Purloined Letter." The subject misrecognizes his position as that of an outside observer, a voyeur unimplicated in the field of vision, separate from the scene of "carceral restraints" that s/he assumes to survey from a distance. Yet, as Wright and slave narrators make clear, African American readers and writers are unable to sustain this imaginary comfort of seeing without being seen. That is, as much as masters and mistresses saw in slave literacy the dangers of a *pharmakon*—where "the *inch*" of slave instruction was likely to turn into "the *ell*" of rebellion (Douglass, *Narrative* 40)—the experience of the literary did not free the black subject in any unambiguous way.

For Wright, this experience is nothing if not a dangerous supplement. To begin with, it counterproductively severs the subject's ties with the black community, which has traditionally provided significant support in the face of racism and discrimination. Having seen Richard's published story in a local paper, his fellow pupils "looked at [him] with new eyes, and a distance, a suspiciousness came between [them]": "If I had thought anything in writing the story, I had thought that perhaps it would make me more acceptable to them, and now it was cutting me off from them more completely than ever" (159–60). Later he notes, "My reading had created a vast sense of distance between me and the world in which I lived and tried to make a living, and that sense of distance was increasing each day" (242). These depictions can be glossed in the light of Henry Louis Gates's argument that, in contrast to most other prominent black autobiographies, in *Black Boy* the narrator's ascent necessitates the demeaning depiction of other blacks as "pitiable victims of the pathology of slavery and racial segregation who surround and suffocate him. Indeed, Wright wills [the narrator's] special self into being through the agency of contrast: the sensitive, healthy part is foregrounded against a determined, defeated black whole" (*Signifying* 182). But clearly Wright also demonstrates the characteristic cost of uplift: "Narratives of ascent," as Gates himself observes elsewhere, "are also narratives of alienation, of loss" ("Two"). In this Wright is not alone among minority writers: Richard Rodriguez, too, points out the "great price" that "education exacted . . . for its equally great benefits" (160).

More importantly, the experience of the literary always carries an incalculable risk for Wright and his predecessors: impeding the subject's adjustment to surrounding realities, it jeopardizes his or her very survival. Douglass writes: "I would at times feel that learning to read had been a curse rather than a blessing.

It had given me a view of my wretched condition, without the remedy" (*Narrative* 42). Similarly, as the black subject of Reconstruction in Du Bois's *The Souls of Black Folk* gets through "'book-learning'" (13) a glimpse of "his power, his mission," this feeling of empowerment is accompanied by anguish. While "the youth of dawning self-consciousness, self-realization, self-respect . . . [sees] in himself some faint revelation of his power, his mission," immediately the reading subject also "fe[els] his poverty; without a cent, without a home, without land, tools, or savings, he had entered into competition with rich, landed, skilled neighbors. . . . He fe[els] the weight of his ignorance,—not simply of letters, but of life, of business, of humanities" (14). In Charles Chesnutt's fictional rendering in *The House behind the Cedars* (1900), reading does not enable the subject to flee; rather, as the result of the experience of the literary "contentment took its flight, and happiness lay far beyond the sphere where he was born" (109).

Wright follows such descriptions in showing how reading consolidates the autobiographical narrator's prison by demonstrating the overwhelming odds against him: "In buoying me up, reading also cast me down. . . . My tension returned, new, terrible, bitter, surging, almost too great to be contained. I no longer *felt* that the world about me was hostile, killing; I *knew* it. . . . I seemed forever condemned, ringed by walls" (239). Subsequently in *Black Boy* the literary acts homeopathically—"I dulled the sense of loss through reading, reading, writing and more writing" (268); "I tried to shut it [news of impending unemployment] out of my mind by reading and writing" (273)—thus taking on the escapist role that alcohol carries for Bessie or religion has for Bigger's mother in *Native Son* (204).

James Baldwin continues this tradition in his mid-1960s observations about education: "to become educated (as all tyrants have always known) is to become inaccessibly independent, it is to acquire a dangerous way of assessing danger, and it is to hold in one's hands a means of changing reality. This is not at all the same thing as 'adjusting' to reality: the effort of 'adjusting' to reality simply has the paradoxical effect of destroying reality, since it substitutes for one's own speech and one's own voice an interiorized public cacophony of quotations" ("Nothing" 391). The difficulty that slave narrators and Wright experience is that there is no definitive form to this reality-to-come, this new symbolic existence. Consequently, they problematize assumptions about the unequivocally salubrious effects of literacy and the literary. They contest what has been called the "autonomous model of literacy," in which literacy and education are equated with the cherished American ideals of freedom and upward mobility (see Salvino 142). Yet, the experience of the literary remains an indispensable tool for Wright. He notes this in a mid-1950s interview: "Writing is my way of being a free man, of expressing my relationship to the world" ("Richard Wright: I Curse" 163).

Even if, for the black reader, the alienating effect of the literary does not lead to the imaginary comforts of the liberal subject, it can be a source of unexpected pleasure. When as an adolescent *Black Boy*'s narrator decides to read his first fictional text to a young woman living next door, the response is one of uneasiness and suspicious bewilderment. As with all the other scenes of writing or reading, he is asked why he had written the story, what its purpose was, and where he had got the idea from. Not being able to answer any of the questions with more than an evasion, he nevertheless experiences a deep sense of satisfaction at her response: "I never forgot the look of astonishment and bewilderment on the young woman's face when I had finished reading and glanced at her. Her inability to grasp what I had done or was trying to do somehow gratified me. Afterwards whenever I thought of her reaction I smiled happily for some unaccountable reason" (116). The narrator's satisfaction stems from the reader's incomprehension. Through his writing, he becomes to a certain extent inaccessible to the woman; his pleasure is that of escaping her "grasp." Writing eludes even the narrator himself: there remains some "unaccountable" excess in the experience of the literary which makes him "smile[] happily." The experience of the literary produces an excess that cannot be accounted for by the calculations of the visible economy.

Through the experience of the literary, the narrator finds cracks in the field of the visible that belie his education in the optical trade. He explains how his "first serious novel"—Sinclair Lewis's *Main Street*—"made [him] see [his] boss": "I had always felt a vast distance separating me from the boss, and now I felt closer to him, though still distant." Through this proximity-yet-distance, this identification-and-alienation, he is able to discern his boss's situatedness within visibility, within the "picture": "It made me . . . identify him as an American type. . . . I felt now that I knew him, that I could feel the very limits of his narrow life" (238).[17] In terms whose Lacanian specificity I will explore in the next chapter, the narrator experiences *an alienation from the symbolic circuits of visibility.* Ong, too, notes the benefits of literacy's alienating experience: "Alienation from a natural milieu can be good for us and indeed is in many ways essential for full human life. To live and to understand fully, we need not only proximity but also distance. This writing provides for consciousness as nothing else does" (82). Alienated, *Black Boy*'s narrator realizes that also white people, such as his boss, are situated within visibility in delimiting ways. Just as black people are described in *Black Boy* and *Native Son* as being placed within a "cramped environment" (*Native* 204) or, like Bessie, having a "narrow orbit" in their lives (123), the white employer is confined within a "narrow life." Through the literary, the narrator can identify (with) the white man, sense the limits of the latter's existence.

The experience of the literary allows the black reading subject what Wright later calls "double eyes" ("Richard Wright, Negro" 90). Splitting the façade of hegemonic reality, the literary reveals the fissure(s) in the Other. If the optical trade demands that the racially marked subject see him- or herself through the eyes of others, the experience of the literary renders double consciousness a productive condition in the search for other perspectives. The narrative of

Black Boy as it was originally published ends with a discussion where reading enables perspectives that are, paradoxically, beyond vision. In a paragraph that was added to conclude the narrative after the second part, "The Horror and the Glory,"had been cut by the publisher, Wright describes the narrator's flight from the South. He credits reading for sustaining him: "It had been my accidental reading of fiction and literary criticism that had evoked in me vague glimpses of life's possibilities" (879). Reading does not open the narrator's eyes to new visions but, much more nebulously, *evokes* possibilities that have not yet been actualized, that await their potential materialization *as* visions. "[I]t was out of these novels and stories and articles," the narrator continues, "out of the emotional impact of imaginative constructions of heroic and tragic deeds, that I felt touching my face a tinge of warmth from an unseen light; and in my leaving I was groping toward that invisible light, always trying to keep my face so set and turned that I would not lose the hope of its faint promise, using it as my justification for action" (879). The experience of the literary intervenes in visibility to the extent that it becomes a haptic experience—the "tinge of warmth"—rather than a visual one ("an unseen light").

With his double eyes, *Black Boy*'s narrator is able to cast a new look at his boss, cracking the seemingly immovable edifice of racial visibility. At times, reading also suggests to him possibilities beyond what is available to vision. If his experiences in the optical trade have all but paralyzed him, the experience of the literary allows, through shifts in perspective, a modicum of mobility. This mobility never approximates the "imaginary" freedom of the novel-reading subject but is always being questioned, threatened, and revised. For Ong, objectivity is one of the outcomes of literacy: "Writing . . . serves to separate and distance the knower and the known and thus to establish objectivity" (114). Yet, for the black reading subject, the experience of the literary never congeals into the imaginary comfort of objectivity and detachment, whose illusions African American writers from Du Bois to Wright have consistently criticized.[18]

LITERARY MALADAPTATION

Wright's commentary on slave-breaking lays bare the shift in racialized violence where the black body disappeared as the primary target and where the agent of the violence was internalized by the racially marked subject. The comparison between Douglass and Wright suggests that, in the system of subjection that the latter describes, the violence of the visible functions more efficiently to imprison racially marked subjects in their "places" than the overt violence—breaking and lynching—depicted by Douglass. Hence, even though one is tempted to laud the diminishing aspect of sheer violence in the transition from Douglass's time to Wright's, one has to heed Foucault's advocacy for resistance in the face of any commonsensical conclusions as to the reasons behind the transition from a society of punishment to one of surveillance. According to Foucault, the disappearance of the spectacle of physical torture in juridical systems of the West has been "attributed too readily and too emphatically to a process of 'humanization,' thus dispensing with the need for further analysis" (*Discipline* 7). A more attuned exploration, he writes, would try to uncover the processes whereby the new disciplinary strategies could penetrate and determine the subjects' consciousness in "economical" and productive ways unrivaled by the strategies of the spectacle. "What was emerging," he concludes, "no doubt was not so much a new respect for the humanity of the condemned . . . as a tendency towards a more finely tuned justice, towards a closer penal mapping of the social body" (78). The aim was "to set up a new 'economy' of the power to punish, to assure its better distribution, . . . so that it should be distributed in homogenous circuits capable of operating everywhere, in a continuous way, down to the finest grain of the social body" (80).

Making her argument with considerably broader material than I do here, Saidiya Hartman observes subjection's tightening grip on the post-Reconstruction African American subject: "It was often the case that benevolent correctives and declarations of slave humanity intensified the brutal exercise of power upon the captive body rather than ameliorating the chattel condition." For the racially marked subject of the late nineteenth century, "emancipation appears less the grand event of liberation than a point of transition between modes of servitude and racial subjection" (5, 6). Indeed, in the nineteenth-century narratives I have been discussing here, self-surveillance and violence of the visible prove to be much more effective deployments of power than the threat and execution of corporeal punishment. Self-breaking emerges as the logical extension and intensification of the practices of corporeal violence. As Henry Blake recognizes, benign masters thwart the slaves' drive for freedom: "''Tis this confounded "good treatment" and expectation of getting freed by their oppressors, that has been the curse of the slave. . . . A "good master" is the very worst of masters'" (Delany 127). Fanon, too, notes that, in the course of occupation, "the more brutal manifestations of the presence of the occupying power may perfectly well disappear. Indeed, such a spectacular disappearance turns out to be both a saving of expense to the colonial power and a positive way of preventing its forces being spread out over a wide area. But such a disappearance will be paid for at a high price: the price of a much stricter control of the country's future destiny" (*Wretched* 142). Again, it is economic utility that dictates the shift from colonial brutality to what Antonio Gramsci would call hegemony: as Fanon observes, such a turn proves "a saving of expense" for colonizers and leads to "a servitude that is less blatant but much more complete" (142). For Lewis Gordon, the colonizer's "call for a nonviolent solution amounts to the preservation of colonialism, or at least a transformation of colonialism into a condition that he will prefer, which amounts to a form of *neo*colonialism" ("Fanon's" 304; see also *Her* 154).

Wright suggests that the function of lynching has been taken over, but not entirely displaced, by the disciplinary practices of self-breaking. From post-Reconstruction to early-twentieth-century America, there occurred "an optical trade" in the strategies of subjection whereby overtly violent practices were subsumed into more subtle yet economical strategies of self-production; lynching and breaking, in other words, were partially displaced by the disciplinary tactics of subjection. Understanding the more subtle functioning of lynching and breaking in twentieth-century America allows us to point out, pace Foucault, the shifting circuits of power. The optical trade, relying on the systematic deployment of what Fanon calls "epidermalized differences," is an apparatus of subjection whose functioning is arguably more uninterrupted and economical because it seeks to make the racialized subject, to paraphrase and recontextualize Thoreau, into his or her own slave-driver. If a Hegelian reading sees in the Douglass-Covey confrontation the "dialectical overcoming" of slavery—or at least a promise thereof—Wright, in revising the optimism that Douglass's "career as a slave" may give rise to, suggests that the racialized subject in the post-Reconstruction era may have come dangerously close to what Kojève, after Hegel, calls "the pure essence of slavery" (56).

For Wright and numerous slave narrators, the experience of the literary produces viewpoints beyond the limited perspective induced through scenes of lynching and other Southern spectacles. Yet, if this experience changes "the look of the world" in displacing the subject's Southern slant with "alien" or "double eyes," it also dangerously wrenches him or her out of joint with symbolic reality. This dislodging of the subject and the *Umwelt* nevertheless characterizes the Lacanian ethics of symbolic change. In contrast to Lacan's explicit dismissal of Darwinism, I suggest that the temporality of this change can be understood in terms of an *evolutionary becoming.* Du Bois suggests the inextricable morbidity and productivity of such maladaptation in *The Souls of Black Folk*'s sole fictional installment, "Of the Coming of John." The story's black protagonist, leaving his hometown for college, experiences a temporal dislocation from all collectivities as he begins to take his studies seriously. Having been once expelled, he returns to school, this time immersing himself into his scholarship, "pausing perplexed where others skipped merrily, and walking steadily through the difficulties where the rest stopped and surrendered" (145). Already out of joint with his surroundings, his alienation becomes more pronounced as he decides, after several years, to make his way back to his hometown. Upon his return, he finds himself at odds with the Negro community. Looking around in his childhood surroundings, he perceives its poverty with new eyes: "a little dingy station, a black crowd gaudy and dirty, a half-mile of dilapidated shanties along a straggling ditch of mud" (148). The community, who has turned up to celebrate his arrival, deems his behavior brusque and dismissive, an impression that is strengthened when the prodigy delivers a speech at his homecoming party at the Baptist Church. The speech—in which he extols the ideals of "human brotherhood and destiny," "of charity and popular education," "of the spread of wealth and work" while denouncing "religious and denominational bickering"—leaves the congregation motionless in their incomprehension and rising indignation at what they consider the young man's dismissal of their spiritual traditions. As he finishes his speech, a hush descends on the crowd: "they sat very still while the clock ticked" (149).

The educated John Jones clearly embodies the double conscious black subject, whose dilemma Du Bois illustrates throughout his work (Sundquist 521), but in "Of the Coming of John" this condition is described in terms of *an evolutionary untimeliness.* The black community's immobility in the face of time's procession—whose relentlessness the ticking timepiece witnesses—returns us to the scene of John's homecoming. In the paragraph describing the uncomfortable and disillusioning encounter between the prodigy and his natal community, the term "monster" is repeated twice: the town folk receive him with "a monster welcome" only to find out that his college years have made him "'monstus stuck up'" (148). Black education can here be seen as "the generation of a kind of productive monstrosity" (Grosz, *Nick* 91) with concomitant dangers. As a monster, John has become maladapted to his environment, black and white alike. In this, his dilemma resembles that of *Black Boy*'s narrator, whose reading and writing alienate him from his surroundings. Neither knows how to act properly. As John discovers, "Every step he made offended some one. . . . [A]ll the time he had meant right,—and yet, and yet, somehow he found it so hard and strange to fit his old surroundings again, to find his place in the world about him" (150). In their literary maladaptation, we might see both John Jones and *Black Boy*'s narrator as representatives of "the unique individual, the one who stands out, who is *exapted*, that is, adapted not so much to present circumstances as to the future" (Grosz, *Nick* 10–11).

Finally, I suggest, then, that we think about the Lacanian ethics of symbolic limits in terms of monstrosities and evolutionary leaps, in terms of the kind of dangerous maladaptation that the experience of the literary courts. This approach would risk proceeding contrary to Lacan's explicit, repeated criticism of evolutionary theory. Already in 1948, he attacks Darwin's system, dismissing it as the product of the culture of European colonialism: Darwin "projected the predations of Victorian society and the economic euphoria that sanctioned for that society the social devastation it initiated on a planetary scale[. H]e justified its predations with the image of a laissez-faire system in which the strongest predators compete for their natural prey" ("Aggressiveness" 27). A few years later, in *Seminar I* (1953–1954), he similarly critiques the thesis of "the struggle for life" as a convenient justification for the expansion of the British Empire: "If it was Darwin who wrought it, that was because he came of a nation of privateers, for whom racism was the basic industry" (177).

While at this stage of his work, Lacan makes a historicist argument against Darwin, later he would oppose evolutionism on theoretical grounds. For him, evolutionary thinking becomes a characteristically Hegelian project whose logic is structured around the telos of development. This argument becomes clear in *The Ethics of Psychoanalysis*: "An evolution that insists on deducing from continuous process the ascending movement which reaches the summit of consciousness and thought necessarily implies that that consciousness and that thought were there at the beginning." In evolutionary thinking, "Being [*l'être*] [is] always implied in being [*l'étant*]" (213–14; brackets in original English translation). According to Lacan, the process of adaptation and development posited by evolutionary theory is identical to the dialectical movement to a predetermined telos. Like dialectics, the evolutionary trajectory appears strictly teleological, proceeding through its ascending movement to "the summit of consciousness and thought." For Lacan, Darwin's work does not represent the Copernican turn as which it is often credited; rather, the evolutionary process, seen in terms of dialectical predictability, consolidates human exceptionality. In a talk given in 1960, he reiterates this critique: "it is not because of Darwin that men believe themselves to be any less the best among the creatures, for it is precisely of this that he convinces them" ("Subversion" 284).

We might note that, in his dismissal of Darwin, Lacan is not alone: also Foucault rejects evolutionism in his late-1960s work. In *The Archaeology of Knowledge* (1969), he criticizes models of history that narrate the past by tracing "evolutive curves" and, which amounts to the same thing, by "projecting teleologies" (12). The same year he insists in an interview: "I am completely opposed to a certain conception of history which takes for its model a kind of great continuous and homogenous evolution, a sort of great mythic life" ("Birth" 66). His rejection is premised on the deployment of evolutionary models in history and politics that has helped naturalize the present state of existence as the culmination of an irrevocable, adaptive process, making the thought of "revolutions" impossible ("Return" 423, 431). To avoid partaking in such models, "progressive politics" should not be envisioned in "evolutionary metaphors" ("History, Discourse" 44).

Yet, "Darwin" arguably gets another hearing in Foucault's work in the subsequent years. The evolutionary vocabulary returns already in 1971, in "The Discourse on Language," with Foucault's references to *monstrosities* in his discussion of the formation of sciences (223–24). The decisive step is taken in "Nietzsche, Genealogy, History" (1971), where Foucault reconsiders evolutionary thinking in terms of Nietzsche's, rather than Hegel's, philosophy. I justify my suggestion that we see symbolic changes in terms of evolutionary leaps with a similar argument: I propose that Lacan's criticism relies on a particular reading of Darwin, one that sees evolutionary theory as marked by the kind of teleological insistence that Foucault, before his genealogical turn, posits on evolutionary thinking. This reading of Darwin needs to be supplemented by the Darwin found in the Deleuzian-inspired work of such recent critics as Keith Ansell Pearson (*Germinal*; *Philosophy*) and Elizabeth Grosz (*Nick*; *Time*). While Lacan links evolutionism to the transcendent movement of the dialectic, Grosz argues that "Darwin provided a model of time and development that refuses any pregiven aim, goal, or destination for natural selection. . . . He refuses anything like the telos or directionality of the dialectic, or a commitment to progressivism in which we must always regard what presently exists as superior to or more developed than its predecessors" (*Nick* 90).

Here we can, then, posit a different Darwin, one whose work is not necessarily in conflict with the Lacanian ethics of potential symbolic change that I suggest we evoke to articulate the experience of the literary in Wright and Du Bois. In different ways, both Lacan and Darwin can be seen not as theorists of adaptation but of becoming, of an open future, an example of which we find in the dilemma of the Du Boisian subject. John Jones's maladaptation renders explicit the limits of symbolic existence, which also concern Lacan's work on ethics. Educated into maladaptation, John, a tragic mulatto of sorts, can find his place in neither the black nor the white world; the time of his existence is wrenched out of joint through the teratogenic experience of the literary. Yet, as a monster, he also embodies a portent or a warning (from the Latin *monstrum* and *monere*) of a future whose otherness cannot be made sense of through present perspectives. As a prodigy or a monster, John suggests a dangerously open future: when such rarely sustainable teratological variations do survive, they do so by precipitating an evolutionary leap that radically transforms the existing horizon of possibilities.

CHAPTER 5

Avian Alienation

Writing and Flying in Wright and Lacan

GINGER. Listen, we'll either die free chickens or die trying.
BABS. Are those the only options?

—Peter Lord and Nick Park (dir.), *Chicken Run*

Flyers are thieves escaping.

—Peter Greenaway, *Flying Out of This World*

Given the emergence of Marx's system in part as a commentary on Hegelian dialectics—turning what Marx considered Hegel's idealist preoccupation with the mind into the economically grounded categories of dialectical materialism—it is not surprising that a number of contemporary theorists of slavery have taken their bearings on the section on "Lordship and Bondage" in *The Phenomenology of Mind*. Continuing the legacy of the "significant number of intellectuals formed by the black Atlantic [who] have engaged in critical dialogues with [Hegel's] writings" (Gilroy, *Black* 54), David Brion Davis, for example, provides a classic Hegelian reading of slavery in *The Problem of Slavery in the Age of Revolution* (1975), calling the *Phenomenology* "a work that contained the most profound analysis of slavery ever written" (558). Davis historicizes the *Phenomenology* by noting its coincidence with the "age of revolution," the beginning of the slaves' "long ordeal of emancipation" (563). While earlier philosophers such as Thomas Hobbes and John Locke had anticipated Hegel in seeing slavery as the lot of the subject submitting to the will of another in a mortal battle between two combatants, Hegel, according to Davis, brought the experience of slavery to "the natal core of man's condition" (559–60).[1]

The most influential Hegel-inflected reading of slavery, however, is Orlando Patterson's *Slavery and Social Death* (1982), whose importance is reflected in the more recent work by Paul Gilroy, Cynthia Willett, Leonardo Cassuto, and Abdul JanMohamed, among others.[2] While also suggesting the limits of Hegel's applicability, Patterson finds the Hegelian idiom, especially as it was politicized by Marx, crucial to his global theory of slavery. With the term "natal alienation," he recontextualizes "a basic category of the Hegelian philosophy" (Marcuse 273), which Marx makes central to his system already in the *Manuscripts of 1844* (esp. 106–19). With natal alienation, Patterson reconfigures the alienation of one's essential, nonexternal characteristics, which Hegel speaks of in *The Philosophy of Right* (1821) (par. 66) as constituting "slavery" or "serfdom." For Patterson natal alienation refers to the slave's "loss of native status," "of ties of birth in both ascending and descending generations," and his or her subsequent existence as "a socially dead person" (5, 7). Slavery, according to Patterson, is instituted as "a substitute for certain death," "usually violent death" (337, 5). The slave is rendered socially dead by a two-stage process in which s/he is "violently uprooted from his [or her] milieu" and subsequently introduced into the slave master's symbolic universe (38). Having neither access to his or her past nor any recognized rights or obligations to kin, the slave is "a genealogical isolate" (5), a being of no stable coordinates. Echoing Marx, for whom the revolution would accomplish the negation of the negation, Patterson speaks in an unmistakably Hegelian (and Kojèvean) idiom of the slave's "need for disenslavement, for disalienation, for negation of social death, for recognition of his inherent dignity" (340).

If Patterson's theory of slavery encapsulates the racial formation[3] of the slave-holding U.S. South, the subsequent shifts in racialization in the postbellum nation, exemplified here by the work of Richard Wright, demand a rethinking of the Hegelian–Marxist concepts. Much like JanMohamed in *The Death-Bound-Subject: Richard Wright's Archaeology of Death*, I suggest in this chapter that the racialized subject in *Native Son* and *Black Boy* may be better understood through the later vicissitudes of the Hegelian alienation, particularly in Lacan's work. I argue that, for Wright, the racialized subject, rather than alienated, is *too firmly embedded* in a structure that prevents him or her any alienated mobility. In the Lacanian idiom, the (white) symbolic order fans out as a self-totalized system; lacking any lack, the Other remains "constantly on [the subject's] back," as Lacan writes in *Seminar X* (qtd. in Fink, *Lacanian* 53). With the overproximity of the unblinking Other, this system determines the racialized subject entirely, or more precisely, allows no subject as such to emerge in the place it assigns to the racialized other.

In Wright as in numerous other African American texts, one of the ways this form of alienation is accomplished is through the experience of the literary and represented, as I will point out, in the trope of flying, of elevation and aviation. The history of contestation around black literacy, pre- and post-Civil War, attests to the impact that reading and writing were considered to have on the subject's sociosymbolic positioning. In the antebellum South, the impediments to Negro literacy provided "a very real enslaving weapon against blacks: legislated into illiteracy, they were held chattel by the power of words in the form of laws legalizing their bondage and tracts confirming their inherent inferiority to whites" (Salvino 147). In the post-Reconstruction movement to black disfranchisement, literacy similarly constituted a technology that was used to control the ex-slaves' and their descendants' access to citizenship and concomitant rights, as, along with property requirements, literacy qualifications were introduced to impede black voting (while the appended "understanding clause" and "grandfather clause" provided loopholes for unpropertied and/or illiterate white subjects) (see Woodward, *Origins* 331–34).

Wright's work and that of slave narrators demonstrate that the value of literacy goes beyond that of basic education, however important, which enables the subject's inclusion in the rituals of societal decision-making. What I call the experience of the literary produces effects that include but are not reducible to those of the status of literacy as a minimum requirement for one's functioning in participatory democracy. The experience of the literary has ramifications for the subject's symbolic positioning, that is, one's relation to the networks of signification in which s/he emerges. Lindon Barrett points to literacy's importance in the intertwining of the racialized subject's cultural position and his or her psychic experiences. Barrett argues that in slave narratives literacy allows one to reach beyond the realm of corporeality, to which the racialized subject has been confined in the Western mind/body schema. Because in the Enlightenment tradition the body has always been the object, never the subject, of thought—because bodies are always thought, never thinking—"African Americans who are forced to live illiterate lives, who are forcibly identified with the limited sphere of the body, are in as manifest a fashion as possible seemingly restricted to being the objects of thought and never its subjects" ("African-American" 419). Barrett suggests that while the importance of the slaves' ability to write their own passes and more efficiently mount counterarguments and counteractions against the system is not to be underestimated, these do not explain the rationale behind the South's injunctions against black literacy. Barrett writes, echoing Henry Louis Gates's and others' studies on the racial logic of Enlightenment philosophy: "if literacy is the most manifest formalization of the life of the mind, if it provides testimony of the mind's ability to extend itself beyond the constricted limits and conditions of the body, then to restrict African Americans to lives without literacy is to immure them to bodily existences having little or nothing to do with the life of the mind" ("Hand-Writing" 324). Literacy provides *an enabling splitting* in the subject's experience—one not unlike, as I will argue, that of Lacanian alienation. It complicates the racialized subject's corporeal experience, making one unavailable as the object of slavery's system of exchange and domination: "Literacy determines for whom the physical, the geographic, and the bodily remain an overwhelming concern and source of identity and for whom it will remain an index of power" ("African-American" 421). Literacy enables one to counter racial visibility, which remained crucial to the logic of antiblack racism after Emancipation; as Houston Baker, Jr., writes, "the mark of Reconstruction's innovative mechanism of White Supremacy remained skin color, *blackness*" (*Turning* 43). I follow Barrett in claiming that literacy and the experience of the literary allow the racialized subject to negotiate the disciplinary visibility of U.S. racial formation, which for Wright mutates but is never overcome in the post-Reconstruction era and the first half of the twentieth century.

In what follows, I begin by explicating the Lacanian understanding of alienation. I follow how this alienation is embodied in Bigger Thomas by linking *Native Son*'s two scenes of writing to Lacan's reading of Edgar Allan Poe's "The Purloined Letter" and to the African American myths of flying Africans and the flying fool. I proceed to consider how the two scenes of writing in Wright's debut novel are reconfigured in his autobiography. If in *Native Son* Bigger experiences an alienation/separation from the white Other, *Black Boy* presents us with a more radical and sustained move against the Other, one that I theorize through Lacan's rereading of the Hegelian Terror. The concomitant choice of "freedom or death" is, of course, posited in numerous slave narratives, including the famous examples of Frederick Douglass and Harriet Jacobs. I argue that this choice is linked to the experience of the literary not only in certain slave narratives but also in the work of W. E. B. Du Bois and Booker T. Washington. Finally, I suggest, contra Russ Castronovo's argument in "Political Necrophilia," that the choice of death, particularly when we understand it psychoanalytically, in terms of the death drive, does not assume a utopian world of withdrawal and noncontradiction but possibly precipitates *the becoming of the death drive*, a dangerous and volatile orientation beyond existing symbolic possibilities.[4] Such possibilities are opened by what I call avian alienation and the subsequent moves along the trajectory of the drive.

Considering the racialized subject's painful and dangerous, yet potentially productive, moment of alienation in Wright's work, then, I am proposing a shift from Patterson's Hegelian framework to psychoanalytic theory in understanding the racialized subject's constitution in the white symbolic order. This shift allows us to see the alienating experience of the literary as *a process of an open becoming*—one whose dangers and potentialities were arguably reflected in the post-Reconstruction debates around black education. In Lacanian idiom, the experience of the literary, as the alienating "uplift" of elevation and aviation, threatens the symbolic order with a possibility of the real's return in the form of ethical violence I discussed in Wright and Fanon in Chapter 3. This dynamic of symbolic aggression is depicted in Lacan's reading of Poe's "The Purloined Letter," which carries numerous intertextual resonances with Wright's texts on writing, flying, and concealment.

LACAN'S ALIENATION AND SEPARATION

Lacan's psychoanalytic use of alienation/separation is not unrelated to the history of reinterpretations of Hegel from Feuerbach and Marx to Kojève and Hyppolite,[5] but, unsurprisingly, significantly modifies the dialectical use of the term. The difference can be found in the way that Hegel and Lacan understand the subject as "propertied." In *The Philosophy of Right*, Hegel distinguishes between "external" properties—one's possessions or fruits of labor—and "those goods, or rather substantive characteristics, which constitute my own private personality and the universal essence of my self-consciousness" (par. 66). Alienation proper refers to the transfer of property of the former order, of "thing[s] external by nature" (par. 65). When alienation concerns nonexternal characteristics, we are dealing with "serfdom" or "slavery" (par. 66). Patterson's natal alienation is a variant of this substantive loss, whose drama Hegel stages in the *Phenomenology*'s "Lordship and Bondage."

While there are thus two forms of alienation in Hegel and Patterson, for Lacan alienation *always* concerns one's being, that essence which Hegel deems "inalienable." In Hegel serfdom is a specific form of alienation, its perversion or travesty; for Lacan alienation unfailingly leads to such radical loss of being, constituting a process "by which man enters into the way of slavery" (*SXI* 212).[6] This difference results from the way that the two theorists stage the scenes of contestation. If Hegel's alienation of slavery is the result of a battle between two subjects—the future slave and master—which can go either way, for Lacan the parties are rather unequally matched. The subject, facing the malevolent demands of the Other, is always on the losing side (Fink, "Alienation" 86). The mugger's demand, "*your money or your life*," illustrates the subject's forced hand at alienation. While the Other's ultimatum is seemingly articulated as an either/or choice, it "has as its consequence a *neither one, nor the other*" (*SXI* 211). For Hegel, "alienation proper is an expression of my will, of my will no longer to regard the thing as mine" (*Philosophy of Right* addition to par. 65). In Lacan's forced choice, there cannot be any question of such "will": regardless of the subject's decision, the outcome is always one's loss of his or her purse. Notably, what Hegel would deem as the loss of external property—of one's "money"—is what for Lacan leads to "slavery." In Lacanian alienation, then, there is no mutual process whereby the combatants could recognize each other on a level field of negotiation between propertied, self-possessed subjects.

More precisely, the Lacanian subject is born only in its confrontation with the Other; Lacan places alienation at the point of the subject's coming into being: "it is in this alienation, in this fundamental division, that the dialectic of the subject is established" (*SXI* 221). In alienation, the subject emerges as meaning through the loss of being, through the loss of him- or herself as property. Lacan continues: "If we choose being"—the suicidal choice of insisting on our purse—"the subject disappears, it eludes us, it falls into non-meaning. If we choose meaning"—if we preserve our life by giving up our property—"the meaning survives only deprived of that part of non-meaning that is, strictly speaking, that which constitutes[,] in the realization of the subject, the unconscious" (*SXI* 211). The choice between "money" and "life" leads to a limited existence, "a life deprived of something," "a life deprived of freedom" (*SXI* 212). Importantly, in the forced choice of alienation *the unconscious* is established.

Concluding that there is "*no freedom without life*," the slave (that is, every subject) is left empty handed, for "there will be no life for him without freedom" (*SXI* 216). Yet, in Lacan, "[p]assage through this impossible point of one's own non-meaning, where it seems that one can say of oneself only 'I am not,' . . . is the fundamental condition of attaining the status of a free subject" (Zupančič, *Ethics* 32). Freedom, that is, may be actualized in the subsequent turns of alienation. Alienation needs to be complemented by an additional process: that of separation. Alienation by itself "functions . . . only to reduce the subject in question to being no more than a signifier, to petrify the subject in the same movement in which it calls the subject to function, to speak, as subject" (*SXI* 207). If alienation, as the loss of being, marks the subject's emergence—its becoming an empty location in the Other—in separation the subject recognizes the lack in the Other. Separation thus functions as "the return way of the *vel* of alienation" (*SXI* 218). From this initial choice, "there is only one exit—the way of desire" (SXI 224). *Desire*—the way out of the immobility of mere alienation—figures as this back-and-forth of alienation and separation, "the superimposition of two lacks" (*SXI* 214). For Lacan, desire is precisely this movement between the lack of the subject and that of the Other. It is represented by the lozenge between the barred subject and the *objet petit a* in the formula for fantasy ($\$ \lozenge a$): the lower half of the diamond marks the alienating movement from the split subject to the *petit a*, while its upper part traces separation as the return in the trajectory of symbolic fantasy (*SXI* 209).

To signal their complementarity, Lacan in his later work presents the processes of alienation and separation as one and the same movement (Fink, *Lacanian* 61). Initiating the dialectic of desire, alienation/separation marks the subject's emergence as an empty place in the symbolic order, which itself is subsequently found lacking. A similar dialectic between the absented subject and the lacking Other is what allows the racialized subject to escape his or her place in the white symbolic network, concretized in *Native Son* by the Dalton household. Bigger's disappearance from, and his successful camouflage within, the white house of Daltonism cannot be explained according to Patterson's Hegelian schema, as the negation of alienation. Rather, I suggest, it is the Lacanian understanding of alienation, a movement that also includes a subsequent "separation," as the subject's emergence as an empty place in the Other, that characterizes Bigger's "transparen[cy]" (*Native* 58). Bigger's experience of immobility and confinement, of the suffocating absence of geographic, psychic, and symbolic mobility—his very lack of subjectivity, perhaps—is negated when he observes how easily he can fool the white gaze, apparently getting away with murder.

BIGGER'S BLUEPRINT FOR NEGRO WRITING

As Horace A. Porter points out, the name Dalton suggests Daltonism, a form of color blindness (91). More precisely, however, Daltonism as a medical condition refers to an inability to distinguish red from green. The name of Bigger's predecessor in the Dalton household is, of course, Green. This suggests that Bigger is, perhaps, Red and that the Daltons, in their color blindness—which names at once their liberal convictions and their inability to discern how race functions—cannot see that their servant Green has been substituted for a Re(a)d one.

In both senses of the homophone, this may seem a dubious argument. It is obvious that Bigger neither has communist sympathies nor has spent any time with books. His lacking class consciousness is exemplified in his resentment toward poor whites, his inability to consider (unlike Reverend Taylor of "Fire and Cloud") the mechanisms of class structuring part and parcel of the same system that sustains racism by rendering it beneficial to a part of the white population.[7] And while his disinterestedness in reading is exemplified in his not having much at all to say about it, his attitude may not be unlike Jake's in *Lawd Today!* (1963): "*Too much reading's bad*. It was all right to read the newspapers, and things like that; but reading a lot of books with fine print in them and no pictures would drive you crazy" (69).

Yet, we find the homophone operative in the logic of the white law: the threat of Bigger's becoming Re(a)d is clearly articulated by the white investigators, for whom being read and being Red have a causal relation. "'Did you ever see him reading anything?'" Britten asks the Daltons' cook, Peggy, trying to find out whether the black servant is a communist spy involved in Mary's disappearance (163). As in *The Outsider* (1953), reading implicates the black subject in criminal activity. In Wright's later novel, District Attorney Houston is finally able to identify Cross Damon as the killer by tracing his past reading: "'I had a brainstorm. I wired Chicago to send me a list of the titles of the books you'd left behind in your room and when they wired back a long list I was delighted . . . That was the first real clue. Your Nietzsche, your Hegel, your Jaspers, your Heidegger, your Husserl, your Kierkegaard, and your Dostoevsky were the clues'" (820; ellipsis in original).[8] Fully aware of reading's ability to inculpate, Bigger is careful to let the white people know that he has no interest in the activity. To exonerate himself and frame Jan Erlone, he dupes the sleuths into considering him un-Re(a)d by ensuring that the communist pamphlets in his room are conspicuously untouched: "Yes, they would have to be stacked neatly. No one must think that he had read them" (101).

Because of his strangely "transparent" (58)—readily graspable *and* evanescent—position in the surrounding field of symbolic "reality," Bigger becomes a masterful reader. Turning out not so much Red as read, he learns to read the white symbolic order in a way that the Red perspective does not allow Jan (or, say, Johnny-Boy in "Bright and Morning Star") to do. If reading—as a disease, a case of "ha[ving] bookworms"—makes one "queer," as Jake avers (*Lawd* 69), its warping influence is synonymous with the enabling "queer sense of power" (*Native* 203) that Bigger experiences as he, having accidentally committed murder in front of the unseeing white gaze, shifts his perspective on the scene of reality before him. Yet, the queerness of this shift always entails the threat of insanity that Jake observes in reading. Taking an awry perspective on the world is an irrational venture in that this turn away from symbolic reality is never distinguished from a debilitating loss of agency and calculability. Thus, from the very beginning, Bigger's black(face) magic threatens to possess him, the conjurer: he finds himself unable to predict the consequences of his new reading of the world. Finally, as he encounters the pathologically paranoid black reading subject in the county jail (290–92), he finds himself looking at an embodiment of the derangement of reading.

In *Native Son* and *Black Boy*, evidence of black reading suggests a subject who, in the idiom of white supremacy, "does not know his place"; and indeed, the experience of the literary allows a shift in the racialized subject's position vis-à-vis the white symbolic order that has immobilized him—a shift that is characteristically that of alienation. The importance of the literary in this process of alienation is emphasized in *Native Son*'s two scenes of writing. In "The Re(a)d and the Black," Barbara Johnson points out one of them: the scene where Bigger composes a ransom note to the Daltons in the presence of his girlfriend, Bessie. As Johnson observes, Bigger's act of writing begins with, or is enabled by, his "pushing the knife out of the way so he could write" (150). He lets go of his blade in order to write; or, we may say, the pen replaces his knife, taking on its protective function. In allowing Bigger to relinquish his weapon, the act of writing repeats the function of a secret interiority impenetrable to the white gaze that Bigger seems to gain after killing Mary. Earlier in the novel, his knowledge of having done the unthinkable, of escaping the Other—embodied in Mrs. Dalton's unseeing stare at the scene of murder—replaced his "knife and gun": "What his knife and gun had once meant to him, his knowledge of having secretly murdered Mary now meant" (127); "His crime was an anchor weighing him safely in time; it added to him a certain confidence which his gun and knife did not" (90).[9] Through his crime, Bigger discerns a split in the Other, an unknowingness in the apparently seamless white symbolic order. As the pen replaces the knife in the ransom note scene, it replicates the function of the secret knowledge that affords him a feeling of self-concealment: "What his knife and gun had once meant to him, his [pen] now meant." While laying down the weapon is a precondition for writing, writing also begins to function as camouflage, allowing Bigger to escape the Other's gaze. Taking hold of the pen, he is able to relinquish his rigid, exhausting posture of vigilant self-defense, instrumentalized in his "knife and gun." In the terms developed in Chapter 2 above, his writing alienates him by allowing him to mobilize paranoid knowledge. If this mobility is that of desire, as Lacan tells us, it places the subject in a position of negotiation with respect to the symbolic law.

The law in itself allows white subjects a distance from the immediate need for self-defense, from the unrelenting watchfulness that characterizes Bigger's life before the murder. During Bigger's trial, the district attorney describes the institution emblematized in the court as a "'sacred law [which] had taken the place of [man's] *gun and knife*'" (341; emphasis added). According to Buckley, this distance separates man from beast in allowing one "'to think and feel in security'": "'the law is strong and gracious enough to allow all of us to sit here in this court room today and try this case with dispassionate interest, and not tremble with fear that at this very moment some half-human black ape may be climbing through the windows of our homes to rape, murder, and burn our daughters!'" (341). The law enables the white subject to position him/herself in a secure, "dispassionate" spectatorial position and thereby to lay down his/her "gun and knife." For the white audience whom Buckley addresses, the law enables a mobility that comes from the subject's distance from the exigencies of survival. Secrecy and writing instantiate this mobility for Bigger: they allow him to relinquish his concrete arsenal and to protect himself in subtler, more "human," ways. In the Hegelian terms developed by Alexandre Kojève, immediate need is modified into the more flexible position of human desire. In Lacanese, the subject emerges via a preliminary alienation from the Other.

This reading of the difference between Bigger's position and that of the white courtroom audience necessitates that we, again, consider the historical specificity of the symbolic order. Rather than seeing, pace Judith Butler, the symbolic law in Lacan as a historically invariant set of foreclosures that render it immutable, such a reading would require us to think about the changeability of symbolic constellations as these are understood by Lacan; it would, in other words, render thinkable such concepts as the *white* symbolic order. Attentiveness to symbolic variability is indeed one way to understand the point of Lacanian ethics: it demands that we remain mindful of the symbolic order's (singular and historically variant) internal limits. As such, "Lacanian ethics is . . . necessarily political in the sense that it takes as its point of reference, acts on behalf of, what remains unsymbolized, unacknowledged, *impossible*, within any given sociosymbolic order. The authentic ethical act, for Lacan, will challenge the limits through which recognized sociality is constituted, aiming at the realization of what appears as impossible within the terms of a given political constellation" (Penney 35). While limits as such are inescapable, their manifestations vary from context to context. In their description of subaltern resistance, Wright and Frantz Fanon suggest that in societies where the color line—embodied in the subject's "corporeal schema"—largely determines the division of differences, race at once enables symbolic logic and functions as the symbolic order's internal point of inconsistency, its extimate core. The law that distributes differences, that shapes the trajectory of desire, is here that of the white symbolic order. The arrangement of the white symbolic order around the impossibility of race simultaneously enables the law's subversion. As Bigger transgresses his place in the white symbolic, he realizes that he can render its law an imaginary construction, blind and rigid, unable to respond to his violent challenge.

If only momentarily, writing effectively conceals Bigger, allowing him to shake off the Other. The ransom demand having been received, his disappearance becomes complete. He is in the kitchen with the cook, Peggy, when Mr. Dalton, carrying the note in his hand, bursts into the room: "The door swung in violently. Bigger started in fright. Mr. Dalton came into the kitchen, his face ashy. . . . Mr. Dalton looked around the entire kitchen, not at anything in particular, but just round the entire stretch of four walls, his eyes wide and unseeing" (160). Not only does Bigger feel partially invisible to others' eyes; this time, his employer becomes literally blind to his presence in his house: Mr. Dalton "look[s] around the entire kitchen, . . . round the entire stretch of four walls," yet missing Bigger, "his eyes wide and unseeing."

As Johnson points out, the black servant is present yet hidden in this scene like the purloined letter in Poe's story of the same name: despite (or, more precisely, because of) being in full view, he remains unseen ("Re(a)d" 149). While Johnson relegates the reference to Poe to a brief aside, I propose we explore this connection more thoroughly, especially because it engages Lacan, who, in 1956, gave a seminar on "The Purloined Letter." While Lacan formulates the process of alienation in the seminar of 1964, *The Four Fundamental Concepts of Psycho-Analysis*, the concept emerges already in his earlier texts, including the essay on the mirror stage and the reading of Poe. In his commentary on "The Purloined Letter," Lacan notes the letter's disappearance as it is dislocated from its place in the symbolic chain. In *Native Son*, Bigger relies on a similar *fading* from the white symbolic network. While Patterson argues through Hegel that the slave experiences a natal alienation, Bigger *emerges as a subject by way of alienation* as he learns to absent himself from the rigorously structured Dalton household and, by extension, the white symbolic order.

In Poe's short story, the Prefect of the Parisian police misses the stolen object in the Minister's apartment because his way of detecting, of looking, is such that he cannot interpret what is before him. Confiding his predicament to Dupin and the narrator, the Prefect boasts of his thorough methods of search. Every inch, every nook and corner of the Minister's quarters has been subjected to the most painstaking work of detection. During the extensive hours of the search, every item of the furniture is explored, mindful of hidden spaces or drawers. As the Prefect explains, "'to a properly trained police agent, such a thing as a *secret* drawer is impossible. Any man is a dolt who permits a "secret" drawer to escape him in a search of this kind. The thing is *so* plain. There is a certain amount of bulk—of space—to be accounted for in every cabinet. Then we have accurate rules. The fiftieth part of a line could not escape us'" (Poe 11). The Prefect's self-assured description of his systematic approach to detection illustrates the kind of imaginary mapping of space that Lacan identifies in *The Four Fundamental Concepts* as the method by which a blind man is able to "grasp" spaces by visualizing them according to the techniques of Renaissance one-point perspective (*SXI* 86).[10]

This perspective is that of the outside observer, the detached ego, whose privilege is inseparable from imaginary blindness. The Prefect's failure in detecting the letter is the result of his having put himself into a position of the Cartesian cogito occupying the geometral point of perspectival vision. As Johnson notes, "[t]he assumption that what is not seen must be hidden . . . is based on a falsely objective notion of the act of *seeing*" ("Frame" 482). In *Native Son*, Mrs. Dalton provides a rather literal incarnation of the Prefect's blindness. Despite her lack of sight, she, like Diderot's sightless observer, is able to "see" around her, including visualizing Bigger's blackness (52). However, the limits of her vision soon become apparent. After Mary's disappearance, she comes to Bigger to inquire about her daughter. As she leaves the room, Bigger realizes that she no longer can "see" him, that he has become invisible and is, in effect, "safe":

> She turned away and he shut the door; he stood listening to the soft whisper of her shoes die away down the hall, then on the stairs. He pictured her groping her way, her hands touching the walls. She must know this house like a book, he though. He trembled with excitement. She was white and he was black; she was rich and he was poor; she was old and he was young; she was the boss and he was the worker. He was safe; yes. (109)

Mrs. Dalton's "vision" is enabled by a perspective fixed around such oppositions as white/black; rich/poor; old/young; the employer/the employee. Adjacent passages contain numerous other references to such binaries: "He was a boy and she was an old woman. He was the hired and she was the hirer. And there was a certain distance to be kept between them" (108); "After all, he was black and she was white. He was poor and she was rich. . . . He felt confident" (109). If Mrs. Dalton can "see," she is able to do so only as long as such enabling oppositions are maintained, as long as everything around her—including her black servant—stays in its "place." From early on, Bigger understands that his confinement is secured through such polarities: "'We live here and they live there. We black and they white. They got things and we ain't. They do things and we can't. It's just like living in jail'" (17). The structures of the white symbolic order immobilize and incarcerate racially marked subjects. Subsequently, this keen appreciation of how the white symbolic functions by distributing subject positions allows Bigger to "rearrang[e] the space of the Daltons' house, [to] mak[e] their space his own" (Scruggs 82).

Poe's Prefect, continuing to detail his failed assignment in the Minister's apartment, tells Dupin and the narrator, "'we not only opened every book, but we turned over every leaf in each volume, not contenting ourselves with a mere shake, according to the fashion of some of our police officers'" (12). Mrs. Dalton's sudden inability to grasp Bigger's role in the events taking place in the white household is similarly described in terms of her failure to *read* her surroundings—or, rather, in terms of her surroundings ceasing to respond to her reading. As she turns away from Bigger, he "picture[s] her groping her way, her hands touching the walls. She must know this house like a book, he th[inks]. He tremble[s] with excitement." Bigger is thrilled as he realizes that he has become unreadable to her, that her "groping" around her house misses his implication in her daughter's disappearance. If Bigger is right in thinking that Mrs. Dalton knows her house *like a book*, she is acquainted with it like the policemen who go through the books in the Minister's library, groping the pages, turning them without reading.

Discussing the reasons behind the Prefect's failure, Lacan continues: "that what is hidden is never but what is *missing from its place*, as the call slip puts it when speaking of a volume lost in a library. And even if the book be on an adjacent shelf or in the next slot, it would be hidden there, however visibly it may appear" (40). Rigorous categories are susceptible to disruption; Dewey's decimal system loses a book even slightly misplaced in a library. Realizing that the Dalton household and, by extension, the white symbolic order is structured around such oppositions as white/black, rich/poor, male/female, master/servant, Bigger knows that once he transgresses these categories, he is lost to the eyes of those who are used to seeing things only according to this particular classificatory system. As Mr. Dalton receives the ransom note, Bigger disappears from the ordered space of the white household. Alienated, he becomes unrecognizable from geometral perspective. His "transparency" ceases to signal his availability as the object of white knowledge and, instead, makes him disappear. He becomes the (alienated) subject who is missing from its place.

The white Other, seemingly ever-present and inescapable, is suddenly riddled with lack, unable to observe that the [B]igger's place has been vacated. Here the movement of alienation, which leaves the place of the subject empty, includes separation, where the superior Other is found incomplete. Lacan suggests that the French term *séparation*, evoking *se parer* (*SXI* 214), signals the skillful self-defensive moves of "parrying" (*parer*) in fencing, of "ward[ing] off or turn[ing] aside a weapon or blow, esp. with a countermove" (*OED*). In realizing the lack in the Other, the subject learns to counter the Other's blows, to respond to them with "adroit [and] evasive repl[ies]" (*OED*). This is what Bigger does as he begins to "play (like) an idiot" in front of the white investigators. As much as *parer* can also be translated as "to adorn" something, Bigger fences with the white symbolic order by way of camouflage, by turning his *servant's livery* into *military fatigues.* Unlike the Hegelian battle for prestige between the slave and the master, the Lacanian understanding of alienation/separation allows us to appreciate such characteristically subaltern guerilla tactics of evasion and tricksterism. For Lacan, all these strategies signal the emergence of the subject: etymologically *séparer/séparation* also suggest the *parturition* of the subject, its coming into being through division (*SXI* 214). What happens to Bigger is not that he overcomes (in however momentary a fashion) his alienation, that he finds his place, but that he becomes, precisely, alienated, something missing from its place, *quelque chose qui manque à sa place.* Through the experiences of writing, he slips away from the "little spot of ground" (*Native* 331) that in the white symbolic order marks his burial site as a subject.

STEALING AWAY

The alienation of writing is figured as flying in *Native Son* and, as will become clear, in African American letters more generally. Following and revising the black tradition that Barrett discusses—that is, signifyin(g) with subtle shifts in perspectives and emphases—Wright suggests that, well into the twentieth century, the experience of the literary retained its centrality in African American efforts at contesting a social reality that took no heed of the Emancipation and Reconstruction as moments that were supposed to have reset the national clock. As described in *Native Son* and *Black Boy*, the structuring of the early- to mid-twentieth-century United States around the color line uncannily keeps alive the supposedly dead and buried racial arrangements of antebellum America. The racialized subject is confined to his or her place in the white symbolic order, a condition that always entails profound psychic ramifications. This condition—that of the subject in the [B]igger's place—is *not* one of alienation. If, as Leo Bersani has argued, contemporary theories present us with a "pastoral view of alienation as a peculiarly modern loss of cultural wholeness and harmony" ("Other" 49), the racialized subject in the white symbolic order does not have access to the fantasy of a de-alienating return to originary integrity. In *Native Son*, consequently, the experience of the literary not so much contests the black subject's alienation in and by symbolic structures as, by instituting a split in the Other, allows the possibility of his or her slippage from the symbolic order's grasp to a dangerously unknown future.

In order to clarify the connection between writing and flying, we may turn to another scene of writing from *Native Son*. Even though the passage is among the best known in the novel—Simone de Beauvoir, for example, cites it in *The Second Sex* (1949) (297–98)—it may not be immediately obvious that it deals with writing. In this early scene, Bigger and his friend Gus, two unemployed black men, are spending their day loitering on the streets of the South Side. As a motion in the sky draws Bigger's attention, he spots an airplane:

> The plane was so far away that at times the strong glare of the sun blanked it from sight.
> "You hardly can see it," Gus said.
> "Looks like a little bird," Bigger said with childlike wonder.
> "Them white boys sure can fly," Gus said. (14)

Houston Baker, Jr., proposes that the plane that Gus and Bigger are fascinated with suggests by contradistinction the "enormous confinement of black life" ("On Knowing" 201). Flying at an indeterminate distance ("'How high do you reckon he is?' Bigger asked./'I don't know. Maybe a hundred miles; maybe a thousand'" [14]), the almost indistinguishable plane represents, according to most readings, the freedom of which the two men are deprived. Simultaneously, the scene underlines the novel's prominent themes of visibility and race in that this freedom is marked by the near-invisibility of the plane. As Gus says, "'You can hardly see it.'" This freedom-as-invisibility contrasts to Bigger's own position in the visual field, where others' inquisitive gazing fixes him to his place. The two men's confinement is emphasized as they watch a pigeon on the street "strutting to and fro with ruffled feathers, its fat neck bobbing with regal pride." As the bird disappears, flying "out of sight over de [*sic*] edge of a high roof," Bigger says, "'Now, if I could only do that'" (18).

Apart from the question of visibility, Bigger's sighting of the plane evokes also another theme crucial to Wright's work in general. The plane, after all, is not just flying; it is writing—skywriting. As the two men gaze at the sky, the plane's vapors spell letters in the sky. The activity of writing is accentuated by the fact that it is the words, rather than the plane itself, that Bigger detects first: "A weaving motion in the sky made him turn his eyes upward; he saw a slender streak of billowing white blooming against the deep blue. A plane was writing high up in the air" (14). When, looking at the plane, Bigger asserts that he "'could fly one of them things'" if given a chance, his friend mocks him, reminding him of the futility of such ambitions: "'If you wasn't black and if you had some money and if they'd let you go to that aviation school, you *could* fly a plane'" (14).

In conjoining flying and writing in these passages, Wright cannily alludes to the way that the post-First World War resistance to black aviation rearticulated earlier white-supremacist arguments against African American higher education. If *uplifting the race* through schooling had been a central aspiration for black Americans since slavery and the Emancipation, black aviation, too, bore a crucial significance for Wright's contemporaries. After the First World War, black activists wanted to see African American men in the role of the heroic aviator, while facing a racist determination to keep the skies a whites-only realm. Pronouncements of African Americans as "physiologically unsuited for military aviation" rearticulated the logic of scientific racism that saw Africans undeserving of higher education. If black uplift through education had been intolerable to countless whites in the post-Emancipation America, similarly "the idea that blacks could master the most advanced machines of the day was nothing less than a provocation to the racist mindset of many Americans" (Hoberman 71, 72). Flying, like education, posed a serious challenge to racist beliefs and practices. Wright's subsequent novel *The Long Dream* (1958) concludes with a scene of flying in which the protagonist Fishbelly, flying to Europe, experiences for the first time the lifting of Jim Crow. The stewardess, "a blond young white woman" (345), leans over him, breaking the taboo of interracial contact that had circumscribed his life in the American South. He realizes: "It was the first time in his life that he had sat surrounded by white men, women, and children with no degrading, visible line marking him off" (346).[11] Bigger and Gus would have been aware of such challenges: as John Hoberman notes, by the 1930s Chicago had become "the mecca of black aviation" (74).

Bigger's subsequent flight has antecedents also in African American slave narratives and folklore. In naming the second part of his novel "Flight," Wright follows the likes of Harriet Jacobs, who calls herself a "bird" (612) and her escape from the Flint plantation "The Flight" (chap. 17), and Pauline Hopkins, who, in her serialized novel *Hagar's Daughter* (1901/1902), similarly describes a slave woman's doomed "flight" from the auction block as that of a "bird" (74).[12] This recurrent punning with the themes of aviation and escape taps into the myth of Flying Africans, whose circulation in diasporic slave communities has been recorded most famously in the Georgia Writers' Project's *Drums and Shadow: Survival Studies among the Georgia Coastal Negroes* (1940) and whose further developments are examined by Melvin Dixon ("'If'"; *Ride* passim), Wendy Walters, and Gay Wilentz. These scholars show the use of the myth throughout the diaspora[13] as "a collective symbol of resistance" (Wilentz, "If" 21), suggesting the subject's "ability to transcend one's condition" (W. Walters 22). Manthia Diawara, too, notes the interlinking themes of aviation and freedom in and beyond *Native Son*: "Black American literature often draws on the theme of flying to construct desire for liberated spaces: Bigger Thomas . . . sees flying as a way out of the ghetto of South Side Chicago; Milkman of *Song of Solomon* (Morrison) reenacts the myth of flying Americans in order to free himself from an unwanted situation" ("Black" 22).

In the economic order of the slave plantation, such flights always entailed a criminal *alienation* in the form of an illegitimate transfer of property. "Stealing away" from the proscribed locations and activities on the plantation was theft, abrogating the master's time and space. In however small ways—as a series of everyday acts of defiance "from praise meetings, quilting parties, and dances to illicit visits with lovers and family on neighboring plantations" (Hartman 66)—this illicit activity of self-appropriation rearranged the geography of the plantation and intervened in its temporality. Stealing away "involved seizing the master's property and asserting the self in transgression of the law" (68). "[Flying] in the face of the law" (69), the self-appropriative act of stealing away also highlighted the crime of theft that the slave economy depended on.[14] Ultimately, of course, it referred to the slaves' escape from their bondage, as embodied in the slave hymn "Steal Away to Jesus," whose coded message Bigger, in flight, is unable to hear (214–15). The hymn included instructions, hidden in plain sight, to slave runaways: the Lord "calls [the slave] by the thunder" because a storm was likely to wipe away the fugitive's footprints; "the green trees bending" suggests spring as the most provident of seasons for flight; and the reference to "tombstones . . . busting" reminded the runaway that graveyards were often used as meeting places for the "conductors" of the Underground Railroad (Tobin and Dobard 138).

We can further note that, as much as in African American history "metaphorical social (dis)placements were and remain frequently avian" (Lhamon 172), in Lacan's reading of Poe the alienating shifts in symbolic positions similarly transpire through the conjoined movements of "stealing," "writing," and "flying." The letter in its symbolic trajectory is propelled by dissemblance and theft: from the Queen's anxious concealment of the letter from his Majesty, to the Minister, who lifts the letter under the knowing gaze of the helpless Queen, to Dupin, who in a sideways glance from behind his tinted glasses detects what the inspectors have missed in the thief's apartment. The coincidence of theft and flight, recurrent in African American letters, occurs also in Lacan's seminar. As Lacan tells us, "The Purloined Letter" was translated into French by Charles Baudelaire as "*La lettre volée*" (29). Punning with the French verb *voler*—meaning, on the one hand, "to steal," and, on the other, "to fly"—he suggests that the letter circulating in Poe's story is not only stolen but also "flying." This doubling is registered to some extent in English in the verb "to lift," and, indeed, in his translation of Lacan's second seminar, Sylvana Tomaselli uses "to lift" for the French "*voler*": "The character in question lifted this letter from the table in the Queen's boudoir" (*SII* 186; see also 197n4).

Unlike the Prefect's pedestrian logic, paranoid self-alienation gives flight to one's cunning, marking a shift in symbolic fortunes. As much as Gus's and Bigger's earth-bound immobility is contrasted to the plane's or the pigeon's ability to fly and disappear, Bigger's consequent freedom is described as, among other things, his sense of being *lifted*. On the morning after the killing, he meets his friends and, as a grand gesture showing off his new position and wealth, buys them each a packet of cigarettes with the money he has taken from Mary's body. He has a feeling like that of "a man risen up well from a long illness" (95), and, as he leaves, feeling the adoration and envy of his friends, "[h]e walk[s] over the snow, feeling giddy and elated" (96). When he is having breakfast with his family after the murder, "[e]lation fill[s] him" (91) as he realizes that others cannot intuit his implication in the crime. He "wishe[s] that he could rise up through the ceiling and float away from this room, forever" (88). Distributing the money he has lifted from Mary's pocket, strutting and ruffling his feathers, Bigger is lifted off the ground. As such, his liberating sense of "being lifted out of oneself" (Rotenstreich 7) recalls pre-Hegelian theories of alienation in the philosophies of Plotinus and Augustine. For them, alienation (*alienatio*, from the Greek *alloiosis*) indeed corresponded to elevation (*elevatio*), denoting the "ecstatic" movement outside oneself, a lifting of the self to, and its merging with, a higher realm (3–4). However, just as the pigeon is a bird whose "regality" can be questioned, the reader cannot but anticipate Bigger's downfall. All the while, we suspect we're witnessing him not so much flying as getting carried away, leaving behind traces—where did he get the money?—that will inevitably lead to his being tracked down.

Native Son's description of alienation is thus markedly post-Hegelian in that Wright refuses to equate writing or the literary with transcendence. As Stephen Michael Best observes, he uses "flight" "not completely, or necessarily, as a sign of escape, but as a trope of *suspension* between poles of black and white, public and private, real and imaginary, past and present experience" (112). "Flight," the title of Book Two of *Native Son*, refers only momentarily to Bigger's avoidance of social or psychic sequestration; ultimately, it comes to denote his doomed escape from a white lynch mob. Indeed, in the context of Bigger's escape and the possible consequences of being caught, we might give a somewhat more literal reading to Best's understanding of the trope of "flight" as "*suspension*" by recalling the terroristic threat of criminalized black male bodies being—literally—"suspended."[15]

Consequently, rather than the Flying Africans, a more appropriate antecedent for Bigger in the African American tradition may be the "flying fool," to whose story Wright explicitly refers in *Lawd Today!* In the folktale, we meet a black man who is denied access to Heaven, St. Peter informing him that "God wasn't home or having any visitors—by which he meant no negroes allowed." When the white gatekeeper turns his back, the man sneaks into Heaven, "st[ealing] himself a pair of wings." Like Bigger's sudden mobility in the white space of the Dalton household, the man steals away in his borrowed wings, until he is "br[ought] . . . down" by a gang of white angels. Having been cast down, he observes: "'Yeah, they may not let any colored folks in, but while I was there I was a flying fool" ("Flying"). The foolishness of black dreams of flight in the white society surfaces as a theme in *Lawd Today!* as Jake gazes dreamily at a movie poster for a "flying picture," imagining himself in a fighter plane: "*Being an aviator sure must be fun, 'specially when you on top of another place and can send it spinning down like that . . .*" (52, 54; ellipsis in original). Yet, in his aggressive get-rich-quick schemes, elicited by the mass culture that, according to Wright and Frantz Fanon, plays a significant role in disciplining the black subject,[16] he turns out "A FLYING FOOL," as he calls himself, penniless and unemployed, at the end of the narrative (215). Similarly, Bigger may get his wings in the white household, but he ends up, like the protagonist of the folktale, "cornered," "br[ought] . . . down" by the white law and order. If the "heavenly police force" on the flying fool's tail reminds us of the lynch mob seeking out Bigger, it is no accident that, having been caught, the black aviator finds himself in up in a tree ("Flying" 118).

SCHOOLING FLYBOY

In spite of Bigger's ultimate downfall, we should not ignore the radical dimension of his momentary alienation. As an accident that, once it has occurred, takes on the aura of an ineluctable event, his crime is recognizable as an act, the kind of an answer of the real that for Lacan typifies ethics. Alenka Zupančič connects Lacan's ethical action, as that which is "grafted on to the real" (*SVII* 21), to what Kant calls a "*revolution*," "rebirth," and "a new creation" (qtd. in Zupančič, *Ethics* 36). Following this description, Bigger's disappearance from and dissemblance with the white symbolic order would be of the order of the ethico-real. As the text repeatedly insists, his destructive actions constitute "an act of *creation*!" (335; see also 90, 205, 242). Bigger's act, to recontextualize Zupančič, "is not simply an outrage, a word of defiance launched at the Other, it is also an act of creation of the Other (a different Other). [Bigger] is not so much a 'transgressor' as the 'founder' of a new order. After [Bigger], nothing will be as it was before" (*Ethics* 204). Jonathan Elmer articulates the creativity of Bigger's violence in terms of a Deleuzian "event" (783–84); its efficacy is extradiegetically reflected in the status of *Native Son* as "a novel from which there was no going back" (Scruggs 69).

Nevertheless, the shift in symbolic fortunes described in "The Purloined Letter"—the thief's entrapment by his strategy of "playing (like) an idiot"—is descriptive of not only Bigger's flight but also his capture. Lacan's observations about the Minister, whose symbolic mastery is reduced by Dupin to imaginary insensibleness, are applicable to Bigger: "we may properly doubt that [the Minister] knows what he is thus doing, when we see him immediately captivated by a dual relationship in which we find all the traits of a mimetic lure or of an animal feigning death, and, trapped in the typically imaginary situation of seeing that he is not seen, misconstrue the real situation in which he is seen not seeing" (44). The avoidance of imaginary capture is only temporary as the subject's symbolic insight turns into another trap. A certain "sliding effect" is almost inevitable in intersubjective triads: "The paradox is that . . . the 'acting accordingly' of the third position tends to catch the subject up in the dynamics of repetition that drag him into the second position, and so forth, without any conscious intention on his part" (Muller and Richardson, "Lacan's" 63). In Poe's story, the second, imaginary position is initially exemplified by the Queen while the Minister occupies the third, symbolic location. Soon, however, the tables are turned so that the Minister finds himself in the second position whereas the third one is taken over by Dupin. What may not be immediately obvious from the story is that, ultimately, Dupin himself slides into the second position (61–62).

If Lacan in the mid-1950s expounds on the repetitive sliding of symbolic structures, we should note the shift in his emphasis over the next decade. By the time of the eleventh seminar, *The Four Fundamental Concepts of Psycho-Analysis*, in 1964, something has emerged in the Lacanian schema that troubles the ineluctability of the letter's symbolic trajectory. De-emphasizing the structures described in "The Purloined Letter," Lacan becomes interested in the inhuman, impersonal real as that which is central to but remains uncontained by both intersubjectivity and the Other. This increasing focus on the real coincides with Lacan's shift away from his earlier, more structuralist influences. In his later work, with the real—a category that does not enter into consideration in the "Seminar on 'The Purloined Letter'"—Lacan seeks to articulate the susceptibility of symbolic structures to other arrangements, their opening onto newness.

If Bigger's alienation lands him in death row, through the experience of the literary Wright's autobiographical narrator gets further in flying/writing. I suggest that at stake in the narrator's literary exploits is the kind of persistence against symbolic injunctions that numerous slave narrators articulate as the revolutionary insistence on "freedom or death," precisely the choice that in *The Four Fundamental Concepts* reconfigures the dynamics of alienation/separation. With the autobiographical narrator's experience of the literary, Wright offers us a continuation of Bigger's violent creativity; the experience of the literary becomes, in its characteristic insanity and criminality, a choice of (symbolic) death. In Lacan's later work, this choice of death stands for the generative force of symbolic de-structuration. With the choice of "freedom or death," we get beyond "(the failure of) tragic transgression" (Chiesa and Toscana 23) that, despite the ethical dimension of Bigger's act, closes the narrative of *Native Son*. Extending Bigger's disruptive act, the narrator of *Black Boy* does not only "parry" with the Other; for him, the experience of the literary becomes "a precondition for a radically new symbolization" (23), marking the search for "an Other-thing [*Autre-chose*]" (*SVII* 212/251). Here emerges the death drive as "a will to create from zero, a will to begin again" (*SVII* 212).

Before being reconfigured, flying, writing, and visibility emerge in much the same terms in Wright's autobiography as they did in *Native Son*. In its two schoolroom scenes, which restage traditional episodes of tutelage in African American letters,[17] *Black Boy* conjoins the themes of visibility and the literary. Being apprehended by the gaze—even when, notably, the gaze is embodied in the narrator's peers and not, as in *Native Son*, primarily in white people—immobilizes the subject, incapacitating his reading (in the first scene) and writing (in the second). Here the narrator has bodily reactions similar to Bigger's as the latter is gazed at by the Daltons. Providing a further link between Wright's two texts, the angst of the second schoolroom scene is disrupted by an event that echoes with some precision *Native Son*'s skywriting episode.

The narrator's first school experience takes place at the Howard Institute. He recalls being "utterly incapable of opening [his] mouth when called upon" in the classroom: "The teacher called upon me and I rose, holding my book before my eyes, but I could make no words come from me. I could feel *the presence of the strange boys and girls behind me*, waiting to hear me read, and fear paralyzed me" (25, 26; emphasis added). Being apprehended by others' looks, the narrator experiences paralysis, his reading impeded. This immobility within visibility is repeated the next time he goes to a neighborhood school. A similar blockage of being "half paralyzed when in the presence of a crowd" (72) occurs as he is called to spell his name and address on the blackboard in front of other pupils:

> I knew my name and address, knew how to write it, knew how to spell it; but standing at the blackboard with *the eyes of the many girls and boys looking at my back* made me freeze inside and I was unable to write a single letter.
>
> "Write your name," the teacher called to me.
>
> I lifted the white chalk to the blackboard and, as I was about to write, my mind went blank, empty; I could not remember my name, not even the first letter. Somebody giggled and I stiffened. (72–73; emphasis added)

The presence of others—the gaze embodied in them—prevents the narrator from reading and writing. His failure is in marked contrast to the adroit actions of the young Booker T. in *Up from Slavery*. During his first day at the institution of Kanawha Valley, the autobiographical narrator performatively wills himself into legitimacy by improvising a father's name:

> When I heard the school-roll called, I noticed that all of the children had at least two names, and some of them indulged in what seemed to me the extravagance of having three. I was in deep perplexity, because I knew that the teacher would demand of me at least two names, and I had only one. By the time the occasion came for the enrolling of my name, an idea occurred to me which I thought would make me equal to the situation; and so, when the teacher asked me what my full name was, I calmly told him "Booker Washington," as if I had been called by that name all my life; and by that name I have since been known. (21)

Whereas the gaze reduces *Black Boy*'s narrator's mind to a "blank," Washington's protagonist performs seamlessly in front of the inquisitive crowd. Because of such oratorical ingenuity—which subsequently allows him to get out of many a such "'tight place'" (97)—Washington grows up to become the most recognized black spokesperson of his time. Wright's narrator never approximates, much less thrives as, such a suave actor in the circuits of visibility and recognition. In the schoolroom scenes, the gaze attributed to the other pupils functions as it did in the passages from *Native Son* where Bigger becomes uneasily aware of his corporeality under the eyes of his white employers. The young boy, standing in front of the class, feels himself "stiffen[ing]," "freeze inside"; his hand "refuse[s] to move"; he "flushe[s] hotly," feeling "paralyz[ed]," with "a storm of emotion surg[ing] through [him]" (72–74). Even if Washington himself may have suffered from similar panic attacks (according to Baker's recent diagnosis in *Turning South Again* [37–39]), unlike Richard he never fails to perform under the gaze.

Black Boy's second schoolroom scene is followed by a spectacle of blissful communality. The class session is cut short when the children hear noises on the street. These noises of celebration, they are told, signify the end of the (First World) War. As the class is dismissed, the narrator joins the celebrating crowds on the streets: "I followed the rest of the children into the streets and saw that white and black people were laughing and singing and shouting. I felt afraid as I pushed through crowds of white people, but my fright left when I entered my neighborhood and saw smiling black faces." The narrator's attention is drawn to the sky where, following other people's eyes, he spots an almost undetectable object. He initially assumes it to be "a tiny bird wheeling and sailing." It is, however, an airplane, as a man who lifts the boy on his shoulders explains: "'Boy, remember this,' he said. "You're seeing a man fly'" (74).

In these scenes, proceeding from the narrator's arrested literacy to the joy of sighting an almost invisible plane in the sky, the central themes of writing and visibility are, as in *Native Son*, connected to the trope of "flying." The intertextual connection between the two narratives becomes obvious when we note that the child's mistake in substituting a bird for the plane is restaged in Bigger's sighting of the skywriter: "'Looks like a little bird,' Bigger breathed with *childlike wonder*" (14; emphasis added).

If his expressions of literacy are stunted by the others' gaze, the narrator learns to negotiate "the look of the world" (*Black Boy* 164, 238) through the experience of the literary. As such, his efforts remind us of Bigger's supple parrying with the Other through writing and concealment. Yet, with the criminal and insane activity of the literary, the autobiographical narrator mounts a more sustained challenge to the symbolic world; I suggest that he does this by continuing the legacy of African American culture where the experience of the literary allows a radical possibility to reconfigure the symbolic realm, articulated in the subject's willing choice of (symbolic) death. If flying/writing constitutes for Bigger the process of alienation (and separation), in *Black Boy* the experience of the literary begins to function not as the alienating *vel* of "your money or your life" but as its radical extension that Lacan encapsulates in the subject's revolutionary insistence on "*freedom or death!*" (*SXI* 213). In this, Wright's autobiographical narrator follows numerous slave narrators. Whereas alienation, instituted by the Other's demand, marks the subject's emergence in the symbolic network, the latter set of choices constitutes the ethical subject's response that, potentially, corners the opponent and precipitates an overhaul of the symbolic system.

LITERARY DISSIPATION

For Hegel, positive freedom requires that the subject act according to "self-conscious, rational self-determination" (Schacht 77)—that the action springs from the self-conscious subject's essential nature, that is, reason. In *The Philosophy of Right*, Hegel establishes that the proper context for such freedom is that of ethical life, whose "system of pure reason" is embodied in the State (Schacht 79). The substance of the State and the substance of the subject are in profound accord; hence, positive freedom finds its expression in the conglomeration of moral customs, the *Sittlichkeit*, of the State's ethical community, made up of mutually recognized and recognizing propertied individuals.

Lacan, on the other hand, thinks freedom by extending the logic of alienation in having the subject counter the choice put forward by the Other—"your money or your life"—with her own impossible, *unreasonable* demand: "freedom or death." Thus introducing what Lacan calls "the lethal factor" into the symbolic pact, the subject possibly derails the symbolic network onto another trajectory, one whose shape is yet to be drawn. Joan Copjec writes that, while the choice of "freedom or death" for Hegel leads to the "freedom of the slave," for Lacan this demand, articulated by the subject to the Other, brings an ethical subject into being (*Imagine* 18; Lacan, *SXI* 212–13). Psychoanalytic thinking thus points to what Bersani calls the subject's "an anti-vital, perhaps even anti-evolutionary capacity to make us love death, to make us see dying as power" (*Death* 65).

The choice of freedom or death resonates with African American history as it was articulated by numerous antebellum black activists: they claimed their revolutionary heritage in deciding to opt for death rather than continuing bondage (see Bruce 271–72). The references to Patrick Henry in Douglass's *Narrative* (including William Lloyd Garrison's preface) (4, 74) are concretized in the fight with the slave-breaker Covey, and in her resistance Jacobs similarly appropriates Henry's "'Give me liberty, or give me death'" as her "motto" (608). When, as Henry Bibb notes in his narrative (1849), the slave law demands that the bondman "submit or die" (15), the slave counters this decree by taking the proposition literally and choosing death. When this choice is made, as James Pennington writes in *The Fugitive Blacksmith* (1849), "no consideration, not even that of life itself, could tempt [the slave] to give up the thought of flight" (120).[18] In the slave narrators' rhetoric, death and liberty are evoked in the same breath, as in the biblical term "deliverance." Whereas Douglass longs for "the glad day of deliverance of the millions of my brethren in bonds" (102), Pennington, to coax his elderly, dying father to Christianity, reminds him that "the moment of thy happy deliverance is at hand" (152). The choice of death as one of freedom is exemplified in the real-life case of the fugitive Margaret Garner's infanticide,[19] as well as in the fictionalized accounts of Clotel's (William Wells Brown) and Hagar Enson's (Pauline Hopkins) suicides. Theirs is a choice that Jacob Green describes in his "song of deliverance" (710) in his *Narrative* (1864):

My soul is vexed within me so
To think I am a slave,
Resolved I am to strike the blow
For freedom or the grave. (718)

Slave narrators often link the experience of the literary to their ability to articulate the radical "avian" alternative of freedom or death. Douglass, for example, is induced to evoke Patrick Henry's revolutionary phrase after the rude awakening he gets from reading. When Douglass has gained literacy, freedom begins to saturate his perspective: "The silver trump of freedom had roused my soul to eternal wakefulness. Freedom now appeared, to disappear no more forever. It was heard in every sound, and seen in every thing" (42–43). This hint of freedom immediately turns into a taste for death: "I often found myself regretting my own existence, and wishing myself dead; and but for the hope of being free, I have no doubt but that I should have killed myself" (43).

Later on, this drive for death is articulated in the fight with Covey: "I had reached a point, at which I was *not afraid to die*. . . . While slaves prefer their lives, with flogging, to instant death, they will always find christians [lower cases Douglass's] enough, like unto Covey, to accommodate that preference" (*My Bondage* 286). An acceptance of death as an answer to the pact of slavery is, then, precipitated in large part by the literary; this experience finally leads to the choice of "freedom or death."

W. E. B. Du Bois and Booker T. Washington similarly link the questions of freedom and death to that of the literary as they articulate their competing programs for post-Reconstruction black education. In *The Souls of Black Folk*, the ascent beyond the Veil is attained through the experiences of the literary and of death, two movements never quite distinct from one another. Du Bois ends his essay "Of the Training of Black Men" with an elegiac scene of transcendence of the Veil through cultural and literary communion: he glides "[a]cross the color line" with writers and philosophers—Shakespeare, Balzac, Dumas, Aristotle—who accept him "with no scorn nor condescension" (74), that is, without the "amused contempt and pity" of the white gaze that accompanies the primal scene of racial self-consciousness in the narrator (11). Here, "wed with Truth," he "dwell[s] above the Veil" (74). In Du Bois, the experience of the literary is figured as a potential moment of transcendence of racially determined experience; so is death. "[T]he dull red hideousness of Georgia" (74), which in "Of the Training of Black Men" is contrasted to the freer realm of the literary, is evoked also in the later installment "Of the Passing of the First-Born," where the narrator recounts the death of an infant. "We could not lay him in the ground here in Georgia," he writes, "for the earth there is strangely red; so we bore him away to the northward, with his flowers and his little folded hands" (133). Yet, the father seeks in vain free soil to bury the child in; instead, he begins to regard death itself as the only available realm uncontained by the world's carceral geography. In this, Du Bois repeats the antebellum affirmation of death as an emancipating release from earthly bondage, its "living death." Considering his dead infant child, the narrator writes: "my soul whispers to me, saying, 'Not dead, not dead, but escaped; not bond, but free.' No bitter meanness now shall sicken his baby heart till it die *a living death*, no taunt shall madden his happy boyhood" (133; emphasis added). His words echo with, for example, those of Solomon Northup, who, observing the painful death of a slave woman separated from her children, writes: "She was *free* at last!" (235). In Du Bois, death is similarly welcomed as a removal of the subject to a happier region "above the Veil" (134).

Death and education, including but not limited to the experience of the literary, as orientations toward a region above the Veil are brought together in the thirteenth chapter of *Souls*, "Of the Coming of John." As Eric Sundquist writes, the short story and "Of the Passing of the First-Born" are "joined together . . . by their shared concern with death and transfiguration" (521). Furthermore, "Of the Coming of John" illustrates the ideas put forward in

"Of the Training of Black Men": its black protagonist embodies the dilemma of the educated black subject. Together the three chapters encapsulate the danger and fecundity of black education not only as a flight from existing incarcerations but also a potentially deadly orientation toward an unactualized symbolic world.

As I suggested at the end of the previous chapter, John Jones returns to his natal community in Altamaha to discover that his education has rendered him a "monster" (148) in the eyes of white and black people alike; he has become maladapted to all available environments. He is initially encouraged in his project to start a school for black children by Judge Henderson, the prominent white citizen in town and the father of the white John, who has also left home to attend a Northern college. While the Judge approves of black education that promotes "'reasonable aspirations'" (151), John unwittingly violates all (symbolic) reason in his actions. Consequently, the town's white people decry "'his almighty air and uppish ways,'" considering him "'a dangerous Nigger'" (151). He has become one of the Reconstruction niggers whose "mighty flighty" (450) ways readers are called to witness and punish in Margaret Mitchell's white-supremacist epic *Gone with the Wind* (1936). Du Bois's story culminates with the flighty John Jones killing his childhood friend and white double, John Henderson, whom he meets molesting his sister. Returning home from the murder site, he announces to his mother: "'Mammy, I'm going away,—I'm going to be free'" (153). Seeking his freedom, he orients himself by gazing at the North Star, a guide for innumerable antebellum black fugitives.[20] Like for slave runaways, freedom for him also entails an active choice of death. Rather than escaping, John returns to the scene of murder and waits for the inevitable lynch mob, headed by the Judge, to deliver him the death that can only be an extension of the symbolic extinction he has undergone through education. He has become alienated from self: while keeping company to his dead namesake and wondering about the fates of his other childhood playmates, he thinks of John Jones, not recognizing himself: "And Jones,—Jones? Why, *he* was Jones" (153). This experience of self-alienation brings to his mind his ec-static experience of attending a performance of Wagner's *Lohengrin*.[21] Like the narrator at the closing scene of "Of the Training of Black Men," he had ascended through high culture, even if he gets a glimpse beyond the Veil through music and not literature: "A deep longing swelled in all his heart to rise with that clear music out of the dirt and dust of that low life that held him prisoned and befouled. If he could only live up in the free air where birds sand and setting suns had no touch of blood!" (147).

If the city where John Jones had attended opera is like a "sea, . . . so changelessly changing" (146), the story finishes with an actual sea as the scene of the death of the two Johns. The sea before John Jones represents an unmappable freedom, to whose appeal Douglass, too, responds in his famous address to the ships at Chesapeake Bay (*Narrative* 59–60). Yet, the music that seems to come from the sea—music that reminds John of Wagner—is indistinguishable from the rumble of the approaching lynch mob bearing "the coiling twisted rope" (154). The sea and death, as topoi of an unactualized beyond, intertwine at the end. Closing his eyes, John turns toward the sea; the last lines of the short story—"And the world whistled in his ears" (154)—leave it undecided if at the end the white mob kills him or if he suicides.[22]

Notably, the musical quotation that opens "Of the Coming of John" is culled from "I'll Hear the Trumpet Sound," a Negro spiritual describing the resurrection of the righteous on Judgment Day. Du Bois may have had the following lines in mind when he chose the song to introduce his story of education, ascent, and death:

> Father Gabriel in that day,
> He'll take wings and fly away . . .
> Good old Christians in that day,
> They'll take wings and fly away . . . (qtd. in Sundquist 523)

Again, the reference is to the myth of the Flying Africans (Sundquist 523). As John follows the North Star to the place of his passing, death in Du Bois is thus linked to the twin figures of education and flying.

In Du Bois, then, the region beyond segregation, beyond a world rent by the Veil, is visited through the experience of the literary—or, in wider terms, higher education and culture—and in death. Despite all their pronounced differences and disagreements, both Du Bois and Washington conjoin the literary with death, even if they draw radically divergent conclusions from this linkage. For Washington, black literary ambitions court death, jeopardizing black life in post-Reconstruction America. If in Du Bois the literary and death allow an ascent, or flight, beyond the Veil, Washington consistently figures "higher learning" as a lethal distance from the exigencies of living; literary ambitions corrode or impede the habits of survival that black citizens desperately need to cultivate in white America. The absurdity and barrenness of book learning is most often figured in the inexplicable pull of "Latin and Greek." Washington contrasts the study of these languages, one of them dead, to the pressing urgency of "life," describing misled students who "knew more about Latin and Greek when they left school, but [who] seemed to know less about life and its conditions as they would meet it at their homes" (*Up* 44). Contrasted to the immediacy of "life," the nonutility of "Latin and Greek," metonymically standing for higher learning, is set against the immediate demands of life. In Dana Luciano's apt turn of phrase, Washington warns the reader against "the necrophilic perversity of those embracing dead letters" (151).

Death delivered by the literary is embodied in the dissipated figure of the black dandy. Washington cites white representations of the outcome of black education: "The white people who questioned the wisdom of starting this new school [at Tuskegee] had in their minds pictures of what was called an educated Negro, with a high hat, imitation gold eyeglasses, a showy walking stick, kid gloves, fancy boots, and what not—in a word, a man who was determined to live by his wits. It was difficult for these people to see how education would produce any other kind of colored man" (57). While he wishes to excise Zip Coon from the minds of his white audience, he suggests that a wrong kind of education was indeed likely to produce such monstrous results: uppity black men and women, putting on airs, choosing the (moral and economic) death of book learning. For Washington, Latin and Greek render the black subject a minstrel character. Black men who get an undue ascent through their misplaced learning are figured as morbid, dissipated hucksters and dandies. Like the Victorian dandy, who "offended an ethic of industry and productivity" (Gagnier 65) by being "too relaxed, too visible, consum[ing] to excess while producing little or nothing" (Dellamora 199),[23] the black dandy actively damages the future of the race. In his 1884 essay "The Educational Outlook in the South," Washington bemoans such "educated loafers": "the proud fop with his beaver hat, kid gloves, and walking cane, who has done no little to injure the cause of education [in the] South," should "be brought down to something practical and useful" (355). Similarly, girls imbued with haughty aspirations through ill-conceived learning end up leading immoral lives; "[going] to the bad" (Washington, *Up* 45), they experience what earlier African American writers had referred to as the condition of immorality's "living death."[24]

Book learning in its countereconomics courts moral degeneracy, dissipation, and death. For Washington, its lethal excess and wastefulness endanger the black subject's place at the table of post-Reconstruction America. Du Bois remains more ambivalent about the potentially generative force of such morbidity. Unlike Washington, he does not seek to placate white fears of black education but admits its dangers, reminding his readership that "education among all kinds of men always has had, and always will have, an element of danger and revolution, of dissatisfaction and discontent" (*Souls* 29).

THE WAGER OF DEATH

This understanding of the experience of the literary as death allows us to complicate Russ Castronovo's critique of the choice of death as emblematic of "the struggle of liberalism to divest political vocabulary of history" (114), which gives us a bodiless, lifeless subject as the epitome of the citizen. In his compellingly argued reading of nineteenth-century discourses of "freedom," Castronovo finds this context-less abstraction of a subject championed by both antislavery and proslavery forces, black and white writers and orators alike. For him, North American discourses around freedom are consequently chronically ahistorical; the nationalized idiom of liberty presupposes a disembodied citizen, unmired in the situational specificities of (primarily) race and gender. As he writes, whether articulated in abolitionist or antiabolitionist tracts, "[f]reedom seems most complete when most disembodied" (121). This ideology of the bodiless subject explains for Castronovo the appeal of the discourse of death, of "political necrophilia," which permeates nineteenth-century debates over freedom, particularly as they were articulated in representations of slavery: death offers an idealized realm of unencumbered liberty; or, rather, it neutralizes the problem of freedom *as* a problem by doing away with the burden of bodies and their histories.

Castronovo thus rejects the absolutist rhetoric of death-as-freedom, instead calling for "a strategy of *anti*freedom to speak against the theoretical imperatives and abstractions of nationalized vocabulary" (139). He argues for the re-historicization and re-embodiment of the subject. To critique the grounding assumptions of American democracy—the privileging of male, white, propertied unmarkedness—and to render visible the everyday labor of contextualized, embodied struggle, we must resist the appeal of death exemplified in the antebellum rhetoric of freedom: death's "transcendent state excludes the very materiality that makes freedom a meaningful relation lived among others" (134).

Consequently, Castronovo argues that Paul Gilroy's endorsement, in *The Black Atlantic*, of the slaves' choice of death uncritically ventriloquizes the "nationalized vocabulary infused with necrophilia" (133). Discussing the slaves' risking of lethal violence toward themselves, Gilroy identifies a "revolutionary eschatology" in which "[t]he inclination toward death and away from bondage is fundamental" (*Black* 68). Rather than selling its readers "the idea of a rationally pursued utopia," the slave writers' "primary categories are steeped in the idea of a revolutionary or eschatological apocalypse" (56). Gilroy reads Douglass's account of his fight with Covey as a subversive reimagining of "Lordship and Bondage" in that the slave's wager of death destroys the self-preservative reason that in Western logic, exemplified by Hegel, leads to the bondsman's subordination. This, for Gilroy, allows us to rewrite "the primary history of modernity . . . from the slaves' point of view" (55). Yet, while the critique of Western post-Enlightenment philosophy in *The Black Atlantic* thus aims to unearth the revolutionary subject of modernism, Castronovo suggests that Gilroy's affirmation of the slave's embrace of death—primarily in the examples of Douglass and Margaret Garner—partakes in "political necrophilia." According to him, Gilroy does not see that the freedom of death requires the kinds of (racially) disembodied and unmarked subjects whose voices have dominated the discourses of Western rationalism. As a result, Gilroy's project of discoloring the unmarked whiteness of Western modernism is mired in a history of appeals whose aim has been diametrically opposed to his.

Through Gilroy's engagement with Lacan, however, we begin to discern why Castronovo's brilliantly executed argument cannot offer a full account of one of the theoretical devices it purports to harness for its support: the psychoanalytic notion of the death drive.[25] For Gilroy, Douglass's decision to go to his death rather than to submit to further abuse undoes the bondsman's reliance on the master's reality. Like Castronovo, who deploys Freud's delineation of the death drive in theorizing the nation's necrophilic passions (esp. 125, 129–30,

138), Gilroy, too, makes an uncharacteristic appeal to psychoanalysis in his attempt to account for the function of death in slave narratives. In positing Douglass as a counterexample to the Hegelian bondsman, he enlists Lacan for support in his project of rearticulating Hegel's philosophical tract from the perspective of the subaltern. He refers to Lacan's essay "The Subversion of the Subject and the Dialectic of Desire in the Freudian Unconscious" (1966) to bolster his stance that the risking of death by the enslaved Douglass reorients Hegel's battle for prestige by making the slave, instead of the master, the one who ups the ante to an all-in wager.

Gilroy correctly identifies "The Subversion of the Subject" as containing one of Lacan's (numerous) dialogues with Hegel. This essay, whose full title announces its Hegelian context, was originally delivered in September, 1960, at a conference on "La Dialectique," where Lacan appeared at the invitation of the prominent Hegelian Jean Wahl ("Subversion" 281). Here Lacan offers a reading of Hegel that had oriented his theory of tragedy in *The Ethics of Psychoanalysis* and that was to inform the description of the processes of alienation and separation in the eleventh seminar, *The Four Fundamental Concepts.*[26] Having contrasted the enslaved subject in *Narrative* to the bondsman in the *Phenomenology*, Gilroy links Douglass's restaging of the battle to Lacan's critique of Hegel. He cites "The Subversion of the Subject" to describe what happens to the scene of confrontation when the slave chooses death rather than the master's reality. Lacan writes:

> death—precisely because it is dragged into the stakes (making this a more honest wager than Pascal's, though Hegel's too is a poker game, since limits are placed on how high the bid can be raised)—simultaneously shows what is elided by a preliminary rule as well as by the final settlement. For, in the final analysis, the loser must not perish if he is to become a slave. In other words, a pact always precedes violence before perpetuating it, and what I call the symbolic dominates the imaginary, allowing us to wonder whether or not murder really is the absolute Master. (296)[27]

Pascal encourages us to wager on God: even if we turn out to be incorrect, we lose nothing; but if God does exist, we will have raked in eternal life. The gambler that concerns Lacan backs a more dangerous proposition: putting everything on one card, s/he forces the (master's) house to reveal its hand. Lacan translates Hegel's earlier scenario, which excludes the slave's death, into psychoanalytic vocabulary by comparing it to the emergence of the subject in the mirror stage. For him, the institution of the Hegelian master–slave relation is characterized by the "specular capture" that, according to psychoanalysis, has its genesis in "the generic prematurity of birth" and the subsequent *méconnaissance* of the mirror stage (296). From a psychoanalytic perspective, the master–slave relation establishes a symbolic circuitry where one's position is susceptible to the kind of "sliding" into imaginary blindness that Lacan describes in his reading of Poe. When death, "the lethal factor" (*SXI* 213), appears, the specular capture of the master–slave dialectic is broken. The Other's constitutive demand, "*your money or your life*," is superseded by another set of options: the slave rearticulates the pact with his choice of "*freedom or death*."

For Castronovo, death constitutes a utopian withdrawal from embodiment and politics, inducing a (color)blindness that sustains dominant historiography. Yet, in "The Subversion of the Subject" Lacan adds a crucial distinction, one that, if accepted, scrambles Castronovo's delineation of the slave's wager: "it is not enough," Lacan writes, "to decide the question on the basis of its effect: Death. We need to know which death, the one that life brings or the one that brings life" ("Subversion" 296). If at stake is death—"the lethal factor"—we have to be clear *which death* hangs in the balance. The endnote Lacan appends to these sentences refers his audience to the recently completed seminar *The Ethics of Psychoanalysis*. This seminar includes the famous reading on Sophocles's *Antigone*, which contradicts Hegel's dialectical rendition of Creon's and Antigone's clash. For Lacan, Antigone's stubborn insistence on the burial of her brother exemplifies an ethical stance that cannot be accounted for in the symbolic terms represented by the laws of the polis and embodied in Creon. By speaking of the death drive, Lacan wants to emphasize the importance not of Antigone's physical death—the law's deadly retaliation—but of her position as not locatable within or explicable by symbolic logic. What concerns Lacan is Antigone's or, in "The Subversion of the Subject," the slave's *symbolic* death as a loss that "brings life."

Similarly, if we are to consider political necrophilia in psychoanalytic terms, we must understand the slave's decision to die not primarily in terms of her biological extinction but as the kind of creative act that also characterizes the inconceivability of Bigger's crime and, as I argue, the experience of the literary in *Black Boy* and slave narratives. As Žižek writes, while symbolic suicide "aims to exclude the subject from the very intersubjective circuit," it can be seen as "the very foundation of a new social link" (*Enjoy* 44, 45). Unlike Pascal's safe bet, choosing death is an insane wager, one that does not make sense according to any existing forms of calculation. By opting for this senseless logic, the slave potentially steps outside of the symbolic pact that binds him to the plantation. The experience of the literary functions, precisely, as such an insane choice in *Black Boy*. Speaking of his adolescent friends, the narrator observes: "Although they lived in an America where in theory there existed equality of opportunity, they knew unerringly what to aspire to and what not to aspire to. Had a black boy announced that he aspired to be a writer, he would have been unhesitatingly called *crazy* by his pals" (188; emphasis added). As in *Up from Slavery*, the insanity of the literary is in its nonutility for symbolic survival. In numerous slave narratives, the encounter with reading similarly brings the narrator face to face with the beyond of language's capabilities. In Douglass, the experience of the literary "sting[s the narrator's] soul to unutterable anguish" (*Narrative* 42), while in Pennington's *The Fugitive Blacksmith* it "grieve[s the narrator] beyond description" (135). As I suggested in the previous chapter, the literary brings such pain because it points toward, without giving a definite form to, an unactualized beyond of current possibilities. The slave subject is left suspended, hanging in mid-air. Douglass concretizes this unactualized something in his address to the ships at Chesapeake Bay. Imagining the beyond in terms of the "'fly[ing]'" ships under whose "'wing'" he longs to be, he "goad[s himself] almost to madness at one moment, and at the next reconcil[es him]self to [his] wretched lot" (*Narrative* 59, 60). If madness refers to the potential creation of a new Other, this names precisely the insanity of Bigger's crime. In the stage adaptation of *Native Son*, when Max identifies Bigger's violent act as one of "creation," of his being born as a subject, Buckley correctly identifies the implications: "He is pleading the prisoner insane, Your Honor!" (Green and Wright 92).

That the insanity of black writing is complemented by its criminality in the white symbolic order is suggested by antebellum statutes proscribing slave education. Similarly, encountering the response to his first published story, *Black Boy*'s narrator muses, "I felt that I had committed a crime" (161).[28] The experience of the literary, as a choice of (symbolic) death, constitutes an incalculable, and hence "insane," crime against the symbolic order. Like in "The Purloined Letter," where "poetry" is linked to insanity (the Prefect's view of poets as "fools") and to criminality (Dupin's admission of his own "guilt" in such "doggerel" [10]), in Douglass and in Wright African American reading and writing constitutes not only "crazy" but also criminal activity.[29] In *Native Son*, such crime and insanity entail the racialized subject's ability to manipulate the field of the visible. Lacan, too, speaks of "the poet's superiority in the art of concealment" ("Seminar" 37), prompting Shoshana Felman to note that "a 'principle of concealment' . . . has to do with poets and thus (it might be assumed) is specifically poetic" (*Jacques* 47). *Black Boy*, however, does not deal primarily with such performances under the white gaze but considers the literary as a potentially deadly withdrawal from the symbolic order.

The experience of the literary does not constitute "labor" in the Hegelian sense. For Hegel, labor is the necessary corollary of the slave's mortal terror of the master. Without labor, this terror remains "inward and mute" (*Phenomenology* 239); only through work does the slave move on and attain consciousness-for-itself. As Kojève points out, through his labor the slave goes beyond, precisely, the *criminality* and *insanity* that characterize the experience of the literary:

> Without work that transforms the real objective World, man cannot really transform himself. If he changes, the change remains "private," purely subjective, revealed to himself alone, "mute," not communicated to others. And this "internal" change puts him at variance with the World, which has not changed, and with the others, who are bound to the unchanged World. This change, then, transform man into *a madman or a criminal*, who is sooner or later annihilated by the natural and social objective reality. (28; emphasis added)

Lacan, too, speaks of work in the *Ethics* seminar, but he connects it to the symbolic authority of Creon, the counterpoint to Antigone as the embodiment of psychoanalytic ethics. He cites the superegoic call: "'Carry on working. Work must go on. . . . As far as desires are concerned, come back later. Make them wait'" (*SVII* 315). For Lacan, this call to labor—which translates as "'Let it be clear to everyone that this is on no account the moment to express the least urge of desire'" (*SVII* 315)—is diametrically opposed to the ethical injunction for the subject to persist in, not to "give ground relative to," one's desire, a stance exemplified by Antigone. Whereas in Hegel the slave labors, in Lacan she *persists*. The slaves' insistent encounter with death should be characterized by what Freud calls *Haftbarkeit*, a term that, according to Lacan, "is perhaps best translated by 'perseverance' but has a curious resonance in German, since it means also 'responsibility,' 'commitment'" (*SVII* 88; qtd. also in Copjec, *Imagine* 16).[30] As Copjec observes, this persistence in the face of death, which Freud distinguishes from *Fixierarbeit*—the repetitive actions posited on the subject by libidinal fixations—marks Antigone's ethical stance in disregarding Creon's orders. Such ethical perseverance in Lacan puts the subject "at variance with the World" (Kojève 28); *Haftbarkeit*, in its orientation beyond the symbolic, can register only as criminal and insane, like Antigone's symbolically unaccountable persistence or the slave's insistence on freedom.

If psychoanalysis ends up stressing the ethics of the death drive—the ethics of the real—this cannot be collapsed with the "nationalized vocabulary of disembodiment" (121) that Castronovo finds in the antebellum rhetoric of political necrophilia. For him, the death drive guides the subject beyond its exhausting engagement with the volatile energies of living, with "striving and contention" (125). Figured as the release of death, freedom is achieved in the zero-degree of tension of the inorganic state beyond pleasure and pain, beyond the vacillations of bound and unbound energies: "[death-as-f]reedom streamlines subjectivity, forging a nationalized vocabulary that privileges word over flesh and exalts utopia over history" (142), Castronovo argues. However, the drive does not function quite as straightforwardly as he presupposes. In understanding the evacuation of energies as the drive's satisfaction, we are, to be precise, mistaking *Triebziel* for *Objekt*, the aim of the drive for its goal. As Copjec reminds us, in psychoanalysis "the death drive achieves its satisfaction by *not* achieving its aim" (*Imagine* 30). According to her, *Todestrieb* itself follows the circuits of sublimation as the proper domain of the drive: "while the *aim* (*Ziel*) of the drive is death, the *proper and positive activity* of the drive is to inhibit the attainment of its aim; the drive, *as such*, is *zielgehemmt*, that is, it is inhibited as to its aim, or sublimated, 'the satisfaction of the drive through the inhibition of its aim' being the very definition of sublimation. Contrary to the vulgar understanding of it, then, sublimation is not something that happens to the drive under special circumstances; it is the proper destiny of the drive" (30). In other words, if we concede its psychoanalytic specificity, the notion of the death drive does not exempt us from wordly, fleshed struggles by freeing the subject from all tension, as Castronovo argues. What he calls "freedom's antagonism to accidents of the flesh" (134) does not find confirmation in psychoanalysis, whose ethics always concerns the "suppurate" excretions of bodily matter (Copjec, *Imagine* 179).

To be fair to Castronovo, Freud is at best ambivalent concerning the distinction between the death drive and the principle of inertia. A Lacanian reading—like the one pursued here—necessarily insists on a clear distinction between the drive and the Nirvana principle (*SVII* 211). For Lacan, the drive's aim of death needs to be qualified. If we speak of the slave's wager of death, we need to clarify the death at stake as symbolic ("Subversion" 296). Similarly, if there is a "[w]ill to destruction" in the drive, this is not distinguishable from a "[w]ill to make a fresh start," "a will to begin again" (*SVII* 212). What Castronovo's reading of the death drive cannot acknowledge is that if the death drive concerns an escape from "reality," this escape is a flight from the reality of *a* symbolic order. Lacan intimates that this symbolic can be rearranged radically, that there is *a becoming of the death drive*, which "has to do with making, with the production *ex nihilo*" Lacan refers to as symbolic creation (*SVII* 225). The drive's "will to create from zero" should be seen as a will for unactualized symbolic potentialities, for some(thing) Other, *quelque chose d'Autre* (*SVII* 212). Simultaneously, in its blind orientation beyond the symbolic, the drive does not obey utopian teleologies, as Castronovo (142) assumes, but is oriented only in terms of the unforeseeability of becoming: here we find "a precondition for a radically new symbolization. . . . [T]he death drive ultimately relies on the law of the *ex nihilo* as the 'will' to *begin* again" (Chiesa and Toscana 23).

THE LITERARY, FLIGHT, BECOMING

In his overview of studies on orality and literacy, Walter J. Ong argues that the transformation from oral to literate cultures is accompanied by shifts in psychic constitution of the subject. According to Ong, the technologies of writing and reading occasion "interior transformations of consciousness" (82): they "engage the psyche in strenuous, interiorized, individualized thought. . . . In the private worlds that they generate, the feeling for the 'round' human character is born—deeply interiorized in motivation, powered mysteriously, but consistently, from within" (153). In Patterson's Hegelian terms, such interiority would be the moment that allows the enslaved subject's negation of natal alienation, his or her emergence as a subject: "The very reflectiveness of writing . . . encourages growth of consciousness out of the unconscious" (150), rendering literacy a "consciousness-raising activity" (151).

Casting Ong's affirmative observations in the context of Wright's and the slave narrators' accounts of literacy and reading reminds us that such work of "consciousness-raising" not only constitutes an uprising against some hegemonic order but also necessitates an abandonment of an existing reality, however injurious and intolerable, for the uncertainties of becoming. Given such unforeseeability, this process is always painful and perilous. Psychoanalysis's counterintuitive ethical decree is for the subject not to labor but to orient her commitment toward that which registers in current symbolic terms as insanity or crime. Gilroy approximates this logic in observing that "in the [slaves'] revolutionary eschatology . . . the moment of jubilee . . . has the upper hand over the pursuit of utopia by rational means" (*Black* 68). Antigone's ethical persistence does not seek a utopia; instead, her ethics of *becoming* needs to be distinguished from the teleology that Hegel articulates as history's ineluctable pull toward the Absolute.

In *Slave Life in Georgia* (1855), John Brown alludes to this necessarily unactualized and unformed space of freedom as his slumbering narrator, in flight from bondage, describes his elation at being disoriented in terms of reality: "I felt so singularly happy, . . . notwithstanding the fear I was in, at not being able to make out where I was, that I could only conclude I was in a dream, or a vision, and for some minutes I could not rid my mind of this idea" (378). Similarly, while the experience of the literary alienates the subject by providing perspectives that are incompatible with the white symbolic order, it does not suture him or her into a readily available Other. Yet, as a suspension of symbolic reality, the experience of the literary may allow the actualization of another symbolic order, the very act that is at the core of Lacanian ethics. As such, the experience of the literary not only institutes the *vel* of alienation, whereby the subject emerges, but simultaneously enables the more radical choice that Lacan—and numerous nineteenth-century black authors—characterize as that of "*freedom or death*."

The difference between a substitution of one structure for another and a more dangerously open becoming can be gauged in the becoming Re(a)d of *Black Boy*'s narrator. In the autobiography, Wright suggests that reading—the experience of the literary—enables a more radical and sustained challenge to white symbolic dictates than becoming Red. Simultaneously, becoming read is more dangerous in that, while communism has an established framework for the subject to situate himself in, the experience of the literary offers no immediate alternative reality to the white symbolic order. Rather, reading merely suspends reality by providing the subject an awry perspective on that which exists: as Douglass discovers, reading "[had] opened [his] eyes to the horrible pit, but to no ladder upon which to get out" (*Narrative* 42). According to Wright, numerous African Americans have found such a ladder in, precisely, becoming Red. He writes in *White Man, Listen!* that, seeking tools of leverage, many have "accept[ed] an ideology in which they do not believe. They [have] accept[ed] it in order to climb out of their prisons. Many a black boy in America has seized upon the rungs of the Red ladder to climb out of his Black Belt. And well he may, if there are no other ways out of it" (20). In an interview, he recognizes his own relation to communism in this: "communism was the only ideology which made some sense of my experience," he says. " . . . It was a way out of a morass" ("One" 241).

Yet, as Wright goes on to detail in the (posthumously published) second part of his autobiography, the ready alternative that being Red presents the subject proves to be its very failing. Despite the Party members' relative lack of immediate racism (302, 351), becoming Red leads the racialized subject into another trap. The numerous African American spokespeople for the Party are described thus:

> Many of their mannerisms, pronunciations, and turns of speech had been consciously copied from white Communists whom they had recently met. While engaged in conversation, they stuck their thumbs in their suspenders or put their left hands into their shirt bosoms or hooked their thumbs into their back pockets as they had seen Lenin or Stalin do in photographs. Though they did not know it, they were *naively practicing magic*; they thought that if they acted like the men who had overthrown the czar, then surely they ought to be able to win their freedom in America.
>
> In speaking they rolled their "r's" in Continental style, pronouncing "party" as "parrrtee," stressing the last syllable, having picked up the habit from white Communists. "Comrades" became "cumrrades," and "distribute," which they had known how to pronounce all their lives, was twisted into "distrrribuuute," with the accent on the last instead of the second syllable, a mannerism which they copied from Polish immigrants who did not know how to pronounce the word. (281; emphasis added)

This *naive practice of magic* reminds us of Roger Caillois's and minstrel theorists' descriptions of the "incantation" that captures the subject. The instrumentalist pretense of being Red soon possesses the subject, rendering him immobile: "Communism, instead of making them leap forward with fire in their hearts to become masters of ideas and life, had frozen them at an even lower level of ignorance than had been theirs before they met Communism" (282).

Like "Bright and Morning Star," *Black Boy*, then, describes how the Red perspective, allowing a new view on the symbolic order, rigidifies into another imaginary posture, thus exemplifying the sliding effect of intersubjectivity Lacan theorizes in his reading of Poe. Tellingly, programmatic communism cannot tolerate the open-endedness of the experience of the literary, its restless becoming. The comrades of *Black Boy*'s narrator are, like the rest of his environment, suspicious and distrustful of reading. They "denounced books they had never read" (282); "I discovered that it was not wise to be seen reading books that were not endorsed by the Communist party" (315). When he is asked to prove his "revolutionary loyalty" to the Party, he responds, "'That's what I'm trying to do through writing.'" He is told that he has confused being read and being Red: "'That's not the way to do it. . . . You must act'" (317). While the Party's exhortation to "act" refers to "taking action," the term inevitably also recalls the form of obsequious "acting" that the white symbolic order demands of racially marked subjects. If he wants to be accepted by the Party, the narrator must go on "acting," heeding the exigencies of the optical trade. But it is impossible for him to adjust to the Party's vision. He cannot accept "the correct vision of life" (327) put forward by the communists, because "[w]riting was my way of seeing, my way of living, my way of feeling" (329).[31]

If Elmer (783–84) sees in Bigger's act an event of the kind Deleuze theorizes in *The Logic of Sense*, the experience of the literary may also be regarded in Deleuzian sense as a flight toward an unactualized future. Of course, Deleuze's term *fuite*—the act of "fleeing," "flowing," "leaking"—does not denote the English "flying" (Massumi xvi). Neither is my intention here to uncritically collapse Deleuze's flight and Lacan's ethical perseverance. Nevertheless, even with the proviso that the two theorists' similarities and differences need to remain an open question, we can recognize in Deleuze's description of flight resonances with avian alienation: "The great and only error [lies] in thinking that a line of flight consists in fleeing from life; the flight into the imaginary, or into art. On the contrary, to flee is to produce the real, to create life, to find a weapon" (Deleuze and Parnet 49). Unlike what Castronovo assumes, Bigger and other African American aviators do not escape life but create one, conjuring weapons with which to dismantle the symbolic and, possibly, precipitate anOther. In *Native Son*'s skywriting scene, writing becomes an act of violence, as, looking at the skywriting airplane, Bigger muses: "'Maybe they right in not wanting us to fly. . . . 'Cause if I took a plane up I'd take a couple of bombs along and drop 'em as sure as hell . . ." (15; second ellipsis in original).[32] Here one can note further intertextual resonances between the scenes of writing/flying in *Native Son* and *Black Boy*. One may assume that, taking place at the end of the First World War, the autobiography's second schoolroom scene closes with the narrator's sighting of not only a plane but a bomber.[33]

Of course, in Poe's tale, too, aggression characterizes the path of the letter: the Minister lifts the letter from the royal boudoir in order to do "harm" to the Queen; Dupin steals the letter to exact a revenge for some past "evil" done to him by the Minister (see Johnson, "Frame" 466–67, 503). Lacan evokes these moments of violence when he notes that Dupin comes to the Minister's apartment "*armed* with a facsimile" ("Seminar" 31; emphasis added). Further echoing the description of Bigger's desire to "drop bombs" when writing/flying, Lacan writes of *la lettre volée* that, as recipients of the stolen/flying letters, we are "*bombarded* . . . with them" (*SII* 198; emphasis added). Famously, the experience of the literary in *Black Boy* expresses the narrator's violence. Reading Mencken, the narrator is "jarred and shocked by the style, the clear, clean, sweeping sentences. . . . [He] picture[s] the man as a raging demon, slashing with his pen, consumed with hate." He realizes: "this man was fighting, fighting with words. He was using words as a weapon, using them as one would use a club. Could words be weapons? Well, yes, for here they were. Then, maybe, perhaps, I could use them as a weapon?" (237). Such moments of avian alienation must not be dismissed as mere flights of fancy, a doomed search for "the airy rights of freedom" (Castronovo 135). Instead, "to flee is not to renounce action: nothing is more active than a flight. It is the opposite of the imaginary" (Deleuze and Parnet 35).

In slave narratives and in Wright, I argue, death points not to abstract ahistoricity (as Castronovo claims) but to the volatility of becoming whose exact shape—whose *specific historicity*—cannot be imagined from within the framework of our current embodied existence. While Castronovo argues that "[s]uicide secures a necrophilic fantasy of innate natural liberty by discounting history" (129), the self-destructive perseverance of an Antigone does not do away with history in favor of "utopia" (142), but *aims at another history yet to be narrated.* Symbolic suicide constitutes not one's happy removal from the anguish of history but (potentially) a creative act of another symbolic. Psychoanalysis would insist that the slave narrators' death drive—their rearticulation of the Revolutionary insistence on "freedom or death"—does not implicate them in the discourse of the disembodied citizen, but constitutes an untimely leap into that which does not yet exist as embodied: a future as radically divergent from the present.

Notes

Epigraphs: Baldwin, "Last" 210; Douglass, *My Bondage* 148.

INTRODUCTION

Epigraphs: Wright, "Interview" (with de Vaal) 155; Green and Wright 61.

1. See Voltaire and Kant. Other early construction workers of race include Francois Bernier, Johann Gottfried von Herder, Johann Friedrich Blumenbach, and G. W. F. Hegel: see the excerpts from their work in Bernasconi and Lott, eds.

2. While W. E. B. Du Bois is one of the earliest and best-known critics to point out the illusory nature of racial categorizations (see his *Africa* 20, and *Negro* 27, 225), Richard Wright, too, clearly recognizes that racial formations are not based on biology: see *White* 80 and "Interview" (with de Vaal) 155–56. Most recently, Paul Gilroy has made a powerful argument for "abolishing" race: see his *Against Race*.

3. Wright himself endorses such work of alienation in our approaches to African American culture: "What new values of action or experience can be revealed by looking at Negro life through alien eyes or under the lenses of new concepts?" he asks in his introduction to St. Clair Drake's and Horace R. Cayton's *Black Metropolis* (1945). " . . . What would life on Chicago's South Side look like when seen through the eyes of a Freud, a Joyce, a Proust, a Pavlov, a Kierkegaard?" (xxxi).

4. On Wertham, see Marriott chap. 3 and Fabre, *Unfinished* 236, 272, 276, 292, 354; on Karpman, see ibid. 271–72, 284. Wertham's "An Unconscious Determinant in *Native Son*" (1944) is the earliest psychoanalytic reading of Wright's work. For Wright's library, see Fabre, *Richard*.

5. See also Claudia Tate's chapter on Wright in her *Psychoanalysis*, esp. 93–94.

6. See West, "Malcolm X" 55; Michele Wallace 55–56; and Singh xv.

7. For a reassessment of Mannoni, see Khanna chap. 4.

8. For examples of this in Freud, see *Three* 49–50, 57n, 66, 88, 91, 168; "On Narcissism" 67, 92–93; "Instincts" 129; "Unconscious," 199–200; "Group" 114, 148, 154ff.; "Moses" 360; "Question" 343; "Outline" 436. Of course, Freud is not alone in posing this analogy: see, for example, Hegel's remarks about Negroes as "a race of children" ("Anthropology" 40) and Africa as "the land of childhood" (*Philosophy of History* 196).

9. See Moore; Tate, "Freud'" 54–57, 59–60.

10. See also Iginla.

11. See Freud, "Über Coca." For relevant discussions of "Moses and Monotheism," see Boyarin, "'Imaginary'"; Santner, "Freud" and "Freud's."

12. See also Gilman, *Freud* and *Jew's*; Boyarin, "'Imaginary'"; and Khanna. Inevitably, psychoanalysis itself was a racially marked science: as Gilman notes, the term "psychoanalyst" functioned for Nazis as a "synonym . . . for 'Jew'" (*Jewish* 13; qtd. in Wilentz, "Healing" 70). For the considerable role of Otto Weininger, and in particular of his best-seller *Sex and Character* (1903), in the construction of Jewishness as a pathology in psychoanalysis and early twentieth-century German culture, see Harrowitz and Hyams, eds., and especially Gilman's "Otto" therein.

13. See also Boyarin, "What?" Hortense Spillers, too, writes that "the 'race' matrix was the fundamental *interdiction* within the enabling discourse of founding psychoanalytic theory and practice itself" ("'All'" 89).

14. In "Freud" (esp. 57), Claudia Tate turns to Rogin's thesis to theorize Freud's use of the primitive.

15. For an argument similar to (if somewhat more nuanced than) Torgovnick's, see Tate, "Freud" esp. 54–55.

16. See Jean Walton's discussion of Marie Bonaparte, Melanie Klein, and Joan Riviere in *Fair*. Walton's argument that early women psychoanalysts "were especially susceptible to mobilizing racial signifiers in the negotiation of their status within [the] social symbolic" (12) points to a similar dynamic of "blackfacing" that Tate and Rogin discuss with respect to Freud and early-twentieth-century Jewish Americans, respectively.

17. Murray mentions Arnold Rampersad's *The Life of Langston Hughes* (1986), Thadious Davis's *Nella Larsen: Novelist of the Harlem Renaissance* (1994), and Keith Byerman *Seizing the Word: History, Art, and Self in the Work of W. E. B. Du Bois* (1994). We may add Margaret Walker's *Richard Wright, Daemonic Genius* to the list. It seems, then, that biographers have taken on the challenge Rampersad put forward in 1988 in "Psychology and Afro-American Biography." Rampersad describes his Hughes biography as "mildly Freudian" (10). On Davis's book on Larsen, see also Tate, *Psychoanalysis* 139–40.

18. Spillers subsequently makes her psychoanalytic influence explicit in "'All.'"

19. See also Bergner, "Politics" 220–25.

20. While all Žižek's work is marked precisely by this engagement of Lacan with politics, Laclau has increasingly provided psychoanalytic readings of his theories of citizenship and radical democracy. His engagement with psychoanalysis is already evident in the classic *Hegemony and Socialist Strategy* (1985), written with Chantal Mouffe, and has become central to his thinking by *Emancipation(s)* (1996), *Contingency, Hegemony, Universality* (2000), written with Judith Butler and Žižek, and *On Populist Reason* (2005). See also Laclau's remarks in Pessoa et al. 14–15. Stavrakakis's *Lacan and the Political* provides a lucid introduction to these questions.

21. See in particular the essays by Merrill Cole, Tim Dean, Seshadri-Crooks, Suzanne Yang, and Žižek.

22. Mellard includes Žižek, Joan Copjec, Elizabeth Cowie, and Juliet Flower MacCannell in the ranks of "the New Lacanians." More recently, Alenka Zupančič, Tim Dean, and Charles Shepherdson have emerged as important contributors to this field.

23. See, for example, her reductive description of "Freud" (348n10).

24. Tate similarly argues that "psychoanalysis has repressed the effects of social oppression on the primary family. There are no neutral cultural contexts for plots of

subjective development." She further contends that "Wright's fictions make [the] erroneous presumptions [of psychoanalysis] about cultural neutrality quite conspicuous" (*Psychoanalysis* 114). Barbara Johnson gives an example of the blindness of (not Freud's nor Lacan's but) Heinz Kohut's psychoanalytic theory to the social in "Quicksands."

25. For Felman too, psychoanalytic reading always necessarily entails the possibility of "unseat[ing] the critic from any guaranteed, authoritative stance of truth" (*Jacques* 35).

26. For Fanon, colonial psychiatry "seek[s] to 'cure' a native properly [by] seeking to make him thoroughly a part of a social background of the colonial type" (*Wretched* 250). See also Baldwin, "Here" 688.

27. See Deleuze, *Spinoza* and *Expressionism* esp. chaps. 11–14 and "Conclusion."

28. See the reviews by Cynthia Davis; Scott Herring, who has minor reservations (158); Matthew Johnson and Clara Jones; Rolland Murray; James Robert Saunders; Sandra Stanley; and Kathryn Bond Stockton.

29. See also Gates, *Figures* 24–58; "Talking"; and Baker, *Blues* 116–22.

30. On application/implication, see Felman, "To Open" 8.

31. The complete autobiography, published in 1991 by The Library of America, consists of the original 1945 volume of *Black Boy: A Record of Childhood and Youth*, excluding its final ten paragraphs, and the posthumously published *American Hunger* (1977).

32. In a contemporaneous review of *Pagan Spain*, for example, the reviewer decrees that Wright's "gifts and insights as a novelist might be better served in reporting such dramas as now unfold in Montgomery, Tallahassee, and Clinton, Tenn. They are tailor made for his talents" (Ottley 56). See also Hyman 2011. Tate discusses the reception of *The Outsider* in similar terms in *Psychoanalysis* 4–5.

33. Baker, "On Knowing" 210–23; Jane Davis; DeCosta-Willis; Trudier Harris, "Native"; Hernton; Keady; Mootry; M. Walker 117–18; Warren; and S. A. Williams. Joyce Ann Joyce defends Wright's representations of women in "Richard," as does Kathleen Ochshorn. For JanMohamed, Aunt Sue in "Bright and Morning Star" "is the one major exception to the general pattern of Wright's misogynistic representations of all forms of femininity" (*Death-Bound-Subject* 73), whereas according to Dennis Evans, *Pagan Spain* includes Wright's "first, and possibly only, sympathetic treatment of women" (167).

34. This is done most notably by James Baldwin in "Everybody's" esp. 32–33; and "Alas" esp. 273.

35. As JanMohamed writes, "it is this category that has been responsible, more than any other single factor, for the general failure of Wright criticism to read adequately the subtext or the latent content of his fiction" (*Death-Bound-Subject* 41). The best-known examples—because coming from two African American literary giants—of this reproach are Ellison's "World" and Baldwin's "Everybody's." See also, Bone 150–51; Dickstein 184–85; Eisinger 64, 68–70; Fiedler 118; Randall Kenan, qtd. in Rowell, "An Interview with Randall Kenan," 143. Michel Fabre questions such approaches in *World* 56–76.

36. Gates discusses the reception of black texts in similar terms in "Talking" 78–80.

37. Only since the 1980s has Wright has received renewed scholarly interest from differing, more theoretically informed perspectives. In addition to the groundbreaking work by Joyce Ann Joyce in *Richard Wright's Art of Tragedy*, Houston Baker

in *Blues, Ideology, and Afro-American Literature*, and Henry Louis Gates in *The Signifying Monkey*, see the subsequent studies of Abdul JanMohamed ("Negating"; "Rehistoricizing"; *Death-Bound-Subject*), Barbara Johnson ("Re(a)d"), Jonathan Elmer, and Biman Basu.

1. A [B]IGGER'S PLACE

Epigraphs: Wright, *Native* 294; Lacan, *SXI* 93.

1. Wright's influence is even less contested in African American letters. According to Addison Gayle, Jr., "no viable literary tradition was possible until after *Native Son*" (24). See also Yarborough x; Littlejohn 21; Lee 5; as well as the examples collected in Reilly, ed 39–99; and in Kinnamon, "How" 124–27.

2. For a particularly condescending note, see Bloom, "Introduction."

3. See also Sanders 2004. For a discussion of the view of Wright as an author possessing too limited and limiting a view of his material, see R. Butler xxx.

4. Wright is not the only "reader of color" to experience such perspectival expansion through literature. In the autobiographical *The Hunger of Memory*, Richard Rodriguez writes of his childhood experiences: "Merely bookish, I lacked a point of view when I read. Rather, I read in order to acquire a point of view" (64).

5. Wright's sympathy with Lamming's work, and with the postcolonial Caribbean in general, is registered in his introduction to the first American edition of Lamming's *In the Castle of My Skin*.

6. In his analysis of *Native Son*'s "spectragraphic" dynamics, Maurice Wallace, too, attends to the dynamics of vision and visibility in Wright's novel (35–46).

7. Wright himself connects Nietzsche to psychoanalysis: in *White Man, Listen!* (6), he discusses perspectivism in connection with the psychoanalytic theory of ambivalence. For a relevant discussion of Nietzsche, see Scheiffele. See also Wolfenstein, who in passing connects Du Bois's notion of double consciousness to Nietzsche's perspectivism.

8. See also Du Bois, *Darkwater* 77. Wright rehearses this famous scenario also in *12 Million Black Voices*: "When [white people] see one of us, they either smile with contempt or amusement" (103).

9. The unconventional spelling in this and the following quotations mark Wright's early attempts at transcribing the black vernacular, an effort which he was to a large extent to abandon in *Native Son*.

10. My reference to Taylor's "lynching" may seem like a misreading in that two central aspects of the twentieth-century understanding of lynching are missing from the text. First, the mob does not kill Taylor. While an older sense of the word refers to a practice of extralegal frontier justice in which the victim was not necessarily put to death (Wiegman 93), at the time depicted in Wright's story, "lynching" did imply killing. However, when he wakes up, Taylor thinks, surprised, "They didnt kill me" (202)—as if the scene was for some reason aborted. Second, without a white audience, the beating does not meet Du Bois's description of lynching as necessarily taking place "openly, publicly, spectacularly" (*Dark* 87). Trudier Harris describes the communal aspect of lynching thus: "A crowd of whites . . . usually exhibit a festive atmosphere by singing, donning their Sunday finery, and bringing food to the place of death. Women and children join the men—women performing their wifely duties and children becoming initiated into the roles they will play in adulthood. . . .

Sometimes the crowd lingers to have its picture taken with the victim" (*Exorcising* xi). Nevertheless, we may note that, after he has been left alone, bleeding and barely able to walk, Taylor has to make his way home through the white residential district of the town—"N Ah gotta go thu a white neighborhood, he thought with despair" (203). The fact that he tries to avoid any contact with the residents—as opposed to asking for help from the people he meets—suggests the community's implication in his punishment.

11. See also François Bernier's description of racial difference in "A New Division of the Earth" 3; Johann Gottfried von Herder's references of "the eye of the anatomist" discerning race (24); and Johann Friedrich Blumenbach's reliance on "eye-witness" accounts (31n13, 35).

12. Wiegman, too, notes that Linneaus, Bernier, Blumenbach, and George Louis Leckerc Buffon "all argued against understanding racial differences as hierarchical" (28). Mosse makes a similar argument about J. B. Antoine de Lamarck's work (18). See also Stepan chap. 1. While Bernier may have been the first one to group peoples in "races" according to their visible differences, Blumenbach or Immanuel Kant are often credited for using the term for the first time in its modern sense. See Bernasconi and Lott viii–ix; Bernasconi, "Who"; West, "Genealogy" 99ff.

13. For Cornel West, however, such "personal preference[s]" evident in the writings of these early commentators and scientists are not negligible but constitute a clear predecessor for white supremacy ("Genealogy" 100). See also Bernasconi, "Who" 15. Yet, the majority of scholars argue that, predating the systematization of racial categories, seventeenth- and eighteenth-century texts are nearly devoid of race prejudice as we understand it today. Nicholas Hudson points out that even if Europeans who explored foreign regions before the eighteenth century were convinced of their superiority to the peoples they saw, they nevertheless did not link this superiority to their race. Indeed, these early travelers often commented on "the relative sophistication of the political and social systems established in other countries" (250). Roxann Wheeler similarly suggests that human variation and hierarchies were conceived in terms of religious and cultural difference rather than race (289). This is supported by C. L. R. James's observation, in *The Black Jacobins*, of the relative lack of racism in seventeenth-century France (37). See also Basil Davidson's description of early European travelers to the Congo (qtd. in Walder 27).

14. In *Exorcising Blackness*, Trudier Harris connects Bigger's trial to the Scottsboro proceedings, where the black defendants were "clearly lynched" (97). Ishmael Reed argues for a similar link between Bigger and a later, alleged legal lynching in his "Bigger and O. J." Considering the proliferation of the "lynching" trope, we should further point out what is perhaps the most striking reversal of the nineteenth- and early-twentieth-century usage of the term: its deployment to describe the trial of a white man for a conceivably racist assault on a black man. With this, I am referring to an extraordinary moment in the Abner Louima court case when the father of Justin Volpe—the NYPD officer who was accused of (and who later admitted to) sodomizing the Haitian immigrant with a toilet plunger or a broom in a police precinct restroom after an arrest—called the widely publicized trial a "modern-day lynching" (qtd. in Waldman).

15. See Delaney for a general discussion of place and race in the U.S. legal history, and Scruggs (chap. 3, esp. 73) for an insightful consideration of the urban geography in *Native Son*.

16. The black protagonists of *Lawd Today!* similarly observe:

"They make us live in one corner of the city . . ."
"... like we was some kind of wild animals . . ."
"... then they make us pay anything they want to for rent . . ."
"... 'cause we can't live nowhere but where they tell us!" (172)

17. Without elaborating, Kalpana Seshadri-Crooks (*Desiring* 33), too, notes the importance of understanding perspective for a Lacanian analysis of race.

18. For introductory accounts of early Renaissance perspective, see Field, *Infinity* 20–42 and Kemp 9–52. For a lucid explanation of Alberti's formulation, see Kemp 342–43.

19. See the plates reproduced, for example, in Field, *Infinity* 121, "Linear" 4, and "Perspective" 240–41.

20. On Alberti's and Piero della Francesca's Euclidean perspectives, see Kemp 22 and 27–28, respectively. The question of whether Euclid was aware of linear perspective (see Knorr) does not concern me here.

21. While Copjec writes that Renaissance perspective is influenced by geometral optics, I wish to reserve this term for what Lacan calls "flat" optics (*SXI* 85). Lacan discusses Desargues's model in the unpublished thirteenth seminar, *L'objet de la psychanalyse* (1965–1966).

22. As Stephen Greenblatt writes, the two men in the painting "are in possession of the instruments—both literal and symbolic—by which men bring the world into focus, represent it in proper perspective. Indeed, in addition to their significance as emblems of the Liberal Arts, the objects on the table [celestial and terrestrial globes, sundials, quadrants and other instruments of astronomy and geography, a lute, a case of flutes, a German book of arithmetic, . . . and an open German hymn book] virtually constitute a series of textbook illustrations for a manual on the art of perspective" (17). See also Baltrušaitis's discussion of *vanitas* in *Anamorphotic Art* 93–100.

23. Note that all the emphases are in the original.

24. While Lacanian scholarship most often names sexuation as the grounding difference organizing the symbolic, I argue in Chapter 3 that race may also function as real difference.

25. Speaking of white "ignore-ance," Patricia Williams, in *The Alchemy of Race and Rights* (1991), provides an account of visual access and transparency that is largely compatible with Wright's analysis: "she didn't like white people seeing inside her"; "What was hardest was not just that white people saw me, . . . but that they looked through me, as if I were transparent" (222). Antonio Viego's comments on "colonizing, dominating, and ultimately racist interpretative practices" are directly relevant to my discussion of Wright: "Racism depends on a reading of ethnic-racialized subjects that insists on their transparency; racism also banks on the faith and conceit that these subjects can be exhaustively and fully elucidated through a certain masterful operation of language" (6).

26. Baldwin, "Many" 76; Bone 150–51; Sanders 2004. There are critics, however, who do see Max's speech as contributing positively to the novel's strength; some of these views are recounted in Hakutani 72–73.

27. A Foucauldian critique of Max's appeal would note his blindness to the fact that the surveillance which finds its "privileged locus of realization" (*Discipline* 249) in

the carceral is by no means limited to prisons or other disciplinary institutions such as the army, the schoolroom, the orphanage, or the monastery. In these, one can observe in concentrated form the strategies of surveillance and discipline in the society at large (180). As Gilles Deleuze points out, "discipline cannot be identified with any one institution or apparatus precisely because it is a type of power, a technology, that traverses every kind of apparatus or institution, linking them, prolonging them, and making them converge and function in a new way" (*Foucault* 26).

28. Assessing the strategies of the spokespersons hired by the Central Committee of the Communist Party to defend the nine African American adolescents sentenced to death in Scottsboro in 1931, Du Bois writes that, for the lawyers, "the actual fate of these victims was a minor matter. . . . All this was based on abysmal ignorance of the pattern of race prejudice in the United States" (*Dusk* 298). The communist involvement in the Scottsboro case divided many notable African Americans, with the NAACP leader Walter White criticizing the lawyers and Langston Hughes supporting them (see Rampersad, *Life* 216–18). Wright himself asserts: "The political Left often gyrates and squirms to make the Negro problem fit rigidly into a class-war frame of reference" ("Introduction," in Drake and Cayton xxix). See also *Native* 65. On the trial's influence on Wright's early work, see Higashida 410–20.

29. Hakutani uncritically adopts Max's own description of his strategy. Max says in his courtroom speech, "'The unremitting hate of men has given us a psychological distance that will enable us to see this tiny social symbol in relation to our whole sick social organism'" (324).

30. On Max's failure, see also JanMohamed, *Death-Bound-Subject* 131–33.

31. Anticipating our turn to postcolonial theory in Chapter 3, we can further note that, as Édouard Glissant has pointed out, "understanding" works hand in hand with colonial conquest. When the globe shrunk with the discovery of new lands, "[u] nderstanding cultures . . . became more gratifying than discovering new lands. Western ethnography was structured on the basis of this need. But we shall perhaps see that the verb *to understand* in the sense of 'to grasp' [*comprendre*] has a fearsome repressive meaning here" (Glissant, *Poetics* 26; brackets in English translation).

2. THE GRIMACE OF THE REAL

Epigraphs: Lacan, *SXI* 107; Huggins 262, 263.

1. That this view dominated the media response becomes clear from any Internet search on the controversy. See also the *New York Times* editorial piece, "Fallout." For a more comprehensive and complicated look on the questions of (African-)American beauty standards and their political meanings, see Adams; hooks; Lester; Mercer, "Black"; Rooks; and P. Taylor.

2. See also Bogle; Boskin 11ff.; Gubar 55; and E. Lott 11, 51–55; Majors and Mancini Billson; and Watkins. For a cultural studies text that considers contemporary African American culture in the context of blackface, see Jefferson. In other words, Daily Paskman and Sigmund Spaeth's pronouncement in 1928 that their book functions "not as an obituary to minstrelsy, but as an advance notice to its permanent life" (240) resonates in uncannily prophetic tones here.

3. Lhamon singles out Saxton's, Roediger's, and Lott's studies.

4. The most significant difference in Mahar's work is his insistence that African Americans were not the exclusive, perhaps not even the primary, target for minstrel

parodies. For him, other nationalities and ethnicities, as well as women, constituted a more important subject for blackface performers and audiences (191, 329, and *passim*). Mahar also dismisses Lott's conclusions about the "interracial desire" that minstrelsy exhibited as too generalized and ultimately unfounded (4, 8). While he seems not to have had access to *Raising Cain*, published a year before his own book, he undoubtedly would have been as uncomfortable with Lhamon's conclusions as he is with Lott's.

5. Betsy Wing, in *Poetics of Relation*, translates the French original *rélation* as "Relation," whereas Michael Dash, in *Caribbean Discourse*, prefers "cross-cultural poetics."

6. For a fictionalized account of minstrel tradition's hybridity, see Wesley Brown, *Darktown Strutters* (1994).

7. In the latter essay, Parry criticizes also Gayatri Spivak's work.

8. On *pharmakon*, see Derrida, *Dissemination* 61–171. Using the latter term, I am thinking of Vicki Kirby's and Rosi Braidotti's (266) work.

9. For other brief references to minstrelsy's alleged black origins, see Paskman and Spaeth 11–12, 30–33, 176, 180, 186.

10. In the later essay "Blackface Minstrelsy, Vernacular Comics, and the Politics of Slavery in the North," Saxton reiterates this reading of blackface minstrelsy.

11. For Saxton, the central tenets of Jacksonian Democracy included "[t]he absolute necessity of white supremacy"; "[w]estward expansionism"; "[e]galitarianism . . . for whites only"; and "the defense of plantation slavery" ("Blackface Minstrelsy, Vernacular Comics" 163; see also "Blackface Minstrelsy and Jacksonian Ideology" 17).

12. Also Michael Rogin's work on Jewish identity belongs to the second stage. In *Blackface, White Noise*, his argues that "Blackface is the instrument that transfers identities from immigrant Jew to American. By putting on blackface, the Jewish jazz singer acquires . . . first his own voice, then assimilation through upward mobility, finally women. . . . Assimilation is achieved via the mask of the most segregated; the blackface that offers Jews mobility keeps the blacks fixed in place" (95, 112).

13. See Paskman and Spaeth 175; Toll 134–35, 195; Watkins 109–111; Woll 1–2.

14. Numerous writers and scholars join Ellison in emphasizing the importance of representations in the history of racism. For a slave in Martin Delany's *Blake*, the hardest work is preferable to being under a white gaze that turns Negroes' lives into something like a minstrel spectacle: "'we'a rather work in de fiel' . . . [c]ase den da would'n be so many ole wite plantehs come an' look at us, like we was show!'" (77). Similarly, W. E. B. Du Bois finds that *Birth of a Nation* constituted a "much more insidious and hurtful attack" on blacks than the actual invasion of Haiti in 1915 (*Dusk* 239); and Boskin argues that minstrelsy representations took over the oppressiveness of legalized slavery after the Civil War (124).

15. See Toll 196, 216; Huggins 246; Watkins 112; Woll 2, 4, 41–42. These dilemmas were not relieved with the demise of the minstrel stage: as Mark A. Reid suggests, stereotypical, minstrelsy-derived roles were accepted by African American actors in early Hollywood films because they created much-needed employment opportunities (23).

16. See also Toll 196, 222–23; Huggins 281–82; Krasner 319–20; and Woll 4ff.

17. See also Deleuze and Guattari, *Thousand* 112, 116, 120. Elsewhere, however, Deleuze and Guattari suggest the productivity of paranoia: "to augment and expand Oedipus by adding to it and making a paranoid and perverse use of it is already to escape from submission" (*Kafka* 10).

18. On Dali and Lacan, see Berressem; Roudinesco 31; I. Gibson 308–10, 366.

19. See, for example, John Forrester's translation of *Seminar I* (177) and Alan Sheridan's translation of "The Mirror Stage" (4). I use Bruce Fink's more recent translation of *Écrits* throughout.

20. As Lacan writes, "the doctrine of discontinuity between animal psychology and human psychology which is far away from our thought" (qtd. in Dylan Evans 121).

21. We can detect the centrality of paranoia for Lacan in that his exploration into human psychology begins with this very question: in 1932, he not only defended his doctoral dissertation centering on a monograph of a woman suffering from paranoid delusions (see Benvenuto and Kennedy chap. 1), but also translated Freud's "Some Neurotic Mechanisms in Jealousy, Paranoia and Homosexuality" for *Revue Française de Psychoanalyse* (Stavrakakis 10).

22. Lacan quotes here Poe's "The Purloined Letter" (15; emphasis Lacan's).

23. The two different types of identification (imaginary/symbolic) suppose two different types of knowledge, which, as Evans points out, are designated by different terms in the French original texts. "Egomiming" or imaginary identification corresponds to *connaissance*, that is, to imaginary knowledge; *savoir*—knowledge in the symbolic—exceeds this kind of miming. This difference repeats the different typologies of the visual field that Lacan maps in his eleventh seminar and that I explored in the previous chapter. Imaginary knowledge is analogous to vision organized around geometral perspective, while symbolic knowledge would be that which only "the subject of representation" can acquire through his or her implication in the field of vision.

24. Here, too, he repeats Mr. Dalton's attitude toward Bigger. As Bigger visits the Daltons' for the first time, the master of the house reminds him: "'And any time you're bothered about anything, come and see me. Let's talk it over'" (44).

25. In *Man, Play, and Games* (1958), Caillois further illuminates the dynamics of danger and protection in human mimicry and "play." While "the inexplicable mimetism of insects immediately affords extraordinary parallel to man's penchant for disguising himself, wearing a mask, or *playing a part*," in the insect world, mimicry refers to something much more organic than it does for humans: "in the insect's case the mask or guise becomes part of the body instead of a contrived accessory" (20). However, as much as animal mimicry entraps its practitioners, the playful, controlled human simulation can accelerate into what Caillois terms *vertigo*, in which the "stability of mind" is destroyed and "a kind of voluptuous panic" is inflicted "upon an otherwise lucid mind" (23). Caillois notes that "play is protection from danger. The actor's role is sharply defined by the dimension of the stage and the duration of the spectacle" (49). However, he goes on to suggest that games cannot always be thus contained but are in danger of contaminating "real life": "simulation in itself generates both vertigo and split personality, the source of panic" (75). The subject may be immobilized in the lethal trap of its mimetic pose.

26. For Lacan, the genesis of paranoia always includes a visible, distinguishable moment at its beginning; see Lacan, *SIII* 17. We must note, however, that here he speaks of paranoia as a pathology. Bigger's paranoid perception of his surroundings cannot be reduced to pathology, which Philip Bolton does in "The Role of Paranoia in Richard Wright's *Native Son*."

27. Let us note in passing the telling ambivalence in Du Bois's chosen term: as Jacques Derrida reminds us, we can think "the gift" etymologically "as good *and* bad, as gift and poison (*Gift-gift*)" (*Given* 81; see also 12). Du Bois's well-known familiarity

with the German philosophical tradition (see Adell chap. 1, and Zamir) suggests that the choice of terminology may have been a conscious one. See also Radano 72.

28. Yet, we can perhaps immediately detect the limitations of Bigger's new position. First, the white person he catches and induces shame in is not, for instance, Mr. Dalton, but, rather, the maid—a servant like himself. (Later, Bigger does detect similar feelings of shame in Mrs. Dalton [130].) Second, rather than being, like the Sartrean voyeur, "reduce[d] . . . to shame" (*SXI* 84), Peggy "was *just a little ashamed* of having been seen in the basement in her kimono" (100; emphasis added).

29. Even after his having been arrested, white investigators are convinced that communist involvement is the deeper truth behind Bigger's crime (250). Such assumptions were made when Chandler Owen and Asa Randolph, the editors of *The Messenger*, were brought to trial for allegedly violating the Espionage Act in 1918: "the magistrate in Cleveland had not believed that the two young black men . . . were capable of writing the articles charged against them. Whites . . . believed that the Red Scare was exclusively white men's business" (D. L. Lewis 17). The white law's belief that "'Negroes never conspire'" (Du Bois, *Dark Princess* 97), in other words, renders the law eminently vulnerable to black(face) conjurations.

30. Silverman traces her theoretical trajectory via a number of texts—Walter Benjamin's, Isaac Julien's, Harun Farocki's, and Cindy Sherman's, among others—which she puts in dialogue with Lacan. As such, her method closely resembles mine. Nevertheless, even though, as I noted in my introduction, a certain violence may be inevitable in any encounter of bodies (of work), one should be alerted to the cost of this violence when such crucial psychoanalytic concepts as the drive, the real, and the *objet a* are entirely eliminated from the resulting theory. For example, in her discussion of *The Ambassadors*, Silverman does not once mention the *objet a*, whose centrality to Lacan's reading of Holbein is clear (*Threshold* 175–78). Similarly, her suggestion that in English we substitute two terms for the French *le regard* aligns her argument more with Judith Butler's theory of performativity than Lacanian psychoanalysis. In Silverman's vocabulary, the *gaze* is a transhistorical human phenomenon, something like a mechanical apparatus carving out culturally validated representations that make up what we recognize as "reality." The *look*, on the other hand, names a function of the embodied subject—"located within desire, temporality and the body" (*Threshold* 160)—that is circumscribed by but may also resist and subvert the gaze: "the look has all along possessed the capacity to see otherwise from and even in contradiction to the gaze. The eye is always to some degree resistant to the discourses which seek to master and regulate it, and can even, on occasion, dramatically oppose the representational logic and material practices which specify exemplary vision at a given moment" (156). We should only note that the division of the visible into a transcendent gaze and a desiring, embodied look goes directly counter to Lacan's theory of the symbolic structuration of desire, in which gaze names the object-cause of desire. For Silverman, the "productive look," always "'errant'" and possibly "transformative," allows the subject's negotiation with the visible (155, 160, 170, 180ff.). For Lacan, on the other hand, it is precisely the *gaze* that allows the subject's ethical relation to the symbolic and the real. Ultimately, Silverman's theory is inassimilable to psychoanalysis to the extent that any critique of her work in Lacanian terms would be pointless. While I do recognize that she may have very little investment in any fidelity to Lacan (and, importantly, that she would not have had access to most of the illuminating texts by the "New Lacanians" from which I have benefited), her approach does exemplify "the peculiar way in which the

theoretical specificity of Lacanian theory is constantly eroded in the very course of its reception" (Shepherdson, *Vital* 8). See also Copjec's critique of Silverman in "Body's" and *Imagine* 209–10.

31. Trubek quotes Melman 21.

32. A more detailed discussion of these passages in *The Ethics of Psychoanalysis* would have to make a distinction between the primordial real and *das Ding*, where the former is the "mythical" outside of the symbolic, while the latter emerges as a product of the processes of signification themselves. *Das Ding*, as Lorenzo Chiesa writes, "is *not* the primordial Real: in the context of Seminar VII, the Thing is in fact a hole effected by the signifier in the primordial Real; hence, it is by definition a *loss* of *jouissance* which, as such, can only be always-already lost for the symbolic subject independently of any positive interdiction" (169). Alenka Zupančič makes a similar distinction, although for her *das Ding* is the primordial real while the *objet a* functions as the intra-symbolic excess of signification: "'the remainder' (what [Lacan] calls the *objet petit a*) is not simply the remainder of the Thing, but the *remainder of the signifier itself* which retroactively established the dimension of the Thing; it is not the remainder of some 'matter' that the signifier was incapable of 'transforming' into the symbolic, it is the remainder, the outcast, the 'spittle' of the self-referential dynamics of signifiers. . . . It is not that after [symbolization] something pre-symbolic is left over, as 'unsymbolizable' or something that 'escapes' symbolization, it is that symbolization, in its very perfection and completeness, produces a surplus which 'undermines' it from within by engendering impasses" (*Ethics* 190–91).

33. Indeed, echoing Lacan's description of the infant's response to its image in the mirror stage, the original French terms in the eleventh seminar's description of *trompe l'oeil* suggest that at issue in the recognition of *trompe l'oeil* is the mobility of paranoid identification: the "delight [*jubilation*]" (*SXI* 112/102) the viewer-subject of the anamorphotic painting experiences reminds us of the child's "jubilant activity [*un affairement jubilatoire*]" and "jubilant assumption [*L'assomption jubilatoire*] of his specular image" ("Mirror" 4/94).

34. Lacan uses the same French term—*grimace*—in the originals: see *SXI* 88 and *Television* 17.

35. My brief gloss of the feminist theory of masquerade here excludes a number of important contributions: see, in particular, Apter chap. 4; Doane, *Desire* and *Femmes* chaps. 1 and 2; Modleski chap. 2; Pellegrini chap. 7; and Russo chap. 2.

36. Bigger becomes conscious of his "blackface" in the street car scene too: "He looked anxiously at the dim reflection of *his black face* in the sweaty window pane. Would any of the white faces all about him think that he had killed a rich white girl? No!" (96; emphasis added).

37. Žižek suggests that the threat of the real is embodied in popular films as "the return of the living dead. This return functions as "the reverse of the proper funeral rite[,] . . . signif[ying] that [the dead] cannot find their proper place in the text of tradition" (*Looking* 23). Not accidentally, in his courtroom speech, Max refers to Bigger as, precisely, a corpse that has risen from its grave: "'Obsessed with guilt, we have sought to thrust a corpse from before our eyes. We have marked off a little spot of ground and buried it. We tell our souls in the deep of the black night that it is dead and that we have no reason for fear or uneasiness. But the corpse returns and raids our homes! . . . [T]he corpse it not dead! It still lives! . . . '" (331). In Lacan's terms, Bigger is an extimate presence, simultaneously "the most intimate" and "the most hidden," "a foreign body,

a parasite" (J.-A. Miller, "Extimité" 122, 123). Max correctly recognizes the burial site—"a little spot of ground" (331)—as similar to the "one little spot" (*Native* 300) that characterizes the [B]igger's place.

38. The terms of the exchange between Jim and Jack are repeated between Tyree Tucker and Dr. Bruce in *The Long Dream*. When faced with the prospect that the bounty of his life-long trickster career is about to be stolen from him, Tyree momentarily flirts with the kind of self-destructive resistance that Jim promotes: "'For twenty years I grinned and slaved and bowed and scraped and took every insult that a man can know to git something, and now they ask me to give it all up! I won't! *I'll die first!*'" Tyree's companion repeats Jack's advice as he tells Tyree to calm down: "'You can't think *straight* felling [sic: feeling] like that, man'" (241; emphases added). On the semantic play of "queer" and "straight" in Wright's work, see my "Queer Guerrillas."

39. Fauset; Hughes; Johnson discusses his "philosophy of laughter" in *Along* 118–20; Du Bois recurrently refers to African Americans' "divine gift of laughter" in his autobiographical texts (*Darkwater* 21, 198; *Dusk* 148, 325; *Autobiography* 228). See also Levine chap. 5.

40. In less offensive tones, Baldwin makes a similar point: "every American Negro . . . risks having the gates of paranoia close on him. In a society that is entirely hostile, and, by its nature, seems determined to cut you down . . . it begins to be almost impossible to distinguish a real from a fancied injury" (*Fire* 362). Similarly, William H. Grier and Price M. Cobbs argue in *Black Rage* (1969): "Black people, to a degree that approaches paranoia, must be ever alert to danger from their white fellow citizens. It is a cultural phenomenon peculiar to black Americans" (173; see also Early 33). In Audre Lorde's terms, the challenge then becomes "how to cultivate our group paranoia into an instinct for self-protection" (82).

41. On late-twentieth-century restagings of blackface, see also Shawn-Marie Garrett: "This kind of work does not say black is beautiful, stereotypes are cruel and shameful, and whites are to blame. Instead, it asks, what is black? what is white? what is between them? what would one be without the other?" (40).

42. See also Patricia J. Williams's (166–67) critical comments on white liberal calls for laughter as a way to "disempower" racism.

3. UNFORESEEABLE TRAGEDIES

Epigraphs: Lacan, *SVII* 244; Baldwin, *Fire* 379.

1. Wright repeats this scenario in "The Psychological Reactions of Oppressed People," in *White* 3.

2. "The eye of another was a kind of cage," Lamming writes in *In the Castle of My Skin*, for whose U.S. edition Wright contributed an introduction. "There was something absolutely wonderful about not being seen" (65, 66). Lamming discusses colonialism and the gaze at length in *The Pleasures of Exile*, esp. the essay "A Way of Seeing."

3. See James Campbell 1–6; Fabre, *World* 182–85; Stovall chaps. 4–6. On the reasons behind Wright's exile, see Stovall 182–85; on the outrage that his exile caused in the American press, see ibid., 219.

4. For a detailed publishing history of Wright's texts in French, see Charles T. Davis and Fabre, eds. 198–202. For the largely favorable reception of *Un Enfant du pays*, *Les Enfants de l'oncle Tom*, and *Black Boy*, see Fabre et al., eds., *French Critical Reception* passim, esp. 73–95.

5. The exact extent and closeness of Wright's and Fanon's friendship is somewhat in dispute. In her biography, Margaret Walker claims that they had a much more long-term friendship than other biographers suggest (8, 246, 299, 319). In a scathing review, "Margaret Walker's Richard Wright," Fabre refutes such claims along with many of the other statements Walker makes in her biography. Walker, in turn, criticizes Fabre's biography (3, 164; see also Giovanni and Walker 88–101).

6. See *Black Skin* 139, 183, 219n6, 222, the last of which is an implicit reference to Wright's *12 Million Black Voices*. See also Fanon, *Wretched* 216.

7. See also Reilly, "Richard" 52; and Singh xxvii–xxviii.

8. Gibson takes the term from the original French title of *Black Skin*'s fifth chapter, "L'expérience vécue du noir," which Charles Lam Markmann renders in English as "The Fact of Blackness" (*Fanon* 212n27; see also Judy 53–54).

9. We should further note the unpsychoanalytic vocabulary in which other readers have couched their criticism. Let's remember, for example, that "ambivalence" (Sharpley-Whiting 28n21), far from denoting a wholesale rejection of and disassociation with an object, names in psychoanalysis a persistent attachment whose threat is compounded by its primal importance. Consequently, if we detect an ambivalence in Fanon's approach to what he found in Lacan, we should insist on exploring the significance of this dialogue, rather than dismiss it.

10. For the periodization of Lacan's work, see Dean, *Beyond* 36–60 and Shepherdson, "Pound" 72n8.

11. See Fink, *Lacanian* 123–25, 186n14; Dean, *Beyond* 52–60.

12. The Algerian *Front de libération nationale* moved its anticolonial battle to the French soil with the 1957 assassination of a former Vice-President of the Algerian Assembly and the bomb and arson attacks on factories, police stations, and oil plants that followed in 1958 (Macey 364).

13. Given my argument below about the role of gender in Fanon's understanding of colonization and counterstrategies, I use the masculine pronoun for the colonized subject of *Black Skin*.

14. Fanon is often said to problematize negritude in his later works, such as *The Wretched of the Earth*. However, it is important to note, as Tony Martin (394) does, that he is critical of the movement already in *Black Skin*.

15. Fanon criticizes Sartre's analogy between the Jew and the Negro (*Anti-Semite* 11, 54). While Sartre writes that "Jew is over-determined" (79), Fanon argues that the black man, unlike the Jew, is never in a position to escape his position: "the Jew can be unknown in his Jewishness. He is not wholly what he is. . . . He is a white man, and, apart from some rather debatable characteristics, he can sometimes go unnoticed" (*Black* 115). For the influence of Sartre's study on Fanon, see N. Gibson, *Fanon* 18ff. and Khanna 139–42.

16. In *The Wretched of the Earth*, Fanon similarly writes that the colonized are "condemned" to "immobility": "The first thing which the native learns is to stay in his place, and not to go beyond certain limits" (52).

17. The translator of *A Dying Colonialism* explains that *haïk* is "the Arab name for the big square veil worn by Arab women, covering the face and the whole body" (36n4).

18. See also Decker 182, and Minces 165–66. Alf Andrew Heggoy, however, insists that "[h]istorically, Algerian women have enjoyed more freedom than is usually admitted by Western authors" (449). Anne-Emmanuelle Berger and Winifred

Woodhull (3ff.), too, criticize Western scholars' tendency to generalize on the veil's significance.

19. See also Alloula 14.

20. See also Silverman, *Threshold* 148. Joan Copjec (*Read* 105) rephrases these insights in Lacanian terminology.

21. On women's position in discourses of anticolonial nationalism, see also Chatterjee; Dubey esp. 3–7; Helie-Lucas 107; and Sharpley-Whiting 20, 58.

22. See also Fernandes 48–49; Heggoy 452, 453; Mernissi vii; Tucker, "Introduction" x, xiv; and Woodhull 22. For contemporary configurations of colonial feminism, see Mohanty and Judith Butler's brief comments about the U.S. invasion of Afghanistan in *Precarious* 143.

23. In *The Wretched of the Earth*, Fanon similarly notes: "The native replies to the living lie of the colonial situation by an equal falsehood. . . . In this colonialist context there is no truthful behaviour" (39).

24. Markmann renders *livrée* as uniform in *Black* 114/112, 187/171; and as livery in 12/30, 34/47.

25. See also the witty reading of Stevenson's classic gothic horror story of Dr. Jekyll and Mr. Hyde in Halberstam chap. 3.

26. One can detect such ambivalence also in the function of *livrée/coat*. The *OED* informs us that "coat" very rarely refers to an animal's hide. The crucial difference between coat and hide, both the outer layers of an organism, is that the dead matter of coat is a more changeable, impermanent layer than the skin. Very often a coat can be shed and subsequently regrown; many animals do this for, exactly, predatory purposes or those of concealment.

27. Similarly, in *Native Son*, the bodily tension that racialization induces in Bigger's body enables his violent action: his "body [is] taut as that of an animal about to leap" (94). The performance of obsequiousness in front of white people simultaneously prepares him for flight or an attack: "His knees [are] slightly bent, like a runner's poised for a race" (201).

28. As Anne-Emmanuelle Berger notes, the Arabic term for a non-veiled woman, *moutabarijate*, literally translates as "fragmented woman" (107).

29. On Fanon and Capécia, see also Bergner "Who" 81–84; Sharpley-Whiting chap. 2.

30. See also Lola Young and Gwen Bergner, who writes that Fanon's depiction of black women in *Black Skin* exposes "his own desire to circumscribe black women's sexuality and economic autonomy in order to ensure the patriarchal authority of black men" ("Who" 81).

31. Juliette Minces writes that the FLN allowed women to participate only as substitutes for men's participation and in order to give the impression of progressiveness to attract the support of the French Left (162–63). For the regression of women's position in post-independence Algeria, see Dubey 25n10; Heggoy 454; Helie-Lucas 110–14; Minces 164, 166–70; Sharpley-Whiting 57–58; Woodhull 12–14; and Zouligha.

32. Fanon's denial of the role of films or novels in the women's imitation should be read in the context of his comments in *Black Skin* on the importance of such Western cultural products in inducing in the colonized a sense of inferiority through an identification with foreign values: see *Black* 140, 152–53n15. The films Fanon refers to are Western because, as Hala Salmane notes, there was hardly any Algerian cinema before the country became independent in 1962 ("Structures" 19). For French cinema on

Algeria, see Salmane, "On Colonial." See also Kaplan and Doane, *Femmes* 227. Wright discusses Hollywood cinema's influence on Africans in *Black Power* 77, 80, 179–81.

33. For analyses of the development of political consciousness, culminating in Sue's character, in the stories of *Uncle Tom's Children*, see Higashida; JanMohamed, "Rehistoricizing."

34. Faith functions for her like the wall/curtain does for Bigger before Mary's murder: without it, "he would be swept out of himself with fear and despair" (*Native* 9).

35. This context also highlights Bigger's tragic dimension. If Bigger plays the paranoid game by identifying with the "coon" of the minstrel stage, he thereby reprises Sue's role of the mammy: his realization of the subversive potential in blackface as "[h]e looked anxiously at the dim reflection of *his black face* in the sweaty window pane" (96; emphasis added) is a repetition of the opening scene of "Bright and Morning Star," where we find Sue "st[anding] with *her black face* some six inches from the moist windowpane" (221; emphasis added). Like Sue, "bent toward a moment of focus, . . . poised on the brink of a total act," after Mary's murder Bigger "felt that he had his destiny in his grasp. He was more alive than he could ever remember having been; his mind and attention were pointed, focused toward a goal" (127). As much as Antigone's impossible act "create[s] a new possibility there where the options seemed to be exhausted" (Zupančič, "Lacan's" 111), in killing Mary, Bigger "create[s] a new life for himself" (*Native* 90; see also 242); it is, like Antigone's, "an act of *creation*!" (335). On Bigger as a tragic hero, see also Joyce, *Richard*. On tragic elements in *Uncle Tom's Children*, see Delmar.

36. For the full-fledged argument concerning the "dialectics of death" in Wright, see JanMohamed, *Death-Bound-Subject*.

37. Here we may also distinguish between fundamentalist terrorism and (what might be called) *real* terrorism against the symbolic order. As Žižek writes, "the 'fundamentalist' act is done for the big Other; in it, the subject instrumentalizes himself for the Other; while an authentic act authorizes itself only in itself—that is to say, it is not 'covered' by the big Other; on the contrary, it intervenes at the very point of inconsistency of the big Other" ("Afterword" 243). Similarly, Sue moves to act only when she finds herself betrayed by—discerns the lethal inconsistency in—all Others.

38. For a clear account of the shifts in Lacan's understanding of the real, see Shepherdson, "Intimate" pars. 34–65. See also Fink's delineation of the two reals in Lacan: *Lacanian* 27.

39. Bigger provides a similar performance for Mr. Dalton's benefit: "He stood with his knees slightly bent, his lips partly open, his shoulder stooped; and his eyes held a look that went only to the surface of things. There was an organic conviction in him that this was the way white folks wanted him to be when in their presence" (42).

40. See also Gates, *Figures* 48–49, 236–50.

41. For a well-known example of black double-voicedness, see F. E. W. Harper 9. See also Wright's discussion of slave songs in *White* 88.

42. For another example, see *The Outsider*, where a black waiter, having scalded a white woman with coffee, apologizes with a voice "so high-pitched that it was ludicrous" (496).

43. Notable in these discussions is an inability to decide whether the effects of passing are subversive or reactionary, whether they destabilize or validate existing symbolic structures. Clearly, like Algerian women, numerous African American passers—from George Winston, who infiltrates a racist white family as their son's educated friend in

Frank Webb's *The Garies and Their Friends* (1857), and Walter White, who investigated lynchings in the 1920s South by passing in white supremacist circles (White 365), to Bigger Thomas and Adrian Piper (esp. 246)—these passers disrupt the symbolic with their gazing: if the veil had threatened the colonizers by allowing Muslim women unreciprocated visual access, passing, in enabling surreptitious entrance behind enemy lines, similarly allows the subject's "seeing without being seen" (Sollors 253). Passing, however, is never purged of the dangers that characterize black(face) magic. The two phenotypically white African American characters in Webb's *The Garies and Their Friends*—George Winston and Clarence Garie—embody the promise and threat of passing. While the former functions as "the subversive mulatto saboteur" (Fabi 38), the latter, as a result of his extended contact with white society, internalizes racism and self-hatred. If Clarence Garie dons whiteface to succeed in the white world after the murder of his family by a white mob, he gradually becomes unable to separate his sense of self from the white values he is forced to embody. While his passing as white provides him opportunities (good boarding school, access to employment) otherwise closed to him, it becomes increasingly difficult for him to retain the double-consciousness that such deception demands of him. In this, he succumbs to the dangers carried by the mobility that blackface performance afforded some nineteenth-century blacks and that I explored in the previous chapter. Clarence Garie begins to believe in his role to the extent that he becomes blind to the emotional warmth and support offered by the African American community (Fabi 39–40). He is also emasculated by his passing: as Fabi writes, in essence his character resembles "the fallen heroines of nineteenth-century popular fiction" (40).

44. Because I argue that the symbolic may be structured around racialization as much as it is around sexuation, I prefer the term symbolic function to "castration" and the "phallus."

45. I follow Fink in referring to sexuated subjects as "man"/"woman," "men"/"women," or "masculine"/"feminine," reserving the terms "male" and "female" for occasions where biological differences are at stake (*Lacanian* 194n24). Given the limitations of space here, my brief account of sexuation should be supplemented by the lucid analyses by Dyess and Dean; Fink (*Lacanian* 105–25); and Shepherdson (*Vital* 72–83), while mindful of the differences in their accounts, which I chart below. See also the essays collected in Barnard and Fink, eds.; and Salecl, ed.

46. For an account of feminist, queer-theoretical and postcolonial readings of the phallus, see Jan Campbell.

47. While Jean Walton, criticizing Copjec's relegation of racial (as well as class and ethnic) differences to the symbolic realm, similarly suggests that sex may not be the only real difference (*Fair* 5–11), her argument is of little use to us here because she does not adequately engage the Lacanian premises of Copjec's approach. The difference between Walton's and Copjec's work can be articulated in paradigmatic terms: while the former represents historicist scholarship, Copjec takes on Lacanian theory as an ontological system. Competently discussing the implicit ways in which gender and race were inscribed into early psychoanalysis, Walton's work never entertains any questions of *being* as they are proposed by psychoanalysis. Consequently, her critique of Lacanian scholars—who pose ontological questions ultimately unarticulable from within an historicist framework—is misdirected. This (unacknowledged) misfit with the ontological paradigm may be the result of her uncritical reliance on Judith Butler's reading of Lacan.

48. I leave unaddressed here the argument about Fanon's androcentric misreading of Capécia. See Sharpley-Whiting, chap. 2.

49. The traffic between symbolic acting and the real act is parallel to the ambivalence in the psychoanalytic notion of the semblant, which is at the same time a defense against the real and an inroad to the failing point of symbolic networks. Jelica Sumic writes: "for Freud, as well as for Lacan, there are two apparently contradictory faces of the semblant that are nonetheless bound together. That is what Lacan in particular insists on: as an artful device the semblant can be considered both as a path to accede to the real, as well as a defence against the real. Not surprisingly, this duplicity of the semblant lends itself to two opposing interpretations. According to the first, the semblant is primarily an artifice useful for triggering a misrecognition or for erecting a barrier against the real of jouissance; according to the second, however, the semblant is nothing but a suppletory device, be it imaginary or sublimatory, destined to support the drive's satisfaction" (17).

50. I have pursued this point in Tuhkanen, "Performativity."

51. For Butler's best-known rejection of the Lacanian real, see *Bodies* chap. 7. She reiterates her criticism throughout her subsequent writings: see Butler, *Undoing*; and her contributions to Butler, Laclau, and Žižek.

52. Gender, according to her well-known formulation, "is itself a kind of becoming or activity" (*Gender* 112). In *Undoing Gender*, too, she refers to "gender as a mode of becoming" (81).

53. Arguing that "a loss of certainty is not the same as political nihilism," she writes in *Bodies that Matter*: "The incalculable effects of action are as much a part of their subversive promise as those that we plan in advance" (30, 241). More recently, in *Undoing Gender*, she has similarly advocated "a futural form of politics that cannot be fully anticipated, a politics of hope and anxiety" (180).

4. THE OPTICAL TRADE

Epigraphs: Thoreau 7; Wright, "*Black*" 81.

1. See Gates, "Introduction" xii; Bontemps xix; Baraka; M. Dixon, *Ride* 59.

2. In conceptualizing my comparison between Douglass and Wright thus, I am obviously indebted to other scholars who have found Foucault's work helpful in thinking about the racial logics of modernity: see Goldberg, *Racist*; Stoler; and Wiegman. Goldberg's and Stoler's emphases are not so much on the dynamics of surveillance as on modern regimes of truth.

3. Butler seeks to retain openness in her system of dialectical turns by refusing the synthesis of the dialectic: see *Psychic* chap. 1. I argue elsewhere that her later work demonstrates the paradigmatic tendencies of her Hegelianism in that her politics become increasingly not about future's openness but about strategies of recognition. See Tuhkanen, "Performativity."

4. Pointing out the dearth of references to the racialized logic of punishment in Foucault's work, Angela Y. Davis, too, encourages caution in translating his studies of incarceration onto the North American scene. Alerting us to the specificities of carceral practices in postbellum United States, where racial slavery, although abolished, profoundly affected the penal code, she reminds us that, whereas Foucault sees a shift from the body to the soul as the focus of European penal forms, "black slaves in the US were largely perceived as lacking the soul that might be shaped and transformed

by punishment." Consequently, "the privilege of punishment"—based as it was on the assumption of the inherent liberty and equality of subjects that could then be rescinded—was applicable only to white subjects (99).

5. For the growth of Jim Crowism in the first decades of 1900s, see Woodward, *Strange* 97ff. For a catalogue of not only the racial riots, lynchings, and legal set-backs that blacks faced during 1900–1924, but also the response of African Americans to such violence, see Berry 98–125.

6. Wright himself writes that toward the end of the second decade "racial conflict flared over the entire South" (*Black Boy* 71).

7. In *Discipline and Punish*, Foucault insists that power in these institutions works not by repressing but by engendering: "punitive measures are not simply 'negative' mechanisms that make it possible to repress, to prevent, to exclude, to eliminate; . . . they are linked to a whole series of positive and useful effects which it is their task to support" (24). Elsewhere, however, he emphasizes the fact that, more than other institutions, prisons are designed for the purposes of elimination. Even if all of us "are caught in a system of continuous surveillance and punishment," prisons form a "part of an eliminative process. Prison is the physical elimination of people who come out of it, who die of it sometimes directly, and almost always indirectly in so far as they can no longer find a trade, don't have anything to live on, cannot reconstitute a family anymore, etc., and, finally, passing from one prison to another or from one crime to another, end up by actually being physically eliminated" ("Michel" 31).

8. Apart from *Narrative* chap. 10, see also *My Bondage* chaps. 15–17 and *Life* chaps. 15–17.

9. Also for Griggs, visibility is a trade. However, his menial job as a window cleaner suggests that, as an economy of the visible, the optical trade allows only certain positions to be occupied by African Americans. This trade keeps Griggs in his "place" in the economical and social structures. In remarking to the narrator, "'You're marked already,'" Griggs himself misreads his own position in the trade in assuming that "markedness" functions to inculpate only those who transgress the economy. In the white symbolic order, "racially" marked subjects are, obviously, "marked" regardless of their adherence to the rules of the optical trade. As Butler notes, "The more a practice is mastered, the more fully subjection is achieved. Submission and mastery take place simultaneously, and this paradoxical simultaneity constitutes the ambivalence of subjection" (*Psychic* 116).

10. The optical trade for colored boys also includes knowing when not to look, as *Black Boy* later illustrates. Working as a bellboy in a hotel, the narrator has to get used to seeing the prostitutes frequenting the premises and, at times, their white customers naked in the rooms. He, as the rest of the black servants, are, nevertheless, expected not to look since "[i]t was assumed that we black boys took their nakedness for granted." On one occasion, the narrator makes the mistake of looking at a white prostitute in the presence of a customer, thus unwittingly transgressing what is allowed for his eyes. He immediately receives a threat from the white man: "'Keep your eyes where they belong if you want to be healthy!'" (193–94). Such scenes demonstrate, as Alice Walker writes, the necessity for black men to "perfect[] the art of doing the most intimate things to and for white people without once appearing to look at them" (*Temple* 35).

11. For descriptions of lynchings whose brutality cannot but remind one of the opening scene of *Discipline and Punish*, see Zangrando 41–42, and Litwack 8–9, 14–16.

12. Mechlin discusses the Pease-Reynolds incident in 286–87.

13. As Eve Kosofsky Sedgwick argues, "The terrorism of the lynch mob would not have been a potent weapon if the Black Americans claiming their rights and freedoms had known, not only that some portion of them would be murdered, but which ones. The genocidal 'solution' was never possible in the American South because the struggle was, precisely, over the control of labor power: only the specifically *disproportionate* effect of terrorism, made possible by the randomness of the violence, gave the needed leverage without destroying the body on which it was to work" (*Between* 88). In the autobiographical *Darkwater*, Du Bois similarly suggests that racism's unpredictability renders it all the more powerful and insidious (223). See also Douglass, *Narrative* 69; JanMohamed, *Death-Bound-Subject* 9; and Zangrando 42.

14. In the self-published *A Primer of Facts Pertaining to the Early Greatness of the African Race* (1905), Hopkins's immediate target of criticism is Jeannette Robinson Murphy's *Southern Thoughts for Northern Thinkers* (1904).

15. See Hopkins, "Famous Men: Senator" 261; "Munroe" 20; "Reminisences [*sic*]" 454.

16. The term is repeated also in Wright, *The Outsider* 492, 497, 526, 675 ("the sight of the world"), 774; and *Father's* 34.

17. We may briefly note that, in Lewis's novel, outsiders to the American small town way of life are, like Wright's narrator, tainted by their bookishness. Explaining her first shock at seeing the ugliness of Gopher Prairie, Carol Kennicott placates her newly wed husband by saying, "'I'm just—I'm beastly over-sensitive. Too many books. It's my lack of shoulder-muscles and sense. Give me time, dear'" (33). Later, one of the town misfits introduces himself to her, "'[I'm u]sually known as "that damn lazy big-mouthed calamity-howler that ain't satisfied with the way we run things." . . . I'm just a book-worm. Probably too much reading for the amount of digestion I've got'" (133–34).

18. In numerous texts, Du Bois described his shift from a posture of scientific objectivity and detachment (*Dusk* 58; *Souls* 63) to one of passionate involvement (*Autobiography* 222; *Darkwater* 21; *Dusk* 67–68). Wright discusses objectivity in *White* 44.

5. AVIAN ALIENATION

Epigraphs: Lord and Park; Greenaway 1.

1. Hegel's importance is not diminished by his repression of the question of slavery as it was practiced in European colonies when he was pondering on the possibilities of human freedom. See Buck-Morss.

2. There are two ways to respond to criticism that deems Hegel's system inapplicable to describe the material struggles between slaves and masters (see Hardt 41–45; Kirkland 309–10n100). First, one can situate, with Frederick Copleston, the "Lordship and Bondage" section in the *Phenomenology* in two frameworks: on the one hand, as exemplifying "a stage in the abstract dialectical development of consciousness," and, on the other, "in relation to history." Copleston writes that "human history itself reveals the development of Spirit, the travail of the Spirit on the way to its goal." He also notes that Hegel identifies one of the stages of the slave–master dialectic with "a name with explicit historical associations": Stoicism (184). Second, and more important, one can emphasize the fact that all contemporary theorists of slavery referring to Hegel work in a philosophical environment indebted to Alexandre Kojève's influential politicization

of the *Phenomenology*. Even if we deem the Hegelian system hostile to the "personalist reading[s]" proposed by theorists of slavery (Hardt 41), we must not underestimate the necessarily Kojèvean emphases in contemporary interpretations that connect revolutionary acts and theories—be they Douglass's or Fanon's—to Hegel. Kojève's insistence on "the perspective of lived experience as the necessary context in which to analyze desire and temporality" (Butler, *Subjects* 73) renders his theory amenable to Patterson's and Davis's readings, as well as to Gilroy's, Willett's, Cassuto's, and JanMohamed's subsequent work. According to Judith Butler, Kojève's rereading of the dialectics of lordship and bondage refused Hegel's vision of the Absolute as a telos determining the process of the slave's becoming: he rejected "Hegel's postulation of an ontological unity that conditions and resolves all experiences of difference between individuals and between individuals and the external world" (*Subjects* 63). His view of history is marked not by Hegel's synthetic harmony of Spirit but by "the struggle for recognition [which] forms the dynamic principle of all historical progress" (64). By drawing on Marx, Kojève gives us a Hegel who is less concerned with Absolute Knowledge than with the way desire, impelled by differences between subjects, translates into historical action. While Davis and Patterson make only passing references to Kojève, their interpretations are necessarily situated in the philosophical landscape formed by his galvanizing rereading. As Butler writes, "Hegel's text is itself transformed by the particular historical interpretations it endures; indeed, the commentaries are extensions of the text, they *are* the text in its modern life" (63).

3. See Omi and Winant 55–56 and passim.

4. Here my argument echoes JanMohamed's in *The Death-Bound-Subject*.

5. On Feuerbach and Marx, see Marcuse 267–322. On Hyppolite, see Butler, *Subjects* 79–92.

6. Apart from *The Four Fundamental Concepts*, see also Lacan's "Position of the Unconscious" for an account of alienation and separation.

7. Bigger's failure in considering class is made obvious early on in the novel: "And rich white people were not so hard on Negroes; it was the poor whites who hated Negroes. They hated Negroes because they didn't have their share of the money. His mother had always told him that rich white people liked Negroes better than they did poor whites. He felt that if he were a poor white and did not get his share of the money, then he would deserve to be kicked. Poor white people were stupid. It was the rich white people who were smart and knew how to treat people" (29).

8. In *The Outsider*, the question is, of course, of a particular kind of reading; in Wright's autobiography, the *very activity of reading* is enough to elicit suspicion.

9. Consequently, when there emerges a threat that his bluff may be called and his secret knowledge exposed he reverts back to concrete weaponry. As Bessie demands to know what has happened to the white girl, Bigger "stiffen[s] with fear. He fe[els] suddenly that he want[s] something in his hand, something solid and heavy: his gun, a knife, a brick" (123).

10. Describing his efforts at finding the letter, the Prefect continues: "'when we had absolutely completed every particle of the furniture in this way, then we examined the house itself. We divided its entire surface into compartments, which we numbered, so that none might be missed; then we scrutinized each individual square inch throughout the premises, including two houses immediately adjoining, with the microscope, as before'" (11–12). The division and numbering of the space within the Minister's house, and the two adjacent houses, recalls the Renaissance method of painting where a plate

of glass between the painter and the object was divided into numbered sections that were then faithfully reproduced onto a canvas (see Alberti 54–57 and Chapter 1 above). "'The thing is *so* plain,'" the Prefect brags and, in a homophonic slip of the tongue, betrays the flatness of his conception of space. His investigative point of view thus coincides with the geometral perspective where "[w]hat is at issue . . . is simply the mapping of space, not sight" (*SXI* 86). Referring to Denis Diderot, Lacan notes that, when this perspective is applied, the absence of sight does not prevent the subject from "seeing."

11. Woodward observes the ways in which aviation would trouble segregation as the logic sustaining the delusionary insistence on the nation's racial borders: "The arrival of the age of air transportation appears to have put a strain upon the ingenuity of the Jim Crow lawmakers. Even to the orthodox there was doubtless something slightly incongruous about requiring a Jim Crow compartment on a transcontinental place, or one that did not touch the ground between New York and Miami. No Jim Crow law has been found that applies to passengers while they are in the air" (*Strange* 117).

12. Like Jacobs, James Pennington in his narrative names one of his chapters "Flight" (chap. 2) and refers to a fugitive as "the flying slave" (118). In "The Freedman's Story" (1866), William Parker describes emancipation as his "fe[eling] like a bird on a pleasant May morning" (755); similarly, Solomon Northup, gazing at birds, writes: "I wished for wings like them, that I might cleave the air to where my birdlings waited vainly for their father's coming, in the cooler region of the North" (189–90). The tragedy of Hagar Enson in turn follows almost verbatim Clotel's thwarted escape: see chap. 25 in William Wells Brown's novel.

13. See Smith-Storey; W. Walters 4; Wilentz, "If" 22–23.

14. The argument that slavery entailed "a theft of labor, life, and liberty that demanded an accounting" (Biondi 6), which was put forward in the late-nineteenth-century arguments for compensation to ex-slaves, has recently resurfaced in the debates around reparations. See www.mdcbowen.org/cobb/archives/000191.html, esp. item 1. (Last accessed August 29, 2005.) In Douglass's eyes, slave masters are mere "robbers and deceivers" (*My Bondage* 228; see also 246–48, 327, 337, 341, 412); John Brown writes in his narrative: "I never considered it wicked to steal, because I looked upon what I took as part of what was due to me for my labor" (342; see also 364). See also Bibb 29; Douglass, *Narrative* 42; Jacobs 573; and Pennington 141, 143.

15. As Wilentz notes, in African American literature, a lynch mob is often escaped by flying ("If" 27).

16. See Wright, *Black Power* 77, 80, 179–81; Fanon, *Black* 140, 152–53n15.

17. Gates notes that "[t]he representation of the scene of instruction of the black author's literacy became . . . a necessary principle of structure of virtually all of the slave narratives published between 1789 and 1865" (*Signifying* 147–48). Calling them "primary scene[s] in Afro-American letters," Robert Stepto writes: "Schoolroom and graduation episodes in Afro-American literature begin to assume their proper stature when we recall not only the laws and race rituals that enforced a people's illiteracy (*vis-à-vis* the written word) but also the body of literature, including most obviously the slave narratives, that express again and again the quest for freedom *and* literacy achieved regardless of the odds" (147).

18. At times slave narrators cultivate life as the source of hope. At one point John Brown's narrator, for example, "resolve[s] to drown [him]self" but recants as he gazes into the river: "the water looked so cold and deep, my resolution was shaken"; "I reflected that as long as I had life, there was hope" (352). However, while he thus

"cl[ings] to hope" (354), he finds it necessary to actively opt for death when he finally decides to flee: he sets off "with a full determination either to gain my freedom, or to die in the attempt" (355). Brown's situation can be compared to Douglass's, who observes: "in thinking of my life, I almost forgot my liberty" (*Narrative* 83). See also Craft 514 and Northup 195.

19. On Garner, see A. Gordon.

20. In 1847 Douglass names his newspaper *The North Star* in recognition of the term's significance as the abolitionist shorthand for freedom.

21. On Wagner and Du Bois, see Berman and Sundquist 522–24, 577–78.

22. Rampersad (*Art* 71, 75) thinks it a suicide; Sundquist (522) remains undecided.

23. For a relevant account of the Victorian dandy, see also Bristow chap. 1; and Moers. For post-Washingtonian reconfigurations of the black dandy, see Glick and M. Miller.

24. See Jacobs 564, 577, 579, 583; Hopkins, *Hagar's* 62.

25. While not mentioning "Political Necrophilia," JanMohamed's argument in *The Death-Bound-Subject*, too, constitutes a pertinent response to Castronovo, especially insofar as the latter points to the drive to exemplify the "ontological cleansing" (Dimock 114: qtd. in Castronovo 116) of the subject in its bodiless freedom.

26. As Fink writes, the final version of "The Subversion of the Subject," published for the first time in *Écrits* in 1966, probably went through several rewritings after its initial delivery as a conference paper in the fall of 1960 (*Lacan* 106–07). Yet, it seems safe to assume that the section on Hegelian dialectics was included in the original draft.

27. Closely analyzing Gilroy's detour through Lacan, Merrill Cole, in "Nat Turner's Thing," provides a forceful critique of what he considers *The Black Atlantic*'s "continuist narrative" of history (262). For him, Gilroy's misquotation of Alan Sheridan's translation symptomatically reveals that the psychoanalytic critique of Hegelianism is inhospitable to Gilroy's framework; Gilroy is skinning his hand to assimilate Lacan to his redemptive historiography. According to Cole, Gilroy, seeing in Douglass's challenge to Covey an example of the slave's wager of death, eclipses the radical dimension of Lacan's ethics. As examples of the ethico-real act of the slave, Cole instead points to Nat Turner's uprising and Garner's infanticide. I diverge from Cole in identifying the ethico-real character of an act not only in Douglass's uprising—whose significance Cole dismisses (264)—but also in the activity exemplified by the literary pursuits of *Black Boy*'s narrator.

28. Note also that the "feeling like a criminal" recurs when the narrator tells his coworkers of his plans to leave the South—which, as he is told, must be a result of "'reading too many of them damn books'" (244, 245).

29. In another story of crime and concealment, Wright repeats this connection between reading/writing and criminality/insanity. Having switched identities with a dead fellow passenger, Cross Damon of *The Outsider* plans his freedom: "He would have to imagine this thing out, dream it out, invent it, *like a writer constructing a tale*, he told himself grimly as he watched the blurred street lamps flash past the trolley's frosted window" (456; emphasis added). Yet, such writerly reconstruction of his life evokes feelings of guilt and fears of insanity in him: "In a way, he was a criminal, not so much because of what he was doing, but because of what he was feeling"; "Maybe this dream of a new life was too mad?" (455, 457).

30. James Strachey translated this term "pertinacity": see Freud, *Three* 167; *Drei* 144.

31. Despite all his liberal failures, Jan Erlone, in *Native Son*, is a hopeful character for Wright in that, in the final analysis, he stands as an anomaly to the blindest aspects of communism. If, as *Black Boy*'s narrator observes, "communism had declared war on human loneliness" (355), Jan's very name signals his difference from the rigidity of the Red perspective: his last name is also Wright's vernacular rendition of "alone"—*erlone*—in the short stories "Fire and Cloud" (187) and "Bright and Morning Star" (241, 246).

32. Here Bigger rearticulates Jake's thoughts in *Lawd Today!*: "*Being an aviator sure must be fun, 'specially when you on top of another place and can send it spinning down like that . . .*" (54; ellipsis in original). See also the stage adaptation of *Native Son*: Green and Wright 27–28.

33. On WWI and black aviation, see Hoberman 70–75.

Bibliography

Abel, Elizabeth, Barbara Christian, and Helene Moglen. "Introduction: The Dream of a Common Language." In Abel, Christian, and Moglen, eds., 1–18.

———, eds. *Female Subjects in Black and White: Race, Psychoanalysis, Feminism*. Berkeley and Los Angeles: University of California Press, 1997.

Achebe, Chinua. *Things Fall Apart*. 1959; rpt. New York: Anchor Books, 1994.

Adams, Michael Vannoy. "Hair: Kinky, Straight, Bald." In *The Multicultural Imagination: "Race," Color, and the Unconscious*. London: Routledge, 1996, 85–100.

Adell, Sandra. *Double-Consciousness/Double-Bind: Theoretical Issues in Twentieth-Century Black Literature*. Urbana and Chicago: University of Illinois Press, 1994.

Alberti, Leon Battista. *On Painting and On Sculpture* (1435). Ed. and trans. Cecil Grayson. London: Phaidon, 1972.

Alessandrini, Anthony C., ed. *Frantz Fanon: Critical Perspectives*. London: Routledge, 1999.

Alloula, Malek. *The Colonial Harem* (1981). Trans. Myrna Godzich and Wlad Godzich. Minneapolis: University of Minnesota Press, 1986.

Andrews, William L. *To Tell a Free Story: The First Century of Afro-American Autobiography, 1760–1865*. 1986; rpt. Urbana and Chicago: University of Illinois Press, 1988.

Ansell Pearson, Keith. *Germinal Life: The Difference and Repetition of Deleuze*. London: Routledge, 1999.

———. *Philosophy and the Adventure of the Virtual: Bergson and the Time of Life*. London: Routledge, 2002.

Apter, Emily. *Feminizing the Fetish: Psychoanalysis and Narrative Obsession in Turn-of-the-Century France*. Ithaca: Cornell University Press, 1991.

Atwood, Margaret. *The Handmaid's Tale*. 1986; rpt. New York: Anchor, 1998.

Awkward, Michael. "Negotiations of Power: White Critics, Black Texts, and the Self-Referential Impulse." In *Negotiating Difference: Race, Gender and the Politics of Positionality*. Chicago: University Of Chicago Press, 1995, 59–91.

Baker, Houston A., Jr. *Blues, Ideology, and Afro-American Literature: A Vernacular Theory*. 1984; rpt. Chicago: University of Chicago Press, 1987.

———. *Modernism and the Harlem Renaissance*. 1987; rpt. Chicago: University of Chicago Press, 1989.

———. "On Knowing Our Place." In Gates and Appiah, eds., 200–25.

———. *Turning South Again: Re-Thinking Modernism/Re-Reading Booker T.* Durham: Duke University Press, 2001.

———, ed. *Twentieth Century Interpretations of* Native Son. Englewood Cliffs: Prentice-Hall, 1972.

Baldwin, James. "Alas, Poor Richard" (1961). Rpt. in *The Price of the Ticket*, 269–88.

———. "The Black Boy Looks at the White Boy" (1961). Rpt. in *The Price of the Ticket*, 289–303.

———. "Everybody's Protest Novel" (1949). Rpt. in *The Price of the Ticket*, 27–34.

———. *The Fire Next Time* (1963). Rpt. in *The Price of the Ticket*, 333–79.

———. "Here Be Dragons" (1985). Rpt. in *The Price of the Ticket*, 677–90.

———. "The Last Interview" (1987). Conducted by Quincy Troupe. In *James Baldwin: The Legacy*. Ed. Troupe. New York: Simon and Schuster/Touchstone, 1988, 186–212.

———. "Many Thousands Gone" (1951). Rpt. in *The Price of the Ticket*, 65–78.

———. "Nothing Personal" (1964). Rpt. in *The Price of the Ticket*, 381–93.

———. *The Price of the Ticket: Collected Nonfiction 1948–1985*. New York: St. Martin's/Marek, 1985.

Baltrušaitis, Jurgis. *Anamorphotic Art* (1969). Trans. W. J. Strachan. Cambridge: Chadwyck-Healey, 1977.

Baraka, Amiri. "*Black Boy* as Slave Narrative, *Black Boy* as Anti-Imperialist Narrative." In *Daggers and Javelins: Essays 1974–1979*. New York: William Morrow, 1984, 172–81.

Barnard, Suzanne. "Introduction." In *Reading Seminar XX: Lacan's Major Work on Love, Knowledge, and Feminine Sexuality*. Ed. Barnard and Bruce Fink. Albany: State University of New York Press, 2002, 1–20.

Barrett, Lindon. "African-American Slave Narratives: Literacy, the Body, Authority." *American Literary History* 7:3 (Fall 1995): 415–42.

———. "Hand-Writing: Legibility and the White Body in *Running a Thousand Miles for Freedom*." *American Literature* 69:2 (June 1997): 315–36.

Basu, Biman. "The Genuflected Body of the Masochist in Richard Wright." *Public Culture* 16:2 (Spring 2004): 239–63.

Baudelaire, Charles. "The Essence of Laughter and More Especially of the Comic in Plastic Arts" (1855). Trans. Gerard Hopkins. Rpt. in *The Essence of Laughter, and Other Essays, Journals, and Letters*. Ed. Peter Quennell (New York: Meridian, 1956), 107–30.

Benvenuto, Bice, and Roger Kennedy. *The Works of Jacques Lacan: An Introduction*. New York: St. Martin's Press, 1968.

Berger, Anne-Emmanuelle. "The Newly Veiled Woman: Irigaray, Specularity, and the Islamic Veil." *diacritics* 28:1 (1998): 93–119.

Berger, John. *Ways of Seeing*. 1972; rpt. London: Penguin, 1977.

Bergner, Gwen. "Politics and Pathologies: On the Subject of Race in Psychoanalysis." In Alessandrini, ed., 219–34.

———. "Who Is That Masked Woman? or, The Role of Gender in Fanon's *Black Skin, White Masks*." *PMLA* 110:1 (January 1995): 75–88.

Berlant, Lauren. "National Brands/National Body: *Imitation of Life*." In *Comparative American Identities: Race, Sex, and Nationality in the Modern Text*. Ed. Hortense J. Spillers. New York: Routledge, 1991, 110–40.

Berman, Russell A. "Du Bois and Wagner: Race, Nation, and Culture between the United States and Germany." *German Quarterly* 70:2 (Spring 1997): 123–35.

Bernabé, Jean, Patrick Chamoiseau, and Raphaël Confiant. "In Praise of Creoleness" (1989). Trans. Mohamed B. Taleb Khyar. *Callaloo* 13:4 (Fall 1990): 886–909.

Bernasconi, Robert. "Who Invented the Concept of Race?: Kant's Role in the Enlightenment Construction of Race." In *Race*. Ed. Bernasconi. Oxford: Blackwell, 2001, 11–36.

Bernasconi, Robert, and Tommy L. Lott. "Introduction." In Bernasconi and Lott, eds., vii–xviii.

———. eds. *The Idea of Race*. Indianapolis: Hackett, 2000.

Bernier, François. "A New Division of the Earth" (1684). Trans. T. Bendyshe. Rpt. in Bernasconi and Lott, eds., 1–4.

Berressem, Hanjo. "Dali and Lacan: Painting the Imaginary Landscapes." In *Lacan, Politics, Aesthetics*. Ed. Willy Apollon and Richard Feldstein. Albany: State University of New York Press, 1996, 263–94.

Berry, Mary Frances. *Black Resistance, White Law: A History of Constitutional Racism in America*. New York: Allen Lane/Penguin, 1994.

Bersani, Leo. *The Death of Stéphane Mallarmé*. Cambridge: Cambridge University Press, 1982.

———. "The Other Freud." *Humanities in Society* 1:1 (Winter 1978): 35–49.

Bersani, Leo, and Ulysse Dutoit. *Caravaggio's Secrets*. Cambridge: MIT Press, 1998.

Best, Stephen Michael. "'Stand by Your Man': Richard Wright, Lynch Pedagogy, and Rethinking Black Male Agency." In *Representing Black Men*. Ed. Marcellus Blount and George P. Cunningham. New York: Routledge, 1996, 111–30.

Bhabha, Homi K. *The Location of Culture*. 1994; rpt. New York: Routledge, 1995.

Bibb, Henry. *Narrative of the Life and Adventures of Henry Bibb, an American Slave*. 1849; rpt. in Y. Taylor, ed., *I Was Born a Slave, vol. 2*, 1–101.

Biondi, Martha. "The Rise of the Reparations Movement." *Radical History Review* 87 (Fall 2003): 5–18.

Bloom, Harold. "Introduction." In Bloom, ed., 1–6.

Bloom, Harold, ed. *Richard Wright*. New York: Chelsea House, 1987.

Blumenbach, Johann Friedrich. "On the Natural Variety of Mankind" (1795). Trans. Thomas Bendyshe. Rpt. in Bernasconi and Lott, eds., 27–37.

Bogle, Donald. *Toms, Coons, Mulattoes, Mammies, and Bucks: An Interpretive History of Blacks in American Films*. Rev. ed. 1989; rpt. New York: Continuum, 1993.

Bolton, H. Philip. "The Role of Paranoia in Richard Wright's *Native Son*." *Kansas Quarterly* 7:3 (Summer 1975): 111–24.

Bone, Robert A. *The Negro Novel in America*. New Haven: Yale University Press, 1958.

Bongie, Chris. *Islands and Exiles: The Creole Identities of Post/Colonial Literature*. Stanford: Stanford University Press, 1998.

Bontemps, Arna. "The Slave Narrative: An American Genre." In *Great Slave Narratives*. Selected and introduced by Bontemps. Boston: Beacon Press, 1969, vii–xix.

Borch-Jacobsen, Mikkel. *Lacan: The Absolute Master*. Trans. Douglas Brick. Stanford, CA: Stanford University Press, 1991.

Boskin, Joseph. *Sambo: The Rise and Demise of an American Jester*. New York: Oxford University Press, 1986.

Boyarin, Daniel. "'An Imaginary and Desirable Converse': *Moses and Monotheism* as Family Romance." In *Reading Bibles, Reading Bodies: Identity and The Book*. Ed. Timothy K. Beal and David M. Gunn. London: Routledge, 1997, 184–204.

———. "Jewish Cricket." *PMLA* 113:1 (Jan 1998): 40–45.

———. *Unheroic Conduct: The Rise of Heterosexuality and the Invention of the Jewish Man.* Berkeley and Los Angeles: University of California Press, 1997.

———. "What Does a Jew Want?; or, The Political Meaning of the Phallus." In Lane, ed., 211–40.

Bradley, A. C. "Hegel's Theory of Tragedy." In *Hegel on Tragedy.* Ed. Anne and Henry Paolucci. 1962; rpt. New York: Harper & Row, 1975, 367–88.

Bradley, David. "On Rereading 'Native Son.'" In *Black Literature: Criticism*, vol. 3. Ed. James P. Draper. Detroit: Gale Research, 1992, 2018–20.

Braidotti, Rosi. *Metamorphoses: Towards a Materialist Theory of Becoming.* Cambridge: Polity, 2002.

Brennan, Teresa, and Martin Jay, eds. *Vision in Context: Historical and Contemporary Perspectives on Sight.* New York: Routledge, 1996.

Bristow, Joseph. *Effeminate England: Homoerotic Writing after 1885.* New York: Columbia University Press, 1995.

Brodhead, Richard H. "Sparing the Rod: Discipline and Fiction in Antebellum America." In *Cultures of Letters: Scenes of Reading and Writing in Nineteenth-Century America.* Chicago: University of Chicago Press, 1993, 13–47.

Brown, John. *Slave Life in Georgia: A Narrative of the Life, Sufferings, and Escape of John Brown, a Fugitive Slave, Now in England.* 1855; rpt. in Y. Taylor, ed., *I Was Born a Slave, vol. 2*, 319–411.

Brown, Laura S. "Not outside the Range: One Feminist Perspective on Psychic Trauma." In *Trauma: Explorations in Memory.* Ed. Cathy Caruth. Baltimore: Johns Hopkins University Press, 1995, 100–12.

Brown, Wesley. *Darktown Strutters.* 1994; rpt. Amherst: University of Massachusetts Press, 2000.

Brown, William Wells. *Clotel; or, The President's Daughter* (1853). Rpt. in *Three Classic African-American Novels.* Ed. Henry Louis Gates, Jr. New York: Vintage, 1990, 3–223.

Brownmiller, Susan. *Against Our Will: Men, Women and Rape.* New York: Simon and Schuster, 1975.

Bruce, Dickson D., Jr. *The Origins of African American Literature, 1680–1865.* Charlottesville: University Press of Virginia, 2001.

Buck-Morss, Susan. "Hegel and Haiti." *Critical Inquiry* 26:4 (Summer 2000): 821–65.

Burgin, Victor. "Geometry and Abjection." In *Abjection, Melancholia, and Love: The Work of Julia Kristeva.* Ed. John Fletcher and Andrew Benjamin. London: Routledge, 1990, 104–23.

Butler, Judith. *Antigone's Claim: Kinship between Life and Death.* New York: Columbia University Press, 2000.

———. *Bodies that Matter: On the Discursive Limits of "Sex."* New York: Routledge, 1993.

———. "Endangered/Endangering: Schematic Racism and White Paranoia." In *Reading Rodney King/Reading Urban Uprising.* Ed. Robert Gooding-Williams. New York: Routledge, 1993, 15–22.

———. *Gender Trouble: Feminism and the Subversion of Identity.* New York: Routledge, 1990.

———. "Imitation and Gender Insubordination." In Fuss, ed., 13–31.

———. *Precarious Life: The Powers of Mourning and Violence*. London: Verso, 2004.

———. *The Psychic Life of Power: Theories in Subjection*. Stanford: Stanford University Press, 1997.

———. *Subjects of Desire: Hegelian Reflections in Twentieth-Century France*. 1987; rpt. New York: Columbia University Press, 1999.

———. *Undoing Gender*. New York: Routledge, 2004.

Butler, Judith, Ernesto Laclau, and Slavoj Žižek. *Contingency, Hegemony, Universality: Contemporary Dialogues on the Left*. London: Verso, 2000.

Butler, Robert J. "Introduction." In *The Critical Response to Richard Wright*. Ed. Butler. Westport: Greenwood Press, 1995, xxv–xxxix.

Byerman, Keith Eldon. *Seizing the Word: History, Art, and Self in the Work of W. E. B. Du Bois*. Athens: University of Georgia Press, 1994.

Caillois, Roger. *Man, Play, and Games* (1958). Trans. Meyer Barash. New York: The Free Press of Glencoe, 1961.

———. "Mimicry and Legendary Psychastenia" (1938). Trans. John Shepley. *October* no. 31 (1984): 17–32.

Campbell, James. "*Un Enfant du Pays*: Richard Wright, St.-Germain-des Prés, the Little Magazines, *J'irai cracher sur vos tombes*." In *Exiled in Paris: Richard Wright, James Baldwin, Samuel Beckett, and Others on the Left Bank*. New York: Scribner, 1995, 1–35.

Campbell, Jan. *Arguing with the Phallus: Feminist, Queer and Postcolonial Theory: A Psychoanalytic Contribution*. London: Zed Books, 2000.

Carney, Faye (general ed.). *Grand dictionnaire francais-anglais*. Paris: Larousse, 1993.

Cassuto, Leonardo. *The Inhuman Race: The Racial Grotesque in American Literature and Culture*. New York: Columbia University Press, 1997.

Castronovo, Russ. "Political Necrophilia." *boundary 2* 27:2 (2000): 113–48.

Césaire, Aimé. *Discourse on Colonialism* (1955). Trans. Joan Pinkham. New York: Monthly Review Press, 1972.

Chatterjee, Partha. "The Nationalist Resolution of the Women's Question." In *Recasting Women: Essays in Indian Colonial History*. Ed. Kumkum Sangari and Sudeshi Vaid. New Brunswick: Rutgers University Press, 1990, 233–53.

Chesnutt, Charles W. *The House behind the Cedars*. 1900; rpt. New York: Penguin, 1993.

Chiesa, Lorenzo. *Subjectivity and Otherness: A Philosophical Reading of Lacan*. Cambridge: MIT Press, 2007.

Chiesa, Lorenzo, and Alberto Toscana. "Ethics and Capital, *Ex Nihilo*." *The Dark God*. Ed. Andrew Skomra. A special issue of *Umbr(a): A Journal of the Unconscious* (2005): 9–25.

Chow, Rey. "The Politics of Admittance: Female Sexual Agency, Miscegenation, and the Formation of Community in Frantz Fanon." In Alessandrini, ed., 34–56.

Cleaver, Eldridge. *Soul on Ice*. 1968; rpt. New York: Dell, 1970.

Cockrell, Dale. *Demons of Disorder: Early Blackface Minstrels and Their World*. New York: Cambridge University Press, 1997.

Cole, Merrill. "Nat Turner's Thing." In Lane, ed., 261–81.

Conley, Tom. "The Wit of the Letter: Holbein's Lacan." In Brennan and Jay, eds., 45–60.

Copjec, Joan. "The Body's Organs and Cindy Sherman's Face." *Lacanian Ink* 14 (1999): 61–69.

———. *Imagine There's No Woman: Ethics and Sublimation*. Cambridge: MIT Press, 2002.

———. *Read My Desire: Lacan against the Historicists*. Cambridge: MIT, 1994.

———. "The Strut of Vision: Seeing's Somatic Support." *Qui Parle* 9:2 (Spring/Summer 1996): 1–30. Rpt. in Copjec, *Imagine There's No Woman*, 178–95.

———. "The Tomb of Perseverance: On *Antigone*." In *Giving Ground: The Politics of Propinquity*. Ed. Copjec and Michael Sorkin. London: Verso, 1999, 233–66. Rpt. in Copjec, *Imagine There's No Woman*, 12–47.

Copleston, Frederick. *A History of Philosophy. Vol. 7: Eighteenth- and Nineteenth-Century German Philosophy*. 1963; rpt. London: Continuum, 2003.

Craft, William, and Ellen. *Running a Thousand Miles for Freedom, or the Escape of William and Ellen Craft from Slavery*. 1860; rpt. in Y. Taylor, ed., *I Was Born a Slave, vol. 2*, 481–531.

Damisch, Hubert. *The Origin of Perspective*. Trans. John Goodman. Cambridge: MIT, 1995.

Davis, Allison. *Leadership, Love, and Aggression*. San Diego and New York: Harcourt Brace Jovanovich, 1983.

Davis, Angela Y. "Racialized Punishment and Prison Abolition." In *The Angela Y. Davis Reader*. Ed. James, Joy. Malden: Blackwell, 1998, 96–107.

Davis, Charles T., and Michel Fabre, eds. *Richard Wright: A Primary Bibliography*. Boston, Mass.: G.K. Hall, 1982.

Davis, Cynthia J. Rev. of Claudia Tate, *Psychoanalysis and Black Novels*. *Legacy* 16:2 (1999): 209–10.

Davis, David Brion. *The Problem of Slavery in the Age of Revolution, 1770–1823*. Ithaca: Cornell University Press, 1975.

Davis, James E. *Who Is Black?: One Nation's Definition*. 1991; rpt. University Park: Pennsylvania State University Press, 1993.

Davis, Jane. "More Farce Than Human: Richard Wright's Female Characters." *Obsidian II* 1:3 (Winter 1986): 68–83.

Davis, Thadious M. *Nella Larsen, Novelist of the Harlem Renaissance: A Woman's Life Unveiled*. Baton Rouge: Louisiana State University Press, 1994.

De Beauvoir, Simone. *The Second Sex* (1949). Trans. and ed. H. M. Parshley. 1952; New York: Vintage, 1989.

De Bolla, Peter. "The Visibility of Visuality." In Brennan and Jay, eds., 63–81.

Dean, Tim. "Art as Symptom: Žižek and the Ethics of Psychoanalytic Criticism." *diacritics* 32:2 (Summer 2002): 21–41.

———. *Beyond Sexuality*. Chicago: University of Chicago Press, 2000.

———. "The Germs of Empires: *Heart of Darkness*, Colonial Trauma, and the Historiography of AIDS." In Lane, ed., 305–29.

———. "Homosexuality and the Problem of Otherness." In *Homosexuality and Psychoanalysis*. Ed. Dean and Christopher Lane. Chicago: University of Chicago Press, 120–43.

———. "Wanting Paul de Man: A Critique of the 'Logic' of New Historicism in American Studies." *Texas Studies in Literature and Language* 35:2 (Summer 1993): 251–77.

Decker, Jeffrey Louis. "Terrorism (Un)Veiled: Frantz Fanon and the Women of Algiers." *Cultural Critique* no. 17 (Winter 1990–91): 177–95.

DeCosta-Willis, Miriam. "Avenging Angels and Mute Mothers: Black Southern Women in Wright's Fictional World." *Callaloo* 28 (Summer 1986): 540–51.

Delaney, David. *Race, Place, and the Law: 1836–1948*. Austin: University of Texas Press, 1998.

Delany, Martin R. *Blake, or The Huts of America* (1859–1862). Boston: Beacon, 1970.

Deleuze, Gilles. *Expressionism in Philosophy* (1968). Trans. Martin Joughin. New York: Zone, 1992.

———. *Foucault* (1986). Trans. Séan Hand. 1988; rpt. Minneapolis: University of Minnesota Press, 1998.

———. *The Logic of Sense* (1969). Ed. Constantin Boundas. Trans. Mark Lester with Charles Stivale. New York: Columbia University Press, 1990.

———. *Negotiations, 1972–1990*. Trans. Martin Joughin. New York: Columbia University Press, 1995.

———. *Spinoza: Practical Philosophy* (1970/1981). Trans. Robert Hurley. San Francisco: City Lights, 1988.

Deleuze, Gilles and Félix Guattari. *Anti-Oedipus: Capitalism and Schizophrenia* (1972). Trans. Robert Hurley, Mark Seem, and Helen R. Lane. 1977; rpt. Minneapolis: University of Minnesota Press, 1998.

———. "Deleuze and Guattari Fight Back . . ." (1972). In Deleuze. *Desert Islands and Other Texts, 1953–1974*. Ed. David Lapoujade. Trans. Michael Taormina. Los Angeles and New York: Semiotext(e), 2004, 216–29.

———. *Kafka: Toward a Minor Literature*. 1975. Trans. Dana Polan. 1986. Minneapolis: University of Minnesota Press, 2000.

———. *A Thousand Plateaus: Capitalism and Schizophrenia* (1980). Trans. Brian Massumi. Minneapolis: University of Minnesota Press, 1987.

Deleuze, Gilles, and Claire Parnet. *Dialogues* (1977). Trans. Hugh Tomlinson and Barbara Habberjam. New York: Columbia University Press, 1987.

Dellamora, Richard. *Masculine Desire: The Sexual Politics of Victorian Aestheticism*. Chapel Hill: University of North Carolina Press, 1990.

Delmar, P. Jay. "Tragic Patterns in Richard Wright's *Uncle Tom's Children*." *Negro American Literature Forum* 10:1 (Spring 1976): 3–12.

Derrida, Jacques. *Given Time: I. Counterfeit Money* (1991). Trans. Peggy Kamuf. Chicago: University of Chicago Press, 1992.

———. *Dissemination* (1972). Trans. Barbara Johnson. Chicago: University of Chicago Press, 1981.

———. *Writing and Difference* (1967). Trans. Alan Bass. Chicago: University of Chicago Press, 1978.

Descartes, René. *Discourse on Method, Optics, Geometry, and Meteorology*. Rev. ed. Trans. Paul J. Olscamp. Indianapolis: Hackett, 2001.

Diawara, Manthia. "Black American Cinema: The New Realism." In *Black American Cinema*. Ed. Diawara. New York: Routledge, 1993, 3–25.

———. "The Blackface Stereotype." In David Levinthal. *Blackface*. Santa Fe: Arena Editions, 1999, 7–17.

———. *In Search of Africa*. Cambridge: Harvard University Press, 1998.

Dickstein, Morris. "Wright, Baldwin, Cleaver." In Ray and Farnsworth, eds., 183–90.

Diderot, Denis. "Letter on the Blind for the Use of Those Who Can See." In *Diderot's Early Philosophical Works*. Ed and trans. Margaret Jourdain. Chicago and London: Open Court Publishing, 1916, 68–141.

Dimock, Wai Chee. *Residues of Justice: Literature, Law, Philosophy*. Berkeley: University of California Press, 1996.

Dixon, Melvin. "'If You Surrender to the Air . . . '" Rev. of Toni Morrison, *Song of Solomon*. *Callaloo* 4 (Oct. 1978): 170–73.

———. *Ride Out the Wilderness: Geography and Identity in Afro-American Literature*. Urbana and Chicago: University of Illinois Press, 1987.

Doane, Mary Ann. *The Desire to Desire: The Woman's Film of the 1940s*. Bloomington and Indianapolis: Indiana University Press, 1987.

———. *Femmes Fatales: Feminism, Film Theory, Psychoanalysis*. New York: Routledge, 1991.

Douglass, Frederick. *Autobiographies*. Notes by Henry Louis Gates, Jr. 1994; rpt. New York: Penguin/Library of America, 1996.

———. *Frederick Douglass: Selected Speeches and Writings*. Ed. Philip S. Foner. Abridged and adapted by Yuval Taylor. Chicago: Lawrence Hill, 1999.

———. *Life and Times of Frederick Douglass, Written by Himself* (1893). Rpt. in *Autobiographies*, 453–1045.

———. "Lynch Law in the South" (1892). Rpt. in *Frederick Douglass*, ed. Foner, 746–50.

———. *My Bondage and My Freedom* (1855). Rpt. in *Autobiographies*, 103–452.

———. *Narrative of the Life of Frederick Douglass, an American Slave* (1845). Rpt. in *Autobiographies*, 1–102.

———. "Why Is the Negro Lynched?" (1894). Rpt. in *Frederick Douglass*, ed. Foner, 750–76.

Drums and Shadows: Survival Studies among the Georgia Coastal Negroes. Savannah Unit Georgia Writers' Project. Athens: University of Georgia Press, 1940.

Dubey, Madhu. "The 'True Lie' of the Nation: Fanon and Feminism." *differences* 10:2 (Summer 1998): 1–29.

Du Bois, W. E. B. *Africa, its Geography, People and Products/Africa—Its Place in Modern History*. 1930; rpt. Millwood: KTO Press, 1977.

———. *The Autobiography of W. E. B. Du Bois: A Soliloquy on Viewing My Life from the Last Decade of Its First Century*. 1968; rpt. New York: International Publishers, 1979.

———. *Color and Democracy: Colonies and Peace*. 1945; rpt. Millwood: Kraus-Thomson, 1975.

———. *Dark Princess: A Romance*. 1928; rpt. Jackson: Banner, 1995.

———. *Darkwater: Voices from Within the Veil*. 1921; rpt. Millwood: Kraus-Thomson, 1975.

———. *Dusk of Dawn: An Essay Toward an Autobiography of a Race Concept*. 1940; rpt. New Brunswick: Transaction, 1991.

———. *The Negro*. 1915; rpt. New York: Humanity Books, 2002.

———. *The Souls of Black Folk* (1903). Ed. Henry Louis Gates, Jr., and Terri Hume Oliver. New York: Norton, 1999.

Dunbar, Paul Laurence. "We Wear the Mask" (1895). In *African-American Poetry of the Nineteenth Century: An Anthology*. Ed. Joan R. Sherman. Urbana: University of Illinois Press, 1992, 402.

Dyess, Cynthia, and Tim Dean. "Gender: The Impossibility of Meaning." *Psychoanalytic Dialogues* 10:5 (2000): 735–56.

Early, Gerald. "Understanding Afrocentrism." *Civilization* (July/August 1995): 31–39.

Eisinger, Chester E. *The Fiction of the Forties*. 1963; rpt. Chicago: University of Chicago Press, 1965.

Ellison, Ralph. "Change the Joke and Slip the Yoke." In *Shadow and Act*, 45–59.
———. "Introduction." In *Invisible Man*. 1952; rpt. New York: Modern Library, 1994, xvii–xxxiv.
———. *Shadow and Act*. 1964; rpt. New York, NY: Quality Paperback Book Club, 1994.
———. "The World and the Jug." In *Shadow and Act*, 107–43.
Elmer, Jonathan. "Spectacle and Event in *Native Son*." *American Literature* 70:4 (December 1998): 767–98.
Essed, Philomena, and David Theo Goldberg, eds. *Race Critical Theories*. Oxford: Blackwell, 2002.
Evans, Dennis F. "The Good Women, Bad Women, Prostitutes, and Slaves of Pagan Spain: Richard Wright's Look Beyond the Phallocentric Self." In *Richard Wright's Travel Writings: New Reflections*. Ed. Virginia Whatley Smith. Jackson: University Press of Mississippi, 2001, 165–75.
Evans, Dylan. *An Introductory Dictionary of Lacanian Psychoanalysis*. London: Routledge, 1996.
Fabi, M. Giulia. *Passing and the Rise of the African American Novel*. Urbana and Chicago: University of Illinois Press, 2001.
Fabre, Michel. "Margaret Walker's Richard Wright: A Wrong Righted or Wright Wronged?" *Mississippi Quarterly: Richard Wright Issue*. Ed. Michel Fabre and Jack B. Moore. 42:4 (Fall 1989): 429–50.
———. *Richard Wright: Books and Writers*. Jackson: University Press of Mississippi, 1990.
———. *The Unfinished Quest of Richard Wright*. 2nd ed. Trans. Isabel Barzun. Urbana and Chicago: University of Illinois Press, 1993.
———. *The World of Richard Wright*. Jackson: University Press of Mississippi, 1985.
Fabre, Michel, Rosa Bobia, Christina Davis, Edwards O'Neill, and Jack Salzman, eds. *The French Critical Reception of African-American Literature: From the Beginnings to 1970: An Annotated Bibliography*. Westport: Greenwood Press, 1995.
"Fallout from the 'Nappy Hair' Furor." Editorial. *New York Times*, December 11, 1998, late ed., A34.
Fanon, Frantz. *Black Skin, White Masks* (1952). Trans. Charles Lam Markmann. 1967; rpt. New York: Grove Press, 1982.
———. *A Dying Colonialism* (1959). Trans. Haakon Chevalier. 1965; rpt. New York: Grove Press, 1990.
———. Letter to Richard Wright, January 6, 1953. Rpt. in Ray and Farnsworth, eds., 150.
———. *Peau noire, masques blancs*. Paris: Seuil, 1952.
———. *Sociologie d'une révolution (L'an V de la révolution algérienne)*. 1959; rpt. Paris: Francois Maspero, 1968.
———. *Toward the African Revolution: Political Essays* (1964). Trans. Haakon Chevalier. 1967; rpt. New York: Grove Press, 1988.
———. *The Wretched of the Earth* (1961). Trans. Constance Farrington. New York: Grove Press, 1986.
Faulkner, Rita A. "Assia Djebar, Frantz Fanon, Women, Veils, and Land." *World Literature Today* 70:4 (Autumn 1996): 847–55.
Fauset, Jessie. "The Gift of Laughter" (1925). Rpt. in A. Mitchell, ed., 45–50.
Feldstein, Richard, Bruce Fink, and Maire Jaanus, eds. *Reading Seminar XI: Lacan's Four Fundamental Concepts of Psychoanalysis*. Albany: State University of New York Press, 1995.

Felman, Shoshana. *Jacques Lacan and the Adventure of Insight: Psychoanalysis in Contemporary Culture.* Cambridge: Harvard University Press, 1987.

———. "To Open the Question." In Felman, ed., 5–10.

Felman, Shoshana, ed. *Literature and Psychoanalysis: The Question of Reading: Otherwise.* 1982; rpt. Baltimore: Johns Hopkins University Press, 1989.

Fernandes, Leela. *Transforming Feminist Practice: Non-Violence, Social Justice and the Possibilities of a Spiritualized Feminism.* San Francisco: Aunt Lute, 2003.

Fiedler, Leslie A. *Waiting for the End: The American Literary Scene from Hemingway to Baldwin.* 1964; rpt. Harmondsworth: Penguin, 1967.

Field, J. V. *The Invention of Infinity: Mathematics and Art in the Renaissance.* Oxford: Oxford University Press, 1997.

———. "Linear Perspective and the Projective Geometry of Girard Desargues." *Nuncius Annali di Storia della Scienza* 2:2 (1987): 3–40.

———. "Perspective and the Mathematicians: Alberti to Desargues." In *Mathematics from Manuscript to Print, 1300–1600.* Ed. Cynthia Hay. Oxford: Clarendon University Press, 1988, 236–63.

Fink, Bruce. "Alienation and Separation: Logical Moments of Lacan's Dialectic of Desire." *Newsletter of the Freudian Field* 4 (1990): 78–119.

———. *Lacan to the Letter: Reading* Écrits *Closely.* Minneapolis: University of Minnesota Press, 2004.

———. *The Lacanian Subject: Between Language and Jouissance.* Princeton: Princeton University Press, 1995.

Fleischner, Jennifer. *Mastering Slavery: Memory, Family, and Identity in Women's Slave Narratives.* New York: New York University Press, 1996.

Flieger, Jerry Aline. "The Listening Eye: Postmodernism, Paranoia, and the Hypervisible." *diacritics* 26:1 (Spring 1996): 90–107.

———. "Postmodern Perspective: The Paranoid Eye." *New Literary History* 28:1 (1997): 87–109.

"A Flying Fool." Rpt. in *The Norton Anthology of African American Literature.* General ed. Henry Louis Gates, Jr., and Nellie Y. McKay. New York: W. W. Norton, 1997, 117–18.

Foucault, Michel. *The Archaeology of Knowledge* (1969). Trans. A. M. Sheridan Smith. New York: Pantheon, 1972.

———. "The Birth of a World" (1969). Trans. John Johnston. In Foucault, *Foucault Live* 65–67.

———. *Discipline and Punish: The Birth of the Prison* (1975). Trans. Alan Sheridan. 1977; rpt. Harmondsworth: Penguin, 1982.

———. "The Discourse on Language" (1971). Trans. A. M. Sheridan Smith. In *Archaeology* 215–37.

———. *Essential Works, vol. 2: Aesthetics, Method, and Epistemology.* Ed. James D. Faubion. Trans. Robert Hurley and Others. New York: Free Press, 1998.

———. *Foucault Live: Collected Interviews, 1961–1984.* Ed. Sylvère Lotringer. Trans. Lysa Hochroth and John Johnston. New York: Semiotext(e), 1996.

———. "History, Discourse and Discontinuity" (1968). Trans. Anthony Nazzaro. In Foucault, *Foucault Live* 33–50.

———. "History and Homosexuality" (1982). Trans. John Johnston. Rpt. in *Foucault Live,* 363–70.

———. "Michel Foucault on Attica: An Interview." Conducted by John K. Smith. *Social Justice* 18:3 (Fall 1991), 26–34.

———. "Nietzsche, Genealogy, History" (1971). Trans. Donald F. Brouchard and Sherry Simon. In *Essential Works, vol. 2*, 369–91.

———. "On the Genealogy of Ethics: An Overview of Work in Progress" (1983). In *The Foucault Reader*. Ed. Paul Rabinow. New York: Pantheon Books, 1984, 340–72.

———. "Return to History" (1972). Trans. Robert Hurley. In *Essential Works, vol. 2*, 419–32.

———. "Truth and Juridical Forms" (1973). Rpt. in *Essential Works, vol. 3: Power*. Ed. James D. Faubion. Trans. Robert Hurley and others. New York: New Press, 2000, 1–89.

Freud, Sigmund. *Drei Abhandlungen zur Sexualtheorie* (1905). In *Gesammelte Werke* 5. London: Imago Publishing, 1942, 27–145.

———. "Group Psychology and the Analysis of the Ego" (1921). In *Pelican Freud Library* 12: 91–178.

———. *Inhibitions, Symptoms and Anxiety* (1926 [1925]). In *Pelican Freud Library* 10: 227–333.

———. "Instincts and Their Vicissitudes" (1915). In *Pelican Freud Library* 11: 105–38.

———. "Moses and Monotheism" (1939 [1934–38]). In *Pelican Freud Library* 13: 237–386.

———. "On Narcissism: An Introduction" (1914). In *Pelican Freud Library* 11: 59–97.

———. "An Outline of Psychoanalysis" (1940 [1938]). In *Pelican Freud Library* 15: 369–443.

———. *The Pelican Freud Library. 15 vols.* James Strachey and Angela Richards, general eds. Harmondsworth: Penguin, 1973–1986.

———. "The Question of Lay Analysis: Conversation with an Impartial Person" (1926). In *Pelican Freud Library* 15: 277–363.

———. *Three Essays on the Theory of Sexuality* (1905). In *Pelican Freud Library* 7: 31–169.

———. "Totem and Taboo: Some Points of Agreement between the Mental Lives of Savages and Neurotics" (1913 [1912–13]). In *Pelican Freud Library* 13: 43–224.

———. "Über Coca" (1884). In *Cocaine Papers*. Ed. Robert Byck. New York: New American Library, 1975, 47–73.

———. "The Unconscious" (1915). In *Pelican Freud Library* 11: 158–222.

Fuss, Diana. *Identification Papers*. New York: Routledge, 1995.

———, ed. *Inside/out: Lesbian Theories, Gay Theories*. New York: Routledge, 1991.

Gagnier, Regenia. *Idylls of the Marketplace: Oscar Wilde and the Victorian Public*. Stanford: Stanford University Press, 1986.

Gallop, Jane. *The Daughter's Seduction: Feminism and Psychoanalysis*. 1982; rpt. Ithaca: Cornell University Press, 1984.

———. *Thinking through the Body*. New York: Columbia University Press, 1988.

Gandhi, Leela. *Postcolonial Theory: An Introduction*. New York: Columbia University Press, 1998.

Garrett, Shawn-Marie. "Return of the Repressed." *Theater* 32:2 (2002): 26–43.

Gates, Henry Louis, Jr. "Criticism in the Jungle." In *Black Literature and Literary Theory*. Ed. Henry Louis Gates, Jr. New York: Methuen, 1984, 1–24.

———. *Figures in Black: Words, Signs, and the "Racial" Self.* 1987; rpt. New York: Oxford University Press, 1989.

———. "Introduction." In *The Classic Slave Narratives*. Ed. Gates. New York: Mentor, 1987, ix–xviii.

———. "Preface." In Gates and Appiah, eds., xi–xvi.

———. *The Signifying Monkey: A Theory of African-American Literary Criticism*. 1988; rpt. New York: Oxford University Press, 1989.

———. "Talking Black: Critical Signs of the Times." In *Loose Canons: Notes on the Culture Wars*. 1992; rpt. New York: Oxford University Press, 1993, 71–83.

———. "The Two Nations of Black America." *Frontline*. Produced by June Cross. Written by Cross and Gates. Public Broadcasting Service. New York, 10 February 1998.

Gates, Henry Louis, Jr., and K. A. Appiah, eds. *Richard Wright: Critical Perspectives Past and Present*. New York: Amistad, 1993.

Gayle, Addison, Jr. *The Way of the New World: The Black Novel in America*. New York: Doubleday, 1975.

Gendzier, Irene L. *Frantz Fanon: A Critical Study*. London: Wildwood House, 1973.

George, Sheldon. "Trauma and the Conservation of African-American Racial Identity." *JPCS: Journal for the Psychoanalysis of Culture and Society* 6:1 (Spring 2001): 58–72.

Gibson, Donald B. "Wright's Invisible Native Son" (1969). In Baker, ed., 96–108.

Gibson, Ian. *The Shameful Life of Salvador Dali*. 1997; rpt. New York: W. W. Norton, 1998.

Gibson, Nigel. "Fanon and the Pitfalls of Cultural Studies." In Alessandrini, ed., 99–125.

———. *Fanon: The Postcolonial Imagination*. Cambridge: Polity, 2003.

Gibson, Nigel C., ed. *Rethinking Fanon: The Continuing Dialogue*. Amherst, NY: Humanity Books, 1999.

Gilman, Sander L. *Freud, Race, and Gender*. Princeton: Princeton University Press, 1993.

———. *Jewish Self-Hatred: Anti-Semitism and the Language of the Jews*. Baltimore: Johns Hopkins University Press, 1986.

———. *The Jew's Body*. New York: Routledge, 1991.

———. "Otto Weininger and Sigmund Freud: Race and Gender in the Shaping of Psychoanalysis." In Harrowitz and Hyams, eds., 103–20.

———. "Sigmund Freud and the Sexologists: A Second Reading." In *Reading Freud's Reading*. Ed. Gilman, Jutta Birmele, Jay Geller, and Valerie D. Greenberg. New York: New York University Press, 1994, 47–76.

Gilroy, Paul. *Against Race: Imagining Political Culture beyond the Color Line*. Cambridge: Harvard University Press, 2000.

———. *The Black Atlantic: Modernity and Double Consciousness*. Cambridge: Harvard University Press, 1993.

Giovanni, Nikki, and Margaret Walker. *A Poetic Equation: Conversations between Nikki Giovanni and Margaret Walker*. 1974; rpt. Washington, DC: Howard University Press, 1983.

Glick, Elisa F. "Harlem's Queer Dandy: African-American Modernism and the Artifice of Blackness." *Modern Fiction Studies* 49:3 (Fall 2003): 414–42.

Glissant, Édouard. *Caribbean Discourse: Selected Essays* (1981). Trans. J. Michael Dash. 1989; rpt. Charlottesville: University Press of Virginia, 1999.

———. *Poetics of Relation* (1990). Trans. Betsy Wing. 1997; rpt. Ann Arbor: University of Michigan Press, 2000.

Goldberg, David Theo. "In/Visibility and Super/Vision: Fanon on Race, Veils, and Discourses of Resistance." In L. Gordon, Sharpley-Whiting, and White, eds., 179–200.

———. *Racist Culture: Philosophy and the Politics of Meaning.* Oxford: Blackwell, 1993.

Gordon, Avery F. "not only the footprints but the water too and what is down there." In *Ghostly Matters: Haunting and the Sociological Imagination.* Minneapolis: University of Minnesota Press, 1997, 137–90.

Gordon, Lewis R. "Existential Dynamics of Theorizing Black Invisibility." In *Existence in Black: An Anthology of Black Existential Philosophy.* Ed. Gordon. New York: Routledge, 1997, 69–79.

———. "Fanon's Tragic Revolutionary Violence." In L. Gordon, Sharpley-Whiting, and White, eds., 297–308.

———. *Her Majesty's Other Children: Sketches of Racism from a Neocolonial Age.* Lanham: Rowman & Littlefield, 1997.

Gordon, Lewis R., T. Denean Sharpley-Whiting, and Renée T. White, eds. *Fanon: A Critical Reader.* Oxford: Blackwell, 1996.

Gottlieb, Erika. *Dystopian Fiction East and West: Universe of Terror and Trial.* Montreal and Kingston: McGill-Queen's University Press, 2001.

Green, Jacob D. *Narrative of the Life of J. D. Green, a Runaway Slave, from Kentucky, Containing an Account of His Three Escapes, in 1839, 1846, and 1848.* 1864; rpt. in Y. Taylor, ed., *I Was Born a Slave, vol. 2*, 683–719.

Green, Paul, and Richard Wright. *Native Son: The Biography of a Young American.* 1941; rpt. New York: Samuel French, 1980.

Greenaway, Peter. *Flying Out of This World.* Chicago: University of Chicago Press, 1994.

Greenblatt, Stephen. *Renaissance Self-Fashioning: From Moore to Shakespeare.* Chicago: University of Chicago Press, 1980.

Grier, William H., and Price M. Cobbs. *Black Rage.* New York: Bantam Books, 1969.

Grosz, Elizabeth. *Jacques Lacan: A Feminist Introduction.* 1990; rpt. London: Routledge, 1998.

———. "Lived Spatiality: Spaces of Corporeal Desire." In *Culture Lab 1.* Ed. Brian Boignon. New York: Princeton Architectural Press, 1993, 179–205.

———. *The Nick of Time: Politics, Evolution, and the Untimely.* Durham: Duke University Press, 2004.

———. *Space, Time, and Perversion: Essays on the Politics of Bodies.* New York: Routledge, 1995.

———. "Thinking the New: Of Futures Yet Unthought." In *Becomings: Explorations in Time, Memory, and Futures.* Ed. Grosz. Ithaca: Cornell University Press, 1999, 15–28.

———. *Time Travels: Feminism, Nature, Power.* Durham: Duke University Press, 2005.

———. *Volatile Bodies: Toward Corporeal Feminism.* Bloomington and Indianapolis: Indiana University Press, 1994.

Gubar, Susan. *Racechanges: White Skin, Black Face in American Culture*. New York: Oxford University Press, 1997.

Haberman, Clyde. "Cry Racism and Watch Knees Jerk." *New York Times* 4 December 1998, late ed., B1.

Hakutani, Yoshinobu. *Richard Wright and Racial Discourse*. Columbia: University of Missouri Press, 1996.

Halberstam, Judith. *Skin Shows: Gothic Horror and the Technology of Monsters*. Durham: Duke University Press, 1995.

Hall, Stuart. "The After-Life of Frantz Fanon: Why Fanon? Why Now? Why *Black Skin, White Masks*?" In Read, ed., 12–37.

Hardt, Michael. *Gilles Deleuze: An Apprenticeship in Philosophy*. 1993; rpt. Minneapolis: University of Minnesota Press, 2002.

Harper, Frances E. W. *Iola Leroy, or Shadows Uplifted* (1892). With an Introduction by Frances Smith Forster. 1988; rpt. New York: Oxford University Press, 1990.

Harper, Phillip Brian. *Are We Not Men?: Masculine Anxiety and the Problem of African-American Identity*. New York: Oxford University Press, 1996.

Harris, Trudier. *Exorcising Blackness: Historical and Literary Lynching and Burning Rituals*. Bloomington: Indiana University Press, 1984.

———. "Native Sons and Foreign Daughters." In *New Essays on* Native Son. Ed. Keneth Kinnamon. New York: Cambridge University Press, 1990, 63–84.

Harrowitz, Nancy A., and Barbara Hyams, eds. *Jews and Gender: Responses to Otto Weininger*. Philadelphia: Temple University Press, 1995.

Hartman, Saidiya V. *Scenes of Subjection: Terror, Slavery, and Self-Making in Nineteenth-Century America*. New York: Oxford University Press, 1997.

Hartnack, Christiane. "British Psychoanalysis in Colonial India." In *Psychology in Twentieth Century Thought and Society*. Ed. Mitchell G. Ash and William Woodward. New York: Cambridge University Press, 1987, 233–57.

Hegel, G. W. F. "Anthropology" (1830). Trans. A. V. Miller. Rpt. in Bernasconi and Lott, eds., 38–44.

———. *The Phenomenology of Mind* (1807). Trans. J. B. Baillie. 1910; rpt. London: Allen & Unwin, 1966.

———. *The Philosophy of History* (1837). Trans. J. Sibree. Chicago: Encyclopædia Britannica, 1952.

———. *The Philosophy of Right* (1821). Trans. T. M. Knox. Chicago: Encyclopædia Britannica, 1952.

Heggoy, Alf Andrew. "On the Evolution of Algerian Women." *African Studies Review* 17:2 (September 1974): 449–56.

Helie-Lucas, Marie-Aimé. "Women, Nationalism and Religion in the Algerian Liberation Struggle." In *Opening the Gates: A Century of Arab Feminist Writing*. Ed. Margot Badran and Miriam Cooke. Bloomington and Indianapolis: Indiana University Press, 1990, 105–14.

Hernton, Calvin. "The Sexual Mountain and Black Women Writers." *Black American Literature Forum* no. 18 (Winter 1984): 139–45.

Herring, Scott. Rev. of Claudia Tate, *Psychoanalysis and Black Novels: Desire and the Protocols of Race. JPCS: Journal for the Psychoanalysis of Culture and Society* 6:1 (Spring 2001): 157–60.

Herron, Carolivia. *Nappy Hair*. Illustrated by Joe Cepeda. New York: Alfred A. Knopf, 1997.

Higashida, Cheryl. "Aunt Sue's Children: Re-viewing the Gender(ed) Politics of Richard Wright's Radicalism." *American Literature* 75:2 (June 2003): 395–425.

Hoberman, John. *Darwin's Athletes: How Sport Has Damaged Black America and Preserved the Myth of Race*. Boston and New York: Houghton Mifflin, 1997.

Hollinger, David A. *Postethnic America: Beyond Multiculturalism*. New York: Basic Books, 1995.

Holloway, Lynette. "School Officials Support Teacher on Book That Parents Call Racially Insensitive." *New York Times* November 25, 1998, late ed., B10

———. "Teacher Threatened Over Book Weighs Switching Schools." *New York Times,* November 27, 1998, late ed., B14.

———. "Threatened Over Book, Teacher Leaves School." *New York Times,* December 1, 1998, late ed., B3.

———. "Unswayed by Debate on Children's Book." *New York Times,* December 10, 1998, late ed., B3.

hooks, bell. "Straightening Our Hair." In *Reading Culture: Contexts for Critical Reading and Writing.* 3rd ed. Ed. Diana George and John Trimbur. New York: Longman, 1999, 220–25.

Hopkins, Pauline. "Famous Men of the Negro Race: Senator Blanche K. Bruce." *Colored American Magazine* August 1901, 257–61.

———. *Hagar's Daughter: A Story of Southern Caste Prejudice*. 1901/1902. Rpt. in *The Magazine Novels*. New York: Oxford University Press, 1988, 1–284.

———. "Munroe Rogers." *Colored American Magazine* November 1902, 20–26.

———. *A Primer of Facts Pertaining to the Early Greatness of the African Race and the Possibility of Restoration by its Descendants—with Epilogue*. Cambridge: P. E. Hopkins, 1905.

———. "Reminisences [*sic*] of the Life and Times of Lydia Maria Child [pt. III]." *Colored American Magazine* May/June 1903, 454–59.

Howe, Irving. "Black Boys and Native Sons." In Baker, ed., 63–70.

Hudson, Nicholas. "'Nation' to 'Race': The Origin of Racial Classification in Eighteenth-Century Thought." *Eighteenth-Century Studies* 29:3 (1996): 247–64.

Huggins, Nathan Irvin. *Harlem Renaissance*. 1971; rpt. New York: Oxford University Press, 1973.

Hughes, Langston, ed. *The Book of Negro Humor*. New York: Dodd, Mead, 1966.

Hutcherson, Warren. Perf. *Comics Come Home 4*, Comedy Central, New York, January 1, 1999.

Hyman, Stanley Edgar. "Richard Wright Reappraised" (1970). Rpt. in *Black Literature: Criticism*, vol. 3. Ed. James P. Draper. Detroit: Gale Research, 1992, 2010–12.

Iginla, Biodun. "Black Feminist Critique of Psychoanalysis." In E. Wright, ed., 31–33.

Irigaray, Luce. *An Ethics of Sexual Difference* (1984). Trans. Carolyn Burke and Gillian C. Gill. Ithaca: Cornell University Press, 1993.

———. *This Sex Which Is Not One* (1977). Trans. Catherine Porter with Carolyn Burke. Ithaca: Cornell University Press, 1985.

Ivins, William M., Jr. *On the Rationalization of Sight with an Examination of Three Renaissance Texts on Perspective*. New York: Da Capo, 1973.

Jacobs, Harriet (Linda Brent). *Incidents in the Life of a Slave Girl*. 1861; rpt. in Y. Taylor, ed., *I Was Born a Slave, vol. 2*, 533–681.

James, C. L. R. *The Black Jacobins: Toussaint L'Ouverture and the San Domingo Revolution*. 2nd ed. 1963; rpt. New York: Vintage, 1989.

JanMohamed, Abdul R. "The Allegory of Manichean Economy: The Function of Racial Difference in Colonialist Literature." In *"Race," Writing, and Difference.* Ed. Henry Louis Gates, Jr. Chicago: University of Chicago Press, 1986, 78–106.

———. *The Death-Bound-Subject: Richard Wright's Archaeology of Death.* Durham: Duke University Press, 2005.

———. "Negating the Negation as a Form of Affirmation in Minority Discourse: The Construction of Richard Wright as a Subject." In *The Nature and Context of Minority Discourse.* Eds. JanMohamed and David Lloyd. New York: Oxford University Press, 1990, 102–23.

———. "Rehistoricizing Wright: The Psychopolitical Function of Death in *Uncle Tom's Children.*" In Bloom, ed., 191–228.

Jefferson, Margo. *On Michael Jackson.* 2006; rpt. New York: Vintage, 2007.

Johnson, Barbara. *The Critical Difference: Essays in the Contemporary Rhetoric of Reading.* 1980; rpt. Baltimore: Johns Hopkins University Press, 1992.

———. "Double Mourning and the Public Sphere." In *The Wake of Deconstruction.* Oxford: Blackwell, 1994, 16–51.

———. *The Feminist Difference: Literature, Psychoanalysis, Race, and Gender.* Cambridge: Harvard University Press, 1998.

———. "The Frame of Reference: Poe, Lacan, Derrida." In Felman, ed., 457–505.

———. "The Quicksands of the Self: Nella Larsen and Heinz Kohut." In *Telling Facts: History and Narration in Psychoanalysis.* Ed. Joseph H. Smith. Baltimore: Johns Hopkins University Press, 1992, 184–99.

———. "The Re(a)d and the Black." In *Reading Black, Reading Feminist: A Critical Anthology.* Ed. Henry Louis Gates, Jr. New York: Meridian, 1990, 145–54.

Johnson, James Weldon. *Along This Way: The Autobiography of James Weldon Johnson.* New York: Viking Press, 1933.

———. *The Autobiography of an Ex-Coloured Man.* 1927; rpt. New York: Vintage, 1989.

Johnson, Matthew V., and Clara B. Jones. Rev. of Claudia Tate, *Psychoanalysis and Black Novels. The Western Journal of Black Studies* 22:3 (Fall 1998): 205–6.

Jordan, Winthrop D. *White over Black: American Attitudes Toward the Negro, 1550–1812.* 1968; rpt. Chapel Hill: University of North Carolina Press, 1979.

Joyce, Joyce Ann. *Richard Wright's Art of Tragedy.* Iowa City: University of Iowa Press, 1987.

———. "Richard Wright's 'Long Black Song': A Moral Dilemma." *Mississippi Quarterly: Richard Wright Issue.* Ed. Michel Fabre and Jack B. Moore. 42:4 (Fall 1989): 379–85.

Judy, Ronald A. T. "Fanon's Body of Black Experience." In L. Gordon, Sharpley-Whiting, and White, eds., 53–73.

Kandiyoti, Deniz. "Identity and Its Discontents: Women and the Nation." In Patrick Williams and Chrisman, eds., 376–91.

Kant, Immanuel. "Of the Different Human Races" (1777). Rpt. in Bernasconi and Lott, eds., 8–22.

Kaplan, E. Ann. "Fanon, Trauma and Cinema." In Alessandrini, ed., 146–57.

Kawash, Samira. "Terrorists and Vampires: Fanon's Spectral Violence of Decolonization." In Alessandrini, ed., 235–57.

Keady, Sylvia H. "Richard Wright's Women Characters and Inequality." *Black American Literature Forum* 10:4 (Winter 1976): 124–28.

Kemp, Martin. *The Science of Art: Optical Themes in Western Art from Brunelleschi to Seurat*. New Haven: Yale University Press, 1990.

Khanna, Ranjana. *Dark Continents: Psychoanalysis and Colonialism*. Durham: Duke University Press, 2003.

Kinnamon, Keneth. "How *Native Son* Was Born." In Gates and Appiah, eds., 110–31.

Kinnamon, Keneth, and Michel Fabre, eds. *Conversations with Richard Wright*. Jackson: University Press of Mississippi, 1993.

Kirby, Vicki. "Viral Identities: Feminisms and Postmodernisms." In *Australian Women: Contemporary Feminist Thought*. Eds. A. Burns and N. Grieve. Melbourne: Oxford University Press, 1994.

Kirkland, Frank M. "Enslavement, Moral Suasion, and Struggles for Recognition: Frederick Douglass's Answer to the Question—'What Is Enlightenment?'" In *Frederick Douglass: A Critical Reader*. Ed. Bill E. Lawson and Frank M. Kirkland. Oxford: Blackwell, 1999, 243–310.

Knorr, Wilbur R. "On the Principle of Linear Perspective in Euclid's Optics." *Centaurus* 34:3 (1991), 193–210.

Kojève, Alexandre. *Introduction to the Reading of Hegel* (1947). Assembled by Raymond Queneau. Ed. Allan Bloom. Trans. James H. Nichols. New York: Basic Books, 1969.

Krasner, David. "Parody and Double Consciousness of Early Black Musical Theatre." *African American Review* 29:2 (Summer 1995): 317–23.

Lacan, Jacques. "Aggressiveness in Psychoanalysis" (1948). In *Écrits: A Selection*, 10–30.

———. "The Direction of the Treatment and the Principles of Its Power" (1961). In *Écrits: A Selection*, 215–70.

———. *Écrits*. Paris: Seuil, 1966.

———. *Écrits: A Selection*. Trans. Bruce Fink in collaboration with Héloïse Fink and Russell Grigg. 2002; rpt. New York: W. W. Norton, 2004.

———. *The Four Fundamental Concepts of Psycho-Analysis* (1973). Ed. Jacques-Alain Miller. Trans. Alan Sheridan. 1977; rpt. London: Penguin, 1994.

———. "The Freudian Thing, or the Meaning of the Return to Freud in Psychoanalysis" (1956). In *Écrits: A Selection*, 107–37.

———. "The Mirror Stage as Formative of the *I* Function as Revealed in Psychoanalytic Experience" (1949). In *Écrits: A Selection*, 3–9.

———. "The Mirror Stage as Formative of the Function of the I as Revealed in Psychoanalytic Experience" (1949). In *Écrits: A Selection*. Trans. Alan Sheridan. New York: W. W. Norton, 1977, 1–7.

———. "Position of the Unconscious" (1966). Trans. Bruce Fink. In Feldstein, Fink, and Jaanus, eds., 259–82.

———. *Le séminaire de Jacques Lacan, livre XI: Les quatre concepts fondamentaux de la psychoanalyse*. Texte établi par Jacques-Alain Miller. Paris: Seuil, 1973.

———. *Le séminaire de Jacques Lacan, livre VII: L'éthique de la psychoanalyse 1959–1960*. Texte établi par Jacques-Alain Miller. Paris: Seuil, 1986.

———. *Le séminaire de Jacques Lacan, livre XIII: L'objet de la 1965–1966*. Unpublished seminar.

———. *Seminar I: Freud's Papers on Technique 1953–1954* (1975). Ed. Jacques-Alain Miller. Trans. with notes by John Forrester. 1988; rpt. New York: W. W. Norton, 1991.

———. *Seminar II: The Ego in Freud's Theory and in the Technique of Psychoanalysis 1954–1955* (1978). Ed. Jacques-Alain Miller. Trans. Sylvana Tomaselli. 1988; rpt. New York: W.W. Norton, 1991.

———. *Seminar III: The Psychoses 1955–1956* (1981). Ed. Jacques-Alain Miller. Trans. with Notes by Russell Grigg. London: Routledge, 1993.

———. *Seminar VII: The Ethics of Psychoanalysis 1959–1960* (1986). Ed. Jacques-Alain Miller. Trans. Dennis Porter. New York: W. W. Norton, 1992.

———. *Seminar XX: On Feminine Sexuality: The Limits of Love and Knowledge: Encore 1972–1973* (1975). Ed. Jacques-Alain Miller. Ed. Bruce Fink. New York: W. W. Norton, 1998.

———. "Seminar on 'The Purloined Letter'" (1956). Trans. Jeffrey Mehlman. In Muller and Richardson, eds., 28–54.

———. "The Signification of the Phallus" (1958). In *Écrits: A Selection*, 271–280.

———. "Le stade du miroir comme formateur de la fonction du Je telle qu'elle nous est révélée dans l'experiénce psychoanalytique." In *Écrits*, 93–100.

———. "The Subversion of the Subject and the Dialectic of Desire in the Freudian Unconscious" (1966). In *Écrits: A Selection*, 281–312.

———. *Television*. Paris: Seuil, 1973.

———. *Television/A Challenge to the Psychoanalytic Establishment*. Ed. Joan Copjec. Trans. Dennis Hollier, Rosalind Krauss, and Annette Michelson/Trans. Jeffrey Mehlman. New York: W.W. Norton, 1990.

LaCapra, Dominick. *Representing the Holocaust: History, Theory, Trauma*. 1994; rpt. Ithaca: Cornell University Press, 1996.

Laclau, Ernesto. *Emancipation(s)*. New York: Verso, 1996.

———. "Identity and Hegemony: The Role of Universality in the Constitution of Political Logics." In Butler, Laclau, Žižek, 44–89.

———. *On Populist Reason*. London: Verso, 2005.

Laclau, Ernesto, and Chantal Mouffe. *Hegemony and Socialist Strategy: Towards a Radical Democratic Politics*. Trans. Winston Moore and Paul Cammack. London: Verso, 1985.

Lamming, George. *In the Castle of My Skin*. 1953; rpt. Kingston, Jamaica: Longman, 1990.

———. *The Pleasures of Exile*. 1960; rpt. Ann Arbor: University of Michigan Press, 1992.

Lane, Christopher, ed. *The Psychoanalysis of Race*. New York: Columbia University Press, 1998.

Lee, A. Robert. *Black American Fiction since Richard Wright*. South Shields: British Association for American Studies, 1983.

Lester, Neil A. "Nappy Edges and Goldy Locks: African-American Daughters and the Politics of Hair." *The Lion and the Unicorn* 24.2 (2000): 201–24.

Levine, Lawrence W. *Black Culture and Black Consciousness: Afro-American Folk Thought from Slavery to Freedom*. New York: Oxford University Press, 1977.

Lewis, David Levering. *When Harlem Was in Vogue*. 1981; rpt. New York: Oxford University Press, 1989.

Lewis, Sinclair. *Main Street*. 1920; rpt. New York: Bantam, 1996.

Lhamon, W. T., Jr. *Raising Cain: Blackface Performance from Jim Crow to Hip Hop*. Cambridge, Mass.: Harvard University Press, 1998.

Littlejohn, David. *Black on White: A Critical Survey of Writings by American Negroes*. New York: Grossman, 1966.

Litwack, Leon F. "Hellhounds." In James Allen et al. *Without Sanctuary: Lynching Photography in America*. Sante Fe: Twin Palms, 2002.

Locke, Alain. "The New Negro." In Locke, ed., 3–16.

———, ed. *The New Negro*. 1925; rpt. New York: Atheneum, 1968.

Lord, Peter, and Nick Park, dirs. *Chicken Run*. Dreamworks Video, 2000.

Lorde, Audre. *Zami: A New Spelling of My Name*. Berkeley: Crossing Press, 1982.

Lott, Eric. *Love and Theft: Blackface Minstrelsy and the American Working Class*. New York: Oxford University Press, 1995.

Luciano, Dana. "Passing Shadows: Melancholic Nationality and Black Critical Publicity in Pauline E. Hopkins's *Of One Blood*." In *Loss: The Politics of Mourning*. Ed. David L. Eng and David Kazanjian. Berkeley and Los Angeles: University of California Press, 2003, 148–87.

Luepnitz, Deborah. "Beyond the Phallus: Lacan and Feminism." In Rabaté, ed., 221–37.

Mabro, Judy. *Veiled Half-Truths: Western Travellers' Perceptions of Middle Eastern Women*. 1991; rpt. London: I.B. Tauris, 1996.

Macey, David. *Frantz Fanon: A Biography*. New York: Picador, 2000.

Mahar, William J. *Behind the Burnt Cork Mask: Early Blackface Minstrelsy and Antebellum American Popular Culture*. Urbana: University of Illinois Press, 1999.

Majors, Richard, and Janet Mancini Billson. *Cool Pose: The Dilemmas of Black Manhood in America*. 1992; rpt. New York: Simon and Schuster, 1993.

Mannoni, Octave. *Prospero and Caliban: The Psychology of Colonization* (1950). Trans. Pamela Powesland. 1990; rpt. Ann Arbor: University of Michigan Press, 1993.

Marcuse, Herbert. *Reason and Revolution: Hegel and the Rise of Social Theory*. 1941; rpt. London and Henley: Routledge, 1986.

Marez, Curtis. "The *Coquero* in Freud: Psychoanalysis, Race, and International Economies of Distinction." *Cultural Critique* 26 (Winter 1993–94): 65–93.

Marin, Louis. *To Destroy Painting*. Trans. Mette Hjort. Chicago: University of Chicago Press, 1995.

Marriott, David. *Haunted Life: Visual Culture and Black Modernity*. New Brunswick: Rutgers University Press, 2007.

Marshall, Cynthia. "Psychoanalyzing the Prepsychoanalytic Subject." *PMLA* 117:5 (October 2002): 1207–16.

Martin, Tony. "Rescuing Fanon from the Critics." *African Studies Review* 13:3 (Dec. 1970): 381–99.

Marx, Karl. *The Economic and Philosophic Manuscripts of 1844*. Ed. Dirk J. Struik. Trans. Martin Milligan. 1964; rpt. New York: International Publishers, 1967.

Massumi, Brian. "Notes on the Translation and Acknowledgements." In Deleuze and Guattari, *A Thousand Plateaus*, xvi–xix.

McClintock, Anne. *Imperial Leather: Race, Gender and Sexuality in the Colonial Contest*. New York: Routledge, 1995.

McCulloch, Jock. *Colonial Psychiatry and "the African Mind."* Cambridge: Cambridge University Press, 1995.

McKay, Nellie Y. "Naming the Problem that Led to the Question 'Who Shall Teach African American Literature?'; or, Are We Ready to Disband the Wheatley Court." *PMLA* 113:3 (May 1998): 359–69.

Mechlin, Jay. "The Failure of Folklore in Richard Wright's *Black Boy*." *The Journal of American Folklore* 104:413 (Summer 1991), 275–94.

Mellard, James M. "Lacan and the New Lacanians: Josephine Hart's *Damage*, Lacanian Tragedy, and the Ethics of *Jouissance*." *PMLA* 113:3 (May 1998): 395–407.

Melman, Miriam. *Trompe L'Oeil Painting*. New York: Rizzoli, 1983.

Meltzer, Francoise. "Introduction: Partitive Plays, Pipe Dreams." In *The Trial(s) of Psychoanalysis*. Ed. Meltzer. Chicago: University of Chicago Press, 1988, 1–7.

Melville, Stephen. "Division of the Gaze, or, Remarks on the Color and Tenor of Contemporary 'Theory.'" In Brennan and Jay,, eds., 101–16.

Mercer, Kobena. "Black Hair/Style Politics." In *Welcome to the Jungle: New Positions in Black Cultural Studies*. New York: Routledge, 1994, 97–128.

———. "Decolonisation and Disappointment: Reading Fanon's Sexual Politics." In Read, ed., 114–31.

Merleau-Ponty, Maurice. "Intertwining—The Chiasm." In *The Visible and the Invisible* (1964). Ed. Claude Lefort. Trans. Alphonso Lingis. Evanston: Northwestern University Press, 1968, 130–55.

Mernissi, Fatima. *Beyond the Veil: Male-Female Dynamics in a Modern Muslim Society*. New York: John Wiley and Sons, 1975.

Miller, D. A. *The Novel and the Police*. Berkeley and Los Angeles: University of California Press, 1988.

Miller, Hillis J. *Reading Narrative*. Norman: University of Oklaholma Press, 1998.

Miller, Jacques-Alain. "Extimité." Text established by Elisabeth Doisneau. Trans. Francoise Massardier-Kenney. *Lacanian Discourse*. Ed. Marshall W. Alcorn, Jr., Mark Bracher, and Ronald J. Corthell. Special Issue of *Prose Studies* 11:3 (Dec. 1988): 121–31.

———. "An Introduction to Seminars I and II: Lacan's Orientation Prior to 1953 (i), (ii), (iii)." In Feldstein, Fink, and Jaanus, eds., 3–35.

———. "On Semblances in the Relation between the Sexes." In Salecl, ed., 13–27.

Miller, James A. "Bigger Thomas's Quest for Voice and Audience in Richard Wright's *Native Son*." *Callaloo* 28 (Summer 1986): 501–6.

Miller, Monica L. "W. E. B. Du Bois and the Dandy as Diasporic Race Man." *Callaloo* 26:3 (2003): 738–65.

Minces, Juliette. "Women in Algeria." In *Women in the Muslim World*. Ed. Lois Beck and Nikki Keddie. Cambridge: Harvard University Press, 1978, 159–71.

Mitchell, Angelyn, ed. *Within the Circle: An Anthology of African American Literary Criticism from the Harlem Renaissance to the Present*. Durham: Duke University Press, 1994.

Mitchell, Margaret. *Gone with the Wind*. 1936; rpt. New York: Warner, 1993.

Mitchell, W. J. Thomas. *Iconology: Image, Text, Ideology*. Chicago: University of Chicago Press, 1986.

Modleski, Tania. *Feminism without Women: Culture and Criticism in a "Postfeminist" Age*. New York: Routledge, 1991.

Moers, Ellen. *The Dandy: Brummell to Beerbohm*. London: Secker and Warburg, 1960.

Mohanty, Chandra Talpade. "Under Western Eyes: Feminist Scholarship and Colonial Discourses." In Williams and Chrisman, eds., 196–220.

Moncayo, Raul. "The Configurations of Sexual Difference across Real, Symbolic, and Imaginary Dimension." *JPCS: Journal for the Psychoanalysis of Culture and Society* 7:2 (Fall 2002): 216–32.

Moore, Henrietta L. "Anthropology and Cross-Cultural Analysis." In E. Wright, ed., 3–9.

Mootry, Maria K. "Bitches, Whores, and Woman Haters: Archetypes and Typologies in the Art of Richard Wright." In *Richard Wright: A Collection of Critical Essays.* Ed. Richard Macksey and Frank E. Moorer. Englewood Cliffs, NJ: Prentice-Hall, 1984, 117–27.

Mosse, George L. *Toward the Final Solution: A History of European Racism.* New York: Howard Fertig, 1978.

Muller, John P., and William J. Richardson. *Lacan and Language: A Reader's Guide to* Écrits. 1982; rpt. International Universities Press, 1994.

———. "Lacan's Seminar on 'The Purloined Letter': Overview.'" In Muller and Richardson, eds., 55–76.

———, eds. *The Purloined Poe: Lacan, Derrida, and Psychoanalytic Reading.* Baltimore: Johns Hopkins University Press, 1988.

Murphy, Jeannette Robinson. *Southern Thoughts for Northern Thinkers.* New York: Bandanna, 1904.

Murray, Rolland. Rev. of Claudia Tate, *Psychoanalysis and Black Novels: Desire and the Protocols of Race. Modernism/Modernity* 6.3 (1999): 161–63.

Nathan, Hans. *Dan Emmett and the Rise of Early Negro Minstrelsy.* 1962; rpt. Norman: University of Oklahoma Press, 1977.

Nelson, Jill. "Stumbling Upon a Race Secret." *New York Times,* November 28, 1998, late ed., A15.

Northup, Solomon. *Twelve Years a Slave: Narrative of Solomon Northup, A Citizen of New-York, Kidnapped in Washington City in 1841, and Rescued in 1853, from a Cotton Plantation Near the Red River, in Louisiana.* 1853; rpt. in Y. Taylor, ed., *I Was Born a Slave, vol. 2*, 159–317.

Ochshorn, Kathleen. "The Community of *Native Son.*" *Mississippi Quarterly: Richard Wright Issue.* Ed. Michel Fabre and Jack B. Moore. 42:4 (Fall 1989): 387–92.

Odeh, Lama Abu. "Post-Colonial Feminism and the Veil: Thinking the Difference." *Feminist Review* 43 (Spring 1993): 26–37.

Omi, Michael, and Howard Winant. *Racial Formation in the United States: From the 1960s to the 1990s.* 2nd ed. New York: Routledge, 1994.

Ong, Walter J. *Orality and Literacy: The Technologization of the Word.* 1982; rpt. London: Routledge, 1991.

Ottley, Roi. Rev. of *Pagan Spain* (1957). Rpt. in Gates and Appiah, eds., 56.

Panofsky, Erwin. *Perspective as Symbolic Form* (1927). Trans. Christopher S. Wood. New York: Zone Books, 1991.

Parker, William. "The Freedman's Story." 1866; rpt. in Y. Taylor (ed)., *I Was Born a Slave, vol. 2*, 741–87.

Parry, Benita. "Problems in Current Theories of Colonial Discourse." In *The Post-Colonial Studies Reader.* Ed. Bill Ashcroft, Gareth Griffiths, and Helen Tiffin. London: Routledge, 1995, 36–44.

———. "Resistance Theory/Theorising Resistance, or Two Cheers for Nativism." In *Colonial Discourse/Postcolonial Theory.* Ed. Francis Barker, Peter Hulme, and Margaret Iversen. 1994; rpt. Manchester: Manchester University Press, 1996, 172–96.

Paskman, Dailey, and Sigmund Spaeth. *"Gentlemen, Be Seated!": A Parade of the Old-Time Minstrels.* Foreword by Daniel Frohman. Garden City: Doubleday, Doran, 1928.

Patterson, Orlando. *Slavery and Social Death: A Comparative Study.* Cambridge: Harvard University Press, 1982.

Pellegrini, Ann. *Performance Anxieties: Staging Psychoanalysis, Staging Race.* New York: Routledge, 1997.

Penney, James. "Beyond *Atè*: Lacan, Ethics, and the Real." *JPCS: Journal for the Psychoanalysis of Culture and Society* 7:1 (Spring 2002): 24–38.

Pennington, James W. C. *The Fugitive Blacksmith; or, Events in the History of James W. C. Pennington.* 1849; rpt. in Y. Taylor, ed., *I Was Born a Slave, vol. 2,* 103–58.

Pessoa, Carlos, Marta Hernández, Seoungwon Lee, and Lasse Thomassen. "Theory, Democracy, and the Left: An Interview with Ernesto Laclau." *Umbr(a): A Journal of the Unconscious* 2001, 7–27.

Petry, Ann. *The Street.* 1946; rpt. Boston: Houghton Mifflin, 1974.

Phelan, Peggy. *Unmarked: The Politics of Performance.* London: Routledge, 1993.

Phillips, Adam. *On Kissing, Tickling, and Being Bored: Psychoanalytic Essays on the Unexamined Life.* 1993. Cambridge: Harvard University Press, 1994.

Piper, Adrian. "Passing for White, Passing for Black." In *Passing and the Fictions of Identity.* Ed. Ellen K. Ginsberg. Durham: Duke University Press, 1996, 234–69.

Poe, Edgar Allan. "The Purloined Letter" (1844). In Muller and Richardson, eds., 3–27.

Porter, Horace A. *Stealing the Fire: The Art and Protest of James Baldwin.* Middletown: Wesleyan University Press, 1991.

Pouchet Paquet, Sandra. "Foreword." In George Lamming, *The Pleasures of Exile,* vii–xxvii.

Quarles, Benjamin. *The Negro in the Making of America.* 3rd ed. New York: Collier/Macmillan, 1987.

Rabaté, Jean-Michel, ed. *The Cambridge Companion to Lacan.* Cambridge: Cambridge University Press, 2003.

Radano, Ronald M. "Soul Texts and the Blackness of Folk." *Modernity/Modernism* 2.1 (1995): 71–95.

Rampersad, Arnold. *The Art and Imagination of W. E. B. Du Bois.* Cambridge: Harvard University Press, 1976.

———. *The Life of Langston Hughes, Volume I: 1902–1941: I, Too, Sing America.* New York: Oxford University Press, 1986.

———. "Psychology and Afro-American Biography." *Yale Review* 78:1 (Autumn 1988): 1–18.

Ray, David, and Robert M. Farnsworth, eds. *Richard Wright: Impressions and Perspectives.* Ann Arbor: University of Michigan Press, 1973.

Read, Alan, ed. *The Fact of Blackness: Frantz Fanon and Visual Representation.* London: Institute of Contemporary Arts, 1996.

Reed, Ishamel. "Bigger and O. J." In *Birth of a Nation 'hood: Gaze, Script, and Spectacle in the O. J. Simpson Case.* Ed. Toni Morrison and Claudia Brodsky Lacour. New York: Pantheon, 1997, 169–95.

Reid, Mark A. *Redefining Black Film.* Berkeley and Los Angeles: University of California Press, 1993.

Reilly, John M. "Richard Wright's Discovery of the Third World." *Minority Voices* 2:2 (Fall 1978): 47–53.

———, ed. *Richard Wright: The Critical Reception.* New York: Burt Franklin, 1978.

Riviere, Joan. "Womanliness as a Masquerade" (1929). In *Formations of Fantasy.* Ed. Victor Burgin, James Donald, and Cora Kaplan. 1986; rpt. London: Routledge, 1989, 35–44.

Rodriguez, Richard. *The Hunger of Memory: The Education of Richard Rodriguez: An Autobiography*. 1982; rpt. New York: Bantam, 1988.

Roediger, David R. *The Wages of Whiteness: Race and the Making of the American Working Class*. 1991; rpt. London: Verso, 1993.

Rogin, Michael. *Blackface, White Noise: Jewish Immigrants in the Hollywood Melting Pot*. Berkeley: University of California Press, 1996.

———. "Francis Galton and Mark Twain: The Natal Autograph in *Pudd'nhead Wilson*." In *Mark Twain's* Pudd'nhead Wilson*: Race, Conflict, and Culture*. Ed. Susan Gillman and Forrest G. Robinson. Durham: Duke University Press, 1990, 73–85.

Ronell, Avital. "The Uninterrogated Question of Stupidity." *differences* 8:2 (1996): 1–22.

Rooks, Noliwe M. *Hair Raising: Beauty, Culture, and African American Women*. 1996; rpt. New Brunswick: Rutgers University Press, 1998.

Rooney, Caroline. "Clandestine Antigones." *Oxford Literary Review* 19:1–2 (1997): 47–78.

Rose, Jacqueline. *States of Fantasy*. Oxford: Clarendon Press, 1996.

Rotenstreich, Nathan. *Alienation: The Concept and Its Reception*. Leiden: E. J. Brill, 1989.

Roudinesco, Elisabeth. *Jacques Lacan* (1993). Trans. Barbara Bray. New York: Columbia University Press, 1997.

Rourke, Constance. "That Long-Tail'd Blue." In *American Humor: A Study of the National Character*. 1931; rpt. New York: Harcourt Brace Jovanovich, 1959, 77–104.

Roustang, François. "How Do You Make a Paranoiac Laugh?" *Modern Language Notes* 12:4 (September 1987): 707–18.

Rowell, Charles H. "An Interview with Larry Neal." *Callaloo* 8:1 (1985): 11–35.

———. "An Interview with Randall Kenan." *Callaloo* 21:1 (1998): 133–48.

Russo, Mary. *The Female Grotesque: Risk, Excess and Modernity*. New York: Routledge, 1994.

Said, Edward W. *Orientalism*. 1979; rpt. New York: Vintage, 1994.

———. "The Text, the World, the Critic." In *Textual Strategies: Perspectives in Post-Structuralist Criticism*. Ed. Josué V. Harari. 1979; rpt. Ithaca, NY: Cornell University Press, 1981, 161–88.

Salecl, Renata. *(Per)versions of Love and Hate*. 1998; rpt. London: Verso, 2000.

———, ed. *Sexuation*. Durham: Duke University Press, 2000.

Salmane, Hala. "On Colonial Cinema." In Salmane, Hartog, and Wilson, eds., 8–13.

———. "Structures of Algerian Cinema." In Salmane, Hartog, and Wilson, eds., 19–23.

Salmane, Hala, Simon Hartog, and David Wilson, eds. *Algerian Cinema*. London: British Film Institute, 1976.

Salvino, Dana Nelson. "The Word in Black and White: Ideologies of Race and Literacy in Antebellum America." In *Reading in America: Literature and Social History*. Ed. Cathy N. Davidson. Baltimore: Johns Hopkins University Press, 1989, 140–56.

Sanders, Roland. "Richard Wright and the Sixties" (1968). In *Black Literature: Criticism*, vol. 3. Ed. James P. Draper. Detroit: Gale Research, 1992, 2003–6.

Santner, Eric L. "Freud, Žižek, and the Joys of Monotheism." *American Imago* 54:2 (1997): 197–207.

———. "Freud's Moses and the Ethics of Nomotropic Desire." In Salecl, ed., 57–105.

Sartre, Jean-Paul. *Anti-Semite and Jew* (1946). Trans. George J. Becker. 1948; rpt. New York: Schocken Books, 1995.

———. *Being and Nothingness: An Essay on Phenomenological Ontology* (1943). Trans. Hazel E. Barnes. New York: Philosophical Library, 1956.

Saunders, James Robert. Rev. of Claudia Tate, *Psychoanalysis and Black Novels: Desire and the Protocols of Race. Modern Fiction Studies* 45.2 (1999): 498–502.

Saxton, Alexander. "Blackface Minstrelsy and Jacksonian Ideology." *American Quarterly 27*:1 (March 1975): 3–28.

———. "Blackface Minstrelsy, Vernacular Comics, and the Politics of Slavery in the North." In *The Meaning of Slavery in the North*. Eds. David Roediger and Martin H. Blatt. New York: Garland, 1998, 157–75.

Schacht, Richard. *Hegel and After: Studies in Continental Philosophy between Kant and Sartre*. London: University of Pittsburgh Press, 1975.

Scheiffele, Eberhard. "Questioning One's 'Own' from the Perspective of the Foreign." Trans. Graham Parkes. In *Nietzsche and Asian Thought*. Ed. Parkes. Chicago: University of Chicago Press, 1991, 31–47.

Schwartz, Susan. "Fanon's Revolutionary Women." *The UTS Review* 1:2 (1995): 197–201.

Scruggs, Charles. *Sweet Home: Invisible Cities in the Afro-American Novel*. Baltimore: Johns Hopkins University Press, 1993.

Sedgwick, Eve Kosofsky. *Between Men: English Literature and Male Homosocial Desire*. New York: Columbia University Press, 1985.

———. "Paranoid Reading and Reparative Reading; or, You're So Paranoid, You Probably Think This Introduction Is about You." In *Novel Gazing: Queer Readings in Fiction*. Ed. Sedgwick. Durham: Duke University Press, 1997, 1–37.

Sedinger, Tracey. "Historicism and Renaissance Culture." In *Discontinuities: New Essays on Renaissance Literature and Criticism*. Ed. Viviana Comensoli and Paul Stevens. Toronto: University of Toronto Press, 1998, 117–38.

Sekyi-Otu, Ato. *Fanon's Dialectic of Experience*. Cambridge: Harvard University Press, 1996.

Seshadri-Crooks, Kalpana. "The Comedy of Domination: Psychoanalysis and the Conceit of Whiteness." In Lane, ed., 353–79.

———. *Desiring Whiteness: A Lacanian Analysis of Race*. London: Routledge, 2000.

———. "The Primitive as Analyst: Postcolonial Feminism's Access to Psychoanalysis." *Cultural Critique* 28 (Fall 1994): 175–218.

Sharpley-Whiting, T. Denean. *Frantz Fanon: Conflicts and Feminisms*. Lanham: Rowman & Littlefield, 1998.

Shepherdson, Charles. "Human Diversity and the Sexual Relation." In Lane, ed., 41–64.

———. "The Intimate Alterity of the Real: A Response to Reader Commentary on 'History and the Real.'" *Postmodern Culture* 6:3 (1996).

———. "Lacan and Philosophy." In Rabaté, ed., 116–52.

———. "Of Love and Beauty in Lacan's *Antigone*." *Umbr(a): A Journal of the Unconscious* 1999, 63–80.

———. "A Pound of Flesh: Lacan's Reading of *The Visible and the Invisible*." *diacritics* 27:4 (Winter 1997): 70–86.

———. *Vital Signs: Nature, Culture, Psychoanalysis*. New York: Routledge, 2000.

Silverman, Kaja. "Fassbinder and Lacan: A Reconsideration of Gaze, Look, and Image." In *Male Subjectivity at the Margins*. New York: Routledge, 1992, 125–56.

———. *The Threshold of the Visible World*. New York: Routledge, 1996.

Singh, Amrit. "Introduction to the HarperPerennial Edition." In Richard Wright, *Black Power*, xi–xxxiv.

Smith, Barbara, and Beverly Smith. "Across the Kitchen Table: A Sister-to-Sister Dialogue." In *This Bridge Called My Back: Writings by Radical Women of Color.* 2nd ed. Ed. Cherríe Moraga and Gloria Anzaldúa. New York: Kitchen Table, 1983, 113–27.

Smith Storey, Olivia. "Flying Words: Contests of Orality and Literacy in the Trope of the Flying Africans." *Journal of Colonialism and Colonial History* 5:3 (2004).

Sokal, Alan, and Jean Bricmont. *Fashionable Nonsense: Postmodern Intellectuals' Abuse of Science*. New York: Picador, 1998.

Sollors, Werner. *Neither Black nor White yet Both: Thematic Explorations of Interracial Literature*. 1997; rpt. Cambridge: Harvard University Press, 1999.

Sophocles. *Antigone*. In *The Three Theban Plays: Antigone, Oedipus the King, Oedipus at Colonus*. Trans. Robert Fagles. New York: Penguin, 1984.

Spillers, Hortense J. "'All the Things You Could Be By Now, If Sigmund Freud's Wife Was Your Mother': Psychoanalysis and Race." In Abel, Christian, and Moglen, eds., 135–58.

———. "Mama's Baby, Papa's Maybe: An American Grammar Book." In A. Mitchell, ed., 454–81.

Stanley, Sandra K. "Black Literature, Desire, and the Psychoanalytic Model." Rev. of Claudia Tate, *Psychoanalysis and Black Novels: Desire and the Protocols of Race. Callaloo* 22:1 (1999): 253–54.

Staples, Brent. "When the 'Paranoids' Turn Out to Be Right." *New York Times*, May 2, 1999, late ed., WK16.

Stavrakakis, Yannis. *Lacan and the Political*. London: Routledge, 1999.

Steiner, George. *Antigones*. 1984; rpt. New Haven: Yale University Press, 1996.

Stepan, Nancy. *The Idea of Race in Science: Great Britain 1800–1960*. Hong Kong: Macmillan, 1982.

Stepto, Robert B. *From Behind the Veil: A Study of Afro-American Narrative*. Urbana and Chicago: University of Illinois Press, 1979.

Stockton, Kathryn Bond. "Reading Details, Teaching Politics: Political Mantras and the Politics of Luxury." *College English* 64:1 (September 2001): 109–21.

Stoler, Ann Laura. "Racial Histories and Their Regimes of Truth." In Essed and Goldberg, eds., 369–91.

Stovall, Tyler. *Paris Noir: African Americans in the City of Light*. Boston and New York: Houghton Mifflin, 1996.

Sumic, Jelica. "On the Path of the Semblant." *Umbr(a): A Journal of the Unconscious* (2007): 11–34.

Sundquist, Eric J. *To Wake the Nations: Race in the Making of American Literature*. Cambridge: Belknap Press, 1993.

Tanner, Laura E. "Uncovering the Magical Disguise of Language: The Narrative Presence in Richard Wright's *Native Son*." In Gates and Appiah, eds., 132–48.

Tate, Claudia. "Freud and His 'Negro': Psychoanalysis as Ally and Enemy of African Americans." *Journal for the Psychoanalysis of Culture and Society* 1:1 (Spring 1996): 53–62.

———. *Psychoanalysis and Black Novels: Desire and the Protocols of Race.* New York: Oxford University Press, 1998.

Taylor, Paul. "Malcolm's Conk and Danto's Color; or, Four Logical Petitions Concerning Race, Beauty, and Aesthetics." *Journal of Aesthetics and Art Criticism* 57:1 (1999): 16–20.

Taylor, Yuval, ed. *I Was Born a Slave: An Anthology of Classic Slave Narratives. Volume 1: 1772–1849.* Chicago: Lawrence Hill, 1999.

———. *I Was Born a Slave: An Anthology of Classic Slave Narratives. Volume 2: 1849–1866.* Chicago: Lawrence Hill, 1999.

Thoreau, Henry David. *Walden; or, Life in the Woods.* 1854; rpt. New York: Thomas Y. Crowell, 1966.

Tobin, Jacqueline L., and Raymond G. Dobard. *Hidden in Plain View: The Secret Story of Quilts and the Underground Railroad.* New York: Doubleday, 1999.

Toll, Robert C. *Blacking Up: The Minstrel Show in Nineteenth-Century America.* 1974; rpt. New York: Oxford University Press, 1977.

Torgovnick, Marianna. *Gone Primitive: Savage Intellects, Modern Lives.* University of Chicago Press, 1990.

Trubek, Anne. "American Literary Realism and the Problem of *Trompe l'Oeil* Painting." *Mosaic* 34:3 (September 2001): 35–54.

Tucker, Judith E. "Introduction." In *Arab Women: Old Boundaries, New Frontiers.* Ed. Tucker. Bloomington and Indianapolis: Indiana University Press, 1993, vii–viii.

Tuhkanen, Mikko. "Performativity and Becoming." *Cultural Critique* (forthcoming).

———. "Queer Guerrillas: On Richard Wright's and Frantz Fanon's Dissembling Revolutionaries." Richard Wright Centennial Issue of *Mississippi Quarterly*, ed. Jerry W. Ward, Jr. (forthcoming).

Turner, Patricia A. *Ceramic Uncles and Celluloid Mammies: Black Images and Their Influence on Culture.* New York: Anchor Books, 1994.

Tyler, Carol-Anne. "Boys Will Be Girls: The Politics of Gay Drag." In Fuss, ed., 32–70.

Verhaege, Paul. "The Collapse of the Function of the Father and Its Effects on Gender Roles." In Salecl, ed., 131–54.

Viego, Antonio. *Dead Subjects: Toward a Politics of Loss in Latino Studies.* Durham: Duke University Press, 2007.

Voltaire, François-Marie. "Of the Different Races of Men" (1765). Rpt. in Bernasconi and Lott, eds., 5–7.

Von Herder, Johann Gottfried. "Ideas on the Philosophy of the History of Humankind" (1784). Trans. Thomas Nenon. Rpt. in Bernasconi and Lott, eds., 23–26.

Wald, Gayle. *Crossing the Line: Racial Passing in Twentieth-Century U.S. Literature and Culture.* Durham: Duke University Press, 2000.

Walder, Dennis. *Post-Colonial Literatures in English: History, Language, Theory.* Oxford: Blackwell, 1998.

Waldman, Amy. "Unremarkable Past and Unspeakable Act." *New York Times* 26 May 1999, late ed., B9.

Walker, Alice. *In Search of Our Mothers' Gardens: Womanist Prose.* San Diego: Harcourt, 1983.

———. *The Temple of My Familiar.* 1989; rpt. London: Phoenix, 2004.

Walker, Margaret. *Richard Wright, Daemonic Genius: A Portrait of the Man, a Critical Look at His Work.* New York: Amistad, 1988.

Wallace, Maurice O. *Constructing the Black Masculine: Identity and Ideality in African American Men's Literature and Culture, 1775–1995.* Durham: Duke University Press, 2002.

Wallace, Michele. *Black Macho and the Myth of the Superwoman.* New York: Dial Press, 1978.

Walters, Wendy W. "'One of Dese Mornings, Bright and Fair/Take My Winds and Cleave de Air': The Legend of the Flying Africans and Diasporic Consciousness." *MELUS* 22:3 (Autumn 1997): 3–29.

Walton, Jean. *Fair Sex, Savage Dreams: Race, Psychoanalysis, Sexual Difference.* Durham: Duke University Press, 2001.

Warren, Nagueyalti. "Black Girls and Native Sons: Female Images in Selected Works by Richard Wright." In *Richard Wright: Myths and Realities.* Ed. C. James Trotman. New York: Garland, 1988, 59–77.

Washington, Booker T. "The Educational Outlook in the South" (1884). In *African-American Social and Political Thought 1850–1920.* Ed. Howard Brotz. 1966; rpt. New Brunswick: Transaction, 1995, 351–56.

———. *Up from Slavery.* 1901. Ed. William L. Andrews. New York: W. W. Norton, 1996.

Watkins, Mel. *On the Real Side: Laughing, Lying, and Signifying—The Underground Tradition of African-American Humor that Transformed American Culture, from Slavery to Richard Pryor.* 1994; rpt. New York: Touchstone, 1995.

Webb, Frank J. *The Garies and Their Friends.* 1857; rpt. Baltimore: Johns Hopkins University Press, 1997.

Webster, Noah. *Essays on Education in the Early Republic.* Ed. Frederick Rudolph. Cambridge: Belknap, 1965.

Wertham, Frederic. "An Unconscious Determinant in *Native Son.*" *Journal of Clinical Psychopathology and Psychotherapy* 6 (July 1944): 111–15.

West, Cornel. *The Cornel West Reader.* New York: Basic Civitas Books, 1999.

———. "A Genealogy of Modern Racism." In Essed and Goldberg, eds., 90–112.

———. "The Ignoble Paradox of Modernity." In *The Cornel West Reader*, 51–54.

———. "Malcolm X and Black Rage." In Wood, ed., 48–58.

Wheeler, Roxann. *The Complexion of Race: Categories of Difference in Eighteenth-Century British Culture.* Philadelphia: University of Pennsylvania Press, 2000.

White, Walter. "The Paradox of Color." In Locke, ed., 361–68.

Wiegman, Robyn. *American Anatomies: Theorizing Race and Gender.* Durham: Duke University Press, 1995.

Wilentz, Gay. "Healing the 'Sick Jewish Soul': Psychoanalytic Discourse in Jo Sinclair (Ruth Seid)'s *Wasteland.*" *Literature and Psychology* 47:1–2 (2001): 68–93.

———. "If You Surrender to the Air: Folk Legends of Flight and Resistance in African American Literature." *MELUS* 16:1 (Spring 1989/Spring 1990): 21–32.

Willett, Cynthia. "The Master–Slave Dialectic: Hegel vs. Douglass." In *Subjugation and Bondage: Critical Essays on Slavery and Social Philosophy.* Ed. Tommy L. Lott. Lanham, MD: Rowman & Littlefield, 1998, 151–70.

Williams, Patricia J. *The Alchemy of Race and Rights: Diary of a Law Professor.* Cambridge: Harvard University Press, 1991.

Williams, Patrick, and Laura Chrisman, eds. *Colonial Discourse and Post-Colonial Theory: A Reader.* New York: Columbia University Press, 1994.

Williams, Sherley Anne. "Papa Dick and Sister-Woman: Reflections on Women in the Fiction of Richard Wright." In *American Novelists Revisited: Essays in Feminist Criticism.* Ed. Fritz Fleischmann. Boston: G.K. Hall, 1982, 394–415.

Winchester, James J. *Aesthetics across the Color Line: Why Nietzsche (Sometimes) Can't Sing the Blues.* Lanham: Rowman & Littlefield, 2002.

Wittke, Carl Frederick. *Tambo and Bones: A History of the American Minstrel Stage.* 1930; rpt. New York, Greenwood Press, 1968.

Wolfenstein, E. Victor. "On the Road Not Taken: 'Revolt and Revenge' in W. E. B. Du Bois's *The Souls of Black Folk.*" In *JPCS: Journal for the Psychoanalysis of Culture and Society* 5:1 (Spring 2000).

Woll, Allen. *Black Musical Theatre: From Coontown to Dreamgirls.* Baton Rouge: Louisiana State University Press, 1989.

Wood, Joe, ed. *Malcolm X: In Our Own Image.* New York: St. Martin's Press, 1992.

Woodhull, Winifred. *Transfigurations of the Maghreb: Feminism, Decolonization, and Literatures.* Minneapolis: University of Minnesota Press, 1993.

Woodward, C. Vann. *Origins of the New South 1877–1913.* 1951; rpt. Baton Rouge: Louisiana State University Press, 1971.

———. *The Strange Career of Jim Crow.* 2nd ed. New York: Oxford University Press, 1966.

Wright, Elizabeth, ed. *Feminism and Psychoanalysis: A Critical Dictionary.* Oxford Blackwell, 1992.

Wright, Richard. *American Hunger.* 1977; rpt, New York: Harper & Row, 1979.

———. "Big Black Good Man" (1957). Rpt. in *Eight Men*, 93–109

———. *Black Boy (American Hunger).* 1945; rpt. in *Later Works*, 1–365.

———. *Black Boy: A Record of Childhood and Youth.* 1945; rpt. Cleveland: World Publishing, 1947.

———. "*Black Boy* and Reading" (1945). Rpt. in Kinnamon and Fabre, eds., 81–82.

———. *Black Power: A Record of Reactions in a Land of Pathos.* 1954; rpt. New York: HarperPerennial, 1995.

———. "Blueprint for Negro Writing" (1937). Rpt. in *Richard Wright Reader.* Ed. Ellen Wright and Michel Fabre. New York: Harper & Row, 1978, 36–49.

———. "Bright and Morning Star" (1938). Rpt. in *Uncle Tom's Children*, 221–63.

———. "Conversation with Richard Wright" (1965). Conducted by Johannes Skancke Martens. Rpt. in Kinnamon and Fabre, eds., 160–62.

———. *Eight Men.* 1961; rpt. New York: Thunder's Mouth Press, 1987.

———. *A Father's Law.* New York: HarperPerennial, 2008.

———. "Fire and Cloud" (1938). Rpt. in *Uncle Tom's Children*, 157–220.

———. "Foreword." In George Padmore. *Pan-Africanism or Communism.* 1956; rpt. Garden City: Anchor, 1972, xxi–xxiv.

———. "How 'Bigger' Was Born" (1941). Rpt. in Baker, ed., 21–47.

———. "I Feel More at Home in France Than Where I Was Born" (1947). Trans. Michel Fabre. Rpt. in Kinnamon and Fabre, eds., 126–27.

———. "An Interview with Richard Wright" (1953). Conducted by Hans de Vaal. Trans. Edward Lemon. Rpt. in Kinnamon and Fabre, eds., 154–59.

———. "An Interview with Richard Wright" (1946). Conducted by Peter Schmid. Rpt. in Kinnamon and Fabre, eds., 106–10.

———. "Introduction." In St. Clair Drake and Horace R. Clayton. *Black Metropolis: A Study of Negro Life in a Northern City*. New York: Harcourt, Brace & Co., 1945, xvii–xxxiv.

———. "Introduction." In George Lamming, *In the Castle of My Skin*. New York: McGraw-Hill, 1953, ix–xii.

———. *Later Works*. New York: Library of America, 1991.

———. *Lawd Today!* 1963; rpt. in *Early Works*, 22–23.

———. *The Long Dream*. New York: Ace Books, 1958.

———. "A Man of the South" (1950). Rpt. *Mississippi Quarterly: Richard Wright Issue*. Ed. Michel Fabre and Jack B. Moore. 42:4 (Fall 1989): 355–57.

———. "The Man Who Lived Underground" (1944). In *Eight Men*, 27–92.

———. *Native Son*. New York: Harper, 1940.

———. "A Negro Novel about White People" (1960). Interview conducted by Georges Charbonnier. Trans. Michel Fabre. Rpt. in Kinnamon and Fabre, eds., 235–38.

———. "One of Uncle Tom's Children" (1960). Interview conducted by Peter Lennon. Rpt. in Kinnamon and Fabre, eds., 239–41.

———. *The Outsider*. 1953; rpt. in *Later Works*, 367–841.

———. "Richard Wright: I Curse the Day When for the First Time I Heard the Word 'Politics'" (1955). Rpt. in Kinnamon and Fabre, eds., 163–65.

———. "Richard Wright, Negro Author, Is Here to Make Home in Paris" (1946). Conducted by Anne Perlman. Rpt. in Kinnamon and Fabre, eds., 90–91.

———. *12 Million Black Voices*. Photo direction by Edwin Rosskam. 1941; rpt. New York: Thunder Mouth's Press, 1992.

———. *Uncle Tom's Children*. 1940; rpt. New York: HarperPerennial, 1993.

———. "White Faces: Agents Provocateurs of Mankind." Rev. of O. Mannoni, *Prospero and Caliban* (1956). Rpt. in Fabre, *Richard Wright: Books and Writers*, 223–25.

———. *White Man, Listen!* 1957; rpt. Garden City: Anchor, 1964.

———. "Why Richard Wright Came Back from France" (1947). Rpt. in Kinnamon and Fabre, eds., 122–25.

Yang, Suzanne. "A Question of Accent: Ethnicity and Transference." In Lane, ed., 139–53.

Yarborough, Richard. "Introduction to the HarperPerennial Edition." In Richard Wright. *Uncle Tom's Children*, ix–xxix.

Young, Lola. "Missing Persons: Fantasising Black Women in *Black Skin, White Masks*." In Read, ed., 86–101.

Zamir, Shamoon. *Dark Voices: W. E. B. Du Bois and American Thought, 1888–1903*. Chicago: University of Chicago Press, 1995.

Zangrando, Robert L. *The NAACP Crusade against Lynching, 1909–1950*. Philadelphia: Temple University Press, 1980.

Žižek, Slavoj. "Afterword: Lenin's Choice." In V. I. Lenin. *Revolution at the Gates: Selected Writings of Lenin from 1917*. Ed. Žižek. London: Verso, 2002, 165–336.

———. "Class Struggle or Postmodernism? Yes, Please!" In Butler, Laclau, Žižek, 90–135.

———. "*Da Capo senza Fine*." In Butler, Laclau, Žižek, 213–262.

———. *Enjoy Your Symptom!: Jacques Lacan in Hollywood and Out*. New York: Routledge, 1992.

———. *Looking Awry: An Introduction to Jacques Lacan through Popular Culture*. Cambridge: MIT Press, 1991.

———. "Love Thy Neighbor? No, Thanks!" In Lane, ed., 154–75.

———. *The Parallax View*. Cambridge: MIT Press, 2006.

———. *The Ticklish Subject: The Absent Centre of Political Ontology*. London: Verso, 1999.

Zouligha. "Challenging the Social Order: Women's Liberation in Contemporary Algeria." In Nigel Gibson, ed., 354–66.

Zupančič, Alenka. *Ethics of the Real: Kant, Lacan*. London: Verso, 2000.

———. "Lacan's Heroines: Antigone and Sygne de Coûfontaine." *New Formations* 35 (Fall 1998): 108–21.

Index

Abraham, Karl, xii
Achebe, Chinua, 67
Alberti, Leon Battista, 14, 15, 16, 28, 39
alienation, xxiv, 128, 148. *See also under* Lacan, Jacques
Andrews, William, 93
Anouilh, Jean, 71
Ansell Pearson, Keith, 130
Atwood, Margaret, 122

Baker, Houston A., Jr., xii, 136, 145, 152
Baldwin, James, xii, xviii, 30, 57, 67, 103, 124, 180n40
Barrett, Lindon, 135
Baudelaire, Charles, 148
becoming, xxiii, 39. *See also* experience of the literary, the
 Butler, Judith, and, 104–5, 110
 Darwin, Charles, and, 129–1
 death drive, the, and, 136, 151, 164
 Deleuze, Gilles, and, 167–68
 Fanon, Frantz, and, 82, 105
 Foucault, Michel, and, 38
 Hegel, G. W. F., and, 109, 110
 Lacan, Jacques, and, 73, 104–5, 110, 128–31, 164–68
 Wright, Richard, and, 84–91
Benjamin, Walter, 102
Bentham, Jeremy, 113
Berger, Anne-Emmanuel, 182n28
Berger, John, 14
Bergner, Gwen, 182n30
Bergson, Henri, 39
Berlant, Lauren, 3
Bernier, François, 9
Bersani, Leo, 145, 154
Best, Stephen Michael, 148
Bhabha, Homi K., 32, 34, 69, 78
Bibb, Henry, 93, 154
Birth of a Nation (film), 176n14
blackface minstrelsy, xxii, 1, 30–40. *See also* minstrel theory
 African American performers of, 37–39
 and ambivalence, 32, 39, 44, 65
 and paranoia, 43, 65
Blake (Delany), 127
Blumenbach, Johann Friedrich, 9
Bonaparte, Marie, xxi
Borch-Jacobsen, Mikkel, 42
Boskin, Joseph, 35, 65, 92
Boyarin, Daniel, xiv
Braidotti, Rosi, 39
Brecht, Bertolt, 71
Brodhead, Richard, 111
Brown, John, 93, 165, 189n18
Brown, Wesley, 93
Brown, William Wells, 154
Brunelleschi, Filippo, 14, 15, 39
Burgin, Victor 15
Butler, Judith, xxiii, 102–5, 109–10, 115, 141, 184n47, 185n3
Byerman, Keith, 170n17

Caillois, Roger, 44–47, 60, 166, 177n25
Cassuto, Leonardo, 134
Castronovo, Russ, xxiv, 136, 158–64, 167–68, 190n25
Césaire, Aimé, xiv, 93

Chesnutt, Charles, 124
Chiesa, Lorenzo, 179n32
Chow, Rey, 81
Cleaver, Eldridge, xiii, xvi, xviii, xix
Cobbs, Price M., 180n40
Cockrell, Dale, 33, 34, 36
Cole, Merrill, 170n21, 190n27
colonial feminism, 77
Copjec, Joan, 15–16, 73, 95, 98, 103, 153–54, 163, 170n22, 184n47
Cowie, Elizabeth, 170n22
critical race theory, 4, 73
  on comparative anatomy, 9
  and psychoanalysis, xxii-xxiii, 40, 103
  and visual epistemologies, xi, 8–10

Dali, Salvador, 39
Damisch, Hubert, 13, 14
Darwin, Charles, 39, 129–31
Davis, David Brion, 133
Davis, Allison, xvi
Davis, Angela Y., 22, 116, 185n4
Dean, Tim, xix, 72, 73, 97, 98, 99, 102, 103, 170n21, 170n22
de Beauvoir, Simone, 145
de Bolla, Peter, 15
Decker, Jeffrey Louis, 82
Delany, Martin R., 127, 176n14
Deleuze, Gilles, xiii, xiv, xvii, xviii, 39, 130, 167, 176n17
  on becoming, 167–68
  on encounter of bodies, xx, xxi
  on flight, 167–68
de Man, Paul, xxv
Derrida, Jacques, 43, 108, 110, 177n27
Desargues, Girard, 16
Descartes, René, 15
  cogito/consciousness, 14, 16, 49, 53, 62, 143
Deutsch, Helene, xii
Diawara, Manthia, 31, 64–66, 69, 147
Diderot, Denis, 4, 15, 17, 28, 143
Dixon, Melvin, 147
Douglass, Frederick, 11–12, 80, 156
  and Covey, Edward, 109, 113–14, 128, 154–55, 159–60
  and experience of the literary, the, 108, 121, 123, 161–62, 165
  and (symbolic) death, 136, 154–55, 159–60
  and Wright, Richard, 108, 111–16, 126, 162, 165
Du Bois, W. E. B., xx, xxiii, 5, 6, 18, 23, 50, 92, 97, 114, 126, 172n10, 175n28, 176n14, 177n27, 187n13, 187n18
  and critical race theory, 10, 169n2
  on double consciousness, xv, 48–49, 74, 117, 129
  and experience of the literary, the, xxiv, 124, 128–29, 131, 136, 155–58
  on laughter, 40, 62
  "Of the Coming of John," 128–31, 155–57
Dürer, Albrecht, 15
Dyess, Cynthia, 99

Ellison, Ralph, xxiv, 20, 32, 35, 36, 37, 38, 76
Elmer, Jonathan, 150, 167
Evans, Dylan, 40, 41
experience of the literary, the
  and becoming, xxiv, 110, 128–31, 164–68
  in Du Bois, W. E. B., 128–31, 155–57
  as flight, 110, 145–53, 164–68
  in slave narratives, xxiii-xxiv, 107–8, 110, 112, 121–24, 128,134–36, 160–68
  as (symbolic) death, 154–58, 161–62
  in Wright, Richard, xxiii-xxiv, 107–8, 110, 112, 119–31 passim, 134–36, 140, 145, 150–53, 160–68

Fabi, Giulia M., 94
Fabre, Michel, xvi, 6, 68, 84, 86
Fanon, Frantz, xviii, xx, xxii, 2, 25, 57, 67–105 passim, 108, 127, 149, 171n26
  on bodily schema, the, 80–81, 141
  on epidermalization, 69, 74–80, 91, 128
  and feminism, 68, 80–84, 105
  and Lacan, Jacques, 68–74
  and negritude, 82, 181n14
  and sexuation, 80, 83
  on veiling, 69, 74, 76–84, 91
  and Wright, Richard, 68–69, 74–76, 81, 181n5
Fanon, Frantz, works of
  "Algeria Unveiled," 31, 69, 73, 76–84, 95, 102
  Black Skin, White Masks, 68, 69, 73, 74–76, 79, 80, 81, 95
  Dying Colonialism, A, 69, 71, 73
  Toward the African Revolution, 82

Wretched of the Earth, The, 69, 73, 79, 95, 118–19
Faulkner, Rita A., 82
Faulkner, William, 69
Fauset, Jessie, 62
Felman, Shoshana, xvii, xviii, xxi, 162, 171n25
Fenichel, Otto, xii
Ferenczi, Sandor, xii
Fink, Bruce, 184n45, 190n26
Fleischner, Jennifer, xxi-xxiii
Flieger, Jerry Aline, 39
flight, xxii, xxiv, 107, 108, 121, 134. *See also under* experience of the literary, the
black aviation, 146
flying fool, 149
flying slaves, 147, 149, 157
FLN (*Front de libération nationale*), 71, 181n12
and women, 82, 83
Foucault, Michel, 38
on evolution, 130–31
on panopticism, 4, 13, 23, 109–14
Foucault, Michel, works of
Archaeology of Knowledge, The, 130
Discipline and Punish, 112–13, 126–27, 186n7
"Discourse on Language, The," 130
"Nietzsche, Genealogy, History," 130
Freud, Anna, xii
Freud, Sigmund, xii, xiv, xxi, 41, 159, 163, 164
Front de libération nationale. See FLN
Fuss, Diana, 83

Gallop, Jane, xvii, xviii, 27, 97
Garner, Margaret, 154, 159
Garrison, William Lloyd, 154
Gates, Henry Louis, Jr., xxi, 93, 123, 135
George, Sheldon, 99–100
Georgia Writers' Project, 147
Gibson, Donald B., 25–26
Gibson, Nigel, 69–70, 71, 72
Gilman, Sander L., xiv
Gilroy, Paul, xxiv, 134, 159–60, 165
Glissant, Édouard, 33–34, 175n31
Goldberg, David Theo, 31
Gordon, Lewis R., 20, 127
Gramsci, Antonio, 127
Green, Jacob, 154
Green, Paul, xi
Greenblatt, Stephen, 58, 174n22
Grier, William H., 180n40
Grosz, Elizabeth, 38, 45, 105, 130
Guattari, Félix, xiii, xiv, xvii, xviii, 39, 176n17
Gubar, Susan, 36, 38

Hakutani, Yoshinobu, 24–25, 26
Hall, Stuart, 9, 68
Harper, Phillip Brian, 94
Harris, Trudier, 172n10, 173n14
Hartman, Saidiya V., 31, 111, 127
Hegel, G. W. F., xvii, 108, 129, 130, 141, 148, 161, 163, 165, 185n3, 190n26, 190n27
and slavery, theory of, 89, 109–10, 128, 133–37, 142, 144, 153–54, 159–60, 162–63, 164, 187n1, 187n2
Henry, Patrick, 154
Herron, Carolivia, 29–32, 63
Hobbes, Thomas, 133
Holbein, Hans, 4, 16–18, 20, 56, 58, 27
Hollinger, David A., 33
Hopkins, Pauline, xxiii, 119, 147, 154
Horney, Karen, xxi
Howe, Irving, 1, 2, 5
Hudson, Nicholas, 173n13
Huggins, Nathan Irvin, 29, 35, 36, 38, 46
Hughes, Langston, 62
Hutcherson, Warren, 63–66
Hyman, Stanley Edgar, 6, 76
Hyppolite, Jean, 136

Irigaray, Luce, xxiii, 57
Jacobs, Harriet, 93, 136, 147, 154
James, C. L. R., 93, 173n13
JanMohamed, Abdul R., xv, 34, 38, 88–91, 115, 134, 190n25
Johnson, Barbara, xiv-xv, xv, 22, 140, 142, 171n24
Johnson, James Weldon, 62, 94
Jones, Ernest, xii
Jordan, Winthrop, 9, 79

Karpman, Benjamin, xii
Kawash, Samira, 102, 103
Klein, Melanie xii, xxi
Kojève, Alexandre, 109, 128, 134, 136, 141, 162

Lacan, Jacques, xi, xxi
on alienation, 40, 99, 115, 125, 134–38, 145
on *Antigone* (Sophocles), xxiii, 71–72, 84, 89–92 passim
on becoming, 73, 104–5, 110, 128–31, 164–68
on colonialism, 129
and critical race theory, xii-xxiii
on (death) drive, the, 21, 89, 159–64
on ethics, xviii-xix, xxiii, xxiv, 13, 24, 55, 70, 73, 89–90, 91–92, 100, 104–5, 128–39, 131, 141, 149–50, 163–65
and Fanon, Frantz, 68–74
on gaze, the, 16, 29, 41, 44–45, 47, 53–56
and Hegel, G. W. F., 160–61
on imaginary, the, xv, 17, 39, 41–42, 70, 123
on imaginary capture/imaginarization, xxii, 17, 27, 39, 41, 59, 63, 65, 78, 85–86, 121, 150
on (mal)adaptation, 40, 44, 100
on mimicry, 32, 39–44, 78
on mirror stage, the, 40–43, 70
on *objet (petit) a*, the, xxii, 16, 40, 53–58, 68, 72, 74, 91, 96–98, 100, 138
on paranoia, xxii, 32, 39–47, 48, 51, 55, 56, 140, 177n21
on psychosis, 45, 43–47
and racialization, xxii, xxiii
on real, the, xvi, xxii, xxiii, 40, 43–44, 55, 58, 60, 68, 70, 73, 89, 96, 97, 150
on Renaissance perspective, 4, 13–17, 53, 142
on sexuation, xxiii, 57, 73, 96–98 (*see also* sexuation)
structuralist phase of, 40, 150
on symbolic, the, xvi, 41–42, 47, 56–57, 70, 72, 101, 128–31
on trompe l'oeil painting, 53–56
and white symbolic order, the (*see* white symbolic order, the)
Lacan, Jacques, works of
"Aggressiveness in Psychoanalysis," 42, 61, 129
"Mirror Stage as Formative of the *I* Function as Revealed in Psychoanalytic Experience, The," 22, 40–43, 44, 53, 142
Seminar I (*Freud's Papers on Technique*), 129
Seminar II (*The Ego in Freud's Theory and in the Technique of Psychoanalysis*), 42, 53, 60, 78
Seminar III (*The Psychoses*), 41, 42, 47, 62
Seminar VII (*The Ethics of Psychoanalysis*), xxiii, 55, 57, 67, 71, 73, 89–90, 129, 160, 161, 163, 179n32
Seminar XI (*The Four Fundamental Concepts of Psycho-Analysis*), 1, 13–17, 20–22, 29, 41, 43–44, 53–56, 78, 98, 137–38, 144, 150–51, 153, 160
Seminar XX (*On Feminine Sexuality*), 57, 73, 95–98
"Seminar on 'The Purloined Letter,'" 41, 78–79, 94, 123, 136, 142–44, 147–48, 150, 160–61, 166, 167
"Signification of the Phallus, The," 57, 96, 98
"Subversion of the Subject and the Dialectic of Desire in the Freudian Unconscious, The," 130, 160–61
Television, 56
LaCapra, Dominick, 100
Laclau, Ernesto, xv, 97, 170n20
Lamming, George, 3, 68, 172n5, 180n2
Lane, Christopher, xv
laughter, 40, 61–66
Levine, Lawrence W., 61–62, 121
Levinthal, David, 64
Lewis, Sinclair, 125, 187n17
Lhamon, W. T., 32, 33, 35, 36–37, 38
Linneaus, Carolus, 9
literacy, 108, 120–26, 134–36, 154, 164, 189n17. *See also* experience of the literary, the
Locke, Alain, 32
Locke, John, 133
Lorde, Audre, 180n40
Lott, Eric, 32, 33, 35, 36, 38
Louima, Abner, 173n14

Mabro, Judy, 76
MacCannell, Juliet Flower, 170n22
Macey, David, 72
Mahar, William J., 33, 176n4
Mannoni, Octave, xiii, 67, 70
Marcuse, Herbert, 109
Markmann, Charles Lam, 78
Marx, Karl, 133–34, 136
McClintock, Anne, 82

McCulloch, Jock, 79
Mechelin, Jay, 118
Mellard, James, 73, 91, 170n22
Meltzer, Françoise, xvii-xviii, xix, xx, xxi
Melville, Stephen, 40
Mencken, H. L., 167
Mercer, Kobena, 30, 70
Merleau-Ponty, Maurice, 28
Miller, D. A., 121–23
Miller, Jacques-Alain, 4, 98
Miller, J. Hillis, xxv
Minces, Juliette, 182n31
minstrel studies. *See* minstrel theory
minstrelsy. *See* blackface minstrelsy
minstrel theory, 32–40, 46, 166
Mitchell, Margaret, 156
Morrison, Toni, 147
Mouffe, Chantal, 170n20
Muller, John P., 41

Nathan, Hans, 33, 35, 36
Nelson, Jill, 30, 63–66
New Lacanians, the, xv, xxiii, 73, 101, 103–5, 170n22
Nietzsche, Friedrich, 4, 39, 130, 172n7
Northup, Solomon, 155, 189n12

Ong, Walter J., 121, 125, 126, 164

Padmore, George, 2, 4
Panofsky, Erwin, 14
Parker, William, 189n12
Parry, Benita, 34, 38
Paskman, Dailey, 34, 35, 36
passing, 94–95, 183–84n43
Patterson, Orlando, xxiv, 89, 115, 134, 142, 164
Pennington, James, 154, 161, 189n12
Phillips, Adam, xix
Piper, Adrian, 184n43
Podhoretz, Norman, 63
Poe, Edgar Allan, 69. *See also* Lacan: "Seminar on 'The Purloined Letter'"
"Purloined Letter, The," 142–44, 162
Pouchet Paquet, Sandra, 3
psychoanalysis, xi. *See also* Freud, Sigmund; Lacan, Jacques
and colonialism, xiii-xiv
and critical race theory, xii-xxiii, xxiii, 40, 103
and ethics, xviii-xix, xxiii, 70, 71, 73
and feminism, xvii, xix, xxiii, 57, 73
and postcolonial theory, 68–74

Quarles, Benjamin, 12
queer theory, 39, 68, 74, 97

racialization, 4, 47, 75, 76, 145
and epidermalization, 69, 74–80, 91, 128
Fanon, Frantz on, 67–105 passim
and Freud, Sigmund, xiv-xvi
and Lacan, Jacques, xi-xii, xxii-xxiii, 73–74, 96–101, 134–38, 184n44
and violence, 7, 111–19, 182n27
and visual epistemologies, 5–22
Wright, Richard on, 5–13, 69
racial sciences, 75. *See also* critical race theory: and visual epistemologies
Rampersad, Arnold, 170n17
Reed, Ishmael, 173n14
Reik, Theodor, xii
Richardson, William J., 41
Riviere, Joan, 57
Rock, Chris, 65
Rodriguez, Richard, 123, 172n4
Roediger, David R., 37
Rogin, Michael, xiv, 170n16
Roheim, Géza, xii
Ronell, Avital, 43
Rose, Jacqueline, xiv
Roudinesco, Elizabeth, 71
Rourke, Constance, 34, 35, 36
Roustang, François, 40, 61, 62, 64

Said, Edward, xix, 76
Salecl, Renata, 95
Salmane, Hala, 182n32
Salvino, Dana Nelson, 122
Sartre, Jean-Paul, 49, 74, 181n15
Saxton, Alexander, 35, 36, 65
Schwartz, Susan, 102
Scottsboro case, the, 23, 175n28
Sedgwick, Eve Kosofsky, 39, 187n13
Sedinger, Tracey, 72
Sekyi-Otu, Ato, 69–70
Seshadri-Crooks, Kalpana, xv, 33, 73, 98–99, 170n21, 174n17
sexual difference. *See* sexuation; Fanon: and sexuation
sexuation. *See also under* Fanon

and racial difference, 57, 68, 95–101
and real, the, 95, 97, 101
Sharpley-Whiting, T. Denean, 69, 76
Shepherdson, Charles, 13, 73, 99, 170n22
Silverman, Kaja, 13–14, 53–54, 178n30
slave narratives, xv, xxi, xxiii-xxiv, 93, 123, 124, 128, 135–36, 147, 150–51, 153, 154, 160–61, 164, 168, 189n17, 189n18
influence on Wright, 107–68 passim
Smith, Barbara, 101
Smith, Beverly, 101
Sophocles, 71
Spaeth, Sigmund, 34, 35, 36
Spillers, Hortense, xv
"Steal Away to Jesus," 147
Stepto, Robert B., 189n17
Stoler, Laura Ann, 112
Sumic, Jelica, 185n49
Sundquist, Eric, 155

Tanner, Laura A., 22, 28
Tate, Claudia, xx-xxi, xxii, 170n16, 170n24
Thoreau, Henry David, 107, 128
Toll, Robert C., 33, 35, 36, 38, 65
Tomaselli, Sylvana, 148
Torgovnick, Marianna, xiv
tragedy, 69, 73, 74
Fanon, Frantz on, 83–84
Lacan, Jacques on, 87–90, 91, 96, 104
and sexuation, 95–98
Wright, Richard on, 85, 87–88, 90–91, 183n35
Trubek, Anne, 54
Turner, Patricia A., 30–31, 65

Viego, Antonio, xv, 174n25
Vignola, Giacomo Barozzi, de, 14, 15
Voltaire, François-Marie, xi, 8, 10

Wahl, Jean, 160
Walker, Alice, 8
Walker, Margaret, xvi, 170n17
Walters, Wendy, 147
Walton, Jean, 170n16, 184n47
Washington, Booker T., xxiv, 136, 152, 155, 157–58, 161
Watkins, Mel, 37, 38, 62
Webb, Frank, 183–84n43
Weininger, Otto, 170n12
Wertham, Frederic, xii
West, Cornel, 173n13
Wheatley, Phillis, 107
Wheeler, Roxann, 173n13
white symbolic order, the, xxii, 4, 13, 18–22, 47, 54, 56–61, 68, 80, 97–98, 100, 101, 108, 112, 121, 134, 136, 137, 138–45, 162, 165
Wiegman, Robyn, 3, 7, 9, 11, 12, 122
Wilentz, Gay, 147
Willett, Cynthia, 134
Williams, Patricia, 174n25
Wittke, Carl, 34–35
Woodward, C. Vann, 111, 189n11
Wright, Richard, xi, xii, xxiv
on "acting," 74, 92–95, 101, 166–67
and communism, 6, 84–85, 121, 165–67
and Douglass, Frederick, 108–16, 126
exile of, 68–69
on experience of the literary, the (*see under* experience of the literary, the)
and Fanon, Frantz, 68–69, 74–76, 81, 181n5
on optical trade, the, 108–9, 111, 114–26, 167, 186n9, 186n10
on perspective, 2–3, 4, 67, 84–87, 108
on (post)colonialism, 67–68, 103
Wright, Richard, works of
"Big Black Good Man," 10
Black Boy, xvi, xxiii, xxv, 2, 69, 107, 111, 114–26, 129, 134, 136, 140, 145, 151–53, 161–62, 166–67
"*Black Boy* and Reading," 107
Black Power, 69
"Blueprint for Negro Writing," 2, 3, 6, 68, 84, 85
"Bright and Morning Star," 6, 69, 73, 84–91, 103, 105, 139, 166, 191n31
Father's Law, A, 3, 85
"Fire and Cloud," 4, 6–8, 11, 75, 84–85, 139, 172n10, 191n31
"Horror and the Glory, The," 126
"How 'Bigger' Was Born," 2, 5
Lawd Today! 139, 149, 174n16
Long Dream, The, 93, 94, 102, 180n38
Native Son (novel), xiii, xxii, xxiv, xxv, 1–2, 5, 7–8, 10–12, 17–28, 32, 45–53, 55–61, 67, 68, 75–76, 84, 85, 100, 121, 124, 134, 136, 138–53, 167, 191n31

Native Son (play), xi, 162
Outsider, The, 52, 139, 183n42, 190n29
Pagan Spain, 171n32
"Psychological Reactions of Oppressed People, The," 92, 94, 95, 103
12 Million Black Voices, 11, 12, 80, 94
Uncle Tom's Children, xxiv, 69
White Man, Listen! 94, 165, 172n7

Yang, Suzanne, 170n21
Young, Lola, 182n30

Zangrando, Robert L., 111, 116
Žižek, Slavoj, xv, xxii, 25, 42, 56, 59, 88, 97–98, 101, 103, 161, 170n20, 170n21, 170n22, 179n37, 183n37
Zupančič, Alenka, 91, 149, 179n32